DISSERTATIONS AND THESES

· FROM START TO FINISH ·

PSYCHOLOGY AND RELATED FIELDS

SECOND EDITION

JOHN D. CONE AND SHARON L. FOSTER

American Psychological Association · Washington, DC

First Printing April 2006
Second Printing November 2006
Third Printing January 2008
Fourth Printing December 2008
Fifth Printing October 2010

Published by
American Psychological Association
750 First Street, NE
Washington, DC 20002
www.apa.org

To order
APA Order Department
P.O. Box 92984
Washington, DC 20090-2984
Tel: (800) 374-2721, Direct: (202) 336-5510
Fax: (202) 336-5502, TDD/TTY: (202) 336-6123
Online: www.apa.org/books/
Email: order@apa.org

In the U.K., Europe, Africa, and the Middle East, copies may be ordered from
American Psychological Association
3 Henrietta Street
Covent Garden, London
WC2E 8LU England

Typeset in Futura and New Baskerville by World Composition Services, Inc., Sterling, VA

Printer: United Book Press, Inc., Baltimore, MD
Cover designer: Mercury Publishing Services, Rockville, MD
Project Manager: Debbie Hardin, Carlsbad, CA

The opinions and statements published are the responsibility of the authors, and such opinions and statements do not necessarily represent the policies of the American Psychological Association.

Library of Congress Cataloging-in-Publication Data

Cone, John D., 1942–
    Dissertations and theses from start to finish : psychology and related
fields / John D. Cone and Sharon L. Foster.—2nd ed.
        p. cm.
    Includes bibliographical references and index.
    ISBN 1-59147-362-4 (alk. paper)
    1. Psychology—Research—Methodology. I. Foster, Sharon L. II. Title.

    BF76.5.C645 2006
    150.72—dc22   2005037694

British Library Cataloguing-in-Publication Data
A CIP record is available from the British Library.

Printed in the United States of America
Second Edition

Contents

Foreword
Gregory A. Kimble   ix

Preface   xiii

Chapter 1.   What Are Theses and Dissertations and
             Why Write a Book About Them?   3

Chapter 2.   Starting Out: Assessing Your Preparation
             for the Task Ahead   11

Chapter 3.   Time and Trouble Management   31

Chapter 4.   Finding Topics and Faculty Collaborators   45

Chapter 5.   Formulating and Communicating Your Plans:
             An Overview of the Proposal   81

Chapter 6.   Reviewing the Literature   95

Chapter 7.   Research Methodology and Ethics   127

Chapter 8.   Measurement   161

Chapter 9.   Selecting the Appropriate Statistics   187

Chapter 10. Collecting, Managing, and Analyzing
             the Data   227

Chapter 11. Presenting the Results   249

Chapter 12. Discussing the Results   269

Chapter 13. Managing Committee Meetings:
             Proposal and Oral Defense   289

Chapter 14. Presenting Your Project to the World   313

Appendix: Selected Ethical Standards Relevant
to the Conduct of Research in Psychology   335

References   345

Index   357

About the Authors   375

Foreword

An Open Letter to Graduate Students

Greetings!

So you entered graduate school. I've been wondering what happened to you. The decision you have made will often bring great satisfaction, and only now and then regret. Finances may make life difficult, but you and your student colleagues are in the same boat. You will find ways to make poverty seem like fun. Soon you will be making friends who will be your friends forever. You are in a good department. You will be mastering the skills to help you cure the miseries of the world. Congratulations!

You asked me for advice about your thesis or dissertation, but I am not sure that I can be useful; my degree is more than half a century older than yours will be. On the other hand, I have been in this field for a long time. So, I will take advantage of the lofty perch to which my years of experience have lifted me and pronounce for you the lessons I have learned—about dissertations, theses, and some other things, as well.

Lesson 1. Graduate departments are in the business of advancing a science and profession. Think of your time there as an apprenticeship, preparing you to contribute to that goal. Possibly, your most important contribution to science will be your thesis or dissertation. It may be the biggest research project you ever do. The experience can be rewarding.

My next few lessons relate to your thesis or dissertation.

Lesson 2. The topic of your dissertation or thesis should match your intellectual style. The social sciences cover a spectrum of exactness—from quantitative rigor to qualitative imprecision. You, in turn, have what psychologists call a certain *tolerance for ambiguity*. This is where a cognitive match becomes important. Choose a topic that is definite enough to make you feel secure but open-ended enough to be exciting.

Lesson 3. Your dissertation or thesis should be part of an established program of research. Your need to be creative may be urging you toward something unique and independent. Not a good idea! You will miss the stimulating interactions that you otherwise would have with faculty and other students working on related problems. You are apt to get inadequate guidance—or no guidance at all. No faculty member knows enough to supervise everything, and such "unique" dissertations usually add nothing to knowledge. Instead, they exacerbate the worst problem of the discipline: its lack of coherence and integrity.

Lesson 4. The spirit of your relationship with your supervisor should be one of collaboration. When you decide on someone you may want to work with, approach that person and ask for general ideas. Go away with one or two of these ideas and return later with thoughts about research. If things go right, the potential sponsor's reaction will be something like, "I was hoping that you'd be interested in that area, and your project is a good start. Here are a few reprints that describe my work on the topic. Don't you think that we need this control group? That additional condition? Let's work more on this together, and very soon. I'm sure that we can work out something of mutual interest." If you find that you can't relate to a faculty member in this way, look for someone else.

Lesson 5. When it comes to writing your dissertation or thesis, be as brief as they will let you be. At your university, there will be an informal lower limit, established by tradition, on what is acceptable. Almost certainly that limit is more than you will need to tell your story. You won't get away with it these days, but the most successful student I ever supervised did a dissertation that was less than 20 pages long.

Welcome it if your chairperson wants to bother with the details of expression. I learned more about writing from Kenneth Spence when I did my dissertation than from all the English courses that I took in college.

Lesson 6. Realize that the methods you are learning are more important than the subject matter. Most "facts" in social science have a half-life of about 5 years. Research design and methods of analysis are more durable. If *operational definition* is a dirty word in your department, avoid it; but, when you describe your research on "self-concept," "the representation of information in memory," "separation anxiety"—whatever, be sure that you provide the information required for someone else to replicate your study.

Be suspicious of those fascinating incidental findings. They may be just an accident of sampling (Type I error). For years, I have watched the unexpected outcomes of research become parts of a theory being tested. Then, tests of the enriched theory produce their own new insights that the theory embraces—and so on, until the system collapses. Unless you have reproduced them, such revelations deserve, at most, a mention in your dissertation.

Now, three final lessons that are more general.

Lesson 7. Become a socialized member of the community of scholars in your discipline. Go to the departmental colloquia—even those outside your field of interest; often, thinking in another area will clarify your own. Interact with the colloquium speakers. Find out what is happening in their universities and where they think the field is going. If there are opportunities to do so, attend conventions; meet some of the scholars whose work you have been reading. Learn about the national associations in your field, and become a student affiliate member of one or two.

Lesson 8. Start becoming a professional. For the next 5 years—4 if you are lucky—your world is the lab and library, but there is life after graduation. Prepare for it. Learn the folklore and the tricks of the trade you're about to enter.

Try presenting a paper or a poster at a convention. You will meet the people who will be your colleagues—or maybe even hire you—later on. You will hear about the cutting edge of research and application in your area of interest.

Learn how to prepare an article for publication in your field, and write something for publication (stick to the refereed journals; the others count against you).

Apply for a national fellowship. If you win one, you have tangible recognition of your worth, and your life as a graduate student will be more comfortable. Also, preparing the fellowship request will be practice for writing grant applications later on.

Lesson 9. This is a lesson I hate to have to tell you, but unfortunately life is real. What if you bomb in graduate school? What if you get Cs in your courses and they put you on probation? What if you hate research (or therapy or teaching) but they insist that you do it? God spare you that predicament; if you find that you are in it, take stock of your resources and ask yourself two questions.

First, is this the field I really want to be in? The first step toward "making it" in this world is to find something you enjoy so much that you would be happy doing it for nothing; the second step is to find someone to pay you for it. Perhaps this field isn't it.

Second, ask yourself if you are cut out for this line of work. Be honest. Growing up continues for a lifetime; mostly, it's a matter of more and more accurate self-evaluation. You should be in a profession in which you can be excellent, not just good enough. If candid self-assessment tells you that you can't be excellent where you are, move on to something that suits your talents better.

Lesson 10. The book that you have in your hands has much useful information. It goes into great detail on the topics of my lessons. You will find the content thoughtful and usually appropriate to your situation. The book raises questions that you'd never think (or dare) to ask and comes to useful answers. You will learn a lot, and if—in the best of all possible outcomes—you become an academic, it will help you in your work with your own students.

Again, let me offer congratulations and the hope that your life in graduate school will be a short and happy one!

Sincerely,
Gregory A. Kimble
Professor Emeritus
Duke University

Preface

We wrote the first edition of *Dissertations and Theses From Start to Finish* almost 15 years ago, when few written guides existed to help students navigate the ins and outs of thesis and dissertation research. When the first edition of this book appeared in print, we only dimly imagined doing a revision. After all, the basic principles of research do not change, nor do the politics of finding a chairperson or the skills required to give a good talk at an oral defense. However, as the years have passed, the field has changed in many ways. New versions of ethics codes, publication manuals, and statistics texts have appeared. New thinking about methodology in the behavioral sciences has also occurred. And, most notably, the information revolution and ubiquity of personal computers and access to the Internet have changed how students and established scholars seek information as well as the tools they use to collect, manage, and analyze data. Confronted with all these changes, the urge to revise struck and we swung into action.

Our major purpose in writing the first version of this book was to help students. We have received many letters, e-mails, and other communications from students (and from the occasional dissertation supervisor!) expressing thanks, so we believed we had accomplished our goal. We also received some constructive criticism and began to realize that some of our material had become out of date. In revising this volume, we have updated each of the chapters in significant ways. Some material that was past its prime was dropped. Other material previously not included was now added, thanks to the suggestions of helpful colleagues who thought it should be. We have also made the volume consistent with 21st-century technology. Sections on reviewing the literature, preparing presentations, statistics, and the logistics of data analysis most strongly reflect these updates. We include a variety of new references and other resources, adding these at the end of chapters so readers will have ways of seeking additional information from our favorite sources. We also include an occasional Web site when we think the information it provides is valuable and the site is likely to last for the near future. We are cautious, however, recognizing that Web sites come and go more quickly than textbooks and journal articles and do not go through the same peer review or vetting process that much print media do.

We retain aspects of the book that students repeatedly tell us they find useful. We continue to be true to our roots in clinical behavior therapy by breaking the dissertation into small, specifiable steps and by including checklists at the ends of most chapters to operationalize the process for our readers. And we insist, and the American Psychological Association has agreed, that the book be published in paperback at a reasonable cost that graduate students can afford. As with the first edition, we hope this version will provide useful structure, ideas, guidance to our readers—and even a chuckle now and then—as they experience the uncertainty, excitement, and ultimate satisfaction of the research process.

Any large project, whether it's a dissertation or a book, cannot be completed without assistance. We are particularly indebted to the many graduate students who have worked with us over the years and shared their trials, tribulations, and triumphs with us. Colleagues, too, have provided valuable feedback on what their students did and did not find helpful about the first version of the book. The staff at the American Psychological Association, Julia Frank-McNeil, Mary Lynn Skutley, Peggy Schlegel, Susan Reynolds, and most recently Susan Herman, helped us identify and modify parts of the text that were too wordy, too long, or unclear. Finally, we continue to appreciate so much the unflagging support of our spouses, Jan Cone and Tom Barton. Busy academics themselves, each was around during the writing of the first edition, and each once again generously assumed more than his or her share of household chores and meal preparation to help us find the extra time required to complete this revision.

DISSERTATIONS AND THESES
· FROM START TO FINISH ·

1

What Are Theses and Dissertations and Why Write a Book About Them?

Let's answer the second question first. We wrote the first edition of this book to help graduate students in psychology and related fields negotiate the thesis and dissertation process from beginning to end more successfully. We also wrote the book to serve as an archival source of the wisdom we have amassed from a combined total of 50 years of supervising theses and doctoral dissertations. Both of us have told graduate students many useful (and some not-so-useful!) things over the years to help them through the process. Until we systematized these suggestions, we, like other faculty members, had to tell each fledgling thesis and dissertation student everything all over again. The first edition of this book compiled the best of our ideas on how to make the process a less mysterious and more exciting educational experience. In this version, we add a few things we left out and update our suggestions in light of new trends in the field. Although we gear our suggestions primarily toward advanced graduate students conducting quantitative research in psychology and related fields, many are useful to the first-time researcher in general.

How This Book Is Organized

The 14 chapters of this book provide the nuts and bolts needed to put together good theses and dissertations. The chapters cannot do it all, of course. The book will be most valuable to the extent it supplements an already adequate graduate education. We do not explain research design or statistics. Instead, we help you apply what you have already learned in graduate school to the practical conduct of research.

In this first chapter we talk briefly about what theses and dissertations are, what they look like, and some of the reasons for writing them. In chapter 2 we ask you to assess your own preparation and commitment. The second chapter contains suggestions about finding out the local norms concerning the thesis and dissertation process, assessing your preparation for such an undertaking, and organizing your life to get to the finished product. Chapter 3 helps you estimate the time you will need to complete your project and anticipate and manage the myriad events that will come along to derail your efforts. Chapter 4 discusses finding a topic and developing a research question and hypotheses. Because this is most often done in collaboration with one or more faculty members, chapter 4 also contains advice about selecting a chairperson and committee members and about thesis and dissertation etiquette in general. Chapter 5 provides an overview of the all-important thesis or dissertation proposal, and chapter 6 follows with suggestions for developing a literature review to accompany it. Chapter 7 discusses what to include in a good method section, along with issues of research ethics and informed consent. Choosing appropriate measures of your dependent variables, selecting statistics, data collection, data analysis, and writing up the results of your research are covered in chapters 8 through 10. Chapter 11 treats the presentation of these results, and chapter 12 handles their discussion. Chapter 13 reviews strategies for handling your proposal meeting and oral defense. Finally, chapter 14 discusses adapting your document for presentation at professional meetings and for eventual submission for publication.

At the end of most chapters, we provide references to additional sources you might find useful if you want to explore topics covered in the chapter in more depth. Although Web sites come and go, we also provide references to particularly useful Web sites that we believe are likely to last. When the topic or reason for recommending the reference may not be obvious, we list these under headings that indicate the topic or provide a brief explanation of the relevance of some or all of the reference.

Some chapters provide checklists that turn our suggestions into concrete steps you can take to move your research forward. You can adapt these checklists to suit your project and you can also use them to keep track of your progress. Finally, in the appendix we include the American Psychological Association's (APA's) ethical standards for conducting research.

The topics we cover follow the sequence you would normally encounter in the thesis or dissertation process. We think you will get the most out of the book by reading the chapters one after the other as you approach each new phase of your dissertation work. It will also be useful to skim the entire book quickly before starting the process so you will have some idea of its contents and where to look for something should you need it in a sequence different from the one we have chosen.

Now let's go back to the first question posed in the title of this chapter: What are theses and dissertations anyway? First, we define them; then we talk a little bit about their history. Finally, we say something about what theses and dissertations in psychology actually look like.

Definitions, Distinctions, and Functions

A check of several dictionaries for definitions of *thesis* or *dissertation* shows that formal definitions often do not distinguish between these terms. Merriam-Webster OnLine (n.d.) defines a dissertation as "an extended usually written treatment of a subject; *specifically*: one submitted for a doctorate." The same source defines thesis as "a dissertation embodying results of original research and especially substantiating a specific view; *especially*: one written by a candidate for an academic degree." Similarly, AskOxford.com (n.d.), a service of the Oxford English Dictionary, defines dissertation as "a long essay, especially one written for a university degree or diploma" and thesis as "a long essay or dissertation involving personal research, written as part of a university degree."

As these definitions reveal, there is no clear distinction between the terms thesis and dissertation. In fact, both definitions of the former include the latter.

In U.S. universities, it has become common to distinguish between dissertations and theses by referring to the work done for a master's degree as a thesis and that done for the doctoral degree as a dissertation. This is not a universally accepted distinction by any means, and some faculty members refer to dissertations as "theses." Throughout this volume, we will use the term *dissertation* to refer to an original piece of empirical research, done as partial fulfillment of the requirements of doctoral (EdD, PhD, or PsyD) programs in psychology and related fields. *Thesis* hereinafter will refer to empirical research conducted en route to a master's degree.

Despite terminological ambiguities, most faculty members agree on the general functions to be served by theses and dissertations. One major purpose is to reveal the student's skill at conducting independent research that makes an original contribution to knowledge on an important topic. Another is to assess the student's mastery of a specialized area of scholarship. Some see the dissertation process as examining mastery of technical aspects of research—knowledge and ability to apply principles of research design, statistics, and so on. Thus, by this interpretation the dissertation process is an examination of your competence to function autonomously as a researcher. The finished dissertation also results in a new and significant contribution to the knowledge in the field. Theses, too, are expected to contribute to the general knowledge. Thesis requirements place less emphasis on originality, however, and candidates are often given more guidance and supervision. Some thesis candidates conduct a systematic replication of already completed research, for example. In addition, thesis candidates rarely operate as independently as doctoral candidates must.

In addition, dissertations and theses have a training function. By conducting these projects, you learn and grow in your research skills and knowledge of the field. You also should expand your ability to think critically, synthesize and extend the work of others, and communicate clearly and professionally. Ideally, the process should also increase your respect for the empirical aspects of the discipline and your pride in participating in the development of new knowledge about important phenomena.

What Theses and Dissertations Look Like

You have probably asked yourself a number of questions about the form your thesis or dissertation is supposed to take. Must you use particular methods? How long is it supposed to be? What format are you supposed to follow? Are there writing style requirements to follow? Let's look at some of these questions.

First, about methods: Although this book assumes your project will involve quantitative research, not all theses and dissertations require this. The traditional terminal degree in psychology, the PhD, virtually always requires an empirical project. Some applied psychology programs offer an alternative terminal degree, the PsyD, or doctor in psychology. PsyD programs explicitly prepare students for careers as practitioners, often in clinical psychology. PsyD programs may require final written scholarly projects that make original contributions to knowledge, and sometimes they call them dissertations. Many practitioner-oriented schools allow alternatives to the traditional empirical dissertation, however. Sanchez-Hucles and Cash (1992) surveyed directors of 40 "Vail-model" programs—in other words, professional clinical psychology programs in the United States, which presumably included a significant number of PsyD programs. Seventy-five percent of respondents said they accept nonempirical alternatives such as theoretical papers, program evaluations, and clinical case reports. Interestingly, approximately half of the students in these programs elected to conduct empirical research to satisfy their doctoral requirements anyway.

As for length, there is a great deal of variability within and between disciplines and within and between universities. Although we do not have objective data on theses, we do know something about the length of dissertations. We recently randomly sampled 100 dissertations completed between 2001 and 2002 selected from Proquest's *Digital Dissertations* database. Psychology dissertations (PhD only) had a mean page length of 190 (excluding outliers of more than 450 pages), with a range of 89 to 612.[1] Considering the standard deviation for our sample was 89.6, a safe estimate is that 85% of present-day psychology dissertations fall between 63 and 317 pages, inclusive of text, tables, appendixes, and related items. Our educated guess is that master's theses would average about two thirds this length, or about 127 pages.

As for format: Yes, there is a format you are supposed to follow. This will be dictated by your particular academic institution. We suggest you get in touch with the person in charge of such matters and learn about your local (i.e., institution-specific) requirements. These people can usually be found in the office of the dean of your graduate school or at your university library. They will usually have a Web site or written materials to give you that will spell out the acceptable format or formats. In addition, they will probably provide you with other useful information, such as timelines, committee requirements, binding fees, and so on. Theses and dissertations in psychology commonly follow the style and format guidelines set forth in

---

[1] We are indebted to Linda Isaac for collecting and analyzing these data.

the *Publication Manual of the American Psychological Association* (APA, 2010). This book has been written in that format and many journals in the behavioral sciences adhere to it. Indeed, we will refer extensively to the APA's *Publication Manual* throughout this book.

Although this is a frequently followed format, it is not universally accepted, even in schools and departments of psychology. Furthermore, even where it is accepted, institutional deviations often exist—for example, in referencing and the placement of tables—and you will do well to discover these early on. In fact, we advise you to learn the institution-specific norms as one of your first priorities. You will save much time and aggravation later by writing and referencing in the accepted format right from the start.

A good place to begin to get a good idea of what your dissertation or thesis will eventually look like is to examine some of those completed by previous students who have worked with the same committee chairperson(s) you are considering. These will provide excellent concrete examples of what you can expect to have to complete. Ask faculty members for some suggestions. Be aware that completed projects can vary in quality, and faculty members might want to direct you to examples that are most relevant to the type of research you are contemplating. Chapter 4 deals specifically with the selection of committee chairs, so don't worry if you haven't yet selected one.

What in general will your final document contain? Most dissertations and theses closely resemble a journal article, but your document will have more detail. It will begin with a table of contents and then launch into a review of the literature. Following this will be your method section, then your results, and finally your discussion. A reference section will contain details on the works cited in the text, and appendixes will provide supplemental material, such as equipment blueprints, consent forms, data recording forms, and sometimes even raw data themselves.

So there you have it. You know what theses and dissertations are and what they look like. The remainder of this book will tell you about the nuts and bolts of the process you will follow to complete this major undertaking. Now, let's turn our attention to what is probably the most important question of this chapter.

Why Do a Thesis or Dissertation in the First Place?

There are many reasons for doing a thesis or dissertation. In the final analysis, you are writing one because your graduate program you are in requires it to obtain a particular degree. There are other good reasons as well, of course. Some are economic: The document might be your ticket to higher income, an academic or applied job, or the beginning of your professional career. Others are intellectual: Research offers many challenges and opportunities to think about and solve conceptual, methodological, and practical problems. Conducting research is also a way to find out more about some psychological or other behavioral science phenomenon that piques your curiosity. Completing a thesis or dissertation can also provide the personal satisfaction of taking on and mastering a complex and challenging task.

Now that you are at this point in your program, take a moment to consider how you view this specific requirement. Is it merely a troublesome hurdle to clear on your way to a degree? Are you looking for the easiest, quickest way to get beyond it? Do you eagerly anticipate gaining useful skills during the project? Do you see it as having any relevance to the work you plan after graduation? Is it an opportunity for you to pursue further research you are already doing and to answer new questions you have been asking yourself?

As cognitive–behavioral therapists know, the way you think about the major research you are about to undertake will contribute to the enjoyment and ease you experience, as well as the amount you learn from it. If you are filled with curiosity about some aspect of psychology or even about the process of doing research in psychology, good for you! You will probably have the stamina to stick with your project from start to finish. You will probably even have some fun along the way. It is useful to concentrate on the positive aspects of the project and to view the hurdles you will encounter as challenges rather than obstacles. You probably haven't gotten this far if you don't enjoy learning. Doing research, for many, is the ultimate learning experience.

Find What Works for You

Before ending this chapter, a word of warning is in order: Some of the advice we offer will not be useful to you. Not every strategy works well for every student, and not every faculty member and department orchestrate the thesis and dissertation process with the same instruments and score. There are almost as many different ways of getting from the beginning to the end of the dissertation process as there are graduate students. The key is finding ways of negotiating the process that work for you. In addition, rules and traditions differ from place to place. Take what we say with some healthy skepticism, and gather information along the way to see whether your local situation is different from what we present in this book. Remember, completing a thesis or dissertation is, in some respects, a rite of passage. As with most such rites, some of the process may seem arbitrary and nonfunctional. If you acknowledge this up front and decide to do what needs to be done whether it makes complete sense or not, you will succeed much more easily and have a lot more fun along the way.

In other words, don't get too intimidated by the thesis or dissertation process. Yes, it's lengthy. Yes, it's involved. Yes, you may never have done anything quite like this before. Yes, it may be scary. And yes, you, like many others, will probably complete the process and earn your degree. Remember, most of the project will involve skills you already have. In addition, your chairperson and committee will be there to help.

One of our students put it well:

> As I come to the close of my graduate process and the completion of my dissertation, one thought keeps coming back to me—that any goal is possible given two factors: 1) the ability to break things down into tiny steps, and 2) the support of family, friends, and the community. (Dionne, 1992, p. iii)

We know you are motivated or you wouldn't be reading this book. Are you ready to act on this motivation? Let's turn to chapter 2 to examine your preparation in some detail and find out what you might do to be even better prepared for the task ahead.

2

Starting Out: Assessing Your Preparation for the Task Ahead

I n the previous chapter we suggested you examine your attitude toward completing a thesis or dissertation. Being in the right frame of mind is important both at the start and throughout big writing projects such as this. There are other types of preparation too. In this chapter we help you assess some of those. Our goal is to help you appraise skills needed to do the job well.

Are You Ready?

To get you started we provide a reality test. By now you have identified good reasons for undertaking a major research project and you are convinced you want to do it. Are you really prepared, though? Complete the Research Readiness Checklist that follows (see Exhibit 2.1) to answer that question better. When you take the test be sure to respond to each of the questions as truthfully as you can. Remember, this is a test of just how realistically you are approaching this process. Be honest with yourself. A "no" answer will provide useful material for reflection when we talk about the implications of your responses. Write your answers on a separate sheet of paper and we will discuss how to interpret them in the next section.

Exhibit 2.1

Research Readiness Checklist

Yes	No	**How Well Do You Write?**
☐	☐	1. Do you get feedback from professors that your writing is easy to follow, that your logic is clear?
☐	☐	2. Do you use correct grammar consistently?
☐	☐	3. Do you consistently spell correctly?
☐	☐	4. Do you know APA format well enough to write with only occasional checking?
☐	☐	5. Do you know how to use a comprehensive word processing program (e.g., WordPerfect, Word)?
☐	☐	6. Do you organize your papers effectively?
☐	☐	7. Do you prepare an outline before beginning to write?

Yes	No	**Do You Have the Necessary Methodological Preparation?**
☐	☐	8. Have you taken two or more graduate level statistics courses within the past 3 years?
☐	☐	9. Have you taken a graduate level course in test construction or measurement theory?
☐	☐	10. Have you taken a course in research design as a graduate student?
☐	☐	11. Have you been required to critique a number of empirical research papers in graduate school?
☐	☐	12. Have you been involved in empirical research as a graduate student?
☐	☐	13. Do you know how to use at least one major statistical software package?

Yes	No	**General Preparation**
☐	☐	14. Have you talked to at least three other individuals about their thesis/dissertation experience?
☐	☐	15. Have you examined theses/dissertations completed by other students in your program?
☐	☐	16. Do you have at least 10 to 20 hours per week to spend on the project?
☐	☐	17. Will this time be available for *at least* 12 to 18 months?

continued

Exhibit 2.1, continued

Yes No

☐ ☐ 18. Do you have the physical space to do uninterrupted writing, data analysis, and so forth?

☐ ☐ 19. Do you have access to adequate bibliographic resources (libraries, databases)?

☐ ☐ 20. Do you have access to faculty/advisor input on a regular basis?

☐ ☐ 21. Do you have the agreement of family/loved ones to support you in this effort?

☐ ☐ 22. Do you own or have access to a computer?

☐ ☐ 23. Do you have adequate keyboarding skills?

☐ ☐ 24. Do you know how to use the databases, literature retrieval mechanisms, and other resources available at your school's library?

☐ ☐ 25. Do you have reasonable time-management skills?

☐ ☐ 26. Do you have reasonable interpersonal/political skills?

☐ ☐ 27. Do you know the formal rules governing the thesis/dissertation process at your school?

☐ ☐ 28. Do you know the informal rules governing this process?

☐ ☐ 29. Have you asked other students about the costs of running their research?

☐ ☐ 30. Have you investigated financial resources available to defray dissertation costs?

Because this checklist is not an empirically validated measure, don't think of it as providing definitive answers concerning your preparation to navigate a complex research project successfully. Instead, use it as an inventory of the important types of preparation you will need to make the journey a smooth one. Basically, this list is a task analysis of the skills and resources that we believe you will need to complete the project effectively and in a timely manner. This leads to a word of warning: Do not let a "no" answer be a stimulus for an anxiety attack. A "no" does not mean you will fail to complete your thesis or dissertation. One of us, for example, would have said no to at least four items before beginning her successfully completed dissertation. Nor does a full complement of yes answers mean that you will sail through the project trouble-free. Rather, use "no" answers to alert you to potential trouble spots that advance planning and preparation could help you avoid. Next we provide some tips on what this preparation might involve.

Interpret Your Responses

To analyze your preparation, let's look more closely at some of the items on the checklist.

Writing. Writing and methodology skills are probably the most important skills you need to complete a thesis or dissertation successfully. If you said "no" to Items 1 and 2, you should seriously consider additional preparation before undertaking your project. Organization skills in writing (Item 1) are an indication of how clearly you think. If you do not organize well, you might have trouble thinking in a logical fashion. And, unfortunately, there are no quick and easy programs to teach this skill. So, if you have reason to believe you do not organize verbal material well, stop and reconsider. You might benefit from specific coursework or tutoring in organizing and sequencing written material. Examine offerings in the English department of your school. Have you ever taken a course in logic? If not, look for one in the philosophy department. Grammatical skill (Item 2) is more specific than organization. If you have consistently received input during your university schooling that you have problems with sentence structure, paragraph organization, writing mechanics, and the proper choice of words, give some serious thought to remediating before beginning your thesis or dissertation. Although some schools permit editorial consultation on theses and dissertations, most stop short of allowing the kind of input serious grammatical deficiencies would require. Unless English is not your native language, faculty will expect you to write the document yourself, not have an editor do it.

You can take several steps to improve grammatical skills. First, make sure you have taken a good course or mastered a good textbook on syntax and the rules of grammar and punctuation. With this basic foundation in syntax and punctuation, one next step toward grammatical proficiency would be to subject a sample of your writing to one of the several good grammar-checking programs that run in conjunction with your word processor. Note that Word™ has a good spelling and grammar checker that includes a number of options that you can elect to occur automatically or on demand. A stand-alone software program, StyleWriter™, is also good. It is available online and can be downloaded to your computer.

Such programs will indicate whether you have violated one or more of hundreds of rules of grammar, made punctuation errors, produced too many long sentences, been too negative, or written in the passive voice. Using one of these programs is almost like hiring a professional copyeditor to review your work. You will be amazed at the thoroughness with which these programs analyze your writing. Even if you typically have been considered a good writer, you will benefit. We all have bad habits that are so automatic we're not even aware of them.

As an example of the type of analysis you will receive from a grammar-checking program, look at the writing sample in Exhibit 2.2. The exhibit shows a paragraph taken from an earlier draft of this chapter.

As you can see, StyleWriter™ provides a rather detailed analysis of this writing sample. One's writing can be improved considerably by subjecting repeated samples to analyses of this type, as the revision of this sample reveals in Exhibit 2.3. Note the word counts at the bottom of these exhibits. Although there is a small reduction in the revised sample, it is usually the case that revising in line with StyleWriter™'s suggestions results in the use of fewer words. You will not get feedback this extensive from your committee or chairperson. About all these busy people will have time to do is comment that your writing needs improvement. They might point out a few specific split infinitives, verb–subject disagreements, and preposition errors, but their job is to teach independent research skills and not writing. It is unlikely that any person could provide the comprehensive feedback available from well-constructed software programs. It is just not humanly possible to keep the thousands of rules available in one's head and recall them at just the right moment, even if time permitted. Russell Shaw discusses the pros and cons of grammar-checking software in an interesting article found online (Shaw, 2002).

A word of warning is in order. Please note that we use a rather informal style in writing this book. It is full of "you's" and contractions, for example, and occasionally a series ending in "and so on." These informalities are not expected in formal writing and would not be acceptable in a thesis or dissertation. Please do not use the writing in this book as an example of a style that would be appropriate in your document.

A final suggestion for improving your writing is to obtain a copy of the most prestigious journal in your field. This should be a journal that publishes empirical research much like what you will be doing in your thesis or dissertation. Select several papers from a recent copy of the journal. Prepare an outline of one of them. Notice how the author(s) organize the paper by concentrating on the headings and subheadings used. Within

Exhibit 2.2

Original Paragraph With StyleWriter™ Corrections Suggested

Writing. Writing and methodology[1] skills are probably[2] the most important skills you need to complete a thesis or dissertation. We'll discuss methodology in a moment. First, let's talk about writing. If you said "no" to Items 1 and 2, you should seriously consider additional[3] preparation before undertaking your project. Organization skills in writing (Item 1) are an indication[4] of how clearly you think. If you do not organize well, you might have trouble thinking in a logical fashion. And, unfortunately, there are no quick and easy programs to teach this skill. So, if you have reason to believe you do not organize verbal[5] material well, stop and reconsider. You might benefit from specific coursework or tutoring in organizing and sequencing written material. Examine offerings in the English department of your school. Have you ever taken a course in logic? If not, look for one in the philosophy department. Grammatical prowess[6] (Item 2) is somewhat[7] more specific than organization. If you have consistently received input[8] during your university schooling that you have problems with sentence structure[9], paragraph organization, and the proper choice of words, give some serious thought to remediating before beginning your thesis or dissertation. Although some schools permit[10] editorial consultation on theses and dissertations, most stop short of allowing the kind of[11] input[12] serious grammatical deficiencies[13] would require[14]. Unless English is not your native language, faculty will expect you to write the document yourself, not have an editor do it.

Words = 241   Style Index: 53 Average   Ave. Sent: 14 Excellent
Passive: 0 Excellent

Note. When working with this software, you can click on the shaded words and see an explanation from *StyleWriter*™ about why the word is flagged. In addition, *StyleWriter*™ advises you of changes to consider. Examples for the first nine shaded words in the sample above are as follows.

[1] Complex Words
Generally prefer simpler words
Use the simpler, more familiar word whenever possible. Simpler words make your writing easy to read. Using simpler words will help to make your meaning clear so your readers can concentrate on the message.
For example:
Please endeavor to ascertain the truth.
Please try to find out the truth.

[2] Redundancies
Avoid wordiness
Improve your writing by making long-winded phrases simpler. You can often replace a phrase with a single word without losing any meaning.
Getting rid of unnecessary words in your writing will make your sentences shorter and your meaning clearer. Economy of words is a mark of good writing.

continued

Exhibit 2.2, continued

StyleWriter highlights redundant phrases and offers shorter, simpler alternatives to remove padding from your writing. Examples:

Redundancies	Advice
at a later date	later (be specific)
due to the fact that	because, since, for, as
in order to	to
in relation to	about, in, with, towards, to, on (or omit)
prior to	before

[3] Complex Words
      Advice: added, extra, more, another

[4] Complex Words
      Advice: sign, signal, mark, hint, suggestion

[5] Confused Words
      Advice: aural = of the ear or hearing
                    oral = of the mouth, voice or speaking, spoken
                    verbal = of words or speech, usually spoken

[6] Misused Words
      Advice: prowess = valor or daring—does not mean skill or competence

[7] Overwriting
      Advice: You can usually omit "somewhat." For example, somewhat older = older

[8] Jargon/Abstract
      Advice: Don't overuse [be specific or edit out]

[9] Jargon/Abstract
      Advice: Don't overuse [be specific or edit out]

Note. From StyleWriter™. Ave. sent = average sentence length. The program rates sentence length in terms of the type of writing selected, with higher numbers being longer sentences and generally more difficult to read.

---

sections of the paper, notice how the different paragraphs are sequenced and how they present the flow of information in a logical way. Finally, notice the sentence structure the author uses. The best way to make sure you attend to these things in enough detail to improve your own writing is to prepare your outline and examine it for organization and structure. Leave space on your outline and copy in the text under each heading. Then copy, word for word, the sentences that support or expand each point in the outline. After doing this for several papers you will be impressed with how much better your own writing becomes. You can do the same thing using dissertations or theses your chairperson designates as particularly well written.

Spelling (Item 3) and style requirements (Item 4) deal with even more specific verbal skills. Happily, although they are important, their absence is not fatal in the budding behavioral scientist. If you own a computer you can put your document through its spell-checking program and catch most

---

Exhibit 2.3

Paragraph Revised After StyleWriter™ Corrections

Writing. Writing and methodology skills are the most important skills you need to complete a thesis or dissertation. We'll discuss methodology in a moment. First, let's talk about writing. If you said "no" to Items 1 and 2, you should seriously consider more preparation before undertaking your project. Organization skills in writing (Item 1) are a sign of how clearly you think. If you do not organize well, you might have trouble thinking in a logical fashion. And, unfortunately, there are no quick and easy programs to teach this skill. So, if you have reason to believe you do not organize verbal material well, stop and reconsider. You might benefit from specific coursework or tutoring in organizing and sequencing written material. Examine offerings in the English department of your school. Have you ever taken a course in logic? If not, look for one in the philosophy department. Grammatical skill (Item 2) is more specific than organization. If you have consistently received feedback during your university schooling that you have problems with sentence structure, paragraph organization, and the proper choice of words, give some serious thought to remediating before beginning your thesis or dissertation. Although some schools allow editorial consultation on theses and dissertations, most stop short of allowing the help serious grammatical deficiencies need. Unless English is not your native language, faculty will expect you to write the document yourself, not have an editor do it.

Words = 236   Style Index: 21 Good   Ave. Sent: 14 Excellent
Passive: 0 Excellent

Note. Ave. sent = average sentence length. The program rates sentence length in terms of the type of writing selected, with higher numbers being longer sentences and generally more difficult to read.

---

of the results of poor skills in this area. If not, you can hire someone to proofread for you. The same can be said for American Psychological Association (APA) format. Some computer programs (e.g., StyleEase for APA Style™) actually do most of the formatting work required. If you don't have such a program, get one or hire an editor familiar with APA style. Better yet, buy the *Publication Manual of the American Psychological Association* (APA, 2010) and learn the proper formatting yourself. Anyone competent enough to complete graduate work can master APA style with a little help from this clear and detailed manual. The APA also publishes a student guide to using APA style (APA, 2010) that can be helpful, although it is geared more toward typical student papers than toward theses and dissertations.

If you are at a school that uses some other style, most likely there is someone who can give you a style sheet or refer you to a Web site or manual that indicates what is acceptable. Ask at your library or dean's office for such a document. Again, a quick search of the Internet will most likely reveal several software programs written to help you conform to your particular style requirements.

Methodology

Items 8 through 13 deal with the adequacy and recency of your methodological preparation. It is probably safe to say that taking two or more statistics classes (Item 8) is an essential requirement for satisfactory thesis or dissertation completion in most departments. (It is not, of course, if you are in a program in applied behavior analysis in which analyses are largely confined to verbal descriptions of the impact of graphically presented results.) If you are not currently fluent in the statistical concepts and tools covered in the usual two-course graduate statistical sequence, you may have to take some remedial steps. Part of the material covered in such courses can be found in chapter 9. Look it over. Does it seem comfortably familiar? Could it be with just a brief review?

If it has been some time since you completed your statistics coursework, you might want to appraise your current skills more systematically. If your graduate program includes tests of statistics as part of its comprehensive exams, ask your advisor if you can take the current version of the test. Explain that you want to know whether you need to take a refresher course. You might accomplish this by auditing the major methodological courses, all or in part.

Before you let statistics phobia scare you away from doing a thesis or dissertation, remember that we said "fluent." We did not say that you must be an A+ whiz in statistics or that you find the material easy. Most students, in our experience, find statistics to be the most challenging and intimidating part of research. Even students who earn As in stats classes may find that they need to review the material or that they sometimes get stumped when it comes to applying what they learned to their own projects. Nonetheless, with adequate guidance, they master this aspect of their thesis or dissertation. The key is obtaining adequate guidance if you have mastered basic statistical concepts and additional training or tutoring if you have not. Thousands of psychologists-in-training have mastered their fear of numbers, and, with some work, you can too.

An affirmative answer to Item 9 (measurement theory) is most important if you are planning a project that will require constructing your own scale. Are you working in an area with nonexistent or inadequate measures of the variables you will be studying? Are you planning to survey the attitudes of a group of migrant workers, for example? Are you interested in violence in gay males' dating relationships but have found there are no good measures of it? If your answer is yes to similar questions, you should be fluent in measure development or test construction concepts. The intricacies of scale construction and validation are myriad and should not be approached lightly. Even if your research does not involve the actual construction of new measures, it is good to be an educated consumer. To make the most informed choice of instruments for the variables you will be studying requires more than passing familiarity with psychometric concepts. If you are unsure of your preparation in this area, take a look at the material in chapter 8.

Have you taken a class in research design (Item 10)? This is important for understanding how to design studies in ways that minimize sources of internal invalidity while maximizing external validity. If these terms sound like Greek to you, we strongly recommend that you review research design principles.

Another outcome of design classes is that you learn to speak the language of research, and to speak it correctly. Ill-prepared students often use the word *confound* when they mean *methodological problem.* Others refer to the *reliability* of a research design or confuse *dependent* and *independent variables.* Correct use of terminology is important for discussing the methodology of your own study as well as others' work. In addition, an incorrectly used term in an oral defense is a signal to committee members that you may not know what you are talking about. This kind of problem invites probing and sometimes antagonistic questioning. Fortunately, it is easily prevented if you make sure you understand research terms and use them precisely.

Which brings us to Item 11—having some experience at reading and evaluating the research literature. All published articles are not equal in terms of their methodological rigor. Part of your job in creating a good study is to sort the good from the mediocre (We can hope the bad never made it into print!) and to make sure your study is in the "good" group. In addition, you will need to be appropriately critical of what others have done (in your literature review) and what you yourself have done (in the discussion section). As with most things, practice makes perfect. Experience in critically reading and evaluating empirical literature in graduate courses has the added advantage of sharpening your thinking skills in general. Meltzoff (1998) fabricated numerous studies with built-in problems and presents these (with answers) if you need more practice.

To some extent, answering positively to Item 12 (research experience) may cover you with respect to the previous four items. If you have been especially active in a program of research that serves as the basis for your own study, you will likely be familiar with the methodology required for conducting that research. If you have been involved less extensively, or if your plans have led you to another area, you might not be as well-prepared. In this case, a thorough appraisal of your competence in statistics and measurement might be in order.

Most graduate programs expose students to computer software designed to take the drudgery out of number crunching in research (Item 13). Among the more popular are SPSS, SAS, and Systat. Find out which of these are available to you and can be used to analyze the data you will eventually produce. If you do not know yet exactly which tests or procedures you will need, just familiarize yourself with what is available for now. You can get more specific after you have designed your project and know the type of data you will be analyzing.

In summary, your writing and methodology skills are the most important determinants of your success in the research process. Before moving on, however, let's look at the implications of some of the other items on the Research Readiness Checklist. Consider Items 16 and 17, for example. Some otherwise realistic candidates are amazed at suggestions that they will need *at least* 10 to 20 hours a week to devote to the effort. And the thought that this might have to extend over 1 to 2 years completely dumbfounds them! In truth, these are probably conservative estimates—at least for dissertations. Davis and Parker (1979) found that 80% of dissertations require 11 to 19 work months to complete. And these figures are based on 175-hour months! Of course, these estimates are subject to local variation, and that is where Items 14 and 15 can be useful. What have others at your school said about the time required to complete their theses or dissertations?

Environmental Support

What about the space to pursue this mammoth undertaking? This is clearly not the time to be eyeing the kitchen table, figuring you can work around the salt and pepper, the toaster, and the morning paper. You are going to be at this awhile, so you will want to choose your work space carefully. Find someplace quiet that will afford uninterrupted privacy for sustained periods of time. Many university libraries provide locked carrels for scholars doing long-term projects.

Both of us have had the occasional student who actually rented an office specifically for doing the dissertation. They planned to do no other work in this office. This exemplifies an important behavior management principle. Behavior that is under the control of narrowly defined stimulus conditions will, other things being equal, become increasingly focused. Researchers in self-control have talked about stimulus control for some time (Stuart, 1977). People with weight problems are told to eat only at the dining room table and (sometimes) only with a white placemat in front of them. Insomniacs are told to sleep only in bed, and only to sleep in bed, thus bringing sleeping more clearly under the stimulus control of the bed. B. F. Skinner had a special desk in his house for writing. He spent several hours at this desk each day, and permitted himself no other activity (e.g., bill paying or personal correspondence) at this desk.

Related to bringing your writing under the stimulus control of a particular location is bringing it under the control of a particular time of day as well. In his later years, Skinner wrote each day between 5:00 and 7:00 a.m. By being consistent in the time you work each day, you increase the chances that a whole host of additional temporally related stimuli will control your writing. The outside light and sounds are likely to be constant (and thus less distracting), as is your biological state. Although for some consistency might be the hobgoblin of little minds, it is more often the godparent of successful theses and dissertations.

You will be much more likely to produce this consistency if you carefully cultivate the support of family and loved ones. Do not neglect these important people. Be frank and realistic with them about your need for sustained periods of molelike behavior. At the same time, arrange occasions when you can be exclusively with them. Children and other family members will be much less likely to interrupt your work if they know you have committed to spend specific times with them and if you keep these commitments.

Computer Access and Skills

What about access to a computer and keyboarding skills (Items 22 and 23)? Are these really all that important? It is hard to imagine anyone asking these questions in this computer age. Yes, they are important. Computer literacy is not absolutely essential, however, and we know of dissertations completed successfully even today by people who cannot type. If you are one of these people, you will need to allow considerable amounts of time for typists to prepare your various drafts. This may help you decide whether to take the plunge and become computer literate—a step we used to consider optional but now consider almost essential.

Time Management

Chapter 3 has lots to say about time management skills (Item 25), an area in which most of us can improve. We have also discussed some of the elements in successful time management in the material on stimulus control earlier in this chapter. Suffice it to say that most deadline workers and procrastinators will face major challenges in completing their dissertations. It's time to start learning new work habits now.

Interpersonal Skills

Items 26 and 27 are related to just how well you are likely to get along with others in your research endeavor. Interpersonal and political skills refer to effective interaction with the key players in this work. The most important, of course, is your chairperson. Do you have the interpersonal skills needed to work effectively with this person? Are you willing to submit innumerable rewrites in response to what seem to you to be petty criticisms? Often students do not appreciate that multiple revisions are required to make a scientific document clear, coherent, and sufficiently detailed. It is said that Sir Isaac Newton knew well the importance of multiple rewrites. He took great care in revising his papers, and would write, cross out, correct, copy all over again, cross out, recorrect, and recopy. When he finished this process he would start all over again. "Thus, he made at least eight drafts of the *Scholium generale* for the second edition [of *Principia Mathematica*]" (Koyre, 1965, p. 262). Are you ready for a similar level of care?

Do you know how to assert your disagreements with suggestions in positive, constructive ways? Or do you typically react in defensive ways to suggestions for change? Do you know how to read the relationships between and among committee members? Are you likely to select members whose failure to get along interferes with your thesis or dissertation? Can you recognize grandstanding in committee meetings so that when it happens in yours you can handle it effectively? If your project requires the support of people in off-campus agencies, do you have the interpersonal resources to obtain and maintain this support? Can you move in and out of these agencies in effective, nondisruptive ways?

If your interpersonal skills are a bit rough, make a list of those situations in which you have difficulty. You may be able to recruit an assistant to help you with situations that involve contact with agencies, for example. The assistant can do most of the interacting if you are not good at it. With situations you must handle yourself, plan to seek advice from other students or faculty who are good at handling such situations. Rehearse effective approaches with a friend and get feedback on your performance.

Formal/Informal Rules

At all schools there are both formal and informal rules governing the entire thesis and dissertation process. There are forms to complete, fees to pay, deadlines to meet, and formats to follow, among other matters. For example, many schools publicize the occurrence of doctoral defenses. These are open meetings to which all members of the academic community are invited. To give notice in a timely way, it is often necessary to impose deadlines for specifying a time and place for the meeting. Is this true at your school? Some schools circulate a form among committee members indicating the time and place of the defense. At that time the committee member is asked to sign the form agreeing to be available and acknowledging receipt of a copy of the thesis or dissertation. Does your school do this? What about the time committee members are given to review the proposal before the proposal meeting is convened? Two calendar weeks is not an unusual amount of time for this. Is there a time period such as this at your school? Find out early what the formal rules are. Ask for a copy of them at the office of the chairperson of your department, the dean of the graduate school, or, if there is no graduate school dean, the dean of the school in which your program is located.

Then there are myriad informal rules. Becoming aware of these will make your life go more smoothly. For example, when should you approach a faculty member about chairing your committee? Do faculty expect you to have a well-developed idea and literature to back it up before you contact them? What if you have discussed ideas with several faculty and like the ideas of one best but really want to work with another? Is it okay to use the ideas provided by one faculty member while choosing another as chair? How complete and carefully proofread do drafts need to be before presenting them to your chair? To your committee? Are there certain blackout periods during which proposal meetings generally cannot be scheduled (e.g., during the last or first weeks of the term or during the summer)? Start finding out about these informal rules early in the process. Discover what they are before getting too far down the path. Talk to other graduate students who have nearly completed the journey. Ask your chair or potential committee members what they know about such rules. There will be no published list to obtain from the dean's office. And although the informal rules are often as important as the formal ones, faculty and more advanced students may not think to mention them unless you ask.

Costs and Resources

It costs money as well as time to do research. Schools and faculty vary widely in the financial support they provide for student research. This can range from no financial support to complete support of all of the student's costs in conducting the research. The latter is most common when a faculty member has large grants and the student's project is subsumed under the objectives of the funded research.

The Association for Support of Graduate Students (ASGS) collected data from 85 students in different disciplines who participated in ASGS e-mail discussions ("Saving Your Thesis When Support Goes Down the Drain," 1995). Most of these students had some sort of tuition assistance, and therefore probably attended more resource-rich institutions. Among the most common expenses students reported were costs incurred for photocopying, paper, and purchase of computers and printer. Additional costs to consider, depending on your project, may be payments to participants and research assistants, as well as costs for procuring copyrighted measures, software, equipment, postage, advertising. You may also have travel expenses. You will probably also have a few fees to pay to file the document, apply for the degree, and the like.

How will you finance these costs? Although you probably do not know your exact topic at this point, it's not too soon to do a little investigation. Some faculty and departments have funds they can draw on to assist students. Some schools have competitive grants for thesis and dissertation assistance. Many national organizations such as the APA and the National Institutes of Health offer dissertation grants and fellowships. Some of these are quite specialized. Your university's grants and contracts office is a good source of information about funding resources, especially once you have narrowed down your topic. Web sites are another source (see, for example, http://www.apa.org/students/funding.html for the APA Web site on sources of funding for education in psychology). Finally, other students who have obtained funding are great sources of information, as are their mentors. For now, just get an idea of how other students ahead of you have handled the costs of their research. If it looks like funding opportunities are likely to be few and far between, think about cutting back on café lattes from your local espresso bar and putting away some money to help with dissertation expenses when the time arises.

Examine Your Cognitive Ecology

In assessing your overall preparedness, it is useful to identify and dispel some common assumptions that will impede your progress. Mahoney and Mahoney (1976) referred to the process of cleaning up irrational thinking as cognitive ecology. The first few irrational thoughts have to do with estimating what it will take to get the job done. Even after everything you have read so far, you may be saying to yourself that if you start now, you can expect to be finished with the entire process in 6 months. You might be thinking the copy editor can get the final draft prepared in 5 days. Or you might be saying you can get all the participants you will need from two elementary schools, or that it will take 2 weeks to get permission from the principals to contact their teachers. If there is anything close to a Newtonian principle governing research, it is that estimates such as these are almost always wrong. In fact, this is true of research in the behavioral sciences in general. Estimates are so often in error that we have found it helpful to invoke the "rule of threes" whenever we make them. Multiply everything you think you'll need by three and your estimates will be much more on target.

A related irrationality is thinking that everything will run smoothly. It won't. Plan for the unexpected. It is going to happen anyway, and you might as well be ready for it. In addition to needing three times more of just about everything to complete the job, you can expect participants to break their appointments, equipment to fail, data to be lost, your chair to take another job and leave the university, among other difficulties. Are you ready for these events? Assess the likelihood of each and prepare contingency plans. If the event is significant and its likelihood great (e.g., your chair leaving) and you cannot develop a plan for working around it with your particular project, you might want to consider an alternative project altogether.

Another irrational thought is that your study must be the definitive work in the area. We are not saying that there is anything wrong with ambition. The problem is the paralyzing implications of the "Nobel laureate" error. If you think yours has to be the definitive study, you are never going to be satisfied that you have researched enough literature, framed the question and hypotheses properly, selected the absolutely best design, or controlled all the important variables. Keep in mind that knowledge grows by increments. Scientific breakthroughs and paradigmatic revolutions (Kuhn, 1970) are rare, and it is even more rare that they are the result of single studies.

The myth of methodological perfection is a related collection of thoughts that impedes research progress. Every study has its faults. These may not be recognized until the scientific community has scrutinized the work closely, but the faults are there. At a minimum there are trade-offs, the most common being that between internal and external validity (i.e., between scientific control on the one hand and generalization to the messy real world on the other). To expect your study to be different is simply unrealistic. We are not saying you should strive for anything less than excellence in pursuing your research. But to insist on methodological perfection when this is unattainable is likely to lead to an unfinished project.

If you still think your research has to be a methodologically perfect, definitive study, you would do well to analyze the function of such thoughts. What are you gaining by thinking them? Will they serve to insulate you from your own and other's criticisms of your lack of progress? After all, who could be faulted for wanting to do the perfect study and for refusing to be a part of anything less? Is it keeping the research process deliberately drawn out so that you can stay in school and not have to face the cold, cruel world of job seeking and economic self-sufficiency?

This chapter is about assessing your preparation for doing a thesis or dissertation. It deals with a number of skill and knowledge issues related to completing the task successfully. Some issues deal with things you can change more or less readily. In this category are the irrational beliefs discussed in the preceding section. Other issues concern areas (e.g., measurement and statistics) in which you might need better preparation. This might be accomplished by taking or reviewing additional courses. Finally, some basic skill areas (e.g., coherent, grammatically correct writing) *require* proficiency to complete a major research project. The guidelines in this chapter will be most useful to you if you approach them in an open, honest, self-appraising way. Answer the questions on the Research Readiness Checklist as forthrightly as possible. There is no shame in acknowledging areas of needed improvement. If the changes cannot be made, better to discover this now than to struggle along in self-defeating ways.

We hope that you have taken this appraisal seriously. Theses and dissertations are complex projects that require many skills. Remember: You do not have to be perfect to complete your dissertation or thesis. It is normal to have to work on areas in which you have less experience or expertise. Most of us muddle through the process one way or another. If you have a history of academic success (and most likely you do), if you apply the skills you have and work on those you lack, you, too, will make it through.

Item 25 in the Research Readiness Checklist asks about your time management skills. Regardless of how good they are, even the best of us run into problems when completing projects as multifaceted as theses and dissertations. For this reason, chapter 3 is devoted entirely to the topic of time and trouble management. It provides useful suggestions for preventing many difficulties and for dealing with those that arise despite your high level of preparation for the wonderful adventure ahead.

Supplemental Resources

Guides for Thinking About and Writing Dissertations and Theses Software

Error Detector: Order from elc.polyu.edu.hk/CILL/errordetector.htm

StyleEase for APA Style: Order from Stylewriter-USA.com

StyleWriter™: Order from Stylewriter-USA.com. For more on Stylewriter™, go to http://www.editorsoftware.com/. You can download a free 30-day trial at http://www.editorsoftware.com/demonstrations/stylewriter-writing-software-demonstration.html or http://www.editorsoftware.com/reviews/RAA/download/stylewriter-trial-form.html.

Books and Web Sites

American Psychological Association. (2010). *Publication manual of the American Psychological Association* (6th ed.). Washington, DC: Author.

Association for Support of Graduate Students. (2005). Web site accessed October 31, 2005, at http://www.asgs.org/

Darley, J. M., Roediger, H. L., & Zanna, M. P. (Eds.). (2003). *The compleat academic: A practical guide for the beginning social scientist.* Washington, DC: American Psychological Association.

Krathwohl, D. R. (1988). *How to prepare a research proposal: Suggestions for those seeking funds for behavioral science research* (3rd ed.). Syracuse, NY: School of Education, Syracuse University.

Meltzoff, J. (1998). *Critical thinking about research: Psychology and related fields.* Washington, DC: American Psychological Association.

✔ **To Do . . .**

Assessing Your Preparation

☐ Complete Research Readiness Checklist

☐ Interpret your responses

— Writing skills

— Methodology skills

— Environmental support

— Computer access and skills

— Time management skills

— Interpersonal skills

☐ Examine your cognitive ecology

3

Time and Trouble Management

In chapter 2, we warned you to expect the unexpected to occur sometime in the course of completing your dissertation. This chapter deals with some of the most common general problems you might encounter in producing a thesis or dissertation and suggests ways to avoid or overcome them. Later, chapter 10 helps you plan the specifics involved in implementing your research. Our goal in both chapters is to help you anticipate and plan the many steps involved in successful research, so that you encounter fewer surprises.

The first issue to address is how to manage your time effectively. Our focus is the logical outgrowth of Einstein's (1974) definition of time as the occurrence of events in sequence. It follows from this definition that effective use of your time means that you are managing sequenced events in an effective way. But what do we mean by "effective"? A synonymous phrase might be "gets desired results." Managing events effectively can be viewed as arranging things to get the results you want. Because most activities in life, especially research projects, involve a sequence of events, managing time effectively means managing these events effectively and accomplishing your goal of a completed thesis or dissertation.

Start With a Goal

Successful completion of a research project starts with a goal. Carefully worded goals contain certain common elements. Most important, they state *what* you want to accomplish and *by when*. For maximum effectiveness, the "what" should be stated in terms of measurable behavior. "Complete my dissertation by June 30, _____" would be an example. Another is "Obtain permission for study from elementary schools by March 1, _____."

The most difficult part of such goal setting is deciding the *when* element. Sometimes this is decided for you. You may have a form of financial support that ends at a specific time, whether you are finished or not. For example, government scholarships to students from foreign countries often include a completion date as one of the terms of the award, after which the student must return to the country to perform some type of work. Obviously, this type of contingency is more exacting than the one that involves simply stopping further monetary support at the end of a specified period. This, in turn, is more exacting than an open-ended completion date, with no contingencies. Careful planning and the effective use of your time are extremely important if you must finish your thesis or dissertation by a specific date.

Estimate Your Time Requirements

Think of your thesis or dissertation as a project. As with any sizable project, there are numerous subprojects or smaller steps to identify, sequence, and accomplish to complete the larger effort. You can increase the ease and manageability of your research by carefully identifying and sequencing the steps involved. So, how can you identify the steps?

First, sit down and reflect on everything you know about the requirements. Remember to consider both formal and informal rules. If you don't know them, find out now. List them in terms of things you have to do. For ease of later sequencing, it helps to put these on 3" × 5" cards, one event per card, beginning with a verb that specifies the action you need to take. For example, participants have to be recruited. Write this as "Recruit participants." Workspace has to be obtained. Write this as "Find (obtain or acquire) a place to work." Bound copies of the final version of the document might need to be presented to the librarian at your school. Write this as "Turn in ____ bound copies to the library." Why start each item with a verb? A verb indicates action and makes it pretty clear who is responsible for the action—namely, you. Compare "Recruit participants" with "Participants need to be recruited." The first is clearly an instruction to you. The second is merely a declarative sentence. So, participants need to be recruited. Isn't that interesting! When you watch the way you talk, you also watch how you behave in other ways. And decisive language is associated with decisiveness in other behavior. Compare the forcefulness of "*Try* to recruit participants" with "Recruit participants." Have you ever invited someone to a party and heard "That sounds great! I'll try to be there"? How much money would you bet on their appearance? Get clear on your intentions and then move decisively to accomplish them.

We routinely require our students to develop individual lists of goals with respect to their project. These are lists of the sequenced steps necessary to take students from where they are at the beginning to a completed dissertation. Many students find this worthwhile because it concretizes the whole undertaking. We do not restrict the number or sequencing of the steps. Although we generally encourage small, easily accomplished events using the "little steps for little feet" principle, students vary considerably in selecting the number and size of the steps in their lists. Some prefer fairly large chunks, for example, "Write proposal." Others prefer smaller chunks, for example, "Outline proposal," "Write first five pages of proposal," and "Turn in first draft to chairperson."

There are two approaches to sequencing the steps in your list. With backward chaining, you begin with the last step (e.g., "Turn in copies at the library") and work backward to the first step. This is most helpful in the planning stages, especially if you must be finished by a particular date. If an exact completion date does not concern you, you might take the more leisurely forward-chaining approach, starting where you are and listing all the steps between that point and the final one, adding dates for each as you go. If you find it too overwhelming to set goals that will cover the entire dissertation, pick an intermediate goal (e.g., "obtain approval of the proposal") and develop steps for that part of the process.

We get as few as six steps in some goal lists and as many as 46 in others. Some inventive sorts have even put their lists in the form of flowcharts, with alternative courses to pursue depending on outcomes at various decision points. For example, one student had these alternatives following "Defend dissertation successfully." "If 'yes,' leave on much deserved trip to Europe with wife and family. If 'no,' start looking through the help wanted ads." A little levity can be a great help at all stages in the process!

As you produce the list of things you must do to complete your project, think of each item as a goal in itself. As mentioned, write each step in the form of a goal, including both the behavior to perform and the date by which you will perform it. If you have started with the date by which you want to be finished, it is relatively easy to work backward from that date and to estimate how long each step should take.

Be realistic in estimating your time. As we noted earlier, most students grossly underestimate the amount of time it will take to turn a research question into a complete proposal. "Two months should be plenty," they might say. Even if the student is the world's fastest writer and has all of his or her literature in hand, what about the time required for the faculty supervisor to read between two and six drafts of the literature review and the method section? How about the time required for committee members to read the proposal? In planning time requirements, first be honest with yourself about what you are likely to accomplish in a given time period. Second, be sure to consider steps in your time line that rely on others (e.g., your committee chairperson, the Institutional Review Board, research assistants). If you are in doubt about time estimates and the sequencing of steps, ask other students about their experience. Ask your chairperson for estimates as well.

Schedule the Work

Once you have identified and assigned realistic completion times to each of the steps in the process, you may find it useful to represent these visually. There are numerous approaches you could take, from simple Gantt charts to more complex PERT (Program Evaluation and Review Technique) analyses. These tools provide a structure for planning. For example, a Gantt chart lays out a list of tasks with a visual time window for accomplishing them. Many project-scheduling software packages (e.g., MS Project™) can be useful in mapping your task. These vary considerably in complexity and thorough-ness, ranging from simple timeline charts to analyses that include cost estimates, conditional completion probabilities, and so on. Unless you are already a project-scheduling whiz kid or have some burning interest in learning such skills, it is probably enough to produce a modest Gantt or time-line chart. (Tablets of blank Gantt charts can be purchased in office supply stores.)

Exhibit 3.1 shows a partial Gantt chart for a research project. List each of the identified activities or steps in the project down the left side of the chart. Do this in the order they will be accomplished. Across the top of the chart list the time unit (days, weeks, or months) to be used in scheduling the steps. The arrows indicate when an activity or step is to be started and when it is to be completed. Activities that occur at a single point in time are indicated by Xs in the example; sometimes they are indicated by triangles. It can be seen that Activity 1, in-class assessments, is to begin the first day of the first week, continue throughout the week, and conclude at the week's end. Activity 2, identifying target children and their desired playmates, also begins in Week 1 and continues to the end of that week. Activity 3, random assignment to groups, occurs once, at the end of Week 1. Activity 9, conduct

Exhibit 3.1

Milestone Chart of Children's Social Skills Research Project

Activity Week:	1	2	3	4	5	6	7	8	9
1. Assess children in classes	→								
2. Identify target children and desired playmates (DPs)	→								
3. Randomly assign to groups	X								
4. Interview DPs of target children in template-matching group (TMG)		→							
5. Develop templates		X							
6. Interview choosers of target children			→						
7. Design target behaviors for TMG		X							
8. Design treatment plan		X							
9. Conduct direct observations				→				→	
10. Implement treatment				→——————————→				
11. Repeat in-class assessments									→

direct observations, occurs during all of Weeks 4 and 8. It is obvious from this example that several events must occur before others, that some occur simultaneously, and that some overlap.

A visual representation of the steps and their temporal relationships to one another makes you aware of the completeness of your planning. It also shows the interdependence of the tasks you need to accomplish. The whole job becomes clearer. The chart also becomes a tool you can use in communicating with others when describing your project. This is especially useful when meeting with representatives of off-campus agencies from whom you hope to recruit participants. It also impresses your committee in proposal meetings. Not only does it aid you in explaining exactly what you plan to do, it also shows your committee that you have thought of everything. Well, almost everything!

The added advantage of even simple computer-scheduling software is that you can get immediate feedback on the consequences of changes in your plans. If you are familiar with spreadsheet software, you know the tremendous power afforded by the automatic recalculation of related values when a single value in the data set is changed. Suppose that you decide you want to take a week off in the middle of your project for some unplanned R & R. You know, a great aunt has decided she just has to go to Hawaii and thinks you're the only one who can accompany her (at her expense, of course). What impact will this have on the entire project? Is it a simple matter of moving every time line a week back? Or is it more complex because of the parallel nature of some of the activities and their conditional dependence on one another? When you schedule, remember it is not set in stone. Logistics problems may force you to alter your plans once you begin the project. This is to be expected. You may not yet know how to estimate time frames and may need to alter your deadlines as you master this skill. Scheduling software helps by showing the impact of such alterations on the rest of the project.

Plan Your Schedule to Free Yourself

At this point, you may be asking why all this fuss about scheduling, time lines, charts, and so on. You want to get on with your research. Is all this fancy planning just a socially acceptable form of avoidance? It certainly can be, of course. On the other hand, an ounce of planning can avoid a pound of problems later on. In the Army, one of us had a sergeant who used to admonish new recruits daily with the five Ps: *prior planning prevents poor performance.* A little time spent initially identifying, sequencing, and time-lining the steps in your research project will save inordinate time and frustration later.

In addition, scheduling time to pursue your dissertation will help it become a regular part of your life. It also clarifies whether your schedule permits you to work on the dissertation on a regular basis or whether you are going to have to adjust other activities to make time for it. In our experience, students who make time in their day-to-day schedule for their dissertations finish earliest and with the least pain. Remember the old story about the tortoise and the hare? Remember who won the race? It's true with dissertations, too.

Equally important is the liberating effect of having a schedule and sticking to it. If you have been conscientious in identifying and scheduling all the steps in your project, you have really done the hard part. Now all you have to do is accomplish each step as it comes up in the schedule. This is why we encourage students to make the steps many and small. A good rule of thumb is to make them small enough to accomplish in a day or at most a week. If you do this, you can enter the steps in your appointment calendar or your personal digital assistant, writing each on the day you have scheduled to accomplish it.

Be sure to specify the outcome you want to produce in behavioral terms or in terms of products having a close relationship to behavior. For most people, "Read five articles" is preferable to "Spend 2 hours reading," and "Read and outline five articles" is even better. A few students, however, have told us they find time goals more useful than specific product goals, probably because they already use their time productively. The key is keeping on schedule by regular work, and taking the steps toward completion one by one.

Once all the steps are entered into your calendar, you can stop worrying. All you have to do is complete each small task as it comes up on your calendar or daily to-do list. It's like the old joke: How do you eat an elephant? One bite at a time! That is exactly how you complete a major research project. In fact, one of us wrote sections of the first edition of this book by planning to complete five pages of her portion every week. By sticking to that plan, she produced about one chapter a month and finished her writing on schedule.

We once had a student who sat down at the beginning of each semester and scheduled all his classes and all of his study, paper-writing, and project times for the classes. Each day of the semester was scheduled. When other students asked how he could stand to live under such a confining schedule, he replied that, on the contrary, he found the entire process quite liberating. Now he didn't need to spend any more time figuring out how he was ever going to get all that work done or worrying about whether he would. He could use that time more productively in (planned!) recreational pursuits, safe in the knowledge that by having a plan and sticking to it all his work would get done. This method would not work for everyone, but the lesson is clear: When you know what you have to do and do it according to schedule, you free yourself for guilt-free enjoyment of other parts of your life.

A final point to remember when constructing your initial schedule is to allow time for your social supports. If your time with significant others is going to be severely limited during particular periods, discuss this with them ahead of time, while you are first making your schedule. They need advance warning and the opportunity to plan alternate activities for themselves during those times. Whenever possible, give them some say in the schedule itself. By being empowered at this stage, they are less likely to feel excluded and resentful later. Balancing professional and personal commitments and priorities is never easy, and it's a particular challenge during the dissertation process to make sure you make time for health and friend- and family-related activities while still committing enough time to your research to complete your education in a timely fashion.

We alluded earlier to the overuse of scheduling and planning as a way of avoiding getting on with the project. Many other behaviors are even more easily seen in this light. There is no cleaner, better organized apartment than that of a dissertation candidate, for example. Procrastination and avoidance (or P and A) should probably be a category in the *Diagnostic and Statistical Manual of Mental Disorders* (*DSM*, of the American Psychiatric Association, 1994), it is so common among those doing theses and dissertations.

We all avoid things to some degree or the other. In the extreme, however, P and A prevent the project from ever being completed. Thus, where dissertations are concerned, the master of P and A becomes the ABD (All-But-Dissertation, or ABT for master's students). To minimize these behaviors, put the following statement on your wall in very large print.

> THE MASTER OF P AND A BECOMES THE ABD.

It can then serve as a daily reminder to keep with the program. Some of our students have taken this suggestion to heart and routinely post their goals on their refrigerators or computers to remind themselves to keep their eyes on the prize.

If you follow the suggestions earlier in this chapter, you are already dealing with P and A. If you have identified small enough steps, sequenced them properly, and written them in your appointment calendar or scheduler, you have arranged the components of a momentum-gathering machine that will propel you through the dissertation process. This is because of the energy that is liberated by completions. Ever notice how simply getting something done gives you the motivation to do other things? This is how it works with research projects as well. By getting each day's small step completed, energy seems to be liberated to do more steps. Doing these in turn produces more energy, and so on. The momentum builds and carries the project forward.

With major research projects, the most common time for procrastinating is in the writing stages, namely, producing a proposal and a final version of the thesis or dissertation. Several factors can operate. If, despite following our sage advice so far, you are still procrastinating, perhaps you are victimizing yourself with some of the following verbal behavior.

1. *"I can't seem to get started. It's so overwhelming."* Feeling overwhelmed is a clue that you have not broken your task into small enough steps. Think about what you can accomplish today toward your goal: Reading five articles? Typing your references? Outlining your method section? Overwhelming tasks can be turned into manageable ones by the simple device of breaking them into small, readily accomplishable steps. If you can't face the one you planned, do something on the project that seems more appealing. Accomplishing that task may give you the energy to tackle the one you originally planned. Do SOMETHING to get into the task.

2. *"I can't work on my research unless I have huge chunks of time, and I won't have those until next summer."* This is a creative excuse for doing nothing until next summer. The truth is, although you might be more efficient if you had large chunks of time, you can still get something done without them. In addition, can't you find at least one 3-hour block of time each week to work on your research? One of us, for example, has set aside a morning a week for the past decade to work on scholarly writing. This time is as sacred as classroom teaching (after all, would you cancel a class you were teaching to do school work for another class? To clean your apartment? To go food shopping?). Over the years, many articles and book chapters were written during these periods. As we have pointed out repeatedly, people complete theses and dissertations by steady work, one page at a time.

It is also important to schedule your dissertation and competing activities to take advantage of times you work best on academic tasks (see Yates, 1982, for more extended discussion). Our students have varied tremendously in how they work best—what times of the day, smaller or larger chunks of time, doing varied or single-focus activities, and so on. Schedule time to do intellectual tasks when your brain is at its best. If you are at your best in the morning, don't make 9:00 p.m. to 11:00 p.m. the time to work on your dissertation! Schedule less demanding tasks when you are likely to be tired or not at your cognitive best.

3. *"I don't know enough (haven't read enough, worked out the problems well enough, or don't have good enough hypotheses) to write anything."* This is a variation on perfectionist thinking: "I can't do it if it is not perfect." You obsess about doing it, and nothing gets written. No written draft will ever be perfect the first time around. Just write it, knowing and planning for it to be imperfect. Then, build in time for revision, to improve the first draft. Recall the grammar checking/editing software described in chapter 2.

More problematic are self-doubts: "I'm not smart enough, will never do enough/do well enough to satisfy my advisor, will be found out as the 'imposter' that I am" (Rudestam & Newton, 2001). This kind of self-talk robs you of your confidence and creates unnecessary emotional behavior and self-directed negative thoughts. It is important to distinguish between the nature of the thesis or dissertation task (which is the reality you face) and what you conclude about yourself (which is your own personal fiction or philosophy). Yes, the dissertation is a challenge, it is scary, and it is the door to your future, which may be even scarier! Yes, it is a long and often demanding task, which will require you to work hard and to push yourself. Yes, drafts that you worked very hard on will come back to you covered with "constructive" comments that you might choose to beat yourself up over. Yes, you will have times when you feel lost, because you WILL (temporarily) be lost. BUT—and this is big BUT—that does not mean you are stupid, an imposter, or not up to the task. Most people doing a dissertation experience these things. These are normal experiences in a challenging process. Don't beat yourself up if you find them difficult. Instead, pat yourself on the back: At least your experiences show you are normal!

4. *"I can work only with deadlines."* Some people learn to goof off unless a deadline is imminent. Then, they pull all-nighters to produce a paper, study for a final, complete a grant proposal, and so on. These people find themselves in deep trouble when the thesis or dissertation arrives, because these projects involve working toward a long-term goal with many steps and (usually) few immediate deadlines. As you have probably realized, a proposal

or final draft is not a project to be pulled off over a single weekend armed with carafes of coffee or bottles of amphetamines. We suggest two solutions for the deadline worker. First, create a series of real and meaningful deadlines for completing portions of your thesis or dissertation. Perhaps your graduate program has these. Some programs, for example, have a rule that clinical students cannot apply for internships without an approved dissertation proposal. If yours does not, perhaps you and your chairperson can create a similar contingency for you anyway. For example, if you are applying for academic jobs, perhaps you and your chair can agree that letters of recommendation will only be sent after a certain step (e.g., data collection or data analyses) is completed. Other professional timelines, such as dates for submitting abstracts to conventions or presenting your results at a job colloquium, may also serve as deadlines for you.

A second strategy involves breaking the deadline habit altogether. If you intend a professional career that involves research and scholarly writing, you will need to reduce your procrastination. So why not start now? If you create and stick with schedules, as outlined in this chapter, you *will* kick the habit.

One useful approach is to arrange your schedule according to the Premack principle, so named because of the psychologist who popularized it. The simple fact is that we can strengthen low-probability behavior by following it with behavior of a higher probability. This is the behavioral principle behind the old, "First you work, then you play" maxim. Do something on your research, then do something you really want or need to do (e.g., shopping or sleeping). Build this "work first, play second" rule into your lifestyle, and your project will be finished much more painlessly.

It is a good idea to build rewards into the research completion schedule initially. After turning in the final draft of your proposal to your committee members, for example, plan a get-away trip with a loved one. But do not leave unless the draft has been completed. If you make your accomplishments rewarding for significant others, too, they will keep supporting you in the overall effort. If you build the rewards into the schedule in advance, you will have them to look forward to. In this way, you will control a lot more on-task behavior than by waiting to finish the task and then deciding what nice thing to arrange for yourself and others.

Finally, ask members of your social support system to encourage you to make progress. Tell your peers about your accomplishments so they can congratulate you. Some students even band together into dissertation support groups to help keep each other on track. Two current students, for example, meet for a day each week to work on their dissertations. They go to the library, work independently at one student's apartment, and so on. Another student joined an online dissertation support group that provided her with many good ideas for breaking though her habits of procrastination. Be careful here, though. These groups should reinforce accomplishments, not commiserate with one another or provide support for "good reasons" for not making progress! Another good idea is to post a graph showing pages written per day (week) on your refrigerator door. People can notice it and make comments appropriate to the data.

Other challenges can arise during dissertation writing that have the potential to disrupt the process. Many people soldier through them with the help of friends, advisors, peers, and books such as this one (see the list at the end of this chapter for some added references that may be helpful). Professional guidance is also available in the form of "dissertation coaches" and therapists who specialize in working with students. If time management or emotional issues seriously interfere with your dissertation or thesis progress, it is worth your time to consider whether professional help might assist you in getting "unstuck" and moving forward.

As we keep repeating, the key to completing a dissertation is forward movement. Although we have offered lots of ideas about scheduling and planning, there are many different roads that all lead to the completed dissertation or thesis. As we've said before, find one that works for you, using your knowledge of yourself, your environment, forethought, and planning, and you will be well on your way.

Supplemental Resources

Bolker, J. (1998). *Writing your dissertation in fifteen minutes a day.* New York: Henry Holt. [This nifty volume focuses mostly on the writing process—how to think about writing as well as how to manage the writing process.]

Burka, J., & Yuen, L. (1983). *Procrastination: Why you do it, what to do about it.* Cambridge, MA: Da Capo Press. [Highly recommended by dissertation coach Mary McKinney, a clinical psychologist who specializes in helping dissertation students and entry-level academics.]

Gantt charts. (2005). Retrieved November 17, 2005, from http://www.ganttchart.com/index. html. [A Web site that provides an overview of Gantt charts and their history.]

Lakin, A. (1974). *How to get control of your time and your life.* New York: Signet Books. [A classic, also recommended by McKinney.]

Tracy, B. (2004). *Time power: A proven system for getting more done in less time than you ever thought possible.* New York: AMACOM.

Yates, B. T. (1982). *Doing the dissertation: The nuts and bolts of psychological research.* Springfield, IL: Charles C. Thomas. [Chapter 2 of this reference addresses self-management and time management and offers good suggestions for self-assessment.]

✔ **To Do . . .**

Managing Time and Trouble

☐ Set goals

☐ Estimate your time requirements

— Identify subgoals and activities

— Break down big tasks into small steps

— Sequence the subgoals/activities/steps

☐ Schedule the work

☐ Minimize procrastination and avoidance

— Avoid common unproductive thinking patterns

— Use the Premack principle

☐ Schedule dissertation times that capitalize on your energy levels

4

Finding Topics and Faculty Collaborators

At last we arrive at the steps involved in getting your specific project under way. Please remember that we sequence these chapters in the order in which we think *most* students deal with dissertations and theses. This order is not sacrosanct. For example, we deal with finding a topic and chairperson in this chapter and writing a literature review in chapter 6. But suppose you do a literature review for a term paper in a course that leads to a researchable topic. In that case, reading chapter 6 followed by this chapter might be more functional for you. Nor do these activities necessarily proceed in a linear sequence, one after the other. We tell you how to word your hypotheses precisely in this chapter, but in our experience, students generally refine and finalize their hypotheses as they meticulously study the literature (chap. 6, this volume) and develop their methodology (chap. 7, this volume). As we say many times, find the sequence and method that works for you and follow it.

Now, let's start with the two most important decisions you will make in planning your dissertation: what to study and who will guide you in studying it. We consider these together because we believe the two decisions are so closely linked.

Selecting a Research Area

Coming up with a researchable idea can be the most difficult step for many graduate students. This can come from two mistaken assumptions. One is the Nobel laureate error just described in chapter 2. The second is the "undergraduate research paper" error, in which students think that any topic they come up with is, by definition, a good topic. Although professors often tolerate unusual or wacky topics for undergraduate research papers, you can expect more than a little skepticism about these topics as a fledgling professional.

Why are these assumptions problematic? The Nobel laureate error reflects unrealistically grand thinking, whereas the undergraduate paper error reflects unrealistically miniscule thinking. As faculty members chairing these projects, we often prefer the Nobel laureate error. It is easier to trim the fat off a bloated research idea than to build up an anorexic one. Both errors reflect poor reality testing. The first at least shows the candidate is willing to work!

These errors are more common in individuals who have not had much firsthand exposure to actual research. Thus, master's students may have more trouble than doctoral students, unless the doctoral student has been sliding through the program deliberately avoiding research involvement or has been in a program without many faculty who are active researchers. If you have been active in research up to now, you probably already have an idea. It probably came as the logical extension of some research you have been collaborating on with faculty and other students. If not, the challenge of coming up with a workable research idea grounded in the literature may be a bit more formidable. If you are a master's student, your chairperson might give you a specific idea. Alternatively, you might replicate and extend work already published. If you are a doctoral student, your idea should be original, and your study must make a novel contribution to the literature.

In reality, there are two steps to coming up with a viable research project for your thesis or dissertation. First, identify the general topic or *area* in which you want to do research—for example, short-term memory, childhood aggression, social support, or information processing. This is relatively easy and can give you something to say when people ask you what your research is about. Once you have a topic, you are ready for the second step—in other words, coming up with a research question and hypotheses. Because these are much more specific, they take more thought. and most students find these skips in the process more difficult than arriving at a general research area.

Select a General Topic Area First

Let's talk strategy for a minute. Students often ask when the topic selection process should start. We generally answer, "the earlier the better." For some lucky few it begins during their undergraduate years. They might have taken a particular course that piqued their interest in a research area. They might have worked as research assistants on some faculty member's or graduate student's research project. They might have selected a graduate program because a faculty member was doing research in the same area. For them, the thesis or dissertation will be the logical extension of a program of study that began years earlier.

Most of us haven't had this experience as undergraduates, however. The direct research experience we had, if any, was probably in an area unrepresented by faculty in our current program. If you have not already done so, we advise you to examine descriptions of faculty research interests. Identify several that sound interesting to you. Find out as much as you can about the studies being done. Also find out as much as possible about the faculty members themselves. Take courses from them. Schedule appointments with them and ask them about their research and whether they have reprints you can read. Read these reprints and see if they describe research you really want to pursue. If they do, find out ways of getting directly involved, preferably before you start your own research. With research, as with many complex skills, direct experience will be a better teacher than simply reading about how to do it.

In the best of cases students start this process at the beginning of their graduate careers. Then their graduate program contributes in significant ways to their own research. Each course they take has some relevance. If they start the process early, they will be able to see that relevance more clearly as they advance through the program.

It is useful to keep an idea log in which you jot down potential research ideas as they occur to you. One of us still keeps one of these and logs ideas for papers, book chapters, research projects, or possible grant ideas on his computer as they come to him in the course of everyday life.

If you are starting early and do not like the experience you have with a particular professor or research program, try another one. There is nothing wrong with having a deliberate plan to work directly with several faculty in the early stages to find out their styles, the type of work they do, and some of the problems and rewards associated with it. Some of the most productive students we have known have systematically worked with numerous faculty during their graduate years. This helped them gain research experience from a variety of perspectives and led to several viable proposal possibilities when they needed to do their own research. If you choose this route, let the faculty know so they will not be surprised or have their research program disrupted by your premature departure.

If you have not had this experience and are further along in graduate school, don't despair. Remember, the first step is only to *identify* a research area, not to plan what you will do for the entire project. The area you pick must meet two key criteria. First, it must interest you enough that you will be willing to spend hours reading about it, writing about it, and analyzing data having to do with the area. Second, you must find a faculty member interested in chairing the project.

To identify an area, think about your classes and professional experience. What topics interest you? What do you find yourself stopping to read in the library when you are supposed to be compiling research for a class? What academic topics come up frequently when you are talking shop with other students and faculty? What term paper did you enjoy writing the most? Did you write it recently enough that you are current in the literature in that area? If so, you might have a head start on the literature review for your thesis or dissertation. We say much more about literature reviews in chapter 6. Some students are strategic about their choice of topic. They think ahead to the kind of work they plan to do as a psychologist and use that to guide their selection of a topic.

Identifying the things you think, read, talk about, or plan to do is a good way of clarifying areas that interest you. Most likely, you will find several of these. You can then identify faculty who share these interests and talk with them about the area. Although we suggest you have at least a general topic area identified before you seek out faculty with an interest in the area, this is not written in stone. Many students reverse this process. In other words, they find a faculty member with whom they like to work, and then identify a topic jointly. If you are planning a thesis, you might ask faculty members if they have projects they would like a student to take on as a master's project. This also provides an opportunity to see what particular faculty members are like, find out what projects might interest them, and make a good impression. In general, it is better to choose a slightly less engrossing area that a faculty member will support than an exotic one that only you find fascinating.

Avoid Going It Alone

Some students, particularly those at the doctoral level, have the impression that their research is supposed to be a solo affair. They spend months developing a research idea and proposal and then approach a faculty member to try to sell it. Yates (1982) described his own experience doing just this, and being devastated when his ideal committee chair rejected the idea as infeasible. In situations like this you are faced with rejecting the advice of the faculty member and trying to find another who will agree it is a terrific proposal or rejecting the idea and starting over. The latter alternative is not high on the hit parade of fun things to do in graduate school.

True, the dissertation is the test of your preparation to conduct independent research. This is not quite so true of master's theses, however, and with neither do you have to generate and develop ideas completely on your own. In fact, solo work at this stage runs a real risk of producing unworkable proposals. Another all-too-frequent occurrence is that you cannot find a faculty person with the expertise and interest in your topic to shepherd you through the rest of the process. We have known students who have gone systematically to every single faculty member of a department with an idea only to find no one who would agree to chair their committee. Thesis and dissertation research is challenging enough without making it into a course in salesmanship as well. We strongly recommend that you avoid going it alone. Use the approaches described above to develop ideas *in conjunction with* a faculty member. If she or he has joint ownership of the idea, there will be a cooperative relationship that will aid enormously in completing the research with minimum hassle.

Selecting a Chairperson

Selecting a chairperson for your project is a crucial step in the thesis/dissertation process and goes hand in hand with selecting a topic. A good chairperson will provide expertise in your topic area, specific feedback on your work, and support—as well as an occasional kick in the pants if you need it to keep going. A poor chairperson will provide few of these and may, in fact, make your life miserable as you negotiate the dissertation or thesis process.

Before approaching a faculty member as a potential chairperson, consider the chair's role. Although the specifics of this role vary from school to school and from chairperson to chairperson, some general functions of the chair are reasonably consistent. First, the chairperson helps the student develop the research idea and methodology. Second, the chairperson provides the first line of quality assurance for the project. Thus, he or she reads and critiques multiple drafts of each section of the thesis or dissertation. Third, the chairperson approves the proposal for and the final version of the project before permitting the student to submit these documents to other committee members.

Most chairs work closely with their students in guiding master's theses. At the doctoral level, chairpersons vary from those who see the dissertation as a totally collaborative process in which they are fully involved to those who want students to report in only when drafts are complete or if they encounter major problems. If you prefer to work independently, hands-off chairpersons are likely to be attractive. If you are like the majority of students, however, you will want a more active chair. If you do, consider three important factors when deciding whom to invite to chair your project: (a) how well you could work with the faculty member, (b) how much expertise he or she has in your research area, and (c) how skilled the person is at the specific tasks required to guide you smoothly to a completed thesis or dissertation. If you choose well, you will work comfortably with your chairperson and obtain specific, timely, and specialized guidance on your project. Working with a good chairperson is like going to a good dentist: The process may not be enjoyable or painless, but it may not be as bad as you anticipate. And the final product is worth it!

Departments usually have rules about who may and may not serve as dissertation or thesis chairpersons and committee members. Except in rare circumstances, chairs must have earned the doctorate themselves. Some institutions allow only individuals who have adequate recent publication records or who have been on the faculty for a certain period of time to assume the dissertation chair role. These rules are based on the assumption that inexperienced faculty members or those without active programs of scholarship will lack the skills to ensure that the doctoral project has sufficient scope, grounding in the literature, and methodological rigor. Rules regarding who may chair master's theses are often but not always more liberal than those regarding dissertations. Furthermore, some schools require special permission if the student wishes to work with a faculty member outside of the student's specialty area or department. Working with a chairperson who is not a faculty member at all may also be prohibited or allowed only under special circumstances (e.g., when a faculty member is willing to act as a nominal chair or as a cochair). Finding out these rules in advance will help you avoid getting your heart set on working with someone who is not eligible to chair a thesis or dissertation. In addition, find out what forms require signatures and have those ready for your chairperson and committee members to sign when they agree to assume those roles. This formalizes the agreement and makes it difficult for them to change their minds later.

Consider the Nature of Chair–Student Collaboration

A dissertation or thesis is a collaborative project between the chairperson and the student. When a final dissertation is archived in *Dissertation Abstracts International,* the chair's and student's names are both listed. Faculty with national and international reputations will be careful about the type of work with which their name is associated. Assuming the responsibility of chairing a dissertation committee is not something most faculty members take lightly. For your collaboration to succeed, you and your chairperson will need to work reasonably well together. This is especially true if you have little research experience and will need a good deal of guidance (often the case with the master's degree). A first step in assessing how well you might work with a faculty member is to examine the match between what you want from your chairperson and your chairperson's notion of the best way to implement his or her role. So what do you want from your chairperson? Do you want someone who will guide you from research area to a specific topic (which will probably be something interesting to the chairperson), or do you want someone who will be happy for you to follow your own inclinations? Will you work best with a chairperson who is highly structured (e.g., sets deadlines and meets regularly with students) or with one who is more *laissez-faire?* Do you want to work with someone who is interpersonally warm and supportive, or are other characteristics (e.g., expertise and professional connections) more important? In short, think about and decide what kind of structure, how much input in terms of topic development, and what sort of interpersonal style you prefer. You can then appraise how well the faculty member's style matches the way you prefer to work.

Think About Potential Chairpersons' Expertise

Some students and faculty assert that your chairperson must know a lot more about your topic than you do. Others disagree with this assertion, maintaining that the role of the chair is to critique your methodology and the logic of the your arguments, not to be an expert in your topic area. Good methodological and analytical skills should be applicable to any topic area, they say. We agree with the last statement. We further agree that students sometimes produce excellent research working with chairpersons who know little about the student's area at the outset of the project. Nonetheless, we believe it is ordinarily in the best interest of both students and the profession for students to find chairs with expertise within the student's topic area. Furthermore, we generally recommend that students develop their specific research questions jointly with a faculty member, working within the faculty member's area of interest. This is particularly important for students conducting research for master's theses, who enter the process with less experience and skill than doctoral students and who generally need more guidance at all stages of the project.

We strongly recommend that you work with a chairperson with expertise in your area, based on our opinion that this will lead to a better product with less time and agony. Faculty members who have worked in an area for a number of years know the literature well. They know what research has and has not been conducted and what is currently being done. This knowledge can prevent you from spending months designing what you think is the ideal study, only to find that someone published your magnum opus the month before in the *Journal of Personality and Social Psychology*. Furthermore, such faculty members will be likely to guide you into a study that makes a contribution to the literature.

Just as important, knowledgeable faculty members will know the ins and outs of doing research in the area. They will know effective participant recruitment methods, the pitfalls in common designs and procedures, and the methodological norms in the area. Thus, you are unlikely to begin a master's thesis that has the scope of a small grant because you are unaware of how time-consuming your procedures will be. Nor are you likely to design a study with a fatal flaw that is due to ignorance of the topic area (your own *and* your chair's). A chair who knows your literature may be able to point you to relevant articles, chapters, and books. A student of ours, for example, once announced that she was going to the library to start her literature search. When she discovered that her chair had two file cabinet drawers full of reprints related to her general topic area, she spent a day with these files and photocopied the articles that she needed, saving many hours downloading articles and searching the stacks.

Another reason for working in faculty members' areas is that these chairpersons will have more investment in your project. Faculty members who care deeply about what you are studying are likely to spend more time with you, think about the project more fully, and generally keep a sharper eye on your progress than those who do not. A sense of ownership often promotes accountability among collaborators, and if you share that ownership with your chairperson, you may reap the benefits of more timely and in-depth feedback and support.

Finally, working with a chairperson with expertise in your area may have practical benefits. Faculty members with active research programs often have laboratory space, equipment, and sometimes even monetary resources (e.g., grant funds to pay participants). Many will let you use some or all of their facilities if you work in their area. In addition, you may be more likely to get a job or internship if your chairperson is well known and respected in the field—and if you do such a good job that he or she writes a stellar letter of recommendation about what a great catch you would be.

Of course, working in faculty members' areas is not without potential drawbacks. Some faculty members may be too controlling, requiring you to do what *they* want, the way *they* want it done, without regard for your ideas or intellectual development. You may find yourself following your chair's instructions rather than developing the skills you need to function autonomously as a researcher. Even at the master's level, which involves considerably less independence than the doctorate, you should be learning new skills rather than functioning as slave labor. Failure to develop research skills at this stage is a particular drawback if you plan a career that involves research, where you will be expected to function well independently and to design your own line of research. In addition, faculty members are sometimes more demanding in an area they know than in an area less familiar to them. These problems are not inevitable, however, and we believe that for most students the advantages gained by working in an area the chairperson knows well far outweigh the possible problems.

If working with an expert chairperson is not an option for you, consider recruiting one or more experts in your area to serve on your dissertation or thesis committee. Look for these experts among members of the department, your academic community, other nearby academic institutions, and community sites. Consulting with these individuals on substantive areas can fulfill some of the functions a knowledgeable chairperson would normally serve.

Appraise Potential Chairpersons' Skills

Chairing a dissertation or thesis committee well requires specific skills. Among these skills are guiding the research process and providing quality control. This means that the chair will read many drafts of your proposal and final write-up, provide feedback on areas that need improvement, and help you solve problems when you are stuck. The chair will also head your committee and, ordinarily, will oversee the proposal meeting and the oral defense of the project. Good chairpersons will make their expectations clear, provide specific feedback (both positive and negative), read and return drafts to you in reasonable periods of time, meet with you to discuss the project, and manage conflicts among committee members if they arise.

Expectations and Feedback

In most departments, some faculty members have high standards, whereas others are less critical and require fewer rewrites, less extensive methodology, and so on. The implications of working with a hard versus an easy chair go far beyond how many hours you can expect to put into the project, however.

We must admit our bias: We both are known for our high standards in working with students. These standards, we believe, have several positive consequences for students. First, if you produce a product that satisfies a chair with high standards, you are less likely to encounter serious problems with your committee, because you and the chair already will have considered the major issues involved in your project and made good decisions. Second, you will be better prepared for your proposal meeting and oral defense, because you and the chair will have discussed many of the major issues your committee members are likely to raise. Finally, a chair you have satisfied is more likely to go to bat for you if a committee member throws you a curve ball.

Beyond considering faculty members' standards, consider whether prospective chairpersons will provide specific feedback and suggestions. Few things are more frustrating than working with someone who tells you to do better but cannot tell you specifically what you need to do to improve. You should not expect faculty members to find specific articles for you, make all your decisions, or rewrite your poor sentences. But you should look for potential chairpersons who can tell you clearly what you need to do to improve as you work through the process.

Timeliness and Availability

Most students receive feedback on several drafts of each section of the thesis or dissertation before chairs give the section the final seal of approval. The timeliness of this feedback is important: Potential chairpersons who sit on drafts of your introduction and method section for months may seriously delay your progress. Similarly, chairpersons should be available to meet with you within a reasonable amount of time to discuss problems you encounter. What is an acceptable turnaround time? We strive for 2-week turnaround on drafts, recognizing that it will take longer during particularly busy periods (e.g., final-exam grading periods, weeks when we will be out of town, and right before deadlines when all students want to finish their projects). Similarly, if a student has a problem to discuss or needs an appointment, we ordinarily schedule it within a week to 10 days.

Several things can get in the way of mentors being available and providing timely feedback as soon as you would like. Think about these things as you consider prospective chairpersons. Popular chairs may have many students vying for their time. Some faculty are extremely busy with grant-sponsored research or extensive travel commitments. Others may have active consulting or clinical practices that compete with students' needs for time. No matter how scintillating your prose, it is hard to compete with a paycheck. Also, many faculty are on 9-month contracts with their schools and may not be available during the summer months.

If you have concerns about any of these matters, bring the issue up with prospective chairs: Ask them what their usual turnaround time is, whether their schedules will allow them to meet with you regularly, how often you should plan to meet if you work together, and so on. We will discuss this further in a later section, when we explore how to get information about prospective chairpersons.

Finally, you might also ask their opinion about electronically submitted drafts. Some faculty prefer paper copy, others prefer digital versions that can be edited on the screen. These will be important things for you to know, especially if you are not that comfortable with computers.

Assertiveness Skills

We hope that you will select a chairperson and committee members who work well together. But what if you don't? Is your chair assertive enough to back you up if a committee member makes unreasonable demands? Will the chairperson help you out if something goes wrong in the external agency in which the study is being conducted? Your chairperson's assertiveness skills are particularly important if your study involves procedures that are difficult to implement, and, thus, you require help gaining agency support, meeting with the human participants research review committee, and so on. Finding an assertive chairperson is also important if your department is a hotbed of interpersonal feuds, and dissertation or thesis meetings become shooting matches between faculty, with students as hapless bystanders. Finally, remember that your project is both an examination of your competence as a researcher *and* a learning experience. In general, the master's thesis is considered more of a learning experience than an examination, whereas the reverse is true for the doctoral project. How well will particular faculty teach you about research as you negotiate the project? Will the person facilitate your growth as a researcher? Will the person do most of the work for you, will you have to find your own way with little guidance, or will you be challenged to learn and grow in your research skills under the tutelage of a skillful mentor?

Investigate Prospective Chairpersons

Three sources provide information about prospective chairpersons. First is your personal experience: You may have taken a class from particular faculty members or talked with them at get-togethers. Better yet, you may have actually worked with the person on research in the past. This is, of course, the best way to get direct information about what it is like to work under the faculty member's guidance.

If you are reading this volume early enough in your graduate career, consider getting experience working with faculty with whom you share common interests, so you can see firsthand how well you work with the person. Working as a paid research assistant or as an unpaid volunteer can provide this information. If you volunteer, make sure that you assess the requirements and degree of contact you will have with the faculty member before you agree to participate. If you are getting involved to see how well you like working with a particular faculty member, you want to have contact with that faculty member—not be shuttled off to be an unpaid research assistant for the postdoctoral student who is working in the person's lab. Doing a master's thesis with someone is another way of gaining information about a prospective dissertation chairperson. If your program requires a thesis, you can gain firsthand experience with a faculty member by doing your master's thesis with someone who might later serve as your dissertation chairperson.

As you think about your previous interactions with prospective chairpersons and what you did and did not like about your experiences, remember there are important differences between the requirements of the chair role and the requirements of other faculty roles. For example, you may have loved Dr. Smith's lecture style. But Dr. Smith will not be lecturing in your dissertation meetings. Think instead about whether Dr. Smith gave you specific, helpful feedback on your paper and returned exams to you promptly. Of course, Dr. Smith may not be cross-situationally consistent, so you need to look at other kinds of data to supplement your own experience.

A second source of information comes from classmates who have worked with the faculty member. Here we are not talking about the proverbial grapevine. The grapevine, like grocery store tabloids, is generally a source of *entertaining* information. Unfortunately, it is not always a source of *accurate* information, largely because the grapevine is created and fed almost entirely by students and therefore tends to be one-sided. In faculty–student matters, as in most of life, there are two sides to every problem, and the truth ordinarily lies somewhere between them. Faculty members who appropriately refrain from gossiping with students never see their points of view reflected in the contents of the rumor mill.

Sure, some faculty reputations are well deserved. The problem, however, is that without credible data it is hard to know whether the reputation—good or bad—is based on fact or on fiction. Rumors do not provide credible data.

For more reliable information, talk with students who have worked under the guidance of prospective chairs. After all, they have firsthand experience with these individuals in chair–student relationships. Get other students to describe their experiences. Talk to more than one to get a decent sample. Ask questions about areas that concern you: How many drafts did they write of each section? How fast did the faculty member return them? How quickly did the faculty member respond to phone calls and e-mail? What kind of feedback did the faculty member give? What kinds of problems did the committee raise, and how did the chair respond? Note that these questions ask about specific faculty behavior rather than student subjective impressions. Although knowing whether the student liked or hated the chair may be interesting, more important is how the chair interacted with the student. Knowing that information, you can decide whether *you* would profit from working with a prospective chairperson, regardless of whether your informant did.

In addition, in evaluating students' reports, be sure to consider the source. Weak students may find intellectually rigorous professors "too picky," whereas strong students think they are stimulating and helpful. It is hard for any faculty member to be supportive enough for extremely needy students.

Remember, chairs are not randomly assigned to students: Selection biases operate. In our experience, strong students often select demanding but fair chairs, weak or lazy students often choose faculty members who will allow them to cut corners, and no one (if he or she can help it) works with irresponsible or autocratic individuals who change their demands from week to week.

A final source of information comes from interviews with faculty members themselves. At some point you will have a short list of possible chairs and questions to ask them. How a faculty member answers your questions provides another valuable source of information. Approaching the faculty member is part of dissertation and thesis etiquette, a topic to which we now turn.

Approach Prospective Chairpersons: Dissertation and Thesis Etiquette I

You've thought about what you want from a chairperson. You've talked with other students. You have one or more possible topic areas. It's time to select a chairperson. As you sally forth, remember that faculty members have choices about the projects they will and will not chair. Even if you have worked in someone's lab, you cannot assume that this faculty member will automatically take on the chair role or that you know the individual's expectations. You need to ask. Most have explicit or implicit guidelines that they follow in making these choices. For example, one of our colleagues once proposed the following criteria to screen prospective dissertation students:

1. The design must involve comparisons.
2. These comparisons must involve hypotheses generated from relevant literature.
3. Some of the measures must use a method other than self-report.
4. The student must have taken at least one course from the faculty member.
5. The student must have the necessary methodological preparation to complete the particular project.
6. The student must have adequate time to (a) work on the dissertation continuously and (b) meet to discuss progress during the faculty member's normal office schedule.
7. The student must plan to reside in the area until the project is finished.

How you approach prospective chairs depends on whether you are still shopping and want more information or whether you have narrowed the list to a specific faculty member with whom you wish to work. In either case, a first step is to make an appointment to discuss chairing your project. In doing this, be direct about your agenda. If you are still shopping around, you might say to (or e-mail) the faculty member something like the following.

> I'm thinking about my thesis (dissertation), and one of the areas I'm considering is _____. I'd like to talk with you about whether you might be interested in chairing something in this area, if I decide on this topic. I'd also be interested in your general approach to chairing theses (dissertations). Do you have time to discuss this with me?

If you know already that you want the faculty member to chair the project, you might say something like the following.

> I'm interested in doing my thesis (dissertation) in the _____ area. I'd like to discuss my specific ideas with you and see whether you might be interested in chairing my project.

Be prepared for the faculty member to ask you some questions on the spot or to give you a quick decision. For example, we routinely ask students we do not know well about their prospective topic and why they are interested in us (rather than someone else). This allows us to refer students with topics in which we have no expertise to other faculty members and saves us (and the student) wasted appointment time. Similarly, we will agree immediately if the topic interests us and we know the student and are willing to work with him or her. We will immediately turn away students if we are overcommitted, not interested in the topic, or not willing to work with them for some reason. If you are far enough along in your thinking, you might ask the potential chairperson if he or she would like to see a brief (2–3 pages) summary of your idea and proposed methodology in writing. This gives the faculty member a sample of how you write, so make sure it is clear and succinct, uses terminology correctly, and is free of typos and other errors.

If the faculty member agrees to meet with you, go to your meeting with an agenda. If you are shopping, ask questions that will help you decide whether this would be a good chairperson for you. Start with a brief mention of your general area of interest, if you have one. Find out faculty members' explicit and implicit rules: how they generally work with students, how much input they generally have in topic development, what kinds of students they work best with, and whether they have any openings currently. Do not necessarily expect a faculty member to agree to chair your project, however, until you have a specific research question. Many are not willing to invest the time and energy involved in chairing a project if they believe the research is trivial or uninteresting. If you lack ideas, ask the faculty member for suggestions or for readings that will assist in formulating a research question. If the faculty member agrees to meet with you further to discuss or develop topics, this is a good first step. It does not necessarily mean the person will chair the project, however.

If the faculty member indicates potential or definite interest in chairing your project and you are still interested, end the meeting by asking, "What should I do next?" This gives the faculty member a chance to make expectations explicit about what you need to do to keep the process rolling. If you are still topic- and chair-shopping, you may want to tell the faculty member that you are considering several topic areas and talking with several individuals and will get back to him or her if you want to discuss the process further, thanking the faculty member for the appointment time.

We cannot emphasize enough the importance of establishing clear, direct communication with a chairperson regarding expectations and roles. Knowing what is expected makes the process less ambiguous for all concerned. Faculty members may or may not provide this explicit information, so students should think about how they can tactfully and directly communicate about issues involved in planning the project. Direct communication early about expectations and roles sets the stage for a good working relationship and helps prevent later problems that are due to mistaken assumptions on the part of either chair or student.

Anticipate Trouble Spots

Several issues can be troublesome when seeking a chairperson. Below, we list three common problems students face, along with our ideas for how to cope with each.

1. *"I worked in Dr. McGee's lab and did my master's thesis with Dr. McGee, but I want to work with Dr. Jones on my dissertation. Is there any way to do this without alienating Dr. McGee?"* Many students fear that leaving someone's lab means that they forgo the goodwill and letters of recommendation from that faculty member. This is not necessarily so. In many schools, students are allowed (in some cases, encouraged) to shift mentors if their interests change or if they wish to get exposure to another research area. Most faculty understand this, although they may be sorry to lose a student they have invested years in training.

In these situations, we recommend discussing the issue with the faculty member you wish to leave, saying something to the effect of the following.

> I'm thinking about my dissertation topic. Although I've learned a lot from working with you, my interests are really in the area of _____. I'd like to talk to Dr. Jones about possibly working together on this, but I wanted to talk with you first to get your reaction.

The gracious faculty member will say, "I'd love to have you, but it's your choice," and there will be no negative repercussions. In fact, faculty members may appreciate your consulting them before approaching someone else. Less gracious but equally direct faculty members may tell you that they put a lot of time into your training and that their payback is for you to do your thesis or dissertation on a topic that interests them. Then, you can decide whether maintaining the faculty member's good will is worth altering your topic and your plans.

2. *"I want to study the influence of sunlamps on worms' turning behavior. This is in Dr. Barton's area, but I don't want to work with Dr. Barton."* This is a problem for at least two reasons. First, unless someone else shares Dr. Barton's expertise, you may not find a faculty member qualified to chair your project. Second, Dr. Barton will likely find out about your topic and figure out that you chose another chairperson for a reason. Dr. Barton may or may not make an issue of this. Moreover, colleagues who are close to Dr. Barton may not be willing to serve as a chairperson or as committee members. In addition, years later people may wonder why you chose someone other than the department's known expert to be your chair. Were you trying to take the easy way out?

We suggest that you consider two questions in thinking through this issue. First, determine your reasons for not selecting Dr. Barton. Is there any way you could arrange the process to minimize the problems you anticipate? Small problems can even be discussed with the faculty member when you shop for a chair: "I'd love to work in your area, but you seem very busy and I know I'll need a fair amount of guidance. If we decide to work together, would it be possible to schedule regular meetings?" Logistical problems can often be solved by open discussion in advance; problems involving irresponsible behavior and a negative interpersonal style are not so easily broached and prevented through advance problem solving. A second question revolves around a realistic appraisal of the consequences of choosing someone other than Dr. Barton. Will Dr. Barton really care? Will Dr. Barton react? Will Dr. Barton's feelings or opinion have any impact on your life after you complete your degree? Many students catastrophize about the impact of not choosing Dr. Barton, when Dr. Barton may be happy not to have another student or may dislike the student as much as the student dislikes Dr. Barton! At the same time, if you intend to pursue an academic career in Dr. Barton's area and Dr. Barton is a national expert, it may be wise to put up with Dr. Barton's idiosyncrasies in exchange for his or her expertise.

Alternatively, you could do your research on another topic. Surely you can find another idea that interests you and that would allow you and Dr. Barton to save face when you select another chair. You can always change your research interests after you complete the thesis or the doctorate.

3. *"I can't find anyone to chair my project."* If this is your problem, consider the cause. In our experience, the most common reason for this problem lies in the student's choice of topic. Faculty members may turn you down because they think your topic is trivial, poorly thought out, or outside their areas of expertise. Students who get their hearts set on a particular research question, develop it without faculty guidance, and present it to faculty members as a *fait accompli* are particularly likely to be turned down on topical grounds. The solution, of course, is to approach faculty members earlier in the process, talk with them about topics that fit their interest areas as well as your own, and let the faculty member know you are flexible and open to feedback about what is important and what is not.

Another reason for failure to find a chair lies in the student's failure to investigate fully: You get your heart set on a particular faculty member and then discover that faculty member cannot take on another student, is going on sabbatical, or for some other reason is unavailable. You then conclude that you "can't find a chair." As disappointing as it may be, you may need to explore other topic areas that would increase other faculty members' interest in working with you.

Finally, some students cannot find mentors because their academic or personal problems drive prospective chairs away. Students who have had repeated difficulty in their training program may find that few faculty members are willing to undergo the projected agony of working with them. If this is your difficulty, you should honestly appraise the situation. First, you will need to identify your contribution to these problems. Have you been unreliable, antagonistic, abrasive, or inflexible? Do you lack basic graduate-level academic skills and need extensive remediation? Second, you will need to decide whether a change in your skills, behavior, or attitude can be achieved in a relatively short amount of time. This may require a commitment to high-quality counseling, therapy, or other professional assistance. If you are able to achieve these two goals, communicate this good-faith effort to a faculty member, show him or her at least one demonstrable change you have made, and ask for another chance. It is difficult to shift a negative reputation, and you may need to work harder and make more compromises than other students to talk a faculty member into taking you on as a student and to overcome his or her negative expectations of you.

If you do not believe you can make the changes required to be successful in your graduate program in a reasonable amount of time, consider either (a) taking a leave of absence to work on the problem or (b) exiting graduate school gracefully and finding a career that suits you better. Although the latter is a drastic step, repeated problems in graduate school are likely to predict similar problems in job situations that have comparable requirements. Is it really worth staying in a profession for which you are not well suited? Or would you be better off cutting your losses and finding something else that capitalizes on your strengths rather than exploiting your weaknesses?

Develop the Research Question

Let's assume you have successfully identified a topic area for your research (e.g., dental phobia, child sexual abuse, depression, HIV prevention), preferably in collaboration with a respected faculty member who will chair the project. You next have to narrow your idea to something doable. To do this you will frame some sort of researchable question within that area. The *form* such questions should take is fairly specific. We will address form later. First, we take up the *source* of such questions.

In general, you want to ask questions that interest the scientific community. It is *not* a good idea to propose a particular study merely because there is a lack of research on a topic. There might be good reasons why no one has published anything on the question. More important, such a rationale does not inform us about why the question should be asked or answered in the first place.

In coming up with a researchable question, keep in mind that it should have a place in the literature. That is, you should know how it fits, conceptually and methodologically. After all, science is the cumulative process of knowledge generation. What will answering this question tell us? Why is this important? True, it may be useful to know what percentages of students in a given school show particular cognitive deficits associated with learning disabilities. This will have little relevance beyond that particular school, however. Of far more interest to others concerned with children would be the correlates of those problems. If you really want to strengthen the study, you will pick variables that have theoretical relevance for particular approaches to learning disabilities as well. Remember, the purpose of research is to produce generalizable knowledge. It will do this best if it builds on research and theory that has preceded it. We will have more to say about this when we talk about hypothesis formulation later in this chapter.

Poor Sources of Research Ideas

Before we turn to good sources of specific ideas, a word of warning: One common way to come up with a research idea is from one's own personal experience. The recovering alcoholic decides to study families of alcoholics. The student with chronic test anxiety chooses to relate test anxiety and type of question to performance on math exams. The 40-year-old parent decides to study the waning sexual interest of busy executive spouses. In fact, many of us are in the behavioral sciences, especially psychology, because of an interest in some aspect of our own experience. Don't get us wrong. This is not a bad reason for being in psychology in the first place. But it is probably not a good idea to plan thesis or dissertation research around something with a high degree of personal emotional relevance. Save these issues for therapy. Research is difficult enough without having it prompt a lot of personal soul-searching every time you pick up the pen or enter a participant's data.

Besides interfering with your progress, personally loaded issues are unlikely to be approached from the detached, objective, analytical perspective necessary in science. You are likely to have a position on the subject that will interfere with your completing the research satisfactorily on a number of levels. The most important of these is the self-fulfilling prophecy phenomenon (Ambady & Rosenthal, 1992). If you are convinced from your personal experience that test-anxious students do worse on multiple-choice than essay questions, for example, you may unknowingly design your study in subtle ways to ensure this outcome. For example, you may inadvertently share your expectation with research assistants who score your essay questions. Research has shown that assistants can be biased to produce data that are consistent with the desired outcomes communicated to them by the experimenter (Kent, O'Leary, Diament, & Dietz, 1974; Shuller & McNamara, 1976). Of course, we do not suggest you would do this deliberately. Nor is this is a problem only for research in personally relevant areas. It is simply that it is more likely in such research.

Choosing a research topic that evokes strong emotional reactions can also interfere with your objectivity in other ways. For example, otherwise helpful suggestions from committee members might be hard to accept if they don't fit your personal understanding of the problem. This can result in your appearing rigid, defensive, and inflexible—characteristics faculty do not view positively.

In fairness, however, we should note that issues of personal relevance can be a good source of research questions under some circumstances. Your motivation is likely to be higher for such topics, and you might know the area in unique ways that might challenge the conclusions of current investigators. The bottom line is that issues of personal relevance should be considered as a source of research ideas only if you can approach them objectively. If you have resolved the emotional aspects of the issue and can approach it in a detached, relatively disinterested and unbiased manner, go ahead. You might make a truly useful contribution.

Better Sources of Research Ideas

As you might have guessed from some of our earlier comments, possibly the best source for new research is research you are already doing, because you will have both knowledge about and experience in the area. Moreover, if you have been collaborating with a particular faculty member on the research, that person will probably have provided suggestions you can develop into a satisfactory proposal. Finally, research often stimulates more questions than it answers, and one of these might easily provide the basis for a thesis or dissertation proposal.

The existing literature, particularly recent literature, is also an excellent source of research questions. Most journal articles end with suggestions for future research. Look for these. If one of them excites you, spend some time thinking about how you might develop the suggestion into a research proposal. Discuss the idea with your respected faculty member or possible-chair candidate and get a reaction. If it is generally positive, and after you have thoroughly researched the topic, get in touch with the author of the paper and find out what she or he is doing currently in the area. Inquire nonchalantly about the specific question you hope to pursue, asking whether the author has already researched it or whether she or he knows of anyone who has. If the answer to both questions is no, probe a bit and see whether the author knows why. After all, it seemed like such a good idea to you!

This little bit of detective work could be worthwhile and could save you much wasted time and possible embarrassment. The author might have discarded the suggestion because a colleague pointed out an inherent flaw in its logic. Or at a presentation at a professional meeting several people in the audience strongly questioned the ethics of pursuing the research in the manner suggested. Or you might hear that several people have indeed followed the author's suggestion and will present their results in the next issue of the *Ratatat Review*. Wouldn't such news be worth the e-mail or telephone call?

Another good source of researchable questions is to apply a paradigm used with one population to another population. For example, Wolfe, Gentile, Michienzi, Sas, and Wolfe (1991) used a scale to assess specific reactions to traumatic events, the Impact of Events Scale (Horowitz, Wilner, & Alvarez, 1979) as the basis for developing the Children's Impact of Traumatic Events Scale. Research on the leadership styles of executive women might easily suggest similar studies with executives who are members of an ethnic group underrepresented in the profession you are studying.

Reviews of the literature in particular areas provide another worthy source of questions. The *Psychological Bulletin* contains such reviews in psychology. The *Annual Review of Psychology* is another source of such reviews, as are *Clinical Psychology Review* and *Developmental Review*. Many edited books contain literature reviews. The authors of reviews appearing in these sources often point out gaps in the research knowledge or correctable flaws within existing studies. Why not propose research that remedies some flaw that has already been acknowledged as important by the scientific community?

Replications of already published research provide an avenue for additional research in some cases. As mentioned earlier, a proposal to replicate a study will be more acceptable for a master's thesis than for a dissertation. There is much reason to recommend replications. If the original study was done in an exemplary way, you will learn much from modeling. In fact, exemplary studies are the only ones you want to attempt to replicate directly, because there is no virtue in repeating the errors of your predecessors. Check the local norms to see whether replications are acceptable master's theses possibilities.

You may also find links between literatures that have been relatively unexplored and be able to link them. Many professionals study the same problems psychologists do, including sociologists, scientists in the communication field, physicians, and others. Even within psychology there are numerous aspects of the discipline that are often not integrated. Pulling together separate but related strands is a challenging but often rewarding way of devising something truly novel.

A final source of ideas comes from other theses and dissertations. We know some faculty who deliberately steer students away from consulting previous theses and dissertations. Partly this is because faculty members sometimes distrust the quality of research supervised by other faculty. Partly it results from the realization that theses and dissertations have not been subjected to the same peer-review process as most published papers and therefore cannot be as confidently consulted as exemplars of competent research. The faculty argue that if the research is good enough it will be published anyway, and the student will encounter it in the literature.

Our own view is that existing theses and dissertations *can* be a good source of some kinds of information for prospective researchers. We routinely suggest that students consult one or two carefully selected dissertations or dissertation proposals. This assignment stimulates reality testing as well as pointing to exemplary projects that could serve as models. We also recommend completed theses and dissertations as references if students are proposing a study that extends a program of research taking off from the previous thesis or dissertation. And, as mentioned in chapter 1, theses and dissertations completed under the direction of a potential chairperson can be an excellent source of concrete information about the finished product that the chair is likely to expect. We do not suggest them as *sources* of ideas, however. Browsing through published literature reviews will probably yield more ideas per hour than theses and dissertations on the library shelf or in *Dissertation Abstracts International.*

Put the Research Questions in Researchable Form

Once you have decided the area of your topic and the general question to be asked, it is time to word the question so that it can be studied. Well-worded questions share common characteristics (Kerlinger, 2000). The easiest criterion to remember is that the question should be just that. Phrase what you are going to study in the form of a question. Second, the question should suggest a relationship to be examined. This will require that the question also specify the key variables to be examined. This is a particularly important characteristic because the purpose of doing research is to advance science. Because science is the study of relationships between variables, if you don't test a relationship, you are not engaging in science, at least as defined in this book. No science, no thesis or dissertation. It is that simple.

For example, suppose that your general research area involves child sexual abuse, and you wish to study the adequacy of children's memory for specific events. Your question might be, "Are children who have not been sexually abused more likely to describe sexual behavior when interviewed with sexually anatomically correct (SAC) dolls than when interviewed with dolls not having secondary sex characteristics?" This is phrased in the form of a question, but does it imply a relationship to be tested? The children are to be interviewed with dolls that do or do not have complete anatomical features. The independent variable is thus the secondary sexual characteristics of the dolls. The verbal behavior of children exposed to dolls with or without these features will be examined for references to sexual behavior. Such references thus constitute the dependent variable. The research question suggests a relationship between the independent and dependent variables. Thus, it meets the second of our criteria.

The third criterion requires that the research question imply the possibility of empirical testing (Kerlinger, 2000). If the question meets the second criterion, namely, suggests a relationship, it is half way to meeting the requirements of the third criterion. It is not enough to suggest a relationship, however, unless that relationship is empirically testable. The principal ingredient of testability is the specificity of the variables being related in the research question. Can the variables be operationally defined? If the variables cannot be operationalized and measured, the question(s) pursued in the research cannot be answered. If they can be operationalized, an empirical test of the relationship suggested by the question can be performed.

Admittedly, these criteria are somewhat arbitrary. Good research can be done without following them exactly. For novice researchers, however, we have found these characteristics to be quite helpful in evaluating and advancing research ideas.

You will probably need to spend some time refining and reworking your research question to make it clear and specific enough to guide your research. This process will force you to think through exactly what you want to know. You may start with a vague question like, "How do parents and teenagers communicate about sex?" This implies no relationship. That is, there are no independent or dependent variables. In discussion with your chairperson, you revise it: "How does parent–adolescent communication about sex relate to impulsive teenage sexual behavior?" You might revise it even further as you decide what specific aspects of communication and sexual behavior you want to study.

Now that you have a question to study, let's talk about the availability of participants for a minute. Participant access is so important, we have had colleagues who advise students to get participants first and then decide what research they want to do. This falls into the pragmatic school of thesis and dissertation advising! If participants are not available, the greatest idea in the world is not going to make a suitable research topic. Are you working (or doing a practicum or an internship) in a setting with a population suitable for your study? Is your mother, father, spouse, or good friend connected with such a setting? Does your potential chairperson have connections you could tap to gain access to participants? As a reviewer of this book pointed out, outsiders to a system usually lack the power to collect data within that system in ways orderly enough to make research possible. So be sure you are sufficiently well-connected to ensure access to the participants you will need. This is particularly important if your research question requires a select group of individuals (e.g., cancer survivors, displaced executives, etc.). It is less important if you could do your study with more readily available populations (e.g., college students).

Develop Carefully Worded Hypotheses

Well-worded research questions that meet these three criteria will help you specify hypotheses. Hypotheses are declarative sentences that conjecture a relationship between two or more variables (Kerlinger, 2000). Well-stated hypotheses are derived directly from the research question. For example, our previous question asked, "Are children who have not been sexually abused more likely to describe sexual behavior when interviewed with sexually anatomically correct (SAC) dolls than when interviewed with dolls not having secondary sex characteristics?" For this question we might hypothesize that, "Nonabused children interviewed with SAC dolls describe sexual behavior more frequently than nonabused children interviewed with dolls without secondary sex characteristics." Note that in both examples, our hypotheses start with the basic research question and develop a specific prediction about the nature of the relationship between the variables identified in the question. Note also that hypotheses are conjectures about relationships existing in the state of nature today. Thus, they are stated in the present tense. We are not hypothesizing about a relationship that might exist some time in the future, so we avoid the future tense.

At this point you may be thinking that to come up with some hypotheses you'll just say how you *think* your results will come out. That is easy enough, right? Well, not quite. You need a rationale for making predictions. That rationale can come from two sources: (a) previous empirical research (including applied and program-evaluation research), (b) theory, or (c) both. If a particular research question has been informed by previous research, the nature of hypothesized relationships will have been suggested by that research and the specific hypotheses to examine should then be fairly obvious. Similarly, theory may suggest certain relationships that can be tested.

Having said all this, it is important to acknowledge that some research areas are so new that hypotheses are difficult to develop. Similarly, some fields (e.g., ethology or astronomy) have a stronger descriptive tradition than others. If you are having trouble coming up with hypotheses and know your literature and associated theoretical framework, talk with your chairperson. Avoid making something up. Science involves originality, but not creative fiction.

In addition, don't expect yourself to know what you predict until you've read the literature. You may think you can predict the outcome after reading a few articles, only to find that literature you read as you delve more deeply into the topic suggests contradictory findings or leads you in slightly different directions. This is normal and is part of the scientific process. Refine or modify your hypotheses as you think and read more about the topic.

A few words about types of hypotheses. Most commonly we read about the *null* and the *research* hypothesis (Ray, 2006). Research hypotheses assert a relationship to be confirmed in the study. Null hypotheses, first identified as such by Sir Ronald Fisher, basically state that there is *no* relationship. Although you are interested in your research hypotheses, statistics cannot confirm them. They can only disconfirm the null hypothesis. The preferences of thesis/dissertation chairs will differ, but most prefer students to include their research hypotheses in their proposal. The null versions are not necessary as they can be inferred quite easily.

Note, too, that it is generally not considered acceptable to proffer a null hypothesis as an expectation for the results of your project. Thus, the hypothesis "Boys and girls do not differ in their interest in science-related stories" would not be considered legitimate. This is because statistics can only disprove the null hypothesis, not prove it. Look for relationships you expect to exist, not the absence of relationships. Of course, it is perfectly legitimate to hypothesize that you will find different relationships in one group or condition than another. Thus, "Gender difference in interest in science depends on the type of science stimulus, such that boys express more interest in science toys than girls, but boys and girls express similar amounts of interest in science-related stories," is a legitimate hypothesis. This is because it predicts a significant interaction between gender and type of science stimulus, something that can be tested with inferential statistics.

As with research questions, the carefully phrased hypothesis indicates the specific relationships to be examined. It also suggests the nature of the relationship. Thus, "there is a relationship between education level and preference for liberal causes" is less desirable than "there is a positive relationship between education level and preference for liberal causes." Hypotheses worded clearly also include a third criterion important to some researchers: the nature of the experimental design. In this example, a correlational design is implied. Another recommendation is to include in the hypothesis the population in which the relationship is to be studied. The hypothesis "There is a positive relationship between education level and preference for liberal causes in executive women" meets this criterion.

This is probably a good place to stop adding more information to hypotheses. It is common for novice researchers to go further, however. A common mistake is to include the specific measures of one's variables in the hypothesis. For example, "There is a positive relationship between education level as assessed by the Horace Mann Scale of Educational Attainment and preference for liberal causes as measured by the ACLU Scale for Consistently Clear Thinking in executive women." It is certainly true that this hypothesis is more specific, although somewhat unwieldy. Although some might disagree with this, we believe that excessive operationalization at this point misses the point of the research. The purpose is to study relationships between variables to build a science. Including the specific measures of the variables places undue attention on the methodology of the study. We are interested in these specific measures only as they operationalize the major variables of the research. As others have noted, "The hypothesis should refer to the variables of interest, *not* to the specific indicators, or the specific empirical definition, used" (Pedhazur & Schmelkin, 1991, p. 179). In general, phrase your hypotheses at the level at which you want to generalize your findings.

Another mistake to avoid is including the name of the particular statistical test in the hypothesis. Thus, "It is predicted that a one-way ANOVA will reveal differences between attorneys, psychologists, and accountants in degree of extrinsic religiosity" loses sight of the basic issue. In this case, we are apparently interested in differences among these professional groups in extrinsic religiosity. How we test for differences between them on our measures is methodological detail that does not belong in the hypothesis and can detract from the primary focus.

Students often ask, "How many hypotheses should I have?" Our answer is "not many." We sometimes see proposals with 10 to 20 hypotheses. Often these involve the administration of some personality inventory and predictions developed for each of the subscales of the inventory. So many hypotheses are a clear sign that the candidate may have (a) bitten off more than he or she can chew, (b) not given the study enough forethought to narrow the specific hypotheses to a manageable number, or (c) lost sight of the forest. Remember Occam's razor when doing your dissertation: Keep it parsimonious. There are simply not that many independent behavioral phenomena out there. More than likely, if you have developed hypotheses for 10 to 20 measures, a factor analysis would find the measures to be correlated and reducible to a smaller number of 3 to 4 independent factors. Science advances when the same phenomena are explained with fewer concepts or variables. Ask yourself whether all the hypotheses you are formulating are really tapping different things. If not, combine and reword them to focus on the essence of the problem being studied. If they are tapping too many different things, you have bitten off too much. Go back to the literature or consult with your chair to whittle down your project to a manageable size.

Exhibit 4.1 summarizes our recommendations concerning hypotheses. This should help you determine when your hypotheses are adequate.

You now have some idea of the design you will need to use to explore the relationships implied by your hypotheses. Moreover, the nature of your hypotheses will direct the selection of statistical tests. A final issue warrants addressing at this point: Are you adequately prepared to carry out the research as you have now clarified it? For example, novice researchers sometimes launch into an area that does not have adequate (or any) measures for its principal variables or constructs. The first thing the candidate proposes is to develop a measure to use in the research. Our favorite questions of such ambitious individuals are (a) "What courses have you taken in scale construction and measurement theory? Any coursework in factor analysis? Generalizability theory?" (b) "How many years have you budgeted to complete this project?" and (c) "Are you prepared to do a thesis or dissertation just developing the measures you need?" The moral is to avoid research questions that are too ambitious for your skills or that will require you to develop or master excessively complex new technical material. Pare down your scope to something manageable.

Exhibit 4.1

Hypothesis Checklist

Yes No

☐	☐	1. Do your hypotheses suggest the relationship between two or more variables?
☐	☐	2. Do your hypotheses specify the nature of the relationship?
☐	☐	3. Are your hypotheses stated in the present tense?
☐	☐	4. Do your hypotheses imply the research design to be used to study the relationship?
☐	☐	5. Do your hypotheses indicate the population to be studied?
☐	☐	6. Are your hypotheses phrased at the level at which you wish to generalize your findings (i.e., do they talk about constructs rather than specific measures)?
☐	☐	7. Do your hypotheses stipulate relationships among variables rather than names of specific statistical tests?
☐	☐	8. Are your hypotheses free of other unnecessary methodological detail?
☐	☐	9. Do you have a manageable number of hypotheses (e.g., 5–6 or fewer)?

Note. Our preferred answer to each question is "yes," unless your chairperson or departmental norms indicate otherwise.

Recruit Committee Members

Once you have a specific research topic, some idea of your likely hypotheses, and a chairperson, the time has come to assemble the rest of your team: your thesis or dissertation committee. Dissertation and thesis committees vary in size, composition, and specific duties, depending on the institution and the degree. Committee members' general roles are reasonably consistent, however, (a) they provide suggestions for improving the proposed study and, later, the final written project; (b) they serve as additional checks on the quality of the proposal and final document; and (c) they take the lead in examining the student during the oral defense. In the thesis defense, the committee ordinarily wishes to ensure that the student understands and can talk intelligently about the research. In the dissertation defense, the committee also assesses the student's competence to function as an independent researcher. Thus, committee members serve partially as consultants and partially as examiners—two vastly different roles. The balance between assistance and inquisition varies from school to school and committee to committee. It also depends on whether the project is a thesis or a dissertation.

Ideally, committee members should provide expertise that supplements the chair's and contribute new insights and ideas that will enhance the research. One of us, for example, will only agree to serve on a committee if she has some expertise regarding the population, the independent variable, or the major dependent variables of the proposed investigation. Committee members' theoretical perspectives and points of view should be reasonably compatible with the student's, and members should have some interest in the topic. Students working closely with an outside agency should consider inviting a doctoral-level person in the agency to serve on the committee. This person typically becomes the student's advocate and liaison within the agency and also provides valuable information about agency regulations as well as feedback about what requests for agency resources are reasonable. Adding a statistics expert to the committee may be useful if you will be using complex statistical procedures and will need more than occasional consultation with this individual.

Committee members should also get along reasonably well interpersonally with the chair. In addition, committee members should be fair, direct, and trustworthy. Although committee members who praise the student privately and then torpedo the project in the oral defense are rare, the experience is traumatic enough that you should gather sufficient information about prospective committee members to ensure this won't happen to you.

Before considering specifics about selecting committee members, find out the written and unwritten rules about committee members' involvement in preparing the proposal and the final written document. Many departments follow the strong-chairperson model in which committee members read the proposal and full write-up only after the chair approves these documents. This approval follows extensive work between student and chair to fashion the document into acceptable form. Members of the committee are expected to be available for consultation regarding specific aspects of the project that fall within their areas of expertise (e.g., specific measurement issues or statistical treatment of the data). They usually do not, however, serve as substitute chairs (the exception to this is when a committee member knows more than the chairperson about the topic area under study and assumes more extensive responsibility than usual for some aspect of the project). The chair, not the committee, consults with the student on the hypotheses, design, measure selection, and other details. Committee members voice their opinions after the chair is satisfied with the proposal, unless they are invited earlier to help solve a problem for which their skills are well suited.

The strong-chairperson model is not the only model, of course. In some schools, committee members assume roles much closer to that of the chair, sometimes reading drafts of the proposal and final project as the student prepares them (we call this the strong-committee model). Our experience in these situations is that members' roles are often ambiguously defined, leaving the student to figure out when and how committee members should be involved. When this process is the norm, students can clarify the process by asking the chairperson to specify what role the chairperson wants committee members to serve. Getting chairs to be specific is important. When and what should committee members agree to read? How many drafts? Will there be a formal proposal meeting? The student should then communicate these expectations to prospective committee members.

Another risk when roles are ambiguous is that the student gets caught between different members' ideas about how to handle particular research issues. This can result in students running from chair to committee member and back again, sometimes misquoting or forgetting what each person has told them about the issue. In these cases, we recommend a family therapy approach: Arrange a meeting among all involved parties and hash out the issues face to face.

Investigate Prospective Committee Members

Many of our suggestions for finding a chair apply equally to committee members: Find out the formal rules about the composition of the committee and who can and cannot serve as a member; talk to students about their experiences with different faculty as committee members; and take information from the rumor mill with a large grain of salt. The grapevine, hungry for juicy tidbits, often creates conflict where none exists. We have been told on occasion that we do not get along with some of our favorite colleagues, on the basis of misinterpretation and speculation! Check out better sources of data (e.g., good students' experiences with different committees). In addition, ask your chairperson about prospective committee members. If your mentor has worked with them, he or she will know how they can contribute to your particular project. It is imperative to discuss prospective committee members with your chairperson *before* issuing invitations. This is because your chair may have specific recommendations and may work better with certain colleagues than with others.

Your chairperson will also guide you regarding *when* to approach committee members. In general, we advise students not to form a committee until they decide on a research question, develop their methodology, and have a reasonable timetable for completing the proposal and conducting the study. Knowing the specific topic is important for obvious reasons. Knowing the time frame of the project is important, too, because faculty members go on leaves of absence and sabbaticals; do not want to be on a dozen dissertation committees, all of which will be meeting during the same week; and so on. Many who are not paid by the school during the summer do not meet with students or participate in proposal meetings or oral defenses during this period. Replacing a committee member can be difficult. Form a committee of individuals who plan to be available during the time frame you propose.

Approach Prospective Committee Members: Dissertation and Thesis Etiquette II

As with chairpersons, we recommend an interview-and-invite strategy with committee members. Contact prospective committee members by telling them first that you would like to talk to them about possibly serving on your committee. Provide a brief overview of your topic, your proposed method, and your timetable for completing the proposal and the final write-up. Ask potential committee members if they would like to see a brief summary of the project in writing. You may also want to tell prospective committee members what you believe they could contribute to the project. If you wish potential committee members to be available for specific tasks (e.g., to consult on statistics or to assist with your methodology), tell them about these requirements (e.g., "I'm hoping you will be able to help me network with schools"). Ask about any special requirements they might have about your project. A committee member who is a statistician, for example, may wish to discuss your statistics with you only *after* you have discussed them with your chairperson. As with the chairperson, issue or finalize your invitation after you have gathered the information you need to make sure the potential committee member is a good fit for your project.

Supplemental Resources

Darley, J. M., Zanna, M.P., & Roediger, H. L. (Eds.). (2003). *The compleat academic: A career guide* (2nd ed.). Washington, DC: American Psychological Association. [A chapter in this book gives insights into faculty–student research collaboration from the faculty perspective. This is also an especially worthwhile book for those planning academic careers.]

Frick, R. W. (1996). The appropriate use of null hypothesis testing. *Psychological Methods, 1,* 379–390.

Oetting, E. R. (1986). Ten fatal mistakes in grant writing. *Professional Psychology: Research and Practice, 17,* 570–573.

Pedhazur, E. J., & Schmelkin, L. P. (1991). *Measurement, design, and analysis: An integrated approach.* Hillsdale, NJ: Erlbaum.

Sternberg, D. (1981). *How to complete and survive a doctoral dissertation.* New York: St. Martin's Press. [A good source for more information on chair (advisor) selection, including avoiding those who might have a propensity for sexual involvement during the process.]

Webb, E. J. (1961). The choice of problem. *American Psychologist, 16,* 223–227.

✔ To Do . . .

Finding Topics and Committee Members

Develop your topic

☐ Select a general topic area

☐ Work with faculty to develop your ideas

☐ Develop the research question

— Consider research in which you have been involved

— Avoid personally loaded topics

— Use recent literature

— Use other theses and dissertations cautiously

☐ Put the research question in researchable form

— Phrase the question as a question

— Make sure the question suggests a relationship to be examined

— Make sure the question is empirically testable

☐ Develop well-worded hypotheses using Exhibit 4.1

Assemble your team

☐ Identify formal rules about chairpersons, and committee members' roles

☐ Identify informal rules about chairpersons' and committee members' roles

☐ Identify what you want from the chair–student collaboration

☐ Identify potential chairpersons' expertise in areas that interest you

☐ Appraise potential chairpersons' skills

— Expectations

— Feedback

— Timeliness and availability

— Assertiveness

☐ Investigate prospective chairpersons

— Consider past experiences with these individuals

  —Talk with classmates

  —Talk with faculty members

☐ Approach prospective chairpersons

  —Identify important issues to discuss with them

  —Communicate clearly

  —Obtain commitment from chairperson

  —Anticipate and prevent trouble spots

☐ Investigate prospective committee members

  —Talk with chairperson

  —Talk with classmates

☐ Approach prospective committee members

  —Provide overview of your study and timetable

  —Obtain commitment from committee members

5

Formulating and Communicating Your Plans: An Overview of the Proposal

At this point, you know what you want to do and have chosen people to guide you in doing it. Next, you need to formalize your plans. In this chapter, we provide an overview of the content and structure of the proposal. The specific components usually included are covered in chapters 6 through 9. Chapter 13 discusses how you present and defend this proposal during a meeting of your committee. First, let's look at some thoughts about what theses and dissertation proposals are supposed to accomplish.

Understand the Functions of the Dissertation or Thesis Proposal

Your proposal specifies what you expect to do and how you will do it. It is important from several perspectives. First, the proposal is the first significant piece of writing you will do on your thesis or dissertation. In a sense, it serves as the training ground and testing period of the research. Producing the proposal will give you firsthand insights into the complexity of the investigatory process and the particular research area you have chosen. Your proposal also provides your chair and committee members evidence of your preparation to carry out the research and of how you operate as a scholar. Because it sets the tone in this fashion, you should approach the process in ways that communicate how you wish to be perceived by your committee members. Do you want to be seen as a helpless person who needs guidance and reassurance at every turn? Are you more interested in being seen as self-reliant, with good judgment about when and when *not* to seek consultation?

Another reason the proposal is so important is that, once accepted by your committee, it serves as a blueprint for what you intend to do. Your proposal specifies exactly how you plan to complete your research. By approving your proposal, your committee members say that if you do exactly as you specified in the proposal, you will have carried out a project that meets their specifications.

In some schools, the proposal is considered an informal contract (see Sternberg, 1981): If you follow your procedures to the letter, your committee cannot, after the fact, ask you to run more participants, follow an adapted procedure, or run another control condition. Some schools actually have committee members sign an approval (following the addition of changes suggested in the proposal meeting) that is then filed with the amended proposal in the dean's or some other administrative office. Years later, when the weary doctoral candidate returns from Fiji with her completed dissertation and none of her original committee members are still on the faculty, there is some proof that the university really did consent to a study on the underwater aerobic exercise of South Sea island octogenarians.

Not all faculty and departments hold the contract view, however. Even those who do are quick to point out that approving the proposal does not mean the final project will also be approved. You must also conduct the study well, analyze the data appropriately, produce an acceptable final version of the study, and so on. Furthermore, most researchers change something that they proposed once they actually implement the study. Nonetheless, it will behoove you to assess local norms about how binding the proposal is, both to students and to faculty.

Your written product is your opportunity to show what you can do as a scholar. Be aware, however, that although creativity and originality are valued characteristics in conceptualizing and conducting research, they are not popular when writing about it. The proposal is no place for you to challenge the departmental rules and come up with your own "improved" way of doing things. Find out the proposal requirements of your department or school. Do it their way and save your creativity for more important challenges.

The proposal seems a formidable obstacle for many students. But, believe it or not, you have probably done a great deal of the work for it already. What you need to do now is organize all those notes you have taken, all those references, and all those measures you've been collecting as you researched your topic and turn them into a single document. In the next section, we give you an overview of what to put into the proposal.

Know the Elements of the Dissertation or Thesis Proposal

So what goes into a proposal? Departments and faculty vary in how detailed they wish the proposal to be. At one end of the extreme, students present an abbreviated literature review and a method section with little detail and few appendixes. At the other end of the spectrum, the proposal is essentially a draft of the first half of the final dissertation, with all relevant supplemental material in the appendixes. If you haven't already done so, ask your chairperson to recommend a couple of proposals for you to use as models. Compare them to the final dissertation versions of the same study to appraise the level of detail the candidates provided in the proposal.

We lean strongly toward including more rather than less detail in the proposal, because of the contract view noted above. A good rule of thumb is to include everything that will go into the complete dissertation (thesis) eventually. Your ideas, references, and insights are relatively fresh and available now, not lost in the synaptic jungle of your brain or the disorganization of your writing space. Put them into the proposal, and you won't have to worry about losing them or recreating them afresh after you have collected and analyzed your data.

Furthermore, putting the details of your study in writing allows faculty to give you feedback on your specific ideas and plans. The more complete you are now, the less room there is for a committee member to say at your oral defense, "Oh—I *assumed* that of course you would do this my way. You didn't? You really need to run all those participants again to correct that egregious error."

Although formal rules as well as chairpersons' and committee members' preferences can vary, a good way to organize a proposal is in terms of three major sections: an introduction (literature review), a methods section, and a results section. Sometimes a data analysis section is included as part of the method section and may take the place of a results section in the proposal. Of course, some material will go before (e.g., title page and table of contents) and after (e.g., references and appendixes) these major sections. Nonetheless, these three sections constitute the heart of the proposal. The material that follows provides an overview of each section. Subsequent chapters (chaps. 6 through 9, this volume) go into much more detail about these sections of the proposal.

Introduction (Literature Review)

In the introduction section, you will talk about the area of your research and include your review of relevant literature. Two general variations of the dissertation literature review predominate. The first is the two-chapter model. This consists of a relatively short chapter (usually the first chapter of the document) that introduces the topic, provides a brief overview, and then states the research problem and sometimes the hypotheses. A longer second chapter provides a critical, integrative review of the literature. The challenge of this model is to present sufficient information in the first chapter for the reader to understand why the research question is important without being redundant with the longer chapter.

The more streamlined one-chapter model combines the material of the two-chapter version into one, but reverses the order of the major sections. It ordinarily begins with a brief introduction to the topic, then launches into a focused literature review that *concludes* with a statement of the problem and hypotheses. A less common version of this model is one that approximates the length of the introductory section of a journal article (4–8 pages), sometimes accompanied by a lengthier, more comprehensive review in an appendix.

Whichever version you choose, your proposal should contain a complete review of literature relevant to your specific topic. In other words, write the literature review that you will include in the final version of your thesis or dissertation (the final write-up will also include the few new studies that get published while you are conducting yours). Although some schools accept abbreviated reviews for the proposal, we strongly recommend writing a complete review at the proposal stage. What is our logic? You will need to do all the work required for a complete review to write your proposal anyway. Otherwise, you won't know whether someone has beaten you to the punch and already explored your idea. A thorough review of the literature also acquaints you with all the nitty-gritty procedural and design details of research in your area, thereby helping you to avoid the mistakes others have made. The precision required to write a review will force you to think through these details in much more depth than if you just read the literature and give a brief overview in the proposal. In addition, if you write a thorough literature review and methodology section, your final project is halfway written! If you leave the review for later, you'll have a demanding writing task left to do at the end of the project. You are not likely to be highly motivated to reread all those articles that you've forgotten while you were collecting your data.

In the literature review, we, as others (e.g., Yates, 1982), recommend using the funnel approach: Start with the general literature in your topic area and gradually narrow your focus to the specific area of research and precise research question you are going to explore. After introducing the subject and reviewing relevant literature, you will lead the reader skillfully to the point at which the rationale for your specific study should seem readily apparent to any reader who stayed awake for the previous material. As mentioned earlier, if writing a one-chapter literature review, you will place your statement of the problem, research question(s), and hypotheses at the close of this chapter.

How long should the review be? In our experience, this varies widely, depending on departmental norms and on how many pages you devote to the wide end of the funnel (i.e., how much you summarize background material versus review it in depth). Our guess is that the modal length of a literature review for a dissertation varies from about 20 to 50 pages. Theses are usually shorter.

Method

Using a cookbook analogy, if your introduction has been carefully composed, the reader now knows why you have decided on chocolate mousse cake for the dinner party you are planning. Your logic and organization in choosing the main course and wine and other accompaniments have been so compelling that no one would dream of selecting any other dessert. Now for the recipe! The method section can be thought of as the "how it is going be done" section of the proposal. The rule of thumb is replicability. Your method section should provide sufficient details so that anyone reading it would be able to replicate your study in all essential aspects. In other words, the cake should come out exactly the same each time someone reads the recipe and attempts to bake it.

There are a number of subsections that are included in nearly any method section. The first subsection will usually be labeled *participants*. Subsequent sections will cover design, independent variables, measures (dependent and other), apparatus, setting, and procedures. Exactly what content you cover, and in what order, will depend on your study. Chapter 7 provides more details about what to include in the method (and other) section(s) of your proposal.

What about length? Again, this depends on how detailed you are, how complex your procedures and design turn out to be, and how much material you locate in the method section and how much in the appendixes. In our experience, most method sections are 15 to 25 pages long for dissertations. Again, theses may be shorter.

Results

The results section is the place where you will present the fruits of your data collection for the world to see. Start this section with an analysis subsection detailing any preliminary analyses you will conduct—for example, checking the reliability of your measures, conducting validity analyses, examining distributions of scores, and so forth. Then describe the statistical procedures you will use to test your hypotheses and address your research questions. You will make statements such as "A 2×2 ANCOVA will be used to analyze the effects of anxiety and task complexity on errors, with GPA serving as the covariate." Indicate that you will provide appropriate tables of means and standard deviations for each of your groups on each dependent variable. If you use analyses of variance (ANOVAs) or analyses of covariance (ANCOVAs), you might include a summary (source) table indicating the main effects, interactions, error terms, and degrees of freedom you will use. Make sure you indicate what statistical test you will use for every score you plan to analyze. Your reader should also know exactly how each variable is to be scored, a topic you will have covered in the method section under measures. Chapter 9 provides guidelines for matching statistics to research questions.

In most departments, a data analysis plan is included either as the final section of the method section (as the statistical analyses portion of the proposal, whose table of contents is shown in Exhibit 5.1, presented later in this chapter) or as a brief "Results" section of the proposal. It is possible to be more extensive than this, however. One way to clarify your results section for yourself (and your committee) is to create a mock results section. For example, you could provide appropriate tables of means and standard deviations for each of your groups on each dependent measure. Present figures to show, graphically, the effects you might find. For example, if doing an ANOVA, you might present figures to show graphically the main effects and interactions that you expect to find if the study turns out exactly as you predict. Figuring this out ahead of time will help you get clear about what you are really doing and will permit you to check computer printouts later for errors. If your design calls for repeated measures on single cases or groups of participants, you should provide figures and tables appropriate to these data. If your study is descriptive and includes correlations among a number of measures, show the correlation matrixes you are likely to obtain.

Show your results in the ideal form. That is, show how they will look if the study turns out exactly as your hypotheses predict. Then show how they will look if the study is a total bust. Finally, show the most likely case—namely, a mixture of positive, negative, and confusing results.

You may wonder why we would include a results section in our suggestions for your thesis or dissertation proposal. After all, almost no one requires this, so why do something you don't have to do? In addition, you are *proposing* to do the research. You haven't done it yet, so where are the results to include in this section?

It might help you appreciate our suggestions if you consider this section as a "hypothesized results" or "hoped for results" section. Although not everyone would agree with the need for a results section in a proposal, we agree with Sternberg (1981) that such a section forces you to think about exactly how you are going to analyze and present your data. By developing a mock results section, you are required to identify in advance the statistical procedures you will use. This will help you discover whether your data are likely to meet the assumptions of the various statistics, whether your data can even be analyzed to answer the questions you have posed, and what type of consultative or other resources you will need at this point in the process. Looking at different ways the data *could* turn out may also help in identifying design weaknesses that you can correct before you run the study.

Doing this should also help you learn more about your statistics in advance of running the study. For example, if your study will require relatively complex path analyses, latent growth modeling, or confirmatory factor analysis, you may need to prepare yourself by learning more about these procedures. You might also want to seek out the appropriate software packages to do the data analyses. Further, you might want to find experts you could call on for occasional consultation when the data are actually available to analyze. This will save you lots of time later. When your data are collected, you can begin your analyses immediately and will not have to stop and decide just what you are going to do and how. Keeping the momentum going on complex, drawn-out research projects is extremely important. In addition, mock results provide just the level of detail needed for busy committee members to understand exactly what you are planning to do.

With this additional detail, they can identify potential snags and help you steer around them before you run into problems.

References

Include a list of the references cited in your proposal. Prepare this list using the format suggested in the American Psychological Association (APA) *Publication Manual* (APA, 2010), unless your school specifies a different format. Be sure to include only those references you actually cited. Some novice writers prepare a reference list that reflects every article they read. Although this may impress your committee and stand as a memorial to your extensive time in the library or on your computer, such a list is overly inclusive. References you read but do not use should be deleted from the list. Once you prepare your references, you can update the list quite easily when you complete your study and you are preparing the final version of your project.

Appendixes

Appendixes are the repository of all that extra detail that might be useful to someone attempting to replicate your study in the future. They also contain information that might be important to committee members to assure them that you approached your task in a competent way. Copies of instructions to participants, consent forms, debriefing scripts, data-collection instruments that are not copyrighted, construction blueprints, wiring diagrams for apparatus, and treatment manuals are examples of the kinds of entries one might expect to find in appendixes that accompany the proposal. Ordinarily, instruments copyrighted by others are not included in an appendix; if you wish to include them, you must obtain written permission to do so from the copyright holder.

Place items in appendixes in the order that the reader encounters them in the proposal. Thus, appendix A would contain a copy of the advertisement placed in the local newspaper for participant recruitment, if this is the first time the reader is referred to material in an appendix. Appendix B would contain the next such referenced material, and so on.

Table of Contents

Once the rest of the proposal is complete, you can produce the table of contents, right? Actually, it can be a good idea to prepare it ahead of time in the form of an outline. This can help you organize your literature review and method sections. It will also help you identify and avoid problems in conceptualizing your material. Preparing the table of contents ahead of time also provides a task analysis or checklist of what needs to be done to complete the dissertation. A carefully prepared, three-level outline or table of contents shows quite clearly what needs to be done (refer to Exhibit 5.1 for an example of this kind of outline). As you complete the different sections, you can obtain immense satisfaction from checking off your accomplishments.

Of course, the table of contents won't have page numbers until the entire proposal is complete. In fact, the table should be regarded as a tentative outline that can be revised as your writing proceeds. When you are ready to insert page numbers (i.e., just before submitting your proposal to your committee), be sure to assign titles to the appendixes as well. Thus, "Appendix A: Instructions to Participants . . . . p. 86" tells exactly where to go to find what the participants are told. (Some dissertations merely indicate that Appendix A begins on page 86 without indicating what the appendix contains. This is unnecessarily shabby scholarship.) Another nice touch is to give the actual page numbers of the appendixes when referring to them in the text. Thus, ". . . were told they would receive relaxation training for 10 minutes at the start of each session (see Appendix A, p. 86)" is much more helpful to the reader than ". . . (see Appendix A)."

Exhibit 5.1 presents a copy of the table of contents for a dissertation proposal one of us chaired. Studying the tables of contents of theses and dissertations your chairperson recommends as models will show you alternate ways of organizing a proposal.

Investigate the General Proposal Process

The process that students follow in preparing a proposal varies from chair to chair and place to place, but there are some general consistencies. The process usually starts when you have (a) nailed down both an idea and a chairperson (not necessarily in that order!), (b) gathered and read the relevant literature, and (c) arrived at a good idea of what you propose to do. You then write the proposal. Some students submit parts of the proposal for review by their chairperson (e.g., lit review, then method section) as they write, while others wait until they have a complete draft to turn in. Your chairperson can advise you on the process he or she usually follows.

Exhibit 5.1

Sample Dissertation Proposal Table of Contents

ASSESSMENT OF AGGRESSION IN CHILDREN: AN EXPLORATION OF SELF AND PEER REPORT METHODS

TABLE OF CONTENTS

CHAPTER I: INTRODUCTION AND LITERATURE REVIEW 4
   Forms of Aggression 5
      Overt Aggression 5
      Relational Aggression 6
      Indirect Aggression 6
      Social Aggression 7
   Gender Differences in Aggression 8
   Rationale for Examining Overt and Relational Aggression 9
   Measures of Aggression 12
      Direct Observation 13
      Teacher Report 16
      Parent Report 18
      Self-Report 19
      Peer Nominations 22
   Summary and Statement of the Problem 26
   Research Questions and Hypotheses 26

CHAPTER II: METHOD AND PROCEDURES 28
   Participants 28
   Protection of Human Participants 29
   Design 30
   Measures 31
      Pilot Version of the Children's Behavior Scale 31
      Peer Nomination Measure 33
      Children's Social Desirability Scale 36
      Sociometric Questionnaire 37
      Friendship Questionnaire 38
   Control Variables 39
      Procedures 40
      Statistical Analyses 43
         Preliminary Analyses 43
         Main Analyses 43
         Exploratory Analyses 44

continued

Exhibit 5.1, continued

References 46
Appendix A: Teacher Questionnaire 54
Appendix B: Demographic Questionnaire 56
Appendix C: Parental Consent Form 58
Appendix D: Child Assent Form 66
Appendix E: Confidentiality Agreement 69
Appendix F: Pilot Versions of Children's Behavior Scale–Self 71
Appendix G: Pilot Versions of Children's Behavior Scale–Peer 79
Appendix H: Peer Nomination Instrument 94
Appendix I: Children's Social Desirability Scale 97
Appendix J: Sociometric Questionnaire 100
Appendix K: Friendship Questionnaire 103
Appendix L: Instructions 105
Appendix M: Blank Pilot Peer Version of Children's
             Behavior Scale 112
Appendix N: Final Questionnaire 114

Table of contents created by Heather O'Shea, 2003. Reproduced by permission of the author.

Generally, your committee members will not read early drafts unless one or more has serious interest and expertise in your area. Your chairperson should provide feedback on what you have written, and you should continue to revise your document until the chairperson thinks it is suitable to give to your committee members. Usually, submitting it to the committee members signals that you are ready for a proposal meeting (see chap. 13, this volume), at which your readers will raise additional issues for you to consider and suggest revisions to the document. After the proposal meeting, you will make the revisions requested by your committee and submit the proposal for any additional required approval.

Somewhere in this process you will also prepare and submit additional documents to secure the approval of your institutional review board (IRB) for the protection of human (or animal) subjects. As a condition of receiving federal money, the U.S. Department of Health and Human Services requires agencies to have formal procedures in place to ensure the humane treatment of individuals receiving services from the agency. This is true whether it be a college, university, hospital, clinic, or public residential facility. Each agency that permits research must have a committee or group of people serving as guardians of individual rights.

The operations of your local IRB are governed by federal regulations and by local rules and traditions. You must apply in writing to your local

IRB and obtain permission to conduct your research before you begin collecting data. The documents you prepare will provide an overview of your procedures and how you will handle the ethical issues involved in any research (e.g., confidentiality, risks of the procedures) and any specific ethical issues pertaining to your study (e.g., use of deception). We have more to say on research ethics in chapter 7.

The timing and nature of these procedures vary from department to department and chairperson to chairperson. For example, one of us worked in a program where the proposal would not receive final approval from the director of the graduate program until the student had secured IRB approval for the study. The other's requirements were the opposite: The student could not submit his or her proposed dissertation research for IRB approval until the committee formally approved the proposal! Consulting with other students, checking dissertation and thesis requirements, and asking your chairperson for information can all help you inform yourself about the normal sequence and timing of key events in the proposal process.

✔ To Do . . .

Writing the Proposal

☐ Understand the importance of the dissertation or thesis proposal

—Identify requirements of department or school

—Find out whether binding the proposal is expected

☐ Know the elements of a dissertation or thesis proposal

—Table of Contents

—Introduction (literature review)

—Method

—Results

—References

—Appendixes

☐ Investigate the general proposal process

—Timetable

—Chairperson preference about drafts

—When to submit proposal to committee members

—Submitting protocol for IRB approval: When and how?

—Departmental requirements

6

Reviewing the Literature

After you find a topic, you must learn more about it. This involves finding, reading, and summarizing (in written form) the relevant professional literature on your topic. Reading and thinking about what others have done and said will teach you about key conceptual and methodological issues in the field. This process will also allow you to see whether another enterprising individual has already done your study. A related benefit is that you can spend hours avoiding writing anything at all by sitting in an armchair and reading.

Locate Relevant Literature

Literature relevant to your research comes from journal articles, books, book chapters, and the Internet. You may also want to examine conference papers, unpublished theses, and doctoral dissertations.

Each of these literature sources contains a large collection of information, however. What are effective ways of sorting through them to extract material most relevant to your particular topic? Several traditional and some more technologically sophisticated methods provide vehicles for locating relevant literature. Although none of these is perfect, using *all* of them together will ensure a reasonably comprehensive literature search. Before starting your search, there are two important suggestions to consider: (a) Rely on primary sources and (b) avoid the popular press.

Use Primary Sources

Look up the original articles (primary sources) and read them yourself. Do not rely solely on others' descriptions of studies and their findings, often referred to as secondary sources. Reviewers too often cite studies erroneously, indicating the authors said something they did not say or did something they did not do. We know—our own work has been cited to support points that opposed the very stand we were taking in the article being cited! In addition, you may not agree with others' conclusions about the paper. Now is the time to stand on your own intellectual feet and draw your own conclusions. We are not saying there is no value in reading others' critiques of original papers. This is best done after reading the original work yourself, however, and then considering whether you agree with the secondary source's opinions.

What if you cannot find the original article because it is in an obscure, difficult to obtain journal or was presented at a conference but not published? Do not cite the article as though you actually read it. Instead, follow American Psychological Association (APA) guidelines to indicate citation of a secondary source (e.g., "Foster, 2000, cited in Cone, 2005").

Avoid the Popular Press

Although *Time* magazine, *Wired*, the *New York Times, Rolling Stone*, and similar sources may be excellent ways of learning what is happening in the world, they are no substitute for scholarly articles in peer-reviewed journals. The same is true of many Internet sites, where the source and accuracy of information can be even harder to discern. Although the information in popular periodicals may be accurate, you cannot evaluate it as you can a journal article in which the methodology is transparent, delineated clearly enough for all to critique.

Information on Internet sites can be tricky because the sites are so variable. At the one extreme are sites created by individual hobbyists who have a point of view to express. At the other are sites where bona fide scientific organizations provide information compiled by groups of scientists based on current literature. Therefore, evaluating Internet information is crucial. Is the site authored by an expert, and therefore similar to a book chapter or review of the literature? Or are the source and the author unclear? Stick closer to the former and stay away from the latter, at least as a source of reliable and valid information.

Identify Key Authors and Journals

A good initial step in compiling relevant literature is to locate key players in your research area and their favorite publication outlets. Who are the Big Names? What journals regularly publish their work? Others who know the area better than you do are good sources of this information (e.g., your chairperson and committee members).

A second excellent source is the bibliography of a recent book or chapter on your topic. Scan the references to locate relevant articles and to find out who's working in the area. Read the book or chapter to orient you to key issues and concepts in the field.

A third effective strategy is to Google the key players in your field. Go to http://www.google.com/ and type in a name to be searched. You can also do this with Yahoo (http://www.yahoo.com), Alta Vista (htpp://www.altavista.com), and other general Internet search engines. This can be an efficient way to obtain up-to-date information on what these people are doing currently in the area, much of which might not yet be published. For example, you might easily find a person's vitae on a university Web site. In addition, you may uncover information about recent presentations or workshops the person has given on relevant topics. A final site worth examining is http://www.guru.net/, an especially useful resource for information on just about any scholarly topic you can imagine.

Use Bibliographic Reference Sources

Various reference sources can assist you with your literature search. *Psychological Abstracts*, for example, contains abbreviated abstracts from psychological journals and indexes these abstracts by topic and author. It is the print version of the PsycINFO database (see below) and is available in the reference section of major libraries. *Dissertation Abstracts International* is a similar reference source for dissertations. The Educational Resources Information Center (ERIC) is a major clearinghouse for information related to education. *Current Contents* is a weekly periodical that lists tables of contents of recent journals and indicates to whom one can write for reprints. Finally, the APA publishes a series of topical *PsycSCANS*, each of which provides abstracts of journal publications in related fields. For example, *Developmental*

PsycSCAN covers journals related to child development. Although *Current Contents* and *PsycSCAN* are not always found in libraries, faculty may subscribe to them and let you borrow their copies. Cooper (1998) described many of these in more detail and provided an overview of how to use several of these reference sources.

One underused reference source bears special mention. *The Social Sciences Citation Index (SSCI)* indexes every article from more than 1,500 professional journals. These represent 50 different disciplines in the social sciences. *SSCI* allows you to look up who has cited a particular article since its publication. It is available electronically in CD format or online as *Social SciSearch*. To use it, you must know the citation for the original article. *SSCI* is useful when you wish to ascertain what has been done since a paper was published: You can track the influence of an article through time and will often find references that computerized literature searches may not locate. *SSCI* is also helpful for locating research containing information about the psychometric properties of measurement devices you might decide to use: Most users of a device cite the original or seminal article on the measurement tool. Read the instructions carefully and ask a reference librarian to help you the first time you use this source; many people find it hard to master *SSCI* without instructions. Cooper (1998) noted that errors in the reference lists in journal articles sometimes compromise the use of *SSCI*. To have confidence that most relevant references get located, he suggested retrieving information on the cited first author, rather than a specific paper of interest. This will lead to a longer list of citations, but it should be inclusive of all citations of the paper, and you can cull the irrelevant ones.

Published bibliographies of references in specific areas within or outside psychology may also prove useful. Librarians in major university libraries can help you locate pertinent bibliographies.

Use Computerized Literature Searches

Computerized databases enable you to search the literature quickly. To use these resources well, you will have to learn how to execute searches. Although search programs differ in their mechanics, most have similar characteristics. First, you must locate *keywords* or *search terms*—words or phrases that you think describe the contents of the papers. This is facilitated in many journals by including keywords or descriptors beneath the abstract on the first page of an article. You then specify these for the search engine and tell it where to look for them, whether in the abstract, title, or body of the paper (where the computer looks for the keywords depends on the particular database).

Authors' names and journal names can also be used as keywords. In addition, you can tell the search engine to look for abstracts that contain more than one keyword. (Usually you list the ones you want, connected by the word "and." The computer then lists abstracts that contain all the words you have listed.) Alternatively, you can use or instruct the computer to pick out papers that contain any one (not all) of the keywords connected by "or." You can scan results of searches on the computer screen, print them, and (sometimes) download them to hard or floppy disks or e-mail them to yourself. Some search engines will automatically e-mail you when new information relevant to your interests appears on the Web. Recent technological innovations such as blogs and podcasts can also be worthwhile sources of information. Presently they tend to be sources for opinion sharing by like-interested participants rather than sources for specific scientific information. See http://en.wikipedia.org/ for more information on blogs and podcasts.

A trap with computerized searches is to believe that you have done an exhaustive literature search this way. The problem is that the search is only as good as (a) your keywords; (b) the extent to which writers (and indexers) in the field use the same words in their titles, abstracts, and so forth; (c) the range of journals the database contains; and (d) the number of years covered by the database.

Finding the right keywords is critical to success. This is by no means easy; not all investigators use the same jargon to describe their studies. For example, a recent search by one of us using the term "trichotillomania" turned up different references than when "hair twirling" was substituted. Thus it is better to start more generally (e.g., hair twirling) rather than limiting your initial search to specific technical terms. Be aware that some programs have professional indexers select the terms by which the article will be indexed. Such indexers might not be familiar with the technical terms of a discipline, however.

If the journal does not provide keywords separately, one excellent way to locate good ones is to find some articles in your area and examine their abstracts. Words that show up frequently are good candidates as keywords. One especially useful feature of many electronic databases is a thesaurus of terms. This allows you to look at terms related to the keywords you select and may give you ideas about topics that relate to your project but that had not occurred to you. You can also consult the thesaurus for more inclusive or more specific categories associated with your keywords.

If you are not familiar with digital databases in your field, a good place to start is with http://researchresources.net/directory/socialscience. This site provides an organized list of hundreds of Web sites related to disciplines in the behavioral sciences and education. Another excellent starting site is http://www.socsciresearch.com/.

Probably the most useful, widely available computerized database in psychology is PsycINFO. PsycINFO is a database of abstracts of psychological literature dating from the 1800s to the present. It includes journals (more than 1,900 titles covered), books and book chapters, dissertation abstracts, and other databases. Full-text coverage of articles is included in Psyc-ARTICLES™, which is linked to PsycINFO in some libraries. This online database contains the full text of more than 31,000 articles from 42 journals published by the APA and several associated organizations from 1988 to the present. Complete articles can be ordered or downloaded for a fee from PsycARTICLES™. This can come in handy when there is an especially important paper that you have to have immediately. *PsycSCANs* were described earlier as print databases. *PsycSCANs Online* are subsets of PsycINFO that include bibliographic citations and abstracts for specific topics, such as developmental psychology or applied psychology. Currently, the APA offers electronic-only *PsycSCANs* in applied psychology, behavior analysis and therapy, learning disability/mental retardation, and psychopharmacology.

Current Contents Connect® is the online version of the *Current Contents®* series of publications mentioned earlier. An especially valuable database for health-related literature is PubMed (http://www.ncbi.nlm.nih.gov/entrez/). This is a service of the National Library of Medicine, and it includes more than 14 million citations for biomedical articles dating to the 1950s. MEDLINE provides most of these citations, although many come from additional life science journals. PubMed includes links to many sites providing full text articles and other related resources. Another especially good source for quick access to full-text articles is Ingenta (http://www.ingenta.com), which, at the time of this writing, permitted one to search 16,719,850 articles from a total of 28,618 different publications. This site can be a good place to locate references for your topic, but you will find the cost of a full-text version quite expensive. It will pay to make a trip to the library instead.

Google Scholar (http://scholar.google.com/) is another online search engine that can help you locate relevant scientific articles; at the time this book was written it was in Beta testing but freely available.

Write for Reprints and Preprints

Once you have identified key contributors in your area, you can also write, telephone, or e-mail them and request reprints. With the advent of electronic versions of papers and e-mail, reprint requests are not as common as they were in the past. Nonetheless, authors will still ordinarily provide hard copies of journal articles for the asking, although some will ask that you pay for photocopying and postage. Also, request chapters, which you may not find as readily as journal articles, for preprints (articles that are submitted or accepted for publication), and for conference presentations. Although not everyone will send reprints of chapters, preprints, and presentations, if you get them, you'll find out what's about to be published. Check the author's current address online using one of the search engines cited earlier or in the membership directories of relevant professional organizations such as the American Psychological Society, the Society for Research in Child Development, or the Association for Behavior Analysis. Membership directories are available in many school or departmental libraries, in psychology department chairpersons' offices, or on your chairperson's bookshelf. A telephone call may be more effective than a letter at prompting a quick response: It's harder to forget or ignore a request from a person with whom you have spoken than from a letter in a low-priority stack of correspondence. An e-mailed request may be even better.

As Yates (1982) pointed out, you can also look in convention programs to find titles of papers that were presented in your area. Many of these studies will be published over the years immediately following the meeting, and locating these studies will help you find out what is in the publication pipeline.

Look at Literature From Other Disciplines

Psychological Abstracts, PsycINFO, and other resources are limited by the journals they include. Your research area may overlap with other disciplines. Medicine, communications, education, and sociology all have journals that publish articles relevant to some areas of psychology. Many disciplines have printed abstract services such as *Psychological Abstracts* that should be consulted if your research area is addressed by more than one discipline. They also have computerized databases you can access.

Scan the Tables of Contents of Key Journals

As you become familiar with your topic area, identify the journals in which most articles in your area have been published. Then look at their tables of contents (usually listed by author at the end of the last issue of each volume) for the past 10 years. This will help you find articles that may be too recent to be in reference and bibliographic materials, and it will serve as a double check on the yields provided by your other methods. Note that tables of contents are included in *Current Contents®* as well. They are also readily available for journals published by the APA at its Web site (http://www.apa.org/journals).

Use Reference Lists

As you scan relevant articles, look at their bibliographies and note relevant references. This is an invaluable source of references you may not have found through other means. Cooper (1998) pointed out a trap with using both the key journals and the reference-scanning approaches. Most researchers in a particular area, according to Cooper, have informal interpersonal and journal networks. Thus, they tend to publish in and cite articles from their journal network, leading to overrepresentation of articles in journals inside the network and undercitation of articles in journals outside the network. This is yet another reason for using multiple methods to conduct a comprehensive literature search in your research area.

Your search is over when you have done all of the above and keep turning up the same articles, repeatedly, as you look at others' reference lists and bibliographical sources. This may not mean you have collected everything ever written on a topic, but you have probably found the major articles produced in the area.

Keep Track of Citations

As we scan published reference lists for relevant articles, we like to copy complete citations (in APA style) onto index cards (one reference per card) or into a computer file. The latter is preferable, especially if you have a laptop or keyboard-enhanced personal digital assistant (PDA) that you carry to the library with you. Get in the habit of typing the citation one time and take the time to learn APA style for different kinds of references you will use in your ultimate reference lists. We cannot tell you how many hours we have spent in our careers trying to track down page numbers of chapters, author initials, and so forth, that we failed to note when we first wrote down the reference. Some colleagues strongly recommend EndNote, a bibliographic database that allows you to organize reference citations and can format references in many different styles, including APA style. A word of warning: Even the best software solutions to easy APA formatting are not 100% reliable. In the end, you will be responsible for the accuracy of your citations. Thus, there is no substitute for learning APA style yourself.

We like to print out references as we are noting articles to look up. If you print three references per 8½″ × 11″ page you can cut the page into three pieces. These serve like large index cards, and the references on them can be used to locate the actual articles or books in the library. The "cards" can be inserted into journals or books to mark pages for photocopying and taking notes. You can even format the card to capture some of the information you might transfer later to a control sheet. Later on, they can be put in alphabetical order and printed out to form your bibliography. Whatever your referencing system, be sure to check the accuracy of each entry as you look up the original work—not all citations in published papers and chapters are accurate.

Critically Read What You Found

After you collect your literature, read it critically. Remember, you are going to synthesize this information into a coherent review that highlights the main themes, strengths, and weaknesses of the work. To do that, you need to get a sense of the forest as well as the trees. Start thinking about how you will organize this literature in a literature review. A good idea is to scan the articles and chapters you have collected (Galvan, 1999). Look for themes and commonalities in the methodologies and conceptual frameworks that authors use. In addition, you probably will not cite every article you read. Which material is most relevant to your study, and which is tangential? Which topics will you really need to cover, and which can you skip? Pay attention to unanswered questions and methodological strengths and weakness of studies you peruse, and keep notes on these. These will come in handy as you write the review. Exhibit 6.1 provides a list of questions you can use to evaluate empirical studies. See Galvan (2004) for other ways of doing this.

With empirical articles, read the rationale for the study (usually in the paragraphs just before the method section), the method, and the results sections most carefully—*not* the conclusions. You should be able to figure out the conclusions for yourself; you can then check whether you agree with the authors about what they said that they found. Don't be surprised if you think the findings have implications the authors do not discuss or if you think the authors overplay some of their findings.

Write down your observations to keep a record of them. If these observations characterize much of the literature, they may lead you to some major

Exhibit 6.1

Guidelines for Evaluating Empirical Studies

Introduction

1. Does the introduction provide a strong rationale for why the study is needed?
2. Are research questions and hypotheses clearly articulated? (Note that research questions are often presented implicitly within a description of the purpose of the study.)

Method

1. Is the method described so that replication is possible without further information?
2. Participants
   (a) Are subject recruitment and selection methods described?
   (b) Were participants randomly selected? Are there any probable biases in sampling?
   (c) Is the sample appropriate in terms of the population to which the researcher wished to generalize?
   (d) Are characteristics of the sample described adequately?
   (e) If two or more groups are being compared, are they shown to be comparable on potentially confounding variables (e.g., demographics)? If they are not comparable, is this handled appropriately?
   (f) Was informed consent obtained?
   (g) Was the size of the sample large enough for the number of measures and for the effect being sought?
3. Design
   (a) If appropriate, was a control group used?
   (b) Was the control appropriate?
   (c) What was being controlled for?
   (d) If an experimental study, were participants randomly assigned to groups?
4. Measures
   (a) For all measures (measures used to classify, dependent variables, etc.), did the authors provide evidence of reliability and validity, either by summarizing data or by referring the reader to an available source that provides the information?
   (b) Do the reliability and validity data justify the use of the measure? Specific evidence is particularly important if a measure is created just for this study.
   (c) Do the measures match the research questions and hypotheses being addressed?

continued

Exhibit 6.1, continued

(d) If different tasks or measures are used, was their order counterbalanced? Do the authors analyze for potential order effects?

(e) Are multiple measures used, particularly those that sample the same domains or constructs but with different methods (e.g., self-report, ratings by others, self-monitoring, or direct observation)?

(f) If human observers, judges, or raters were involved, was interobserver or interrater agreement (reliability) assessed? Was it obtained for a representative sample of the data? Did the two raters do their ratings independently? Was their reliability satisfactory?

5. Bias and Artifacts

(a) Was administration and scoring of the measures done blindly (i.e., by someone who was unaware of experimental hypotheses)?

(b) If a quasi-experimental study, do the authors include appropriate steps to rule out competing explanations of the findings?

(c) Were procedures constant across participants in all groups? Were any confounds introduced as the result of using different procedures? How troublesome are these?

6. Independent variables

(a) If an experimental study, was there a check that the independent variable was manipulated as described?

(b) If an intervention study, did a sufficient sample of therapists or change agents implement the intervention (i.e., to enhance generalizability)?

(c) If more than one treatment or condition are being compared, did the authors document that these conditions differ in ways they are supposed to differ? Are they the same in every other way (e.g., length, qualifications of therapists or change agents)? If not, is this confound likely to influence the conclusions seriously?

(d) What aspects of the procedures and independent variables limit the external validity of the study?

Results

1. Do the data fulfill the assumptions and requirements of the statistics (e.g., homogeneity of variance for repeated-measures analyses of variance)?

2. Were tests of significance used and reported appropriately (i.e., with sufficient detail to understand what analysis was being conducted)?

3. In correlational studies, did the authors interpret low but significant correlations as though they indicated a great deal of shared variance between the measures? Are the correlations limited by restricted ranges on one or more measures? Do the authors provide means and standard deviations so that you can determine this?

continued

Exhibit 6.1, continued

Guidelines for Evaluating Empirical Studies

4. If there were a large number of statistical tests performed, do the authors adjust the alpha level or use appropriate multivariate techniques to reduce the probability of Type I error that could be due to the large number of tests performed?
5. Do the authors report means and standard deviations (if relevant) so that the reader can examine whether statistically significant differences are large enough to be meaningful?
6. For multivariate statistics, is there an appropriately large ratio of participants to variables (at least 7 for every dependent variable used in an analysis)?

Discussion

1. Do the authors discuss marginally significant or nonsignificant results as though they were significant?
2. Do the authors overinterpret the data (e.g., use causal language to integrate correlational findings or interpret self-report of behavior as equivalent to direct observation)?
3. Do the authors consider alternative explanations for the findings?
4. Do the authors have a "humility" section that mentions the limitations of the research (including methodological problems)? Do the authors point out aspects of subject selection, procedures, and dependent variables that limit the generalizability of the findings?
5. Do the authors "accept" the null hypothesis?

Note. From "A Reader's, Writer's, and Reviewer's Guide to Assessing Research Reports in Clinical Psychology," by B. A. Maher, 1978, *Journal of Consulting and Clinical Psychology, 46,* pp. 835–838. Copyright 1987 by the American Psychological Association.

insights about your topic. Group the papers into categories as you scan the collection.

You will end this process with pages and pages of photocopied and downloaded articles and chapters or—if you can't afford to make copies—with pages and pages of notes (or stacks of note cards) taken from articles and chapters. We recommend the former, despite the expense, mainly because you never know when you'll have to go back to an article to seek a detail you failed to write down in your notes. And if you plan to continue research in the area, photocopies and PDF files of articles provide a good beginning library that you will use again and again. If you go the note route, be sure to include complete details on the methodology in your notes: Details that do not seem important now may become important later as you try to reconcile discrepant findings and search out potential confounds in others' procedures. One idea is to develop a list of information that you will note about every article you read (e.g., number and characteristics of participants, independent variables, etc.). You can even systematize this into a prepared "control sheet" on which to record specific details from each study. An example of a control sheet used by one of us in keeping track of literature he was reviewing in behavioral parent training is presented in Exhibit 6.2. This kind of systematic approach makes it less likely that you will forget to record certain details of a particular paper that you need later. (Cooper [1998] provides an extended discussion of control ["coding"] sheets.) Note that technology can once again be your friend. You can use word processing programs (e.g., OpenOffice, Word) to create control sheets as a form that can be completed on your PDA or laptop as you encounter particularly relevant papers. You can also do this with a database program such as Filemaker™. A real time-saving feature of using technology such as this is the ease with which you can search for particular information (e.g., that paper that used remote auditory prompting; all studies using children under 6) from among the dozens you unearthed in your library and Internet sleuthing.

If you copy someone's words into your notes, *put them in quotation marks and write down the page numbers where they appear.* It is easy to forget later which notes you wrote in your own words and which were quotes or close paraphrases. Even if you do it by accident, using others' words without appropriate citation is plagiarism. We discuss this topic again at the end of this chapter.

Finally, avoid the trap of overreading, a popular procrastination strategy. Memorizing or taking copious notes on every article published in your area is not necessary before starting to write your review. Experience suggests that you may need to read the literature at least twice, but in different ways. You will scan it the first time to learn about the key issues in the field and to decide what material is relevant and how to organize it. You will consult selected articles and chapters again and in more detail as you write the review and realize that you need to know more about what particular authors did and found. Expect this focused rereading once you begin to put your ideas on paper, but don't use your reading as a way to avoid writing.

Exhibit 6.2

Sample Control Sheet for Recording Information From Research Article

Author(s): _____

Title: _____

Source: _____

Availability: _____ on file _____ requested _____ unavailable

Type of Study: _____ single family _____ multiple family

Problem Behavior(s): _____
_____

Number of children directly involved: _____

Type of dependent measure and on whom taken: _____
_____

Observation of behavior by Experimenter (E): _____ yes _____ no

Locus of Observation by Experimenter (E): _____ home _____ clinic _____ lab
_____ residential facility _____ school

Number of therapy (training) sessions: _____

Design: _____ case study, no measurement
_____ case study with measurement: _____ pre _____ during _____ post
_____ time series (0 0 0 X 0 0 0)
_____ equivalent time samples: _____ A-B _____ A-B-A _____ B-A-B
_____ other
_____ multiple baseline (sequential) design
_____ single group, no measurement
_____ single group with measurement: _____ pre _____ during
_____ post
_____ single group time series (0 0 0 X 0 0 0)
_____ single group, equivalent time samples:
_____ A-B _____ A-B-A _____ A-B-A-B
_____ A-B1-A-B2 _____ B-A-B _____ other
_____ two-group classic (experimental vs. control)
_____ more than two groups: control, treatment, and other treatment
comparisons
_____ two or more groups: other treatment comparisons, no untreated
controls
_____ factorial design
_____ other: _____

Follow-up: _____ yes _____ no
amount of time since termination mode: _____

Comments: _____
_____
_____

Get Ready to Write

Before you start to write, get one feature of your written thesis or dissertation clearly in mind: *You are not writing for yourself.* You are writing for an audience. You know what you know, but your committee members cannot see directly into your brain. Nor do most of them know the literature as well as you do; some may be completely unfamiliar with the topic. Thus, your job in writing the literature review is to educate your committee about the topic. In so doing, you can also convince them that you are a competent researcher: Show them that you have integrated the material you read and that you have evaluated the quality of the information. After finishing your literature review, committee members should understand the research questions, procedures, and findings that characterize the field. They should also know the weaknesses of past studies, gaps in the literature, and what needs to be done to move the field forward. By the time they read your final sections, the rationale for your research question should be obvious, as should be the ways you are attempting to improve on past methods, designs, and procedures. If you have organized the review skillfully, you will have led the reader to the conclusion that the absolutely best next study to be done in the area is the one you are proposing.

Investigate Length and Format Parameters

Before you put pen to paper or fingers to keyboard, find out the local norms for reviews of the literature in projects like yours. These vary widely across schools, and it is important to know the parameters of what you are writing before you begin. Chapter 5 described differences between the one- and two-chapter organizational models—important format distinctions that will influence how you organize your material.

Literature reviews vary considerably in length as well as format. Ask your chairperson how long and how comprehensive the literature review is expected to be: This determines how you define the scope of what you cover. Note that we tell you to *ask your chairperson* rather than looking at others' literature reviews. This is because, as paradoxical as it may seem, it is easier to write excessively long reviews than to limit their scope and be concise. Thus, faculty often complain in private about 40- to 50-page (and longer!) literature reviews but let students keep producing them, when 20 to 25 pages would suffice to demonstrate the student's skill at synthesizing a body of literature. Personally, we prefer briefer, more focused reviews to lengthy treatises that try to cover everything and do so poorly. An added advantage of shorter reviews lies in their potential for publication: Many journals will not accept more than 25 to 30 pages of text, so you might as well get used to being succinct.

Write a Preliminary Outline

To get an idea of what you want to cover and how, make an outline or list of the major headings you plan to use in your literature review. Next to each, indicate the approximate number of pages you plan to allocate to each section. Exhibit 6.3 shows one student's working outline for a literature review for a dissertation studying the relationship between ethnicity, gender, and types of strategies older elementary school children use to manage conflicts with their peers. This outline is typical in terms of the section page allocations we recommend for a one-chapter literature review of about 25 pages. But because norms and preferences can vary so widely, be sure to ask your chairperson for feedback about your organization and page allocations.

Note that the outline in Exhibit 6.3 follows the funnel approach we described in chapter 5. It begins with the general context and gradually becomes more specific, ultimately focusing on specific criticisms of existing studies and leading to the specific rationale for the study being proposed.

A preliminary outline will let you see how long your chapter will be if you write it as planned and whether you need to limit or expand your scope. Even if you hate outlines or find they have never worked for you, at least make a list of what you think you need to cover and about how many pages you will devote to each area, so you can see whether your scope is too broad or too narrow. You can also get feedback from peers and your chair about whether your logic and organization seem clear. An added advantage of an outline or list is that having a concrete list often reduces the anxiety and procrastination associated with the seemingly amorphous and enormous task of writing a literature review. Look at your page allocations and remember that all you are really doing is writing a series of 5- to 10-page papers (the subsections of your review) with a lot of transitions to connect them. How many 5- to 10-page papers have you knocked off in your academic career? These are just more of the same.

Don't be surprised if your outline changes as you write the review. The author of the outline shown in Exhibit 6.3, for example, had to cut one

---

Exhibit 6.3

Literature Review Outline and Page Allocations

Dissertation topic: Relationship of ethnicity and gender to type of conflict resolution strategy and peer conflict outcome in 9- to 12-year-old children

<u>Outline</u>
  I. Introduction (2–3 pages)
     A. Historical context of peer conflict research
     B. Importance of conflict in development
     C. Definition of conflict
  II. Toddlers (ages 6 months–3 years; 2 pages)
     A. Issues of conflict
     B. Resolution strategies
  III. Preschoolers (ages 3–5 years; 5 pages)
     A. Incidence and duration of conflicts
     B. Issues of conflict
     C. Resolution strategies
     D. Outcome
     E. Gender differences
  IV. Early childhood (ages 5–9 years; 5 pages)
     A. Incidence and duration of conflicts
     B. Issues of conflict
     C. Resolution strategies
     D. Outcome
     E. Gender differences
  V. Late childhood (ages 9–12 years; 2 pages)
     A. Goals
     B. Strategies
  VI. Ethnicity (2 pages)
     A. Cooperation/competition research
     B. Conflict resolution styles
  VII. Summary and critique (3–5 pages)
  VIII. Statement of the problem and hypotheses

Note. Outline prepared by Avid Khorram, California School of Professional Psychology, San Diego, December 1991. Reproduced with permission of the author.

section ("toddlers") because she had a great deal more than two pages of material about ethnicity. Many of our students reorganize their review once they think through the details of the argument they would make for their study. Think of your outline as a way of helping you get started and organize your material, but be flexible about altering it as you begin to write.

Limit the Scope of Your Review

After putting page numbers on your outline you may wonder, "How can I get all that information into only 25 pages?" If this is your problem, chances are you are making two mistakes. First, you may think you must cite everything you read and cover everything related to the topic: history, theory, old research, new research, speculations, anecdotal evidence, and so on. Not a good idea! A more functional approach is to examine the literature that guides the rationale and methods of your study. You need to know all that background information and be able to answer questions about it, but you do not need to demonstrate that knowledge in writing for the committee. An evaluation of the current state of the field should suffice.

Incidentally, students often ask how far back their review should cover, sometimes hoping they can ignore anything that was published more than 10 years ago. We reply that they should *read* relevant empirical information, regardless of its age, to get a broad view of the development of the field. Their review, however, is likely to emphasize recent literature (usually the most recent 5–10 years), because this will describe the current state of the field. Earlier work that is seminal or highly important should also be included, of course.

If you are still wondering how to cram everything into 25 pages, you may be making a second mistake. Perhaps you are not limiting explicitly the scope of what you will write about. Although you do not need to cite every article you read, you *do* need decision rules for what you include and what you leave out. "I like this study" and "I didn't understand the statistics in this one" are not good reasons. Limiting the literature to a particular group of participants (e.g., by age, race, gender, or other characteristic relevant to the study you are proposing), by type or quality of design (e.g., only controlled studies), or by independent or dependent variables may be appropriate, depending on the literature you are reviewing. State your criteria for inclusion specifically and as far in advance of writing as you can, to avoid allowing personal biases (e.g., "This one doesn't really support my ideas") to sneak into your selections (Cooper, 1998). Be sure to write these criteria into the introduction to your literature review, too.

As an example, Julie planned a study to evaluate a program to teach children to deal effectively with peer provocation. She amassed huge literatures on peer rejection and its correlates, social-skills training programs, and generalization of behavior change from skill-training programs to the natural environment. After some thought and discussion, she realized that few social skills studies addressed peer-provocation problems directly, that much of the literature on correlates of rejection was tangential to her project, and that the conclusions of the literature on generalization should be incorporated into her review of why certain studies failed, rather than being reviewed study by study. Most of her 25 pages would be devoted to reviewing studies that attempted to teach social skills to intellectually normal children with identified excesses in negative behavior. The rest of the literature would be mentioned in passing, if at all. By limiting the populations and the topics she would cover, writing the review became far more manageable.

Lisa, another student, encountered a different problem. She was interested in the effects of therapist self-disclosure on adolescent involvement in therapy. She found large literatures on self-disclosure in therapy with adults, on self-disclosure in personal relationships (adults and adolescents), on the effects of different kinds of therapy for adolescents, and theoretical writings on the effects of self-disclosure in personal relationships. She found little, however, that was specific to her topic. What should she include in her literature review? Lisa decided to review the literature on self-disclosure in adult therapy to justify her independent variable and highlight the innovations in her methodology. She also reviewed the role of self-disclosure in adolescents' personal relationships to make a case for why self-disclosure might play a useful role in therapy. She did not need to review the theoretical literature, adolescent treatment outcome studies, or the adult interpersonal relationships literature, although she might integrate key points from these literatures as they contributed to her analysis of the two areas of research she would cover in depth.

Organize the Literature

Writing the preliminary outline required you to organize and synthesize material from all those articles, chapters, and books—something you should also have been thinking about as you read those materials. Now you finalize your preliminary outline and add detail to it. You can group the literature into manageable, coherent subgroupings in several ways. Below we list some of the most common.

1. Cover studies that examine *related independent variables* together. If, for example, you are reviewing different strategies for enhancing organizational

effectiveness, grouping them by types of strategies may provide a good, easy-to-follow framework.

2. Organize your studies by examining *related dependent variables* together. If you are looking at the characteristics of adult children of alcoholics, for example, you could review studies examining personality, then those examining drinking patterns, then those examining relationship skills, and so on. Alternatively, you could group findings on this population by *assessment method*: self-report, ratings by others, direct observation, and so on.

3. Organize by *type of design*. Ordinarily, this kind of coverage begins with weaker and then progresses to stronger designs. Thus, present uncontrolled case studies before controlled designs, relational studies before experimental, and cross-sectional before longitudinal. Paul's (1969) classic chapter describing research on systematic desensitization exemplifies this organizational strategy.

4. Organize around *theoretical premises*. This method is useful if your study tests competing explanations of a phenomenon or if different theoretical threads all lead to the formulation of your research question. For example, Wolfe (1986) studied fathers' interactions in families with conduct-disordered and non-conduct-disordered children. She organized her literature review around the ways in which fathers could influence the etiology and maintenance of children's disruptive behavior, from a social learning perspective (see Exhibit 6.4 for the major sections of her literature review).

These strategies describe only a few of the many ways of organizing literature. Select an organizational framework that highlights important aspects of the literature, particularly ones you wish to address or improve on in your study. For example, suppose your study improves on past research by using direct observation instead of self-report methods. By presenting findings and studies according to the methods used to assess the dependent variables, you may clearly show the reader the absence of research using direct observation. Remember the funnel: Work from the general to the specific.

It is also a good idea to use subheadings liberally. These show you have thought carefully about the major sections of your review, and they help the reader understand the logic of your organization. Another good practice is to provide summaries as you go along. These can be especially useful after one or several especially long or complex sections. Remember, your goal is to educate your reader and establish good arguments for why your study is an important next step in your area.

Exhibit 6.4

Organizing a Literature Review Around Theoretical Premises

1. Introduction and literature review 1
   1.1 Father involvement in parent training 2
   1.2 Father–child interaction 7
        a. Interaction patterns 7
        b. Father involvement in child management 9
   1.3 Influence of father–mother relationship on
       child behavior 11
        a. Role of social support 12
        b. Role of marital conflict: Overview 15
        c. Role of marital conflict: Poor problem solving 18
        d. Role of marital conflict: Poor modeling 22
        e. Role of marital conflict: Disruption of
           child management 23
   1.4 Summary and conclusions 26

Note. From *Paternal and Marital Factors Related to Child Conduct Problems,* by V. V. Wolfe, 1986, Doctoral dissertation, West Virginia University. Reprinted with permission of the author.

Start Writing

You are now ready to put pen to paper or fingers to keyboard. Organize your notes or photocopies, pull out your outline, and write individual sections of the review.

Beware of writer's block at this point. This malady affects many students, even those who regularly produce literature reviews with little difficulty for class assignments. Sometimes this block results from the mistaken assumption that your review must be perfect. All relevant studies must be cited and all insights must be brilliant before you dare hand a draft of your review to your chairperson, says this unrealistic self-talk.

Not so. Most students hand in and revise several drafts of their literature reviews before they are finished. No matter how polished your prose, your chairperson will have suggestions and expects that the first draft will need work. Everyone's first draft needs work. Because it is impossible for your draft to be perfect, give yourself permission for your work to be improvable.

Remember, this is a learning experience. If your manuscript were without flaw on the first try, there would be nothing left for you to learn.

Another difficulty students sometimes encounter when they begin to write results from their mistaken assumption that they must start at the beginning, write the introduction, and then proceed sequentially. This is the old "linear way is the only way" fallacy. They then sit before the page or the computer for hours as the words to begin the document elude them. Alternatively, several of our students have told us that they haven't written the introduction until after they wrote the bulk of the review—that way they had a good sense of the general thrust and organization of the review, and could provide a much better overview. Bolker (1998), a clinical psychologist who has counseled writers, suggests that for most people writing might be better characterized as a "messy" process, one that is not necessarily linear but *is* characterized by consistently putting words on paper, even if those words get shuffled around and some of the paper sees only the trash.

If you find it hard to start with the introduction, start with a section that comes more easily. If paragraphs don't come easily, write the ideas you want to cover first and then build paragraphs around them. If you can't figure out good transitions between studies, describe the studies first and write the transitions later. The key is to write whatever you can, because tasks that seem impossible one day may be much easier the next. Getting started is more important than completing sections one by one in a specified order. It is also well to remember that revising your words is easier than writing the words in the first place. Write something, anything—then sequence, integrate, and polish it later.

In addition, several of the ideas we mentioned in chapter 3 may be useful here. If you encounter problems getting started, set small goals. Set *product* rather than *process* goals. A product goal indicates what you must accomplish: "Write one page," "Summarize and critique one key article." A process goal indicates what you must do, but not the end product: "Work on dissertation for 2 hours." To accomplish the latter goal, all you have to do is stare at your computer, not actually produce anything! Small product goals help you see progress and work more efficiently.

You can also reward accomplishing small product goals with small rewards. Remember the Premack principle mentioned in chapter 3? Any behavior that is higher in probability than writing your dissertation or thesis can serve as a reward. For many writers, that's almost anything! In writing this book, for example, we often said to ourselves, "I'll get a cup of coffee after I finish 3 pages," "I'll read that magazine after I type this table," or "I'll call my friend after I edit this chapter." These examples show that rewards need not be expensive or time-consuming to be motivating.

Write the Introduction

Begin your literature review with a brief introduction. The introduction should do just that—introduce and make a brief pitch for the topic, introduce key concepts and terms, and describe the scope and organization of the review. A brief introduction might occupy about 3 pages in a 25-page literature review.

A good way to end the introduction is with a paragraph that lays out the scope of the literature review. Sometimes referred to as an *advance organizer*, this material should describe both the literature you will cover and the sequence the reader can expect to follow. In addition, if you omit studies to keep the length of your review manageable, let the reader know your criteria for inclusion or exclusion and why you selected them. For example, suppose a whole group of studies on your topic area was later found to have a particular methodological problem, and you do not think you have the space to cover these studies. The final paragraph of your introduction could say,

> The remainder of the chapter that follows critically reviews contemporary literature regarding _____. Early studies in the area (e.g., _____) generally concluded that _____ (2004). As _____ (2004) and _____ (2005) pointed out, however, these studies all failed to distinguish between _____ (2004), and _____ (2004), and thus, their conclusions are suspect. Later studies have corrected this flaw, and will be the focus of the review that follows. Initial sections discuss _____. The review concludes with a summary and critique of existing literature, followed by a discussion of the specific research question and hypotheses suggested by the review and examined in this thesis (dissertation).

Write the Subsections of Your Literature Review

After the introduction, you will have subsections that review and synthesize portions of the literature. Note that these subsections are consistent with whichever overall organizational approach (e.g., by independent variable, by dependent variable, by design type) you selected earlier. Perhaps the easiest approach is to introduce the section, then describe relevant studies one by one, grouping related studies together. Some writers follow a chronological sequence, citing earlier research first. Provide comparable information for each study: participants, independent variables, dependent variables, design, and findings. Mention noteworthy details (e.g., methodological problems, ethnicity or gender of participants) that will form the basis for themes in your analysis. Then go on to the next. Use parallel organization, describing the aspects of each study in the same way. As Bem (1995) noted, "repetition and parallel construction are among the most effective servants of clarity. Don't be creative; be clear" (p. 174). Pull the material together with a summary and overall critique at the end of the subsection.

This one-by-one method requires considerable skill to keep it from being incredibly boring and reading like a series of index cards typed up one after the other. Liberal use of transitions helps. Identifying and developing important themes as you go along helps, too. Brief comparisons of methods and findings help link studies together and highlight their progression as well as similarities and differences among them. A study-by-study literature review by Inderbitzen-Pisaruk and Foster (1990) illustrated the use of these kinds of phrases. In the following illustration we remove the content of the paragraphs, reprinting only transitional and integrative phrasing from a brief portion of the review (note, however, that one reviewer who examined this paper when it was first submitted criticized it for being too much like an annotated bibliography!).

> Kuhlen and Bretsch . . . [description of study]. . . .
>> In a study that more clearly specified behaviors necessary for. . . .
>> Unfortunately, these two studies are dated, and therefore. . . .
>> In addition, both. . . . This leads to uncertainty about whether. . . .
>> This [uncertainty] has been addressed in more recent studies. Interestingly, despite changes in adolescent culture over the past four decades, [results] have supported those of [study just described]. For example, . . . (Inderbitzen-Pisaruk & Foster, 1990, pp. 426–427)

A second method of organizing subsections of a literature review groups weaker studies or studies that share similar methods, reviews them only briefly, and devotes greater attention to seminal, prototypical, or stronger studies. With this method, a section might begin with a few paragraphs that provide an overview of a large number of studies, their findings, and the strengths and weaknesses they share as a group. Later paragraphs then devote greater individual attention to more important studies.

A third way of organizing subsections of your literature review discusses studies by their findings. This type of review contains less description of individual studies than those presented previously. Instead, the writer uses findings to support the logical series of points developed in the review. This is the most difficult type of review to write, because you must develop your points logically and use literature in an even-handed way to consider the support (pro and con) for your ideas. This multifaceted consideration of the literature may be most appropriate when your study will pit different theoretical explanations against one another or when your selection of variables is guided more by theory than by atheoretical empirical findings.

The three methods of writing a literature review just described involve qualitative analysis and synthesis of the literature. A fourth, quantitative alternative involves systematically scoring studies for particular characteristics and conducting a meta-analysis. With a meta-analysis, results of studies that investigated the same issue are grouped statistically to evaluate the characteristics of the group of studies as a whole. Thus, those studies using direct observation dependent measures can be compared with those using informant ratings or self-report in terms of the overall significance (effect size) of their findings. Although meta-analyses appear frequently in review journals, they are unusual in thesis and dissertation literature reviews (probably because doing one is like doing an empirical study, but with journal articles as "participants"!). Thus, we do not cover them. Cooper (1998), Hunter and Schmidt (2004), and Rosenthal (1991) described meta-analytic procedures concisely but in good detail. Lipsey and Wilson (2000) provided a wonderful how-to guide that should be on the bookshelf of any first-timer. In addition, Rosenthal (1995) provided a detailed description of writing meta-analytic reviews of the literature.

Synthesize and Critically Analyze the Literature

Some of the most frequent complaints of professors are that graduate students do not analyze and synthesize the literature they review (Association for Support of Graduate Students, 1995). Novice literature reviewers often provide excessive description coupled with inadequate critical analysis. Do not simply describe what you read. Instead, synthesize the literature. What patterns do you see in investigators' findings? Are findings consistent? If not, why not? Consider potential explanations, including methodological, design, and population differences among studies and assumptions that may be erroneous about how the independent variables operate or relate to the dependent variables. By the end of your literature review, your reader should have a good idea of the patterns of findings and methods that characterize your area of research.

In addition, you should evaluate the literature critically. Which studies are best, and why? Which studies are worst, and why? Consider methodological as well as conceptual strengths and weaknesses. Remember the checklist in Exhibit 6.1. Just because something is published does not mean it is free of methodological problems. Help the reader see the methodological issues that future studies in your area should address. Highlight topics that merit further study. If you kept a record of problems and issues as you read the literature, consult it for ideas about what to say.

Use a professional tone in commenting on others' work. Obviously, you will not want to trash your chairperson's work. Less obvious is the fact that you should not overstate your criticisms of others who think differently from you. Ad hominem criticisms (criticizing the *person* rather than the *work*) are never appropriate. Be evenhanded, and remember that all research has strengths as well as weaknesses.

Your analysis and synthesis of the literature should pave the way for your study. By the time your reader finishes the bulk of the literature review, the rationale for what you propose (your questions) and why you propose to do it a certain way (your method) should be obvious. Thus, your synthesis should highlight important unanswered questions (i.e., the ones you are proposing to examine). Similarly, your critiques should emphasize methodological problems with past studies you plan to correct with your study. Think of this as developing your argument. Think like a good lawyer: You want to point out to the jury (your readers) how pieces of evidence are relevant to the case you are trying to make as you proceed.

You can integrate statements that synthesize and evaluate the literature into the review in several ways. First, use integrative transition sentences and phrases to help readers see patterns as they read the document. For example, note how the following paragraph ties a group of studies together and highlights major similarities and differences with the study about to be discussed.

> Although most studies described thus far used relational designs, Smith and Jones (2001) explored the issue of _____ with an experimental design. Their findings were remarkably similar to those of previous relational studies.

Second, use comparative and evaluative phrases. Some evaluative comments are unique to a particular study. These fit best when you describe the study.

> The authors failed to replicate others' findings. Unfortunately, the small N in some of their groups (as low as 8) may have seriously limited their power to detect significant effects.

Other comments pertain to a whole group of studies but not to the area as a whole, and you can cover them as you end a particular section of the review.

> Most of these studies share similar strengths and weaknesses. (Elaborate these.) Despite their methodological problems, most tentatively point to similar conclusions. (Tell what they are.)

In addition to analyzing and integrating the literature throughout the review, you may wish to include a final summary and critique subsection. This subsection can specify unexplored topics worthy of future study as well as strengths and weaknesses of past literature. Go beyond a summary of what you have already said. Instead, weave together the threads you have been developing in the rest of the review. Most important, use this section as a logical precursor to your statement of the problem and hypotheses sections.

If you need examples, peruse journals that publish literature reviews, such as *Psychological Bulletin, Clinical Psychology Review*, and *Developmental Review*. Some edited books contain chapters that provide integrative overviews of the literature. Examine the structure and organization of different reviews, and see how different writers integrate and analyze the literature. Studying others' writing may give you ideas for how to write your own review. A useful set of papers on review writing was published as a symposium in the *Psychological Bulletin* in 1995. As part of this, Bem (1995) provided interesting observations on differences between dissertation literature reviews and those written specifically for professional journals.

Introduce Your Study and Hypotheses

If you write a one-chapter literature review, subsections such as statement of the problem and research questions and hypotheses will follow your summary and critique subsection. If you write a two-chapter version, these subsections will usually follow a general introduction to the problem area and to your specific topic. In the two-chapter version, the introduction to your specific topic will precede your literature review and should therefore summarize the material you plan to cover in your literature review. The introductory material in a two-chapter version should also provide a rationale for your topic, indicating why your study will make a novel contribution to the field. Remember in writing this section that your readers will read this material before the literature review, so make it clear enough to stand by itself.

Regardless of whether you use a one- or two-chapter format, your statement of the problem subsection should introduce the rationale for your study. You should also provide a brief overview of your population, design, independent variables, and dependent variables. This will help the reader understand the specific research questions and hypotheses to follow.

Chapter 4 described how to state research questions and derivative hypotheses, and your written presentation of these should reflect these suggestions. In addition, if the rationale for a particular hypothesis is not obvious, briefly give the reason for your prediction, saying something such as, "This hypothesis is based on Smith's (2004) findings that _____." As chapter 4 suggested, you should be able to form hypotheses related to your major research questions. You may, however, have certain secondary comparisons for which deriving hypotheses may be difficult (e.g., if the area is new or if previous findings conflict). If you truly have no basis in research or in theory for making a prediction, you have several options. First, you can simply state that this is the case and offer no directional hypotheses. As an alternative, you could subdivide your research questions into those that address the primary purposes of your study (for which you offer hypotheses) and those that are secondary (for which you offer no hypotheses). Finally, you could drop the particular question as part of the formal study. We prefer the first or second of these, provided, of course, that the question is worth asking in the first place. Different chairs have different views on how to handle this, so check with your chairperson.

Write Additional Subsections

Most schools require that dissertations include the subsections we have just covered. In addition, some require additional material such as definitions of terms, descriptions of limitations of the study you propose, and discussion of the theoretical orientation underlying the study. Check your local requirements for any additional material you must cover as you prepare your literature review.

Be Careful Not to Plagiarize

Earlier we mentioned plagiarism. Its definition bears repeating. To plagiarize, according to Merriam-Webster OnLine, is "to steal and pass off (the ideas or words of another) as one's own: use (another's production) without crediting the source" (Merriam-Webster, n.d.). Lifting someone's words without quotation marks is obviously plagiarism. So, however, is closely paraphrasing another's sentences. So is presenting another's *ideas* as though they were original to you. Copying paragraph organization—or a general way of organizing a topic—is also plagiarism. Find your own way of organizing ideas in your own words. Limit direct quotes, and acknowledge others' ideas and organizational frameworks when you cite or borrow them. If you are in doubt, ask a colleague or your chairperson for feedback.

Revise, Rewrite

Be prepared to revise and rewrite your initial material. Do this after rereading it yourself, and later, after receiving feedback from your chair. New ideas will occur to you and you will find holes in your own logic. In addition, your chairperson (and peers, if you ask for their comments) will give you feedback to improve the paper. Be open to this feedback; these critics are on your side! Your readers will see ambiguities that are perfectly clear to you, but remember that you are writing for them, not for yourself. In addition, your goal is to have a solid document that can stand up to examination by the academic community. Look at this as a chance to improve your writing, sharpen your thinking, master an area of literature, and produce a first-rate document, rather than as an evaluation of your personal worth or a chance for your writing to serve as someone's punching bag. The thinking and writing skills you hone as you develop your thesis or dissertation will benefit you no matter what career path you choose.

Remember that pulling together the information you found in your literature search into a coherent, focused review does more than just help you get a major writing task out of the way. It also should sharpen your thinking about your topic and help you see conceptual and methodological themes in the literature. In addition, the process should lead you to identify methodological issues and possible procedures for your study. In fact, writing your literature review and working out your methodology go hand in hand: As you work out the methods, you think about the literature differently, and vice versa. Your method section will describe the choices you make about how to conduct your research. Chapters 7 and 8 assist you in articulating those choices on paper as you prepare that part of your proposal.

Supplemental Resources

Galvan, J. L. (2004). *Writing literature reviews: A guide for students of the social and behavioral sciences* (2nd ed.). Los Angeles: Pyrczak.

Heppner, P. P., & Heppner, M. J. (2004). *Writing and publishing your thesis, dissertation, and research.* Belmont, CA: Thompson-Brooks/Cole. [Similar to this book, this reference has additional examples of writing.]

On Plagiarism

Plagiarism: What it is and how to avoid it. Retrieved February 4, 2005, from http://www.indiana.edu/~wts/pamphlets.shtml. [A brief pamphlet with examples of what is and is not plagiarism, provided by Writing Tutorial Services at Indiana University (Bloomington).]

Sandler, R. B. (2000). *Plagiarism in colleges in the USA.* Retrieved February 2, 2005, from http://www.apa.org. [Written by an attorney, this essay provides an overview of plagiarism from a legal perspective.]

On the Writing Process

Bolker, J. (1998). *Writing your dissertation in 15 minutes a day.* New York: Henry Holt. [Overview of the author's ideas about how to write in general and strategies for writing a dissertation in specific.]

Vernoff, J. (2001). Writing. In K. E. Rudestam & R. R. Newton (Eds.), *Surviving your dissertation* (2nd ed.). Thousand Oaks, CA: Sage. [Interesting speculation on causes of problems with writing, plus suggestions for writing the dissertation.]

✔ To Do . . .

Reviewing the Literature

☐ Locate relevant literature

— Identify key author and journals

— Use bibliographic reference sources

— Use computerized literature searches

— Obtain reprints and preprints

— Look at literature from other disciplines

— Scan tables of contents of key journals

— Use reference lists from articles, chapters, and books

— Use primary sources

— Avoid the popular press

☐ Critically read the literature

— Identify themes

—Identify strengths and weaknesses of individual articles

—Identify strengths and weaknesses of field as a whole

—Collect photocopies or notes

☐ Prepare to write

—Investigate length and format parameters

—Make a preliminary outline

- Limit the scope of your review

- Organize the literature you will cover

- Include page allocations

☐ Write the review

—Write the introduction

—Write subsections

- Use transitions and integrative phrasing

- Synthesize and critically analyze the literature

☐ Introduce your study and hypotheses

☐ Be careful not to plagiarize

☐ Revise and rewrite

7

Research Methodology and Ethics

In this chapter, we elaborate the elements of the method section that we introduced in chapter 5. Then we discuss ethical principles governing research in psychology and examine the process involved in designing and conducting studies in accord with these principles. The process includes obtaining informed consent, protecting confidentiality of data, and debriefing participants. We also cover negotiating the requirements of institutional review boards (IRBs) for the protection of human and animal participants.

Be aware that this chapter is not an instruction book on research design, procedures, and ethics. It will not tell you, for example, whether it is better to use a correlational or a group design for your research or whether you have thought of all the appropriate controls. If your background in research methodology is rusty, scanty, or otherwise lacking, examine the supplemental resources listed at the end of this chapter. This bibliography will point you toward information that will help you bone up on material you never learned or cannot remember.

Know the Elements of a Method Section

The *Publication Manual of the American Psychological Association* (APA, 2010) describes three basic subsections of a method section: participants or subjects, apparatus, and procedure. Although this organization works for some studies, most need additional elements. We describe different aspects of methodology that should be included in a complete method section. Not all are relevant to all studies, of course. Similarly, although the order we suggest works for many method sections, it does not work for all of them. Before dealing specifically with the components of method sections, let's say a few words about designs.

Design

This is not one of the subsections explicitly identified for the method section by the *Publication Manual.* That is because it is probably better to place your first specific reference to design elements in a paragraph or two just before the method section. Possibly, you gave an overview of your design when you wrote the "statement of the problem" section of your literature review. Be flexible about placement, however, and put the design information where it seems to make the most sense for your particular project. We prefer to describe the design before the method section because the nature of the design you are using will influence all of the method section elements, and this placement will help the reader understand the choices you describe. Often, however, you will need a "design" section somewhere in the method section as well, particularly if your design is complex or needs more explanation than an overview can provide.

What should you include in describing your design? First, make clear whether it is of the within- or between-participants variety. If the variation needed for studying the relationships involved in your study comes from changes in the same participants over time or across situations, you are using a within-participants approach. If the variation comes from differences between participants at a single point in time, you are using a between-participants approach. Another important point to elaborate is the general class of your design. Experimental, quasi-experimental, correlational, longitudinal, and single-participant are the major classes. If you are fuzzy about these distinctions, see Shadish, Cook, and Campbell (2002), who provided a classic treatment of the differences between major design approaches.

Once you have clarified the basic nature of your approach, you are ready to present the details of your particular design. In describing your design, it is useful to provide both labels (e.g., a two-group, true experimental design; A-B-A-B withdrawal design; Solomon four-group design; correlational design; survey research) and descriptions of what you plan to do. Avoid confusing design and statistics in this subsection. "A one-way ANOVA will test the differences between the groups . . ." is a statement of the statistical test to be used, not the design. A statement like this should be placed in the analyses portion (in the results section) of the proposal, described in chapter 5. A better design statement would be, "Children will be assigned randomly to high- and low-reward conditions and math facts of high and low difficulty in a 2×2 factorial design." Another example of a design statement is, "A multiple-baseline design will be used, in which family one will be instructed to implement positive household rules initially, then family two will implement them, and finally family three will do so."

If you plan to administer multiple measures, make a plan for their order (e.g., counterbalancing) and describe this here. If groups will be matched for certain participant characteristics (e.g., gender, IQ, or problem severity), describe how this will be accomplished. If you have forgotten why counterbalancing and matching may be important, dust off your old research design text and reacquaint yourself with these concepts.

A diagram or chart can help describe designs that are complex or hard to follow. Shadish et al. (2002) provided good examples for designs involving between-participants comparisons. Hayes, Barlow, and Nelson-Gray (1999) gave many examples for designs involving within-participants comparisons. Figure 7.1 shows a complex but informative diagram of a study by Sobell, Bogardis, Schuller, Leo, and Sobell (1989).

Participants

In the participants subsection, you should answer three questions: (a) Who will participate? (b) How many will participate? and (c) How will they be selected? If they will be sorted into groups based on some participant characteristic and not randomly assigned (as, for example, when a participant variable such as age, diagnostic classification, or performance on a specific task is used to classify participants and that classification is an independent variable), indicate how this classification will be made.

Studies vary considerably in the details they include about participants. Remember that your participants represent a subset of some larger population to which you wish to generalize your findings. They should be selected and described in ways that reassure us that they do, indeed, represent this population. For example, if participants are human, it is a good idea to

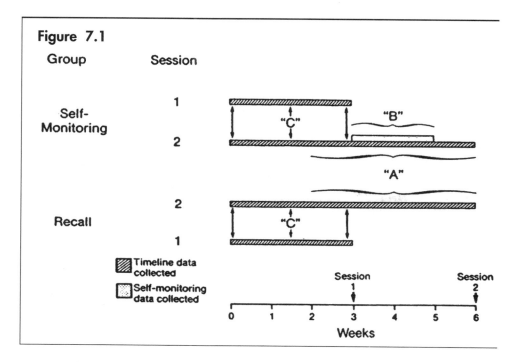

Diagram of experimental design indicating when time-line and self-monitoring drinking data were gathered from both groups of participants, the temporal placement of sessions, and the data sets used in the major statistical analyses (designated by letter in the figure). Contrast A was a between-subjects analysis that used Session 2 time-line data to test for reactivity of self-monitoring. Contrast B was a within-subjects analysis performed using Session 2 self-monitoring and time-line data from participants in the self-monitoring group; it compared data gathered from the same participants for the same time period using the time-line versus self-monitoring method. Contrast C compared each participant's Session 2 time-line with data provided by that participant for the same time interval in Session 1 (usually 21 days). Reprinted from "Is Self-Monitoring of Alcohol Consumption Reactive?" by M. B. Sobell, J. Bogardis, R. Schuller, G. I. Leo, and L. C. Sobell, 1989, *Behavioral Assessment, 77*, p. 451, Copyright 1989, with permission from Elsevier.

provide information on major demographic characteristics such as gender, age (mean and range), race/ethnicity, geographic area represented, socio-economic status, source (e.g., university undergraduate classes or mental health clinics), and basis for participation (e.g., voluntary, paid, or course credit). Depending on the nature of your study, you will want to include other information, such as intellectual functioning (mean and range on a standard IQ measure), scores on any selection variable (e.g., depression, anxiety, or percentage overweight), disability status, diagnosis, and sexual orientation. If a participant characteristic is an independent variable, you should describe it completely, including how you will determine that the person has or lacks this characteristic. In addition, you should describe participant characteristics that will disqualify one from participating (i.e., your exclusion criteria and how you operationalize them).

The novice researcher sometimes gets confused about just who the participants are in the study. The distinction can become difficult when different groups of people are used at different times in the research. For example, in constructing a scale to assess problem spending, one of our students used consumer-credit experts to judge the adequacy of various responses to specified problem situations involving how people handle money. She used these judgments to weight the responses of individuals taking the instrument to establish preliminary norms. Because the primary thrust of the research was to develop a reliable and valid instrument for identifying problem spending, the individuals who provided the data relevant to reliability and validity were considered the participants. The individuals providing the adequacy ratings were referred to as *judges*. Of course, she needed to describe the characteristics of the judges in detail somewhere in the method section as well. In general, the individuals described in the participants subsection are those who provide the data to test the specific hypotheses of the study. Individuals involved in producing instruments or collecting data (e.g., raters or observers) are not considered participants.

Describe your sampling strategy and how you plan to recruit participants. Will you advertise in the local paper? Put up notices around campus? Sample birth registers? Describe exactly what you will do. Put copies of your proposed wording for inviting participants to participate in an appendix.

If nonhuman participants are involved, similar issues need to be addressed. State the number of animals you will use, their genus, species, and strain number, if available. Information on the source of animals is also useful (e.g., supplier, stock designation). Finally, indicate their gender, age, and weight, and describe their general condition. A description of any essential details of their history, care, and handling should also be included (APA, 2010).

Be sure to design a method to keep track of the number of potential participants contacted as well as the number who actually participated, including the number screened out because they met your exclusion criteria. The representativeness of your participants is crucial to the external validity of the study. Therefore, in the final document report not only these figures but also any information you can obtain related to the differences between volunteering and nonvolunteering individuals. If participants drop out prematurely, you will want to cite the percentage and explain why they dropped out.

When deciding whom to select as participants and how to select them, a good rule of thumb is the "representativeness" rule. That is, consider the larger population of individuals you want your participants to represent. To whom do you wish to generalize? When you are clear about this, design procedures to attract those people. To check your success, gather supplemental information to see how closely your participants match the characteristics of that population. Likewise, there may be participants to whom do you not wish to generalize. For example, a study of elementary-age children would not necessarily care whether its results applied to older children. To use your time and other resources efficiently, include procedures and measures that will allow you to screen out individuals who are not appropriate for your study.

The specific nature of your design will also have implications for decisions about whom to include and exclude. In general, more homogeneous populations are likely as a group to have less variable scores on your measures than heterogeneous populations. This is because extraneous participant characteristics that are related to scores on your measures are more likely to occur in the heterogeneous population. On the one hand, variability in independent and dependent variable scores is generally prized in purely correlational designs in which r and its variants (e.g., multiple regression statistics and factor analysis) will be used. This is because restricted ranges on variables being correlated limit the values correlations can obtain (Anastasi & Urbina, 1997).

On the other hand, you may be comparing discrete groups in your study, using ANOVA and related approaches. In this case, extraneous and variable participant characteristics, unless they are controlled, will contribute to your error variance. This will require you to have a more potent independent variable to detect significant findings than if extraneous variance is limited. In these cases, it makes sense to limit your population. Identify characteristics that are not particularly important to generalizing your findings (e.g., socioeconomic status) but have been shown to correlate with your major dependent variables (e.g., intelligence). Participants can then be restricted to a certain subpopulation, based on these characteristics (e.g., all individuals within a relatively narrow socioeconomic range).

Variability in participant characteristics can also be handled in two other ways in group designs. You can control some of it by adding one or more participant characteristics as independent variables in your design. For example, if you are concerned about socioeconomic status in your study of the effects of watching "Sesame Street" on preschool reading test scores, you could add socioeconomic status as an independent variable. Of course, this would add to the total number of participants you would need. A second way to handle this problem is statistical: Measure socioeconomic status and see if it correlates with your dependent variable after your data are collected. If it does, you might use socioeconomic status as a covariate in subsequent analyses.

From this material, it should be obvious that you will need to collect information on your participants, in part to exclude ones you decide not to study and in part to provide adequate descriptions of those you include. Particularly important information has to do with participant characteristics that could provide alternative explanations for your anticipated results or be inadvertently confounded with your independent variables. Pick potential confounds by looking in the literature: What participant variables correlate with your dependent variables? These are good nominees as potential confounding variables. You should measure them and later analyze to see whether they can be ruled out as explanations for your findings.

You will also need to indicate how you will measure the participant characteristics you plan to assess. If you will include a demographic data sheet and two questionnaires to gather participant information, indicate this and refer the reader to an appendix for copies of instruments that are not copyrighted. You will also describe the psychometric properties of these instruments, either here in the participants subsection or later in a measures subsection.

Last, we turn to an early question virtually every student asks: "How many participants do I have to have?" One way is to look at the literature and see what the norm is. This is the easy way, and unfortunately, except for individual organism designs, it is not a good one. Repeated reviews of even the most prestigious professional journals indicate that most group-design studies use too few participants to have sufficient statistical power to detect all but the most powerful effects (Rossi, 1990).

What is the preferred way to figure out how many participants you really need? There are two things to consider when answering this question. The first involves the statistics you plan to use. Some analyses have rules of thumb for estimating the minimum participants-to-variables ratios required to yield stable findings. If you are using multiple regression, factor analysis, multivariate analyses of variance (MANOVA), discriminant function analysis, or related statistics, here's one way to figure out what you need to meet the minimum requirements from a statistical rules of thumb standpoint: Count the number of scores your dependent variables will generate. Sort these into subsets. Each subset should contain the names of the scores you will need in a particular analysis. For example, you may plan one MANOVA involving three different dependent variables assessing aggression. This is your first subset. A second subset contains five demographic variables to be used in a second MANOVA, and so on. Count the number of dependent variables in each subset. Select the number that represents the largest number of scores in any subset (in the example just given, this would be five). Then multiply this number by some number between 7 and 20 that you select in concert with your chairperson (conservative statisticians will require even more than 20 participants per variable, whereas liberal ones will go as low as 7). This is the minimum number of participants your statistics require.

Statistics experts sometimes criticize rules of thumb as being too simplistic (e.g., MacCallum, Widamon, Zhang, & Hong, 1999). The second and better way to figure out how many participants you should recruit requires attention to the *power* of your statistics. Power is not related to rule of thumb derived numbers of participants. Instead, power is a concept referring to the likelihood the statistics you use can detect the effects of the independent variable. Power is a function of three things: (a) your sample size, (b) the magnitude of the effects of your independent variable(s) (i.e., how much of a difference your independent variable makes in relation to the dependent variable in question), and (c) the alpha level you select. Power analyses allow you to estimate how many participants you will need to detect small effects, medium effects, and large effects. Given a fixed number of participants and alpha level (ordinarily $p < .05$), the larger the effect you can expect from your independent variable, the less the power (read "fewer participants") needed to detect it.

To calculate power analyses for group designs, you first need to figure out the smallest effect you care to detect. You will learn quickly that detecting tiny effects can mean that you will need thousands of participants (see Cohen, 1992). A good way to approach this is to ask, "What is the minimum effect that would be meaningful in this area?" In the clinical arena, this is often a moderate effect: Smaller than moderate effects may be too small to be of any practical significance. Whether this is the case, however, will depend on your field of study. In fields in which we know a great deal about factors that affect the dependent variable, such as some aspects of medicine, documenting a small effect can be important.

To do your power analysis, you will have to have various pieces of information. First, you will need to select the level of power you wish to have in your study; .80 is a reasonable value. Second, you also need to know the analyses you will be conducting (ANOVA? regression? correlation?). In addition, you need to have a precise idea of where you will look in your analysis to find out whether your data support the prediction. For example, it's not enough to know that you will do a 2×2 ANOVA. You also need to know whether your hypotheses predict main effects or interactions. Similarly, with regression, you need to figure out whether you are predicting that all of your variables together will predict an outcome (i.e., the overall R^2 will be significant) or whether each of your variables will add significant unique variance (i.e., its beta will be significant). You will judge your power based on the parameter of the statistic you will use to assess whether your findings are significant.

Third, power calculations require estimates of actual numbers that are based on guesses about what your data will look like when they are collected. For example, if you are using parametric statistics, you may need to come up with means, standard deviations, and ds (i.e., effect size values). If you are using correlational statistics, you may need to provide values of the correlations you anticipate. How, you may ask, can I get these numbers before doing the research? You cannot, of course, at least not precisely. But you can estimate what these might be, based on pilot data you collect or published studies that used the same dependent variable and related independent variables. You then use these in formulas that allow you to calculate the number of participants you will need. Cohen (1988) and Keppel and Wickens (2004) explained how to calculate power analyses. Thomas and Krebs (1997) reviewed a number of statistical programs for PCs that will compute power. An Internet site for interactive exercises in performing simple power analyses is http://calculators.stat.ucla.edu/power calc/. Software freely available at this site will perform the analysis for you instantly after you provide some of the values mentioned. Be forewarned, however, that the names for some of the analyses do not match customary terminology in psychology.

In addition, Cohen (1992) provided a brief, readable discussion of power analysis as well as tables you can use to estimate the number of participants you will need to detect small, medium, or large effect sizes at the $p < .01$, .05, and .10 levels. The tables cover t tests, correlations, tests of proportions, chi-square, ANOVA, and multiple-regression statistics. Another easy to use source is Murphy and Myors's (2004) *Statistical Power Analysis*. Although mostly geared toward estimating power rather than "guesstimating" effect sizes, then calculating N, they also provide an appendix that allows the reader to estimate the needed N based on estimates of d values or percentage of variance you expect to account for. This is extremely handy because meta-analysts Lipsey and Wilson (2000, Appendix B) provided formulas for calculating d (or d equivalents) from a wide range of statistics you might find in the published literature. Furthermore, conventions exist for expected sizes of *d*: .20 is considered small, .50 is medium, and .80 is large (Lipsey & Wilson, 2000; Murphy & Myors, 2004). None of these sources covers less widely used or more complex statistics (e.g., hierarchical linear modeling); for these, consult the statistical literature on the analysis and find an expert who can advise you.

Setting and Apparatus

Describe the general context in which the research will take place. If these characteristics are common, you need not specify them in detail. In a controlled experiment, however, give the general dimensions and furnishings of any experimental room and indicate the position of the experimenter and the participant (e.g., "The study took place in a 9 ft. × 12 ft. experimental room with the participant and experimenter seated and facing each other across a 4-ft.-wide table"). Such details would generally not be necessary for studies involving data collected from groups of participants in college or elementary school classrooms, however. Also, because journal space is more limited than dissertation space, these details would be eliminated in preparing your dissertation for publication. If a particular piece of apparatus is used to present stimuli or afford participants a way of responding and it is unique to this study, describe it in detail and include construction plans (either in the text or an appendix). If the apparatus is commercially available, include the brand and model number.

Independent Variables

Indicate how you will operationalize your independent variables, and place this information either in the design subsection, the procedures subsection, or in a subsection of its own. Where you put this depends on the complexity of your independent variables: More complex ones, such as an intervention project or exposure to a specific set of stimuli, may require a separate subsection, or even an appendix that describes the independent variable in detail (e.g., a treatment manual).

Regardless of where you place this information, certain details are essential. In addition to stating how you will operationalize your independent variables, also include how you will ensure the integrity of these variables. In other words, describe how you will determine that they are manipulated consistently and as planned (cf. Billingsley, White, & Munson, 1980; Kazdin, 2003). This may involve manipulation checks by judges (e.g., ratings of therapist or experimenter behavior to ensure that they did what they were supposed to do) and precautions taken by the experimenter (e.g., observing sessions through a one-way mirror). If your study involves instructional manipulations (e.g., to make your participants think they are winning a game played single-handedly against a two-person team in another room), include some way of assessing whether they really believed these manipulations.

Sometimes manipulation checks can be quite complex. One of our students, for example, was interested in whether fourth-grade girls would be rated as more socially competent by peers if they engaged in higher frequencies of certain behaviors thought important to the peers (Hoier, 1984; see Hoier & Cone, 1987, for the published version). Increases in these social behaviors served as the independent variable, and ratings of competence served as the dependent variable. To make sure the social behaviors actually were increased, Hoier made videotapes of the experimental sessions. Trained observers then scored the videotapes. It was important to describe the reliability of this scoring system in the method section of the proposal. Whether information about manipulation checks such as this one would be placed in the independent variables subsection or a measurement subsection depends on where the material will be clearest for the reader.

Be sure to explain who will serve as the experimenter. An abundance of literature shows that any experimenter or data gatherer who will interact with participants should be unaware of the experimental hypotheses, so this person should not be you unless you can use creative methods to keep yourself unaware concerning who is in which condition. One of our less affluent students, for example, managed to do this cleverly. She was evaluating the discriminative validity of a new questionnaire assessing beliefs associated with personality disorders. She classified participants into diagnostic groups using a standardized structured interview. This interview took about an hour to administer and required extensive training. She did not want to pay someone to conduct these interviews. At the same time, she needed to make sure that if she served as the interviewer, she would not know the participants' probable diagnoses. She therefore arranged that clinicians would refer potential participants to her but not inform her of their probable diagnoses. That way she could conduct the interviews herself and remain unaware of diagnoses given the participants by the clinicians.

If you cannot remain blind as to your participants' status on factors that might bias your interactions with them, and you cannot afford to hire an experimentally naïve person to collect your data, several options are available to you. If you are in a university setting, perhaps you can give independent study credit to an undergraduate for acting as your experimenter. Or perhaps you and an equally poor colleague can trade services: Your friend will be your experimenter, and you will be his or hers (be aware, however, that you cannot then discuss your project in detail with this person for social support!). A final and least preferred option is to act as the experimenter yourself, using some procedure to ensure that you do not treat participants in different conditions differently. This might include administering a questionnaire that all participants complete about the experimenter or audiotaping experimental sessions and having raters unaware of the hypotheses evaluate them.

If implementing the independent variable requires skill or elaborate procedures, indicate how you will train your experimenters and ensure their competence before and during the study. This is particularly important with studies that involve interventions, animal surgery, and use of experimental confederates who have to act out certain scripts.

Finally, include information on control procedures you have instituted to prevent confounds. For example, if participants will view a series of videotaped stimuli, indicate how you will control for possible order effects. If different experimenters implement different levels of the independent variable, how will you ensure that levels of this variable, and not experimenter differences, influenced the results? Provide the information necessary to convince your reader that your conditions differ on the independent variable only, and nothing else. To do this will, of course, require that you figure out potential confounds in advance and eliminate them or assess the effects of their presence.

Dependent Variables (Measures)

The measures or dependent variables subsection provides details about the data collection devices you will use. Chapter 8 describes what to look for in decent instrumentation. Here we mention the information to provide about these devices once you have selected them.

Describe readily available instruments by name, author, and date of publication (if published). Include a copy of unpublished measures in one or more appendixes to the proposal; be sure to obtain written permission to reproduce the measure if it is copyrighted. In addition to stating where the measure has appeared in the literature, describe what it looks like (i.e., its topography). That is, paraphrase or quote the instructions to the participant, describe representative test stimuli or items, and state the response alternatives provided (e.g., yes–no or 1- to 4-point ratings). You might want to include representative items in a table to make them readily available to the reader, even if the entire instrument is reproduced in an appendix. Of course, if you are using a well-known instrument such as the Minnesota Multiphasic Personality Inventory—2, you generally won't need to go into detail because most readers will be familiar with it. Items from some tests (e.g., Wechsler Adult Intelligence Scale—Revised) cannot be reproduced in publicly available documents for test-security reasons. Ask your chairperson if you are unsure whether your measures would be considered well known. Finally, describe how the measure will be scored. If it yields more than one score, indicate the score(s) you intend to use.

In addition to describing the topographic characteristics of your measures, include information about their psychometric properties. It is generally not enough to state that the scores you intend to use from the instrument have been found to be reliable and valid. Reliability and validity are relative. Show that you have selected instrumentation that is appropriate for answering the specific questions of interest in your particular project. A score shown to be reliable by someone else might not be adequately reliable for your anticipated use.

The term *reliability* is too general to be informative, anyway. There are different types of reliability or generalizability (Cone, 1977; Cronbach, Gleser, Nanda, & Rajaratnam, 1972; Foster & Cone, 1995) that will be more or less important for your particular study. For example, if you will assess your participants before and after some intervention, the temporal stability (e.g., test–retest reliability) of your instruments will be an important characteristic. Their internal consistency may be of less concern. Moreover, if mean changes in groups of participants from pre- to post- are at issue, you will want to know something about the stability of mean scores, not just that an instrument has been shown to be stable over time. Similarly, a retest interval of 2 weeks might give you some information about the temporal stability of your measure, but if your intervention is going to take considerably longer, you might need to look further to find literature showing your instrument's performance over periods longer than 2 weeks.

In addition to examining different types of reliability, you will want to present some data on the validity evidence relevant to your measures. For example, when using a self-report measure, it is important to examine the extent to which it has been shown to have discriminant validity (Campbell, 1960). Convergent validity information should also be mentioned. Other types of validity (e.g., criterion-related, construct, treatment, and discriminative) will be more or less important, depending on your particular research. We say more about these in chapter 8. Remember to focus on the *scores* you intend to use. Many measures can be scored in different ways, and these scores are not equally reliable and valid. You don't need to discuss the psychometric properties of scores you don't intent to use.

These suggestions deal with measures of your dependent variables. What about your independent variable? As mentioned earlier, you should take steps to ensure that your independent variable does indeed occur at the level you intended. One place to indicate the steps you will take is the measures subsection (the independent variable or procedures subsections are alternatives). Similarly, measures you use to describe your participants can be described either here or in the participants subsection. In deciding where to put this information, ask yourself, "What will be easiest for the reader to follow?"

In addition, if you plan to use humans as observers or judges, indicate who they will be (e.g., undergraduates); how they will be recruited, selected, and trained; and how you will know that they are ready to be let loose on the real data (see Tryon, 1998, for practical guidelines for direct observation, most of which can be extrapolated to other uses of human judges). Indicate, furthermore, what percentage of data will be checked for interobserver or interjudge agreement (at least 20%, selected randomly from each condition or participant, is our minimum) and how agreement will be calculated. Cone (1999a) and Hartmann (1982) provided reviews of the myriad different statistics that can be used to calculate interjudge agreement and presented some formulas (see also House, House, & Campbell, 1981, for a discussion of others). Finally, indicate the procedures you will use in assessing interrater or interobserver agreement. Try to make sure observers or raters do not know who will check agreement and when, if possible, because this knowledge leads to inflated agreement estimates (Romanczyk, Kent, Diament, & O'Leary, 1973).

A final piece of information to include when using observations or judges' ratings is a complete description of the category system (including definitions) and procedures (including data-collection sheets) they will follow. Ordinarily, you should summarize these in the method section and provide a copy of the coding manual or guidelines and scoring sheets in an appendix. If you develop the instrumentation de novo in your study, you may not have information on the psychometric properties of its scores. In this case, we highly recommend a pilot study. If you cannot collect pilot data before your proposal meeting, be sure to include information in the proposal about how you plan to obtain reliability and validity information during the course of your research. In most cases, this should be done before collecting the data needed to answer the main research questions. The reason for this is simple. Suppose you collect reliability and validity data on your instruments at the same time you are collecting data to answer the main research questions. If your data show that your measure is poor, how will you interpret your primary research data? If the data do not turn out the way you hypothesized, the fault may lie in your instrumentation, not in the logic underlying the hypothesis. In other words, your measures are not sufficiently reliable or valid to answer your particular research questions. Cone (1992) provided a more detailed discussion of this issue.

Procedure

In this subsection, describe the actual steps you will take to obtain data from your participants. Walk the reader through the process just as a participant will experience it (Yates, 1982). Start at the beginning. If a research assistant will telephone or screen participants from a list of volunteers, indicate this and state exactly what participants will be told on the phone. If your study involves mailing questionnaires or other information to the participants, state how this will be done. Describe the procedures to be followed when participants arrive at the data collection site, including who will be responsible for each of the procedures. For example, if participants will be randomly assigned to an experimental or control group, state how randomization will occur. Be particularly alert to protecting against participant reactivity to experimental conditions and other forms of participant bias, such as the infamous Hawthorne effect (cf. Ray, 2006). Tell participants only what they need for informed participation. Be aware of the double-blind approach to minimizing experimenter bias and use it if possible.

Describe your procedures for ensuring informed consent. Include the human participants review process you will follow, and place a copy of the informed consent form you will use in an appendix. Describe the process you will use to debrief participants after they have participated. Compose a script for this, and place it in an appendix. Don't forget to offer the participants a chance to obtain a summary of the research findings. A good way to do this is to provide a box for them to check on the consent form if they are interested in receiving such a summary (include a place for their address as well).

Provide the word-for-word instructions you will be using with each participant. If different groups will receive different instructions, indicate how instructions will differ, and put copies of all instructions in an appendix.

Tape recording instructions and playing these for participants ensures standardization and helps avoid experimenter burnout, communication of boredom or impatience, or any of a number of normal (but idiosyncratic) experimenter reactions that might inadvertently affect the outcome of the study. Recall our earlier recommendations concerning integrity checks.

Finally, if your design calls for posttreatment assessment or follow-up, be sure to describe how these will be accomplished. When will they occur? Will participants be brought back? Will they be telephoned, contacted only by mail, and so on?

Be Familiar With Research Ethics in Psychology

This section treats research ethics in some detail to assist you in conducting your own research in as ethically sensitive a manner as possible. We first outline the ethical principles governing the conduct of research in psychology. Then we turn to practical suggestions for implementing the principles.

The professional conduct of psychologists, whether practitioner or researcher, whether student or seasoned veteran, is governed by the ethical principles and standards promulgated by the APA (2002). The Appendix reproduces Standards 2.05, 3.04, 3.08, 4.01, 4.02, 4.04, 4.07, 5.01, 6.01–6.02, 8.01–8.15, those most directly relevant for research. The essence of these principles and standards is that, when psychologists conduct research, they do so competently and with the welfare of participants of paramount concern.

In discharging the responsibility to respect the welfare of participants, our interpretation of the Ethics Code, together with our years of responding to the requirements of institutional review boards (IRBs) leads us to the following recommendations. Please be aware that these are not specific principles and standards of the code, but rather our own paraphrasing and synthesizing based on our joint experience.

1. Evaluate the ethical acceptability of the research.
2. Assess the degree of risk involved for participants.
3. Ensure the ethical conduct of the research by you and others involved in it.
4. Obtain a clear, fair, informed, and voluntary agreement by participants to participate.

5. Avoid deception and concealment unless absolutely necessary and justifiable.
6. Respect the participant's right to decline or withdraw from participation at any time.
7. Protect the participant from any physical harm, danger, or discomfort possibly associated with the research procedures.
8. Protect the participant from any emotional harm, danger, or discomfort possibly associated with the research procedures.
9. Debrief the participant after data collection has been completed.
10. Correct any undesirable consequences to individual participants that result from participating in the study.
11. Maintain strict confidentiality of any information collected about a participant during the research in accord with agreements reached with the participant while obtaining informed consent.

If your research involves the use of nonhuman animals, the most important of the ethical principles is Standard 8.09, "Humane Care and Use of Animals in Research." In conducting such research in the ethically most acceptable way you must observe the following.

1. Conform with all laws and professional standards pertaining to acquiring, caring for, and disposing of the animals.
2. Ensure that a psychologist trained in research methods and experienced in animal care supervises the use of the animals and is ultimately responsible for their health, comfort, and humane treatment.
3. Ensure that all individuals involved in the research have been specifically trained in research methods and ways of caring for, maintaining, and handling the particular animals being used.
4. Minimize any discomfort, infection, pain, or illness to the animals.
5. Use procedures involving stress, pain, or privation only if alternatives are unavailable and the research goal is justified by the practical, educational, or scientific value expected.
6. Perform any surgery under appropriate anesthesia and use procedures to prevent infection and minimize pain both during and after surgery.
7. Proceed rapidly, using appropriate procedures and minimizing pain, with life-terminating procedures when it is appropriate to terminate an animal's life.

Implement the Ethical Standards in Your Research

If your behavior as a researcher follows these standards, you will be acting in an ethically responsible way. This section gives you some suggestions in this regard. More details appear in *Ethics in Research With Human Participants* (Sales & Folkman, 2000). Chapter 8 in Nagy's (2005) *Ethics in Plain English: An Illustrative Casebook for Psychologists* provides interesting vignettes that bring life to the code.

Determine Ethical Acceptability

The first requirement is that the research you plan to undertake be ethically acceptable. How do you find out if it is? A simple test is to examine the principles just listed. Can your research be done if you adhere to each of them? If it can, it is probably ethically acceptable. If it cannot, it still may be ethically acceptable, but you will have to take some extra steps to determine this and to assure yourself and others that it is.

Deception and concealment in research raise particular concerns about ethical acceptability because they can only be used when "absolutely necessary and justifiable." As an example, imagine a study that involves a task in which the participant competes against other individuals. To exercise precise control over the other individual's performance, the experimenter might actually program a computer to compete against the real participant. Participants might be told the individuals against whom they are competing are in other experimental rooms. They will be communicating with each other but will not be able to see one another. Unbeknownst to the participant, the persons in the other rooms are really a computer.

Clearly, you are deceiving the participant in this experiment. Is this inconsistent with the prohibition against deception, or can you establish that the research is important and that it cannot be done without the deception? Frequently deception can be avoided altogether with a little ingenuity or statistical sophistication on your part (Kazdin, 2003). For example, pilot testing in the example just given might reveal that groups told they were competing against a computer performed comparably to those told they were competing against real people. If the research question involves whether competition is critical, showing that computer and people competitors are equivalent eliminates the need for deception. Simply tell your participants they are competing against a computer.

Unfortunately, as this example illustrates, doing a thorough job of ensuring that controversial research methods are ethical can be time-consuming and is often beyond the resources of the fledgling researcher. Performing a pilot study such as this may not be realistic if you want to finish your project and receive your degree while you are still able to walk across the stage at graduation.

The challenge of showing that your research is ethical is another reason to plan a study within the context of a research area that is currently viable in the literature. If you have a body of research on which to draw, chances are that most of those studies have been done in ways consistent with the APA's ethical principles. You can refer to precedents in the established literature to assure yourself, your IRB, committee members, and others that you are conducting your own research ethically. Of course, it is not enough simply to refer to existing literature to prove that your research is ethical. You will need to address each of the principles and be able to assure your committee and your institution's IRB that you are moving forward ethically.

Plan Informed Consent Procedures

Participants' informed consent is a key element in ethically conducted research. Informed consent is a process, and includes both informing prospective participants of what their participation in the research will likely entail and obtaining their written agreement to participate.

One part of the consent process involves giving the participant (or the participant's parent or guardian if the parent is younger than 18 years of age) an informed consent agreement or form. The exact contents that must be included in consent forms will vary from place to place, in keeping with institutional variations in IRB procedures. Based on our experience with a variety of IRBs and our interpretation of the APA Ethics Code, we consider the following to be the minimum essential elements of any consent form:

1. a description of the study and its purpose;
2. the information the participant will be asked to provide, if any;
3. a description of what the participant will be asked to do and how long it will take;
4. a description of potential risks and benefits to individual participants;
5. a statement that participation is voluntary and that the participant can withdraw at any time without penalty;

6. reassurance that all data will be confidential and a description of any circumstances in which the researcher would have to forgo confidentiality;

7. the name and phone number of a person the participant may call to get further information about the research;

8. the name and phone number of a person (other than the researcher) the participant may call if he or she has any complaints as a result of participating in the study;

9. information regarding whether and what compensation will be provided;

10. if the study examines an experimental treatment, a description of alternatives to the research;

11. explanation that a summary of the results/findings will be available if wanted; and

12. places for the participant and researcher to sign the form.

Exhibits 7.1 through 7.4 provide samples of consent forms for different situations involving human participants. Exhibit 7.1 is for a study in which adults consent for their own participation. Joseph Severino designed this dissertation to investigate the effects of hate crimes, using an analog methodology. Gay and straight males were asked to listen and "think aloud" in response to audiotapes depicting a physical assault that did or did not include antigay language. Severino was particularly concerned that males with severe trauma history might face risks of reactivation of trauma, so he screened for this when recruiting participants and ruled out participants who had particular sorts of trauma history. In addition, the tapes contained graphic language, and he informed participants of this.

Exhibit 7.2 shows how a parent consents for his or her teenage son or daughter to participate. Because the research is conducted in a school setting, the form is sent home for the parents to sign. Exhibit 7.3 is an assent form for the teenage participants in the same study to sign. Exhibit 7.4 is an assent form used with younger children (from Grades 4–6) for a different study. It illustrates appropriate language modification for younger children.

In the event you are working with children or other individuals who are not considered legally able to give informed consent, a parent or legal guardian must sign the form. The prospective participants should also be given an opportunity to assent or refuse after you have described the study in simple terms and have asked them directly if they want to participate. In addition, children can be asked to sign an assent form (see Exhibit 7.4),

Exhibit 7.1

Sample Adult Consent for Participation in Research

Alliant International University, San Diego Campus
10455 Pomerado Road
San Diego, CA 92131
Institutional Review Board, (555) 555-5555

Men's Responses to Crime
You are being asked to participate in a research study. However, before you consent to be a volunteer, we want you to read the following and ask as many questions as necessary to be sure that you understand what your participation will involve.

INVESTIGATOR
The name of the student conducting this research is Joseph Severino, MA. The faculty member who is supervising the research is Sharon Foster, PhD.

PURPOSE OF THE RESEARCH
The purpose of the study is to gain a better understanding of people's responses to various types of crimes. In response to crime victimization, individuals engage in a number of thought processes as they attempt to cope with their experience. The goal of the present study is to obtain a clearer picture of the thought processes that individuals engage in after they have experienced different types of victimization.

DURATION OF PARTICIPATION IN THE RESEARCH AND NUMBER OF PARTICIPANTS
If you agree to participate, it will take around 60 to 90 minutes of your time and you will not need to return unless you would like to speak with the primary investigator about your experience in the study. A total of about 80 participants will be involved in this study.

PROCEDURES TO BE FOLLOWED DURING THE RESEARCH
If you choose to participate in this study, you will first be asked to fill out two questionnaires, which ask about traumatic experiences that you may have had in the past. Filling out these questionnaires may bring up upsetting or disturbing memories for those who have experienced traumatic events in the past. These questionnaires may be all that is required of some individuals. In addition to the two questionnaires, you will also be asked to listen to an audiotape dramatization of a crime and to imagine yourself as the victim. At various points, you will be asked to describe what your thoughts would be if the crime were happening to you. Your description will be recorded on audiotape. All recording instruments will be visible and no recording will take place without your knowledge and consent. In addition to verbal feedback you will be asked to fill out two more questionnaires about your reactions.

continued

Exhibit 7.1, continued

Sample Adult Consent for Participation in Research

RISKS

The risk in this study is that you will be exposed to material that is potentially upsetting, arousing, and/or anxiety-provoking. The vignettes in this study include content such as pejorative language and descriptions of violent acts, which you may find offensive, insulting, frightening, and/or disturbing. The violence does not involve sexual acts or serious injury, however. You may stop the tape and quit the study at any time without penalty. In addition, you will be asked to recall traumatic events from your past, which may result in the resurgence of memories that upset you.

BENEFITS OF THE RESEARCH

There may not be any direct benefit to you from this study, but the investigators hope to learn more from the study that may help other individuals later on.

ALTERNATIVES TO THIS RESEARCH

If you choose to participate in this research, there is no other alternative procedure other than what is described. However, you do not have to participate in the research and you may choose to withdraw your participation at any time without any consequence.

CONFIDENTIALITY

You have a right to privacy, and all information identifying you will remain anonymous and confidential. Your answers on all questionnaires, recordings, and paper measures will be coded with numbers, and only the primary researcher will have access to the names. No identifying information will appear on any material. Any information obtained in connection with this research that can be identified with you will remain confidential and will not be disclosed without your permission or as required by law. The results of this study may be published in scientific journals or be presented at psychological meetings as long as you are not identified and cannot reasonably be identified from it. However, it is possible that under certain circumstances, data could be subpoenaed by court order.

QUESTIONS ABOUT THE RESEARCH

If you have any questions you can contact Joseph Severino at 555-555-5555 at any time. Please feel free to ask any questions you may have before signing this form.

SUBJECT COMPENSATION FOR PARTICIPATION

As compensation for your participation in this study, you will receive a free movie pass. In addition, your name will be placed in a lottery for a chance to win your choice of a Game Boy or a portable TV.

continued

Exhibit 7.1, continued

PREVIOUS RESEARCH PARTICIPATION
I have participated in the following research studies within the last three months:

_____

_____

PARTICIPANT RIGHTS AND RESEARCH WITHDRAWAL
Your participation in this study is voluntary. You may refuse to participate or withdraw once the study has started. You will not lose any benefits to which you are otherwise entitled nor will you be penalized. We have tried to explain all the important details about the study to you. If you have any questions that are not answered here, the researcher will be happy to give you more information.

SIGNATURE AND ACKNOWLEDGEMENT
My signature below indicates that I have read the above information and I have had a chance to ask questions to help me understand what my participation will involve. I agree to participate in the study until I decide otherwise. I acknowledge having received a copy of this agreement and a copy of the Subject's Bill of Rights. I have been told that by signing this consent form I am not giving up any of my legal rights.

SIGNATURE OF PARTICIPANT _____ DATE _____

SIGNATURE OF WITNESS _____ DATE _____

SIGNATURE OF INVESTIGATOR _____ DATE _____

Note. From *Gay and Straight Men's Attributions to Simulated Antigay and Nonbias Victimization,* by Joseph Severino. Unpublished dissertation proposal, 2002, California School of Professional Psychology, Alliant International University, San Diego. Used with permission of the author.

similar to a consent form but in simpler language. From our perspective, if *either* the legal guardian or the potential participant declines, the individual is automatically excluded from the study.

Other populations besides children need special protections to ensure their consent is voluntary. These include individuals with mental retardation, prisoners, homeless individuals, active military personnel, employees, and students. With some of these, limited competency to understand what they are agreeing to is an issue, as it is with children. With others, a form of indirect coercion needs to be guarded against. For example, employees may think their superiors expect participation and that their job security is at

Exhibit 7.2

Sample Parental Consent for a Child to Participate in Research

Dear Parent or Guardian,

I would like to ask your permission for your daughter to participate in a study looking at how girls may influence one another's attitudes and behaviors about eating, weight, and shape. The project is titled, "Peer Concern and Influence on Body Image Related Concerns," and is a dissertation being conducted as part of the requirements of obtaining a doctoral degree. Specifically, I will be looking at how important body image and dieting behaviors are to girls and their friends and how this relates to their eating habits, how much they compare themselves to one another, and their feelings about their appearance.

What is involved? The study will include about 150 girls from high schools in San Diego. Girls who participate will come to one or two sessions to fill out several questionnaires. During the session, each girl will be given a list of the participants in her class and will be asked to indicate which of the girls she "hangs out" with the most and how well she knows each of her friends. Girls will be asked to fill out several questionnaires related to their interactions with their friends, and the attitudes and behaviors of their friends. They will also report on how they feel about their own appearance and eating behaviors. Each girl's height and weight will also be measured privately. The time required to complete the session(s) should be no more than 60–70 minutes.

Potential benefits and concerns. I will do my best to accommodate your daughter's schedule so that she does not miss important school lessons; however, she may have to make up some schoolwork, depending on the teacher's schedule. Your daughter is not expected to experience significant discomfort as a result of participating in this study. She may feel slightly uncomfortable answering some of the questions, as they will be asking her to discuss her eating habits and feelings about her weight and shape, but she does not have to answer any questions she does not wish to answer. Benefits of her participation include gaining a better understanding of how peers influence one another with respect to eating behaviors and body image so that we can focus both on prevention and treatment programs. Information about eating problems that sometimes affect teenage girls will be provided for all participants. Each girl will receive a movie pass as a thank you for her participation in the study.

Participation is voluntary. Your daughter's participation in this study is voluntary. There will be no penalty if you do not wish for your daughter to participate in the study, and she may withdraw at any time from the study or refuse to answer any questions. This project has been approved by the Institutional Review Board for the Protection of Human Subjects at Alliant International University.

Confidentiality. All information will be held as confidential as is legally possible. Only the researchers will see the questionnaires. No names will be on any of the questionnaires. Instead, names will be replaced with identifying numbers. Each

continued

Exhibit 7.2, continued

girl will be informed that her answers will be kept confidential. However, if it is revealed to me that a participant in the study is doing something that is potentially dangerous to herself or to someone else, I am required by law to investigate this and possibly report it. This will be made clear to each girl who participates in the study. The chances of this occurring are small, but it is important that you be informed of the limits of confidentiality before you make your decision.

Questions? I would appreciate it if you would return this form whether or not you wish for your daughter to participate, so that I know the information has reached you. You may keep the attached copy of the letter for your records. If you have any questions, please feel free to call me, Erin Anderson (555-555-5555). I can arrange for you to see the questionnaires in advance if you wish. The supervisor of the study, Dr. Sharon Foster, can be reached at (555) 555-5555. The Institutional Review Board at Alliant International University can also answer questions about the rights of participants in research. They may be contacted at (555) 555-5555. In addition, both you and your daughter, if you choose to participate, will receive a copy of the participant's Bill of Rights. The Bill of Rights is a handout that explains what your daughter's rights are as a participant in a research study. It is important to note, however, that some of the provisions on this handout are not applicable for this particular study.

Thank you for your consideration.

Sincerely,

Erin K. Anderson, MA
Doctoral Student
California School of Professional Psychology

Please check ALL the appropriate boxes and send this form back to the school with your daughter:

☐ I have read and understand the permission letter. I give my consent for my daughter to participate in this study if she wishes to do so.
☐ I have received a copy of Miss Anderson's letter for my records.
☐ I would like more information about the study before deciding whether my daughter may participate in the study. Please call me at _____ .
☐ I do not wish for my daughter to participate in the study.

Parent signature/Date _____

Teenager's name _____

Please send this form back to school with your daughter. Thank you!!

Note. From *Peer Influences on Body Image Related Concerns: The Role of Social Comparison,* by Erin K. Ferma. Unpublished dissertation, 2005, California School of Professional Psychology, Alliant International University, San Diego. Used with permission of the author.

Exhibit 7.3

Sample Assent Form for Adolescents

Study Title: Peer Influence on Body Image Related Concerns
Investigators: Erin Anderson, MA (555-555-5555)
            Sharon Foster, PhD (555-555-5555)

I am being asked to help Miss Anderson with a project. The goal of this project is to understand better how important body image and eating behaviors are to girls and their friends.

If I decide to participate in the study, my part in the project would take about 60–70 minutes total and take place in one or two sessions. These sessions would require me to indicate who my closest friends are after being given a list of all the girls in my class. In addition, I would fill out several questionnaires related to my interactions with my friends, and the attitudes and behaviors of my friends, and answer several questionnaires about how I feel about my own appearance and eating behaviors. I would also have my height and weight measured. I understand that all this information is very private and will be kept confidential.

I understand that all of my information and answers will be kept confidential. I understand that if I miss a part of a class to participate in the study, I will have to make up the work I miss, and that I may miss a part of my extracurricular activities if the study takes place after school. I also understand that by participating in this study, I may understand better how I influence my friends and how that influence affects their attitudes and behaviors, as well as my own. In addition, I will receive a movie pass as a thank you for being in the study.

This project has been explained to me and I have been allowed to ask questions about it. I understand that I do not have to fill out the questionnaires if I do not want to and no one will treat me badly. I can stop part of the way through and skip the questions I don't want to answer. I understand that all of my information and answers will be kept private and confidential. However, I also understand that if I indicate that I am doing something that is potentially dangerous that could hurt me, then this information will no longer be confidential and the investigator will be required to report it to my parents. I have read this form, understand the project, and agree to participate.

Student signature/Date _____

Investigator/Date _____

Note. From *Peer Influences on Body Image Related Concerns: The Role of Social Comparison,* by Erin K. Ferma. Unpublished dissertation, 2005, California School of Professional Psychology, Alliant International University, San Diego. Used with permission of the author.

Exhibit 7.4

Sample Assent Form for Children

Assent Form

I understand that I have been asked to be in a research project looking at how girls think, feel, and behave toward other girls. I will meet in a small group with other girls and the interviewer for about 60 minutes. During this meeting, I will be asked about behaviors that girls I know do. I will also read stories about things girls do together and will answer questions about these stories.

I understand that I do not have to answer any questions I do not want and can go back to my class early if I want. I can decide to stop being in this project at any time. It will not make any difference in my grades, and no one will be mad at me if I choose not to participate in this project. If I feel bad about anything I am asked to do in this study I can talk to Ms. Laverty Finch about it. If I do decide to participate in this study, I will receive a small gift after our meeting.

I understand that my answers are private and the interviewer will not tell anyone what I said. I will also keep my answers private and I won't talk to the other kids about what I said in the interviews.

If I have any questions I can ask them now or have my parents or teacher call Ms. Laverty Finch at (555) 555-5555 or Dr. Foster at (555) 555-5555, ext. 555.

My signature below means I have read and understand this form and I agree to be in this study.

_____

Signature of Child   Date

_____

Signature of Interviewer   Date

Note. From *The Relationship Among Relationally Aggressive Behavior, Emotion and Social Cognitions in Preadolescent Females,* by Cambra Laverty Finch. Dissertation, 2001, California School of Professional Psychology, Alliant International University, San Diego. Used with permission of the author.

risk if they decline. Requiring college students to involve themselves in research to satisfy the criteria of a particular course can be viewed as a limited form of coercion (Neuman, 1997), particularly if no alternatives are available for those who do not wish to be research participants. Seek assistance in ethically recruiting individuals from special populations such as these from your chairperson or your school's IRB.

In addition, special ethical considerations may arise when you involve ethnic minority populations in your research. Indeed, given our increasingly pluralistic society, you quite likely will have members of diverse racial and ethnic groups in your research unless you purposely design the research to study particular groups. Numerous concerns can be important, such as how you categorize your groups and the applicability of your constructs and measures to diverse groups. You will want to be sure to avoid inappropriate generalizations when minority individuals make up only a small part of your sample and it is impossible to test whether the results hold equally well for different groups (see Foster & Martinez, 1995, for a general overview). When ethnic minority groups are a primary focus of your research, additional special considerations apply. Fisher et al. (2002) provided extensive discussion of issues involved in creating and using culturally informed and respectful consent and confidentiality procedures in research with children. This discussion is relevant to research with adults as well.

It is important to attend to the reading level of any consent form you use. Be sure that it does not exceed the level of the lowest reading proficiency you are willing to include in your research. Research evidence suggests many consent forms are written at a level much higher than the reading levels of participants. For example, in medical settings it has been noted that the average consent form requires reading proficiency that is five to six grade levels above that of the average patient (Hochhauser, 1999). It is easy to get estimates of the reading level of your consent. Many word processing programs have reading level calculators built into them. For example, Word™, the program used in writing this book, provides a Flesch–Kincaid grade level estimate of 8.7 for the two sentences immediately preceding this one.

As a procedural matter, signing the informed consent form usually occurs as the first order of business when the participant appears for the initial experimental session. If school children are participating, the form will commonly be sent home with the child to be returned with a parent's signature. Ask the parent to return the form after assenting *or* declining. This way you can be sure the parent at least received the form.

Some researchers (e.g., Clarke, Lewinsohn, Hops, & Seeley, 1992; Roberts, Lewinsohn, & Seeley, 1991) have successfully used passive consent procedures in the past. In the Clarke et al. (1992) study, for example, parents of potential participating children were given the opportunity to refuse their child's participation by returning a decline card to the researchers. Children were enrolled in the study if their parents did not return the card. Of course, the children were also given the opportunity to decline participation themselves after the procedures were explained to them. Such procedures might lead to higher levels of participation than more active approaches. If you are considering the passive tactic, however, be sure you have the approval of your IRB for the protection of human participants first, and discuss the potential ramifications with your chairperson. Be aware that passive consent procedures can be controversial. One researcher, a story goes, used them for a study involving controversial procedures with school children. A parent complained after data were collected, and ultimately the researcher had to destroy data from hundreds of participants. There is also evidence of educational and racial bias in the use of passive consent procedures. That is, researchers report higher percentages of less well-educated individuals and minorities in studies with passive consent than those with active consent (Dent, Galaif, & Susman, 1993). Include additional items on consent forms depending on the preferences of the IRB at your particular school.

Examine Risk to Participants

Thinking about potential risk to participants is a crucial part of planning ethical research and seeking IRB approval. You must assess the extent of any risk posed to people, whether physical, emotional, or other, by participating in your project. This can generally be ascertained from existing literature if researchers have used procedures comparable to those you plan to use. In a few cases, the potential harmful nature of research procedures has actually been studied directly (cf. Bell-Dolan, Foster, & Sikora, 1989). You can refer to the results of such studies in designing your voluntary consent form. In most cases, however, potential risks have not been studied directly and must be inferred from the literature. In this event, you should refer to the body of literature and indicate that there have (or have not) been any reported instances of physical, emotional, or other types of harm to participants in the "dozens of studies reported in the literature using these procedures," or words to that effect.

In our experience, novice researchers sometimes underestimate risks, but a more common problem is that they overestimate the likelihood that people will become distressed as a result of participating in their research. For example, we have seen draft IRB proposals that talk about concerns that participants might become upset answering completely innocuous questionnaires simply because questions ask about a person's bad habits, negative moods, or the like. It is important to remember that the benchmark for "minimal risk" is the degree of risk a participant would encounter in a routine physical or psychological examination. People are routinely asked for personal information when they talk to a psychologist, so we assume that reporting normal, everyday information will not be unduly distressing.

After all, would *you* be significantly distressed if asked to report how often you have negative thoughts about yourself, for example? Is there really much likelihood that your participants will become upset? At the same time, asking for highly sensitive information (e.g., about one's sexual habits, use of illegal drugs, etc.) might be more problematic or pose greater risk. When in doubt, talk with others in the profession to gather their assessment of likely risks.

Know the Operation of Your Local Institutional Review Board

The procedures followed by the IRB in overseeing research will typically be published. You should get a copy of these and read them. They will include the steps you must follow in having your research approved *before* beginning to collect data.

Because IRB procedures usually cover pilot testing as well, it is important to examine them early in your planning. Pay particular attention to the dates of IRB meetings and the deadlines and rules for submitting proposals. If the meetings occur only monthly, missing one meeting could mean a delay of as much as a month in getting started. Look also at the different categories of research to make sure exactly what the requirements are for your particular case. Perhaps the research you plan is actually exempt from IRB review or can be subjected to an expedited review. When data are being obtained only from archival sources or when you are using relatively benign surveys, or observing public behavior, or evaluating normal educational practice, as examples, it is usually the case that full IRB review will not be necessary. Rely on the experience of your chairperson or other committee members. They will be knowledgeable concerning the process and politics of the local IRB and will have sage advice for navigating them successfully.

Incidentally, it is important to know the timing of IRB approval relative to proposal meetings. Some schools require the student to obtain that approval before holding a proposal meeting. That is because there are occasionally substantial changes necessary to respond satisfactorily to IRB concerns. These can have implications for fundamental aspects of the research, including the basic question and hypotheses. The committee does not want to have to convene again to consider such changes. Other schools expect the proposal meeting to result in changes to the planned project that are significant enough that the IRB will be evaluating a different proposal than would have been submitted before the committee's input. These schools are likely to require IRB submissions to occur after the proposal meeting.

Whether it comes before or after the proposal meeting, anticipate difficult steerage through the IRB process if the research you are planning is the least bit controversial. An interesting example relevant to this comes from some research in the area of children's social skills that Sharon Foster attempted to conduct some years ago. The procedure involved having children nominate their three most and three least liked peers. One of the members of the IRB was especially insistent that such a procedure was potentially harmful, arguing that the process would call attention to disliked children and that peers might respond to these children even more negatively than usual as a result of the nominations. Foster argued that no data showed the procedure to be harmful, although only one study had directly addressed the issue. Because of the limited data, Foster decided to recruit the concerned IRB member's assistance in designing a study to test this concern. To reassure the IRB, a study could be designed that would examine whether children were negatively affected by the nomination procedure. The IRB member with particular concerns gave permission for such a test, and a student conducted the study as a master's thesis. Incidentally, no negative effects emerged as a result of the nominations (Bell-Dolan et al., 1989), and IRB members were less reluctant about the procedures subsequently.

Plan to Monitor Research Ethics Continually

Designing an ethically acceptable research project and convincing others (e.g., IRB and your committee) of this are basic to beginning data collection. The job of ensuring ethical conduct of the research does not end here, however. In fact, it is just beginning. When you start to collect data, you will need to make sure that you and anyone assisting you with your research behaves in an ethically acceptable fashion at all times. Now is the time to think about how you will protect confidentiality, make sure participants are fully informed about the research, and so forth. Think about how you will do this and build it into your proposal. We will come back to this topic in chapter 10, when we talk about implementing your research.

Two useful sources for additional details about research ethics include the *Publication Manual of the American Psychological Association* (APA, 2010) and the ethical principles of psychologists pertaining to research (see Appendix, this volume). If your studies are in a field other than psychology, it is likely that it has a similar set of ethical principles with which you should become familiar. The basic methodological and ethical principles discussed in this chapter cut across disciplines, however, and it is important to understand them as you formulate your methodology.

Supplemental Resources

Research Design

Barlow, D. H., & Hersen, M. (1984). *Single-case experimental designs: Strategies for studying behavior change* (2nd ed.). Elmsford, NY: Pergamon Press.

Hayes, S. C., Barlow, D. H., & Nelson-Gray, R. O. (1999). *The scientist practitioner: Research and accountability in the age of managed care* (2nd ed.). Boston: Allyn & Bacon.

Kazdin, A. E. (2003). *Research design in clinical psychology* (4th ed.). Boston: Allyn & Bacon.

Kerlinger, F. N. (2000). *Foundations of behavioral research* (4th ed.). New York: Harcourt Brace.

McBurney, D. H. (2004). *Research methods* (6th ed.). Belmont, CA: Brooks/Cole.

Miller, D. C. (2002). *Handbook of research design and social measurement* (6th ed.). Newbury Park, CA: Sage.

Ray, W. J. (2006). *Methods: Toward a science of behavior and experience* (8th ed.). Pacific Grove, CA: Brooks/Cole.

Shadish, W. R., Cook, T. D., & Campbell, D. T. (2002). *Experimental and quasi-experimental designs for generalized causal inference*. Boston: Houghton Mifflin.

Solso, R. L., & MacLin, M. (2002). *Experimental psychology: A case approach* (7th ed.). Boston: Allyn & Bacon.

Weisberg, H. F., Krosnick, J. A., & Bowen, B. D. (1996). *An introduction to survey research, polling, and data analysis* (3rd ed.). Newbury Park, CA: Sage.

Power Analysis

Cohen, J. (1988). *Statistical power analysis for the behavioral sciences* (2nd ed.). Hillsdale, NJ: Erlbaum.

Cohen, J. (1992). A power primer. *Psychological Bulletin, 112,* 155–159.

Murphy, K. R., & Myors, B. (2004). *Statistical power analysis* (2nd ed.). Mahwah, NJ: Erlbaum.

Research Ethics

Cone, J. D., & Dalenberg, C. (2004). Ethics concepts in outcomes assessment. In M. E. Maruish (Ed.), *The use of psychological testing for treatment planning and outcomes assessment* (3rd ed.). Mahwah, NJ: Erlbaum.

National Institutes of Health. (2005a). *Guidelines for the conduct of research involving human subjects at the National Institutes of Health.* Retrieved November 7, 2005, from http://ohsr.od.nih.gov/guidelines/graybook.html. [Web site for National Institutes of Health Guidelines for research involving human subjects.]

National Institutes of Health. (2005b). *Regulations and ethical guidelines.* Retrieved November 7, 2005, from http://ohsr.od.nih.gov/guidelines/45cfr46.html. [Actual federal guidelines involve research with human participants; this site provides special guidelines for children, prisoners, pregnant women, and neonates.]

✔ To Do . . .

Writing the Method Section

☐ Write the different subsections of the method section

— Design

— Participants

— Setting and apparatus

— Independent variables

— Dependent variables (measures)

— Procedure

☐ Follow research ethics in psychology

— Read ethical guidelines

— Write consent and assent forms

— Find and complete an IRB proposal

— Submit the IRB proposal, make any changes, and obtain approval

— Monitor the conduct of your study to ensure ethical practices are maintained throughout

8
Measurement

In this chapter, we discuss operationalizing your dependent and independent variables. Some of these operationalizations will take the form of
the measures or instruments you will use in your study. We discuss the
characteristics of good measures and suggest places to look for measures
and information about them. In addition, we suggest what to do when
the psychometric adequacy of the scores you plan to use has not already
been established.

Operationalize Your Variables

If you are at the point of considering a thesis or dissertation, you probably
know what operational definitions are. If not, avail yourself of a good text
in research design (e.g., McBurney, 1990; Ray, 2006; see the list at the
end of chap. 7, this volume, for additional suggestions) and review the
relevant sections.

Your method section will describe how you plan to objectify all of your
variables, both dependent and independent. For example, suppose you plan
to examine the differences between high, middle, and low socioeconomic

families on cohesiveness. How will socioeconomic status be established? How will cohesiveness be measured? Or suppose you want to look at differences in nursing care provided to children with diabetes mellitus versus similar children with other chronic medical conditions. How will you determine the status of your participants with respect to diabetes? If you predict nursing care will vary depending on the nurses' previous experience with or knowledge about diabetes, how will you assess experience or knowledge? As another example, imagine you are interested in whether adults molested as children are more likely to have psychological problems than similar adults not so molested. How will you define and assess molestation? Will you lump different forms of it into a single category? Will you distinguish between abuse and molestation? If so, how? If you are studying racial or ethnic differences on some variable, how are you defining race or ethnicity? What about mixed-race individuals? Will degree of acculturation into the dominant culture be an issue? If so, how will this be assessed? If you are going to expose participants high and low in "appraisal anxiety" to high-, medium-, and low-stress public speaking situations, how will you manipulate stress? Just as important, how will you determine the success of your manipulation? If you are going to describe whether obese patrons at a restaurant eat more carbohydrates in fast food restaurants than nonobese patrons, how will you make your observations?

The answer to most of these questions is that you will use an objective instrument of some type. The instrument may be a short, rather gross categorization of participants into socioeconomic levels or racial groups. Or it may be a lengthy, rather specific index of appraisal anxiety or some other personality characteristic. Whatever its nature, your operational index will need to have certain qualities to be acceptable to the scientific community. Let's look at these for a moment.

Know Important Characteristics of Potential Instruments

The major requirements of any measure used in scientific research are that it (a) be chosen wisely, (b) have certain psychometric characteristics (i.e., reliability and validity) for the population you intend to study and for the scores you plan to use, and (c) be adequately direct. With respect to choosing wisely, we refer to whether the measure fits the variables that interest you. If you are concerned with conflict in marital relationships, for example, your measure should reflect this. Thus, before selecting measures you will need to define your variables precisely. *Conflict* is a rather general term and could refer to a number of behaviors. These might involve interaction with one's spouse or they might not. A person could be having many conflicting thoughts about staying in the relationship, for example. If the construct as you view it does concern interaction between spouses, is this verbal conflict, physical conflict, or both? It will be easier to choose the right measure if you know precisely what it is you want to assess than if you don't. This is true of any of the constructs you plan to study, whether they are independent or dependent variables. All anxiety is not created equally. There are many different ways of viewing it. Ethnicity is not ethnicity is not ethnicity, either. Furthermore, you cannot rely merely on the name a measure has been given by its developer. You must examine its content to determine whether it assesses the construct in ways consistent with the definition you will use in your study.

You should also think about whether you are interested in behavior (including motor actions, the experience of thoughts and feelings, and physiological reactions) in its own right or as an index of some hypothetical construct. This distinction has important implications for how you evaluate the data on the characteristics of a particular measure (Foster & Cone, 1995). If you are concerned about measuring participants' behavior, your measure should reflect the participants' actions in the real world. If constructs are your interest, whether your measure directly reflects reality will be less important than that it correlates appropriately with other measures in the same nomological (theoretical) net as your constructs. Because assessment of behavior is less familiar to most students than assessment of hypothetical constructs, we will spend a bit more time on issues involved in assessing it than on issues involved in assessing constructs.

So let's assume behavior is your interest. If so, a good measure will be one that is adequately direct. A direct measure assesses *the* behavior of interest, at the *time* and *place* the behavior occurs naturally (Cone, 1978). In the marital conflict example discussed earlier, you might have chosen to focus on verbal forms of conflict. One way to assess verbal conflict would be to ask your participants about it in an interview. Other forms of assessment include administering an appropriate self-report measure, having others who know the couple well rate each member on verbal conflict, having the couple self-monitor (i.e., observe and record their conflict at home), or having trained observers watch the couple and record all instances of verbal conflict.

These alternative types of assessment can be arrayed along a continuum representing the degree of topographic, temporal, and spatial similarity between the behavior that interests you and the behavior reflected in the particular assessment method you are using. Normally, you will be interested in participant responses that are as close as possible to those that occur naturally. This is because you want your data to have real-world implications. You will want your study to have as much external validity as possible. Direct measures enhance external validity. It does not take a rocket scientist to appreciate that asking someone to tell you about something he or she did at some other time and some other place is likely to produce lower quality data than you would get from observing actual performance.

Unfortunately, directness relates in an inverse fashion to cost. To have trained observers watch people in their natural environments is difficult. Direct observation involves spending hours developing and standardizing an observation code, finding and training observers, gaining access to the participants' natural settings, observing them unobtrusively in those settings, and reducing the observers' data to usable form. Compare this with a few hours to develop a structured interview and meeting with and administering it to someone. Even if you train interviewers, tape-record the interviews, and produce transcripts from the tapes, you will still invest much less than if you had chosen the direct observation approach.

Even less cost would be involved if you used self-report measures. Instead of training interviewers, transcribing tape-recording, and scoring the transcriptions, why not merely ask your participants to respond to a limited set of descriptive statements describing their behavior? Why not, indeed, has been the answer of many a researcher, novice and otherwise. In fact, self-report measures are so common that they are generally the first form of assessment we think of when launching the search for objective measures. In the example given earlier, we could ask our couple to respond *true* or *false* to statements asking whether they "argue about money," "raise their voices in front of others," and so on. When we do this, we make the important assumption that what the couple says corresponds to some degree with other important forms of behavior. Unfortunately, research looking at the correspondence between reports of what people *say* they do and what they *actually* do indicates this assumption is often false (Bellack & Hersen, 1977; Shiffman, 2000). Furthermore, it is now clear that retrospective self-report is subject to a whole host of biasing factors, many of which are the product of normal cognitive processing (Stone et al., 2000).

That is not to say that scores on self-report measures do not relate to scores from other measures. They often do, especially to scores on other self-report measures. We are merely pointing out that the common practice of using self-reports as substitutes for more direct forms of assessment has not received much support in the research literature. Indeed, many researchers openly acknowledge that self-reporting may not mirror other behavior. However, only a few take the next step to *determine* whether it does.

We encourage you to consider alternatives to sole reliance on self-report measures. Informant ratings offer an improvement in objectivity, for example. This is because the data are provided by individuals with less personal investment in how their ratings are to be used. They are still indirect, however, as they rely on reports of others about behavior that has occurred at other times and places. In addition, they have well-documented difficulties, some of which mirror those of self-reports, including inaccurate recollection, halo effects, generosity bias, and different interpretations of what is being measured, to name a few (e.g., Cairns & Green, 1979; Cronbach, 1990).

Self-observations (also sometimes called "self-monitoring" or "ecological momentary assessment") provide yet another alternative. These are more direct than interviews, self-reports, and ratings by others because they require the participant to observe and record the occurrence of the behavior of interest and to do so at the *time* and *place* of its occurrence. Although self-observation lacks the objectivity afforded by the independence of the assessor and the assessed, you can mitigate this problem by having the participant focus on very well-defined, specific responses. You can sometimes determine the accuracy of self-observation just as you can determine the accuracy of observation by others (see Johnston & Pennypacker, 1993, for descriptions of how). Self-observations using personal data assistants such as palm pilots have become increasingly used to sample daily activities, moods, and the like, particularly in behavioral medicine (Smyth & Stone, 2003), and these methods have been used with adolescents as well (e.g., Whalen, Jamner, Henker, & Delfino, 2001). Cone (1999b) edited a series of articles on self-observation in the journal *Psychological Assessment* in 1999. Stone, Kessler, and Haythornthwaite (1991); Foster, Laverty Finch, Gizzo, and Osantowski (1999); and Christensen, Barrett, Bliss-Moreau, Lebo, and Kaschub (2003) all described decisions and issues involved in planning self-observation systems.

Finally, we recommend you consider direct observation as a way of assessing your variables. True, it is a costly procedure, as we mentioned earlier. There are ways of using direct observations that are less costly than others, however (Cone, 1999a; Foster, Bell-Dolan, & Burge, 1988). For example, rather than having trained observers travel to natural contexts and station themselves unobtrusively to collect data, you could record (using video- or audiotapes) the behavior for later analysis. Or observers could watch participants in research rooms from behind one-way mirrors. Although such an approach removes the behavior from its natural context, it is still likely to yield higher quality data about actual performance than some of the less direct methods just described. Video- or audiotaping the behavior at the same time will provide a relatively permanent record that you can rescore repeatedly to produce highly objective data.

As this discussion indicates, you can measure the constructs in your study in several different ways. In the next section, we describe some sources to consult to find existing measures. If you are lucky enough to find existing measures of your variables in the literature, you can avoid the work of developing one and establishing its psychometric adequacy. This assumes, of course, that the measure you locate produces scores that are psychometrically sound. We said earlier that good measures are ones that are chosen wisely, are adequately direct, and produce scores that demonstrate appropriate psychometric characteristics (e.g., reliability and validity) for your purposes and for the population you wish to assess. Note that we said "produces scores," "for your purposes," and "for the population you wish to assess." This underscores an important principle: Reliability and validity are conditional. They depend on the nature of the construct you wish to assess, the scores you use to assess it, your purpose, and your population. A test–retest reliability correlation of .60 over 2 weeks may be fine for a state measure like mood but not for a measure of a presumably stable trait like intelligence. A measure of depression may have adequate content validity as a screening measure but inadequate content if its purpose is diagnosis or treatment monitoring. A measure shown to have good predictive validity for assessing achievement in White students may not do as well for Black students. In the next section, we review important psychometric characteristics and offer some suggestions and minimal criteria for evaluating measures you might be considering. Space does not permit us to present an entire course in test construction or measurement theory. Most of these concepts should be familiar to you, although you might not have thought about them in the context of your own particular research project. The literature provides many excellent treatments of these issues (Anastasi & Urbina, 1997; Cronbach, 1990; Cronbach et al., 1972; Guilford, 1956; Kaplan & Saccuzzo, 2005; Nunnally & Bernstein, 1994).

Evaluate the Reliability of Scores From Prospective Instruments

The essential criterion for any instrument, whether in the physical or behavioral sciences, is that it produces data that are reliable. Over the years, measurement scholars have defined different forms of reliability (Kaplan & Saccuzzo, 2005). You have heard of these before: test–retest or temporal reliability, alternate-form reliability, internal consistency, and so on. In 1972, Cronbach and colleagues proposed consolidating various forms of reliability under the general rubric of generalizability theory. Essentially, what they noted was that the different types of reliability all have to do with different ways in which one may generalize the data from measuring devices. The various ways of viewing the reliability of scores from measuring instruments differ from one another both conceptually and practically. As a result, it is not informative to say in your method section that you chose a particular instrument because it is reliable. Indeed, it is not technically correct to say so, as it is the *scores* on a measure, rather than the measure itself, that have certain psychometric properties (Thompson, 2003). The statement to make is that these scores have the psychometric characteristics necessary for your own research. To make this assessment is not easy, if it is done correctly. It requires a clear understanding of your subject matter and just how you plan to study it. For example, if you are studying a psychological construct, different psychometric issues will come up than if you are studying behavior from a natural science perspective (Foster & Cone, 1995; Johnston & Pennypacker, 1993).

Assume you are studying a psychological construct. What are your assumptions about it? Is it supposed to be relatively consistent across time? Across situations? Is it best revealed in the verbal behavior of the participant or in motor or physiological responding? Is it a relatively unitary construct (e.g., anxiety) assumed to underlie and determine responses to your measure, or one made up of multiple dimensions (e.g., behavioral health) that in their aggregate define the construct itself? In the first case, your basic measurement model is an effects indicator model. In the second, it is a causal indicator model (Bollen & Lennox, 1991). Be sure you know the implications your basic measurement model has for the types of reliability your scores should demonstrate.

Your answers to these and other questions will bear on the types of psychometric information to examine when selecting among possible measures. Ideally, you will be able to identify the information you need in advance, select a measure with scores that has it, and present the information to support your choice in your method section. At the very least, you should say more than the measure has adequate evidence supporting the reliability and validity of its scores for your population and purpose. It is a good idea to say that, for your purposes, "the following types of reliability data are needed." Then state what they are. Document their existence for the scores you plan to use. Finally, repeat the process for validity, a subject to which we now turn.

Evaluate the Validity of Scores of Prospective Instruments

In addition to producing scores on your variables in consistent ways, you will want these scores to mean something. Whether they do is contained in the evidence for their validity. An instrument may produce highly reliable data that do not relate to anything. In other words, you may have a measure with reliable scores that are not valid. Incidentally, contrary to what you might occasionally see in textbooks, the reverse is not possible within the context of classical measurement theory. To be valid, scores must be reliable. What we mean by validity is the extent to which scores on a measure relate to scores on other measures. This is more general than the hackneyed definition that scores on a measure are valid if they measure what they are supposed to measure. They may not do this at all well and still have a great deal of validity in the larger sense meant in this volume.

As with reliability, scores may be valid in different ways. A measure has *face validity* if it looks to the participant like it is appropriate for the purposes at hand. *Content validity* refers to how well the measure samples the universe of content relevant to the construct or behavior being assessed, omits irrelevant content, and contains a balance of indicators of the construct (Haynes, Richard, & Kubany, 1995). Thus, item selection, category definitions, and so on are key issues. Content validity is often assessed formally by expert judgments.

Scores have *construct validity* if they enter relationships required by the theory underlying the construct they presumably reflect. They have *convergent validity* if they relate to scores on other ways of assessing the same behavior or construct. They have *discriminant validity* if they do *not* relate to measures from which theory would require them to be independent. They have *discriminative validity* if they produce expected mean differences between groups, and so on.

Criterion-related validity refers to the extent to which scores can be used for their intended purposes. Scores on a measure have criterion-related validity if they allow prediction of scores on other measures (i.e., criteria), usually of a practical variety. If scores on the criterion are available at the same time as scores we are validating, we refer to *concurrent validity*. If they have to be obtained some time in the future, we refer to *predictive validity*.

Which of these types of validity will be necessary for the scores on your measures? Why are these particularly appropriate? Perhaps your study is designed to provide just this information. If so, what type will it be addressing and why?

The types of validity you need to show depend, as with reliability, on the nature of your subject matter, your population, the specific scores you intend to use, and the research questions you are pursuing. If you are studying a psychological construct (e.g., hostility, anxiety, altruism, or chauvinism), you will need evidence of content and construct validity, at a minimum. For example, if your study deals with altruism, it will examine relationships between altruism and some other variables. What is the source of these anticipated relationships? The correct answer is someone's theory concerning altruism. To test the relationships properly will require using a measure of altruism that meaningfully taps the construct as it is understood in the relevant theoretical writings. This meaningfulness resides in the research literature dealing with the measure's construct validity (cf. Grusec, 1991).

If your subject matter is behavior, especially as studied from a natural science perspective, you may not be especially concerned with construct validity in the sense just described. Instead, you will be more likely to focus on the content of the measure. You will want to be satisfied that it contains stimuli likely to set the occasion for samples of behavior that are representative of larger populations of that behavior that are not feasible for you to study directly. Moreover, you will want to know the extent to which the behavior produced by the instrument is representative of what you might expect to see at another time or place. We discussed how well data generalize to other assessment occasions as temporal stability. How well data might represent what can be expected in other contexts deals with their generalizability across settings (Cone, 1978). For example, if you observe positive verbal interchanges between spouses in the laboratory, are they representative of what you might have seen had you observed them at home?

As with reliability, it will not be enough to state in your method section that your measure is valid. Instead, describe what forms of validity are important for your purposes and then provide evidence that they exist for your particular scores. You will most certainly do this if your research involves a validity study itself. This is because to make the case for doing the research you will have provided an extensive review of the measurement literature relevant to the device you plan to use. Any study needs this scrutiny. You always need to know whether a measure assesses the variable of interest and whether it does so consistently for populations like the one you intend to study. In the absence of this vital information, research findings are extremely hard to interpret.

You will find information about the psychometric properties of scores produced by a measure in four places: (a) manuals describing the measure, (b) chapters or review papers evaluating the measure, (c) papers specifically evaluating the psychometric properties of the measure, and (d) papers using the measure. Be aware that the last of these might not mention in the abstract or introduction that psychometric data are presented. Because this is not the primary focus of the study, these data are likely to be hiding in the method section. In addition, some studies that do not even mention psychometric issues might provide findings relevant to the validity issue. For example, repeated findings that self-report measures of anxiety and depression correlate highly cast doubt on the discriminant validity of scores on these measures, at least as scores presumably tapping distinct affective domains. These findings have contributed to theoretical reconceptualizations of these constructs (see Barlow, 2002; Barlow, Allen, & Choate, 2004).

Look Broadly for Decent Measures

We have described the basic assessment methods you can use to operationalize the variables in your research. We have also discussed important characteristics good instruments will have. Where do you look for such instruments? If you are working in an active research area, you will probably use measures that are common to it. If you are braving new frontiers, it might not be clear from the existing literature just what the best measures would be.

Several published compendia provide valuable information about assessment instruments. The best known of these is the *Mental Measurements Yearbook* (Plake, Impara, & Spies, 2003). Published by the University of Nebraska Press, this volume reviews hundreds of tests of various types. Now in its 15th edition, the *Yearbook* has been around since 1938 when Oscar K. Buros initiated it. Many researchers refer to the collection simply as *Buros*. In addition to descriptions of the measures, the more than 500 reviewers in *Buros* provide commentary on their psychometric adequacy.

A related source of information about potential measures is *Tests in Print VI* (Murphy, Plake, Impara, & Spies, 2002). Unlike *Buros, Tests in Print* does not provide actual reviews of the instruments, although it refers readers to reviews in the *Mental Measurements Yearbook*. It does include listings of all commercially available tests, however, and is a good source for locating addresses and journal articles relevant to a particular measure. In addition, it includes information about a test's purpose, individuals for whom it is appropriate, and administration times.

If you are planning to use a more behaviorally focused measure, Hersen and Bellack's *Dictionary of Behavioral Assessment Techniques* (Hersen & Bellack, 1988) can help. Although a bit dated, this volume provides descriptions and reviews of 286 devices and is a good source of introductory information about a measure. More than 200 researchers provide reviews and references to writings in which the original instrument can be found. The measures themselves are not presented in this or in any of the sources we describe. Do not be put off by reference to *behavioral* in the book's title. It includes many instruments that are indistinguishable from traditional, trait-oriented forms of assessment long familiar to personality and clinical psychologists everywhere.

Sweetland and Keyser published an extensive collection of references to tests in 1983 (Sweetland & Keyser, 1983), repeating this publication for a total of 10 volumes between 1983 and 1994. They indexed and provided descriptive information on more than 3,500 instruments. The measures are divided into those relevant to business, education, and psychology. The series can be a good source for identifying promising instruments and consulting the references associated with each to find out more about them. The volumes provide much information on reliability, validity, and norming procedures.

Sweetland and Keyser (1997) also provided a brief reference to commercially available tests organized by subject. More than 700 tests are included. Each entry describes the purpose of a test, enough information to permit evaluating the test's appropriateness, cost, availability, and publisher. If you are working with a clinical population or variables common thereto, the *Handbook for Psychiatric Rating Scales* (Research and Education Association, 1981) might be worth consulting. This volume provides reliability and validity information for each of the rating scales included, along with descriptions of the scales, the types of client for whom the scale would be relevant, and references to consult for further details. Additional books to consult for information about specific measures include those by Fischer and Corcoran (2000a, 2000b) and Robinson, Shaver, and Wrightsman (1991). Antony, Orsillo, and Roemer (2001) is a good source for measures on anxiety, and Nezu, Ronan, Meadows, and McClure (2000) provide a description of numerous measures of depression for which there is some empirical support. If your research involves children's behavior at school, Kelley, Reitman, and Noell (2002) can be helpful. An excellent source of information available online can be found at the Buros Center for Testing's Web site (http://www.unl.edu/buros). Here you can examine an extensive amount of information on tests. *Test Reviews Online* provides the monthly updates and reviews appearing in the *Mental Measurements Yearbook* series for a fee. Users may download reviews and descriptive details of more than 2,000 tests. Note, however, that the *Mental Measurements Yearbook* database is available on CD at many academic libraries. It contains the text of the most recent *Mental Measurements Yearbooks*, and is updated every 6 months.

A particularly good source if you are doing research in behavioral medicine is the Health and Psychosocial Instruments (HaPI™) database. HaPI™ provides information on unpublished instruments, includes more than 8,000 measures, and is updated quarterly. HaPI™ is now distributed on CDs and is available to libraries and others who subscribe to the service. Most of the measures are relevant to behavioral medicine and assess such variables as pain, quality of life, and medication efficacy. HaPI™ also covers measures used in medically related disciplines such as psychology, social work, occupational therapy, physical therapy, and speech and language therapy. Finally, it provides a bibliography of instruments that one can order through the Behavioral Measurement Database Service (BMDS) Instrument Delivery service.

Another good source of information on tests that are not commercially available is the Educational Testing Service (ETS) database. The ETS test collection is said to be the largest in the world, including a library of 20,000 tests and other measurement instruments developed from the early 1900s to the present.

Finally, if none of these sources proves helpful, you can always fall back on PsycINFO. Searching its databases using terms describing your variables or synonyms thereof will at least put you in touch with relevant research. If you are lucky, some of the references will provide psychometrically sound ways of measuring the variables. Before doing this, though, there is one last resource you might examine. Goldman and Mitchell (2003) published a directory that includes unpublished, not commercially available measures that have appeared in approximately three dozen good journals. You might find a measure here with enough initial psychometric information to warrant use in your study, and there is likely to be no charge to use it.

Know What to Do If Vital Psychometric Information Is Unavailable

Suppose you have selected your measure and searched high and low for evidence to support its psychometric adequacy with your population. You have not found any. Suppose also that no alternative measures exist that you can use. What do you do? If you have understood the material presented earlier, you know the types of psychometric characteristics your measure needs to show. Let's look at some of the more important of these and see how you might proceed if they are lacking.

Scorer Reliability

A reliably scored instrument is essential to any research. Even if the literature shows that your measure *can* be scored reliably, you will want to provide evidence that it *has* been in your particular study. We mentioned this point earlier and repeat it here for emphasis. If you are using a self-report method, have a second person independently score some portion, say 25%, of the answer sheets. If the two sets of scores disagree, identify the problem and correct it. If you are using structured interviews, record them all, if possible, and have independent coders score the tapes themselves or their transcripts. As mentioned in chapter 7, at least 20% should be double-scored. If the 20% to 25% you check show problems, intervene. Maybe the two coders have different definitions of the categories you are using. Maybe one or both have just gotten careless. Retraining or increased incentives for accuracy might be needed, and everything coded thus far (not just the reliability data) should be rescored after intervention.

If you are using ratings by others, compare the ratings of two independent raters on 20% to 25% of the same participants. You might do this with a simple correlation, although more precise information will be provided by a percentage agreement measure of some type. For example, you might define an agreement on each rating-scale item as both raters marking the same point on the scale. Or you might be more liberal and require only that they be within one scale point of each other. Count the number of agreements and divide by the total number of ratings to obtain percentage agreement. Even better is a kappa coefficient that corrects for chance agreement (von Eye & Mun, 2005). Use a level of precision in your reliability checking that is at least as precise as the scores you will use in your analyses. For example, if you are using total scores on a "social cues awareness" measure to assign participants to groups, it is important to show independent scorers produce comparable total scores. They may not agree at the individual item level, but their scores should lead to the same assignments.

If you are using a direct-observation coding system, consider supplementing it with video- or audiotape recording to produce permanent records of the participants' behavior. Multiple observers working independently can code these, and you can compare their data. Again, some percentage of the observations should be selected randomly and agreement calculations performed. If video- or audiotape recordings cannot be made, it is best to use independent observers working in pairs, continuously checking their agreement. Train a cadre of observers to be available at any time so that the same observers are not always working together. This will prevent consensual drift by the observer pair in their definitions of the behavior. If you cannot take such seemingly elaborate precautions, you can use a single observer, periodically checking this person with a second observer. This is not the ideal arrangement, however, as the primary observer's behavior is often affected by the presence or absence of the "checker" observer (Romanczyk et al., 1973). If you go this route, train observers to high levels of agreement so that even if they observe better when assessed for agreement than when alone, they are good enough that you can tolerate some slippage.

Just because you obtain your data from some archival source (e.g., patient files in a hospital or records from a county courthouse) do not assume you can ignore scorer reliability. You might think it is a routine matter to determine chronicity of schizophrenia by subtracting a person's date of first hospitalization from the current date. The file might have different dates of initial hospitalization depending on where you look in it, however. Further, you or your assistants may not reliably perform the simple tasks of recording such a date or subtracting one date from another. Always check such steps in the production of data for accuracy. A key element in ensuring that your data are scored reliably lies in rater and observer training. Get lots of practice stimuli (e.g., pilot data) that are similar to what you expect your "real" participants will provide. Work the bugs out on this material before letting your raters or observers loose on your precious research data. Ensure that your judges, working independently, show good agreement on practice material before you give them real data to score. It is wise to overtrain them so their agreement is 10% to 15% higher than the lowest you would accept in your study, because agreement frequently drops when raters and observers begin collecting "real" data (Romanczyk et al., 1973).

Temporal Stability

You can take several steps if data on the temporal stability of scores on your measure are not known yet are required by your particular research question. One would be to perform repeat administrations of the measure over the appropriate interval of time before beginning your actual study. Then correlate the scores of your group of participants between the two assessment occasions. In other words, establish the temporal stability of the scores yourself. Alternatively, you could design your study to control for the possible effects of score changes associated merely with the passage of time. For example, you could include an untreated, assessment-only control group. Or you might use a more sophisticated design that would include such a group and others (e.g., Solomon four-group). Another possibility would involve repeated assessment of your participants over time before and after the introduction of your independent variable. In this within-participants approach, each participant serves as his or her own control for changes in scores associated merely with practice or the passage of time. Note that this approach tells you whether there are absolute score changes over time for one or a group of participants assessed repeatedly. As we discussed earlier in this chapter, mean changes can occur even though stability is high when assessed with correlational analyses.

Item Reliability

Internal consistency estimates are among the easiest characteristics to establish for new instruments, so your particular choice is likely to have this important information. If not, you can usually calculate it yourself from existing normative data (e.g., in a test manual). Use Kuder–Richardson Formula 21 (Kaplan & Saccuzzo, 2005; Nunnally & Bernstein, 1994) to do this. If you expect high internal consistency for the measure of your construct but the internal consistency of the scale is low, you have a problem. If you go ahead and use the scale anyway, you will have some difficulty interpreting your data. This is because an instrument with low internal consistency measures multiple things. Two identical scores that are based on responses to different items in the scale will mean different things.

You cannot protect yourself by running the study and then computing internal consistency estimates. Suppose they are low? It will be too late to modify the measure to improve matters, and you might not want to do this anyway. To improve internal consistency, you would have to organize elements of the instrument in new ways, fundamentally altering the structure of the instrument and rendering available norms and validity information inapplicable. If data concerning internal consistency are unavailable at the outset and you want to proceed with your chosen measure, use a sample of participants large enough to permit you to factor-analyze the scale after the fact. You can then develop scores for your participants on each of the emerging factors. The factors that are most conceptually consistent with your theoretical and practical understanding of your constructs would then be used as your dependent variables. Of course, there would be no norms or validity information for these newly developed scales. Moreover, a reasonable factor analysis requires a good-sized sample, as mentioned in chapter 7. Depending on the number of items in your scale, this could mean 100 participants at a minimum, double that if you want to replicate your factor structure. Of course, this number increases if your analysis involves more items or measures. A better solution may be to collect pilot data on a lesser number of participants and check out your internal consistency before you begin.

This discussion applies largely to the use of self-report ratings and informant ratings methods, but it is applicable to all assessment methods, at least on a conceptual level. Space does not permit us to wander into this interesting arena in any detail. Homogeneity of an assessment instrument can be important regardless of method and of whether your subject matter is a psychological construct or an actual behavior itself. For example, imagine you are performing direct observations of the predatory behavior of free-ranging tarantulas. You will be assuming the several specific responses you code are all members of the same predatory behavior class. If some deal with nesting, some with foraging, and some with reproduction, how will a single score be meaningful? How will you show this?

Convergent and Discriminant Validity

We mentioned convergent and discriminant validity earlier, but did not discuss them in detail. These are especially relevant when one uses self-report measures to tap psychological constructs. This is because new self-report measures often lack discriminant validity. That is, they correlate substantially with already existing measures of pervasive individual difference variables. Some of these pervasive variables include intelligence, socioeconomic status, years of education, and the tendency to say socially desirable things about one's self. Purveyors of new measures must show that they are not simply additional ways of measuring these variables (Campbell, 1960). Because of the pervasiveness of social desirability response sets, for example, new self-report measures must be shown to be independent of social desirability (Edwards, 1970). There are already plenty of good measures of social desirability in the literature, and we do not need another one. Make sure your scale has been correlated with social desirability and shown to be unrelated or at least to have only a modest relationship. In doing this, be alert to the fact that different ways of assessing social desirability (e.g., Crowne & Marlowe, 1960; Edwards, 1957; Wiggins, 1959) are not interchangeable (Edwards, 1990; Helmes & Holden, 2003). Indeed, Paulhus (2002) suggested that three distinct processes can contribute to distorted self-presentation: impression management, self-deception by enhancing one's positive qualities, and self-deception by denying negative qualities. Each of these has different correlates with measures of personality (Paulhus, 2002). Be aware that the Edwards version of this variable has been the most pervasive in self-report assessment. Thus, be sure your measure is at least independent of this type of social desirability. There may be other response sets (e.g., need for approval; Crowne & Marlowe, 1960) with which you want to compare your measure, but the most pervasive is social desirability.

If your instrument has not been shown to be independent of social desirability, you should address this in your research. The first way to do this is to reduce demand characteristics that may increase the likelihood of at least some kinds of biased self-presentation (e.g., make responding anonymous; see Paulhus, 1991, for additional suggestions). Another would be to include a measure of social desirability along with your other measures and compute the correlation between them yourself. Be sure to determine which form(s) of social desirability are most problematic. If the correlation is nonsignificant, social desirability can be eliminated from the interpretation of your results. If there is a correlation, however, you first want to consider what degree of relationship between social desirability and your measure you would expect based on previous literature and theory. For example, depressed individuals are known to distort information in a negative direction (Beck, Rush, Shaw, & Emery, 1979), and therefore a negative correlation between self-reports of depression and social desirability might be expected and even tolerated. Of course, a high correlation would make your measure suspect. If one or more forms of social desirability are not supposed to correlate with your measure, you may want to control for the effects of social desirability statistically, using partial correlation or ANCOVA procedures. You might also consider filtering out those participants with social desirability scores that are high enough to make the rest of their data suspect.

Convergent validity is also important. Campbell and Fiske (1959) articulated the requirement for convergence across measures many years ago. Noting that scores on any instrument are, in part, a function of the characteristics of the instrument itself, these authors suggested using multitrait–multimethod matrixes to sort out this method variance, establishing both convergent and discriminant validity in the process. The importance of convergent validity for measures of constructs cannot be emphasized enough. The structure of our language builds in relationships between concepts automatically. When we use language-based assessment instruments, constructs will likely relate to one another at least partially because of this structure. The validity evidence for a given measure should involve more than correlations resulting from the fortuitous use of common assessment methods. If there really is a construct underlying the scores on a given instrument, logic requires it to be assessable in more than one way. The reason for this is that, if a single measure completely operationalizes a concept, the concept is no longer hypothetical. Because being hypothetical is a cardinal characteristic of psychological traits, without it, one is not dealing with a trait. This is the basis for saying that relationships between assessment alternatives establish the convergent validity of the alternatives and extend the construct validity of the underlying psychological variable at the same time.

If convergent validity has not been established for your scores or with your population, you will have to address this in your own research. The simplest way to do this would be to provide alternative ways of assessing your variables and compare these after you collect the data. If different methods correlate, you can use them interchangeably or in some combination in your data analyses. If they do not, you may have to treat the data from each separately, leading to some interesting material for your discussion section.

By alternative assessment methods, we are not referring to a second self-report measure, a second informant rating, and so on. Self-report data should be supplemented with informant ratings or direct observation data, for example. Sometimes collateral data sources can be used effectively. If, for example, self-reports of drinking are one of your measures, you might compare these with reports from informants such as a spouse or roommate or friend. Or you might use unobtrusive measures such as the number of empty beer cans or liquor bottles in the trash (Webb, Campbell, Schwartz, & Sechrest, 1966). Some behaviors have direct products or traces that can be used for corroboration. Self-reported homework completions or time spent working on one's thesis or dissertation are obvious examples. Look at problems completed correctly or pages written to support the verbal measure.

Generalizability Across Settings

If you are assessing a person's performance, you will be especially concerned about whether data collected with your anticipated measure in one situation can safely be generalized to others. Most likely, you will have to examine this issue yourself. Alternatively, you could rely on one of the researchers' most used caveats that goes something like, "caution should be exercised in interpreting these results because it is not known whether participants would have performed similarly in their homes (classrooms, neighborhood, etc.)." If your study is an applied one, you are probably conducting it in the setting of eventual interest anyway, and setting generalizability is a moot issue. If you are dealing with psychological constructs, their cross-setting generality is often assumed and rarely tested. This is an issue worth pondering, especially if you are concerned with the ecological validity of your research.

Adapt Others' Measures With Caution

What if you wish to adapt others' measures for your own purpose? For example, you may have found a wonderful scale for assessing assertiveness and wish to alter it for use with individuals diagnosed with multiple personality disorder by asking the person to fill it out with reference to each personality. This, of course, means altering the instructions and focus of the instrument.

Will its original psychometric properties still be relevant? You cannot be sure. Logically, the less you change an instrument, the more you should be able to assume that its properties would stay the same. For example, administering only certain Minnesota Multiphasic Personality Inventory—2 (MMPI–2) subscales could reasonably be expected to yield subscale scores that would be the same as subscale scores derived from the same items embedded in the full MMPI–2. However, you cannot be sure unless you gather some data to assess whether this is so. One way to do this would be to conduct a pilot study. Scores on the shortened versus full MMPI–2 could be correlated (as when assessing alternate-form reliability). And, as indicated previously, additional measures that would help you assess the validity of the altered instrument could be built directly into your research project itself.

Avoid Common Errors in Evaluating and Selecting Measures

Several common errors pervade descriptions of measuring devices. Avoid these. First, do not assume that the name of an instrument captures what it measures. Many fledgling and even some experienced researchers fall into the trap of assuming the name of a measure indicates what it assesses. This is not necessarily the case. Examine the content of the measure carefully: It may be misnamed, at least as you understand the construct being assessed. This is an error in logic known in psychology as the *jingle fallacy* (Kelley, 1927).

To assume that a name mirrors a measure's content is a particular problem with questionnaires that have subscales derived using factor analysis. Putting it simply, a factor analysis looks at the data, sorts out what is most closely associated with what, and shows the investigator what these relationships are mathematically. The investigator determines which items hang together closely enough to be considered a factor. Item content has nothing to do with the mathematics of factor analysis. What this means is that items that load on the same factor may (or may not) tap widely different content. The investigator then must inductively figure out a name that seems to fit the items. Unless the creator of the measure has used confirmatory factor analysis to test whether a group of conceptually related items hang together, the name is the researcher's a posteriori creation. Do not assume that it reflects scale content faithfully, or that the scale captures the construct adequately.

In addition, do not assume that a significant correlation is a high correlation. Many consumers of psychometric literature make this mistake. A significant correlation between two measures of the same construct may or may not support the validity of the measure being investigated. The magnitude of the correlation, not its statistical significance, is important. A self-report measure of work productivity and a mechanized assessment of the same variable may correlate .20 and be significant at $p < .05$, but the measures have only 4% of their variance in common. Does this really indicate that you can substitute one for the other?

Also, do not assume that a self-report measure assesses behavior because it correlates with other self-report measures. As we indicated earlier, Campbell and Fiske (1959) long ago pointed out the fallacy in assuming that correlations between measures that used the same method to assess the same construct "proved" the validity of a new measure. Method variance (i.e., the tendency for some of the variation in scores on measures to be a result of the measuring instrument itself) could explain the results. When two self-report measures involve the same method, their scores may be related because of this shared approach to assessment. The true test of an indirect measure of behavior (e.g., self-report) is whether it correlates with a more direct assessment of the same phenomenon. In general, correlations between different ways of assessing the same thing should exceed those between different things assessed with the same method.

Finally, do not use single-item measures. Single-item measures of any construct or behavior are notoriously unreliable. Nonetheless, beginning researchers often persist in assuming that a participant's answer to a question such as, "Were either of your parents alcoholics?" is a good way to classify the individual as one who grew up in an alcoholic family. This is a particular problem when measuring participants' characteristics, either to describe them or to classify them (e.g., as an independent variable). Similarly, designers of new questionnaires often want to interpret their instruments by looking at individual item responses. Unless you can show that individual items are reliable and valid, do not do this.

Get Copies of Instruments

To examine the content of an instrument you are considering using, you need to obtain a copy of the measure. This often turns out to be surprisingly difficult. Journal articles rarely publish copies of measures, and although some are available from commercial publishers, many are not.

To obtain a copy of a measure that interests you and that is not commercially available, contact the creator of the instrument and request one. Make sure to find out the person's current address. Professional directories such as the *American Psychological Association Membership Register* and member listings of other professional organizations (e.g., Society for Research in Child Development and American Psychological Society) are updated regularly and should help you locate the individual. Often the easiest way to find someone quickly is merely to Google him or her. When you find the person, inquire whether the instrument is copyrighted. If so, you must obtain permission in writing to use the measure.

If you cannot find the author, if the author fails to respond to your request, or if you just want to hedge your bets, find someone else who has used the measure in published research. This person must have found a copy of the measure, right? Ask your chairperson, too, about colleagues who might use the instrument. Then track down the user and ask for a copy. Use your advisor's name (with permission) to enhance the chances that the person will respond to your request. Remember, though, that if you are having this much trouble locating a copy of the instrument, it is likely to be relatively unknown. This can mean it there is little information about the critical psychometric characteristics we have discussed in this chapter.

Supplemental Resources

General Measurement Textbooks and Articles

Anastasi, A., & Urbina, S. (1997). *Psychological testing* (7th ed.). Upper Saddle River, NJ: Prentice Hall.

Butcher, J. N., Graham, J. R., Haynes, S. N., & Nelson, L. D. (Eds.). (1995). Special issue: Methodological issues in psychological assessment research. *Psychological Assessment, 7,* 227–413.

Campbell, D. T., & Fiske, D. (1959). Convergent and discriminant validation by the multitrait–multimethod matrix. *Psychological Bulletin, 56,* 81–105.

Cronbach, L. J. (1990). *Essentials of psychological testing* (5th ed.). New York: HarperCollins.

Kaplan, R. M., & Saccuzzo, D. P. (2005). *Psychological testing: Principles, applications, and issues* (6th ed.). Belmont, CA: Wadsworth.

Nunnally, N. C., & Bernstein, I. H. (1994). *Psychometric theory* (3rd ed.). New York: McGraw-Hill.

Thompson, B. (Ed.). (2003). *Score reliability: Contemporary thinking on reliability issues.* Thousand Oaks, CA: Sage.

Questionnaire Methods (Self-Report, Ratings by Others)

DeVellis, R. F. (2003). *Scale development: Theories and applications* (2nd ed.). Thousand Oaks, CA: Sage.

Edwards, A. L. (1970). *The measurement of traits by scales and inventories.* New York: Holt, Rinehart & Winston.

Fink, A. (2002). *The survey handbook* (2nd ed.). Thousand Oaks, CA: Sage.

Paulhus, D. L. (1991). Measurement and control of response bias. In J. P. Robinson, P. Shaver, & L. S. Wrightsman (Eds.), *Measures of personality and social psychological attitudes* (pp. 17–59). San Diego, CA: Academic Press.

Schwarz, N., & Oyserman, D. (2001). Asking questions about behavior: Cognition, communication, and questionnaire construction. *American Journal of Evaluation, 22,* 127–160.

Stone, A. A., Turkan, J. S., Bachrach, C. A., Jobe, J. B., Kurtzman, H. S., & Cain, V. S. (Eds.). (2000). *The science of self-report: Implications for research and practice.* Mahwah, NJ: Erlbaum.

Direct Observation

Bakeman, R., & Gottman, J. M. (1986). *Observing interaction: An introduction to sequential analysis.* Cambridge, England: Cambridge University Press.

Cone, J. D. (1999). Observational assessment: Measure development and research issues. In P. C. Kendall, J. N. Butcher, & G. N. Holmbeck (Eds.), *Handbook of research methods in clinical psychology* (2nd ed., pp. 183–223). New York: Wiley.

Suen, H. K., & Ary, D. (1989). *Analyzing quantitative behavioral observation data.* Hillsdale, NJ: Erlbaum.

von Eye, A., & Mun, E. Y. (2005). *Analyzing rater agreement: Manifest variable methods.* Mahwah, NJ: Erlbaum.

Unobtrusive Measures

Webb, E. J., Campbell, D. T., Schwartz, R. D., & Sechrest, L. (1966). *Unobtrusive measures: Nonreactive research in the social sciences.* Chicago: Rand McNally.

Self-Observation

Christensen, T. C., Barrett, L. F., Bliss-Moreau, E., Lebo, K., & Kaschub, C. (2003). A practical guide to experience-sampling procedures. *Journal of Happiness Studies, 4,* 53–78.

Cone, J. D. (Ed.). (1999). Special section: Clinical assessment applications of self-monitoring. *Psychological Assessment, 11,* 411–498.

Foster, S. L., Laverty-Finch, C., Gizzo, D., & Osantowski, J. (1999). Practical issues in self-observation. *Psychological Assessment, 11,* 426–438.

Stone, A. A., Kessler, R. C., & Haythornthwaite, J. A. (1991). Measuring daily events and experiences: Decisions for the researcher. *Journal of Personality, 59,* 575–607.

✔ To Do . . .

Selecting the Appropriate Measures

☐ Operationalize your variables

☐ Evaluate the reliability of prospective instruments for

—Interrater reliability (scorer reliability)

—Test–retest reliability (temporal stability)

—Alternate form reliability

—Internal consistency (item reliability)

—Determine which forms of reliability are most appropriate for your study

☐ Evaluate the validity of prospective instruments for

—Face validity

—Content validity

—Criterion-related validity

• Concurrent validity

• Predictive validity

—Construct validity

• Convergent validity

• Discriminant validity

• Discriminative validity

—Determine which forms of validity are most appropriate for your study

☐ Look broadly for decent measures

—Use measurement compendiums

—Use computer-based databases

—Use the published literature

☐ Plan what to do if vital psychometric information is unavailable

—Scorer reliability (interrater reliability)

—Temporal stability

—Item reliability (internal consistency)

—Convergent and discriminant validity

—Generalizability across settings

☐ Adapt others' measures with caution

☐ Get copies of measures

9

Selecting the Appropriate Statistics

Nothing strikes terror into the heart of many beginning researchers like the word *statistics*. Even students who breezed through required graduate statistics courses in rigorous training programs sometimes claim total ignorance of all things numerical when asked to select suitable statistics for their own research.

Why is it that even the best students sometimes have difficulty with this topic? Methods typically used to teach statistics are part of the problem. Statistics teachers often take one of two approaches: (a) mathematical or (b) cookbook. The mathematical tradition teaches derivations of formulas and the conceptual underpinnings of statistical analyses. The cookbook tradition teaches how to do statistical calculations. In our experience, neither addresses the important issue of matching statistics to the research question being asked and the hypotheses being tested—a topic on the cusp of traditional research design and statistics courses. Another part of the problem is "mathematics anxiety," a repertoire fostered by early disparagement of one's math ability or failure experiences in mathematics classes (many of which may have resulted from poor teaching and not poor student skill). Math anxiety, in turn, can lead students to avoid opportunities to use numbers and thus miss the chance to develop self-confidence in this area. Avoidance and a resulting lack of practice lead students to depend on others to select statistics for their projects. As a result, they never learn to become independent in this area.

This chapter helps nervous students sort out which statistics are most suitable for their research designs. We strongly recommend that you read this chapter and follow its suggestions *before* you complete your dissertation proposal instead of putting off the dreaded statistics questions until after you collect your data. That is why we place this chapter *before* the chapter on collecting the data, rather than after it. We have been faced too often with the unpleasant task of advising students who have already collected data that they have statistical nightmares on their hands because they did not think about their statistics when they selected their measures and designed their study.

We assume that you would like to avoid this unfortunate situation. We also assume you have taken the usual statistics courses and are familiar with at least the names of different statistics and their general uses. Thus, in this chapter, we do not go into how to calculate, derive, or program particular analyses. Moreover, we cover mainly statistics designed to examine (a) differences between two or more discrete groups of individuals and (b) relationships between variables within a single group of individuals. For most of the strategies we discuss, we assume that your study involves independent (or predictor) and dependent (or criterion) variables that you are able to identify. The chapter ends with a brief discussion of model-testing analyses. Model-testing statistics may be appropriate if your study explores the underlying structure of a set of variables or examines a set of relationships among variables considered simultaneously.

We do not cover every one of the hundreds of statistical tests available. Noticeably unmentioned are specialized approaches used in subdisciplines. Among the more common procedures we omit are sequential analysis and other time-series procedures, meta-analytic techniques and specific statistics for calculating effect sizes, complex longitudinal analyses (e.g., hierarchical linear modeling), multilevel modeling, and survival analysis. Nor do we cover all the controversies involved in using particular statistics. Instead, we survey widely used statistics and their potential role in your analytical plan. To the statistical sophisticate, our coverage will likely seem too simple. To the less experienced, it may seem extremely complex.

Our goal in this chapter is to help you get some idea of potentially suitable statistics for your research. Once you select what might be right for your study, you will need to supplement the material to make sure you understand the statistics you have selected and to ensure that they are the most appropriate for the analyses you have to perform. How can you prepare to deal with the statistical analyses you will be conducting?

Beef Up Your Statistical Knowledge Early

If you are at an early stage in your graduate career, get involved in research and volunteer to take some responsibility for data analyses. Then work closely with the faculty member or research director. Ask questions about why particular analyses are more suitable than others. Taking responsibility for handling the statistics of a study will also force you to learn about parameters and options relevant to the statistics you use. It will also have the related practical benefit of starting your systematic desensitization treatment for statistics anxiety!

Another step to take is to start looking for statistics books that speak your language. Dozens of books cover every conceivable statistical topic. In addition, many professors put descriptions of statistical methods online for students to use. Books and Web site information vary in complexity, focus, balance between mathematical and explanatory material, depth of coverage, and (sometimes) terminology and symbol systems. As a consequence, different material will be more or less user-friendly to you. Your task is to find information that is understandable to you. Throughout this chapter, we refer to statistics books that we find useful. We also provide suggestions for additional resources at the end of this chapter. In addition, some manuals for major computer programs provide good statistical information. The key is finding resources that explain what you need in ways that you understand. Even the two of us disagree sometimes on the statistics books we find most comprehensible!

Examine Your Study First: Create an Analysis Plan

As a first step in choosing suitable statistics, identify the purposes you want your analyses to serve. Initially, you should specify clearly the various questions you want your statistics to answer. The logical place to start is with your research questions and hypotheses. You need to go beyond this, however, because you will probably use statistics for more than just testing your hypotheses. For example, you may wish to examine the relationships among various dependent variables or to check that your three experimental groups do not differ in demographic characteristics. In the section that follows, we itemize a series of steps for figuring out what kind of analyses may meet your needs. We suggest that you proceed through the steps listed for *each* analysis you plan.

After you make a list of the questions or objectives you wish your analyses to address, make a list of each and every variable you plan to analyze to answer each research question and test each hypothesis you've listed. For example, if your question is, "What are the demographic characteristics of my sample?" list each piece of demographic data you plan to examine. Next determine how you will score your measures to get a number for each participant on each variable. Do the same thing for your dependent and independent variables. You should wind up with a list of questions. Under each question will be a list of scores that will be involved in the analysis.

Note that we said "scores" not "measures." It is not enough to say "MMPI–2," for example. The Minnesota Multiphasic Personality Inventory—2 produces dozens of scores. Surely, you won't look at each and every one, so list the specific scores you plan to analyze.

Don't be surprised if you get confused. Confusion can be a signal that you need to clarify how each measure will generate numerical data. If so, pull out a copy of each instrument, make up mock data for a few participants, score the data, and examine the results. How many scores does each instrument produce? Which will you use in your analyses to address your hypotheses and research questions? Add these to your list of variables. At the end of this process, you should have one list of questions you intend to answer with statistics and a second list of variables that those statistics will use in one way or another.

We like to separate analysis plans into a preliminary analyses section and a hypothesis-testing analyses section. *Preliminary analyses* are those analyses you will do to (a) examine the characteristics of your data; (b) examine the properties of your measures (e.g., reliability, validity); (c) check for potential confounding variables; and (d) test the assumptions of the statistics you plan to use for testing your hypotheses. *Hypothesis-testing analyses* use statistics that will allow you to examine whether your data support your predictions. For the moment, just list the questions/hypotheses you wish to examine, along with the specific variables you will use for each. Later, you can fill in the name of the specific analysis you will use to answer the question or test the hypothesis. Exhibit 9.1 shows portions of an analysis plan Colette Lord (2005) developed for her dissertation study on the relationship between indirect aggression and perceptions of social support in the elderly.

Next, choose one of the questions you intend to answer with statistics. Indicate the specific independent and dependent variables (scores) involved in answering this question. For example, if your question is, "Do attention-deficit hyperactivity disorder (ADHD) and non-ADHD boys and girls differ in their recall of social material?" you would list diagnosis (ADHD vs. non-ADHD) and gender (scored as boy or girl) as the independent variables and the recall score as the dependent variable. Then ask yourself (a) will this question be answered by comparing scores for groups of participants? or (b) will it be answered by relating scores on the different variables to one another in a single group of participants? With the example just given, the answer would be yes to the first question: You want to compare boys and girls, ADHD and non-ADHD groups, and so on. This will require some sort of statistic that compares the scores the different groups obtain. Statistics that compare groups are typical of between-groups, within-groups, and mixed experimental and quasi-experimental designs. A group comparison statistic can be appropriate if you are comparing either (a) the scores of different discrete groups of individuals (e.g., males vs. females) or (b) the scores of the same group of individuals but taken at different points in time (e.g., pre- vs. posttreatment) or under different conditions.

Designs that require group comparison statistics use independent variables that the researcher defines in ways that require participants to fit into discrete groups. Each group is called a *level* and has a name. In our example, gender has two levels (boy and girl), because you want your analyses to consider boys and girls separately and to compare them. Diagnosis also has two levels (ADHD and non-ADHD). If the researcher had not been interested in gender differences, gender would not have been an independent variable and the researcher might not have examined gender differences in the analyses.

If you want to treat your participants as a single group and examine associations among scores, a correlational design might be most appropriate. This would be the case, for example, if the research question asked, "What is the relationship of health beliefs (assessed by a single score on a multi-item questionnaire), social support (assessed by a single score on a multi-item questionnaire), and adherence to a medication regimen (assessed by the average of periodic blood-level assay values)?" This research question treats all participants as a single group. They are not sorted into separate discrete groups (levels). Participants' scores on social support and

Exhibit 9.1

Sample Dissertation Analysis Plan: Indirect Aggression and Social Support Among Elderly Retirement Community Residents

PRELIMINARY ANALYSES:

1. Deal with missing data
   —use means to replace missing item values in self-report questionnaires
   —look for patterns if there are large amounts of missing data
2. Examine distributions of scores/data screening
   —look at the range, minimum and maximum scores for all scores to be used
   —if anything looks out of whack investigate for potential errors in data entry
   —identify non normal distributions of variables
   —identify potential outliers
3. Examine reliabilities of all scores to be used in analyses
   —obtain alphas for indirect and direct aggression scores for measures
   —eliminate items that reduce reliability of scales, rerun reliability analyses
      —continue to do this until the reliabilities of the scale are satisfactory
   —change scale formation syntax to reflect these changes
   —obtain alphas for all social support total scores and subscale scores
4. Examine potential covariates/control variables
   —run ANOVAs with all aggression and support subscales as dependent variables; independent variables: gender (2 levels), marital status (2 levels), retirement community membership (6 levels), dining room use (2 levels), romantic relationship (2 levels), contact with kids (2 levels), living alone (2 levels), living in a detached home (2 levels)
   —look at bivariate correlations of all aggression and social support subscales with: years of education, age, months living in retirement community, current and prior income, number of people who did not know the participant well enough to rate on peer nomination instrument

HYPOTHESIS TESTING:

Hypothesis 1: Convergent and discriminant validity of the measures of aggression.
   —look at pattern of bivariate correlations of subscales of aggression measures across methods

Hypothesis 2: Self and peer reports of indirect aggression use will predict overall perceptions of available emotional support and emotional support available from the retirement community.

continued

Exhibit 9.1, continued

—hierarchical multiple regression—dependent variable/criterion variable: Social support measure total score. Block 1: enter covariates, Block 2: enter self-report indirect aggression score, peer report indirect aggression score

—hierarchical multiple regression—dependent variable/criterion variable: Social support retirement community subscale score, Block 1: enter covariates, Block 2: enter self-report indirect aggression score, peer report indirect aggression score

—Check for violations of the assumptions for regression

—normality: assess if residuals are normally distributed

—look at the frequency distribution histograms

—homoscedasticity: look at the normal probability plot of the residuals

—look at a plot of predicted vs. obtained residuals

—look at scatterplot of the standardized residuals and standardized predicted values generated by the regression analyses

—linearity: look at scatterplot of the standardized residuals and standardized predicted values generated by the regression analyses

—multicollinearity: look at correlations among predictors and tolerance values

Note. Portion of analysis plan created by Colette Lord for *Indirect Aggression and Social Support Among Elderly Retirement Community Residents* (Lord, 2005). Lord adapted indirect and direct aggression scales for use with elderly retirement community populations, examined their reliability and validity, and related indirect aggression use to social support. Her data were gathered in independent living facilities of retirement communities. Her actual analysis plan listed SPSS commands, names of specific variables, and analyses related to tests of additional hypotheses and exploratory questions. Analysis plan adapted with permission of the author.

health-belief measures will be related to their adherence scores. In correlational designs, variables can be continuous or discrete, although they are most often continuous. We will look for correlational statistics to answer association or relationship types of questions.

Several complex correlational statistics involve model testing. Structural equation modeling and linear growth modeling are examples of model-testing statistical approaches. One principal way in which these techniques differ from other types of statistical analyses is in how they test hypotheses. In many group-comparison and correlational statistics, one seeks to reject the null hypothesis and looks for results that indicate that the test statistic differs significantly from zero. Model testing, in contrast, tests how well your actual data fit a model (theory) that you believe describes the relationships between variables. Here the statistics reveal the extent to which your data fit the model you designed or support your theory.

Many students have trouble at this point because they have not completely worked out their design. Some research topics can be approached with either a group comparison *or* a correlational design. Suppose, for example, you are interested in whether children with high IQs experience more problems with their peers than do children with lower IQs. You could study this in two ways: (a) collect IQ scores and peer interaction scores and examine the relationship between them (i.e., correlate them) or (b) sort children into IQ groups with two or more levels (e.g., high IQ and average IQ) and look at differences between the groups in their peer interactions using a group comparison statistic.

If you are not certain which you are doing, look again at the design section of your proposal (see chap. 7, this volume), and clarify what you intend to do. Correlational designs are often most appropriate when you conceptualize your independent variables as natural continua (e.g., intelligence) or if you wish to examine the best combinations of independent variables to predict a single dependent variable. Some researchers also hold that correlational designs are more appropriate than group comparisons when you do not manipulate your independent variables. In addition, creating groups by dichotomizing or trichotomizing on continuous measures and then using group-comparison instead of correlational statistics results in loss of statistical power when relationships between variables are linear (Cohen, 1983). Group-comparison designs are more appropriate than correlational designs when the independent variables are natural categories (e.g., ethnicity, gender) or are based on variables combined in a nonlinear fashion (e.g., psychiatric diagnosis, which is usually based on presence, absence, or degree of several behaviors). Group comparisons are also generally more appropriate when you manipulate the independent variable.

The second thing to figure out is which of your dependent variables are suitable for parametric statistics. Examples of parametric statistics are ANOVA, multiple regression, Pearson *r* correlations, and *t* tests. Parametric statistics involve the assumption that the underlying distribution of scores in the population you are sampling is normal. (Particular parametric tests have additional requirements, as well.) An oversimplified but common rule of thumb is that ordinal and categorical data cannot meet these assumptions and should be analyzed using a nonparametric approach. Exceptions to this rule exist (e.g., Myers, DiCecco, White, & Borden, 1982), however. Nonetheless, continuous data are more likely to meet the requirements of parametric statistics than are categorical data. Thus, look at parametric analyses first when dealing with continuous data. If the characteristics of your data violate the assumptions of the parametric analysis, you may need to consider nonparametric alternatives (e.g., using Chi square instead of a *t* test or ANOVA). This is especially true if the analysis is not robust (i.e., does not react well) to your particular violations of its assumptions and if you cannot minimize the impact of these violations (e.g., by data transformations).

The choice between parametric and nonparametric analyses is usually determined by the nature of your *dependent* variable. Examine each dependent variable one by one. Not all variables will have the same characteristics. A common error, for example, is to assume that you can use the same analysis to test whether two or more experimental groups are equivalent on age, ethnicity, gender, years of education, and other demographic variables. Age and education are usually analyzed with parametric statistics. Gender and ethnicity are usually examined with nonparametric statistics because they are categorical variables. Similarly, you may use entirely different statistics to answer different questions in your study. Don't assume one test will do it all!

At this point, you should have a list of questions you will use statistics to answer. You will also have a list of independent and dependent variables for each question. For each dependent variable, you will have indicated whether a parametric or nonparametric test is more appropriate. Finally, you will have indicated whether the question involves grouping the participants and comparing the groups (group-comparison statistic), relating scores on one or more measures in a single group (correlational statistic), or testing a specific model that involves multiple independent and dependent variables considered simultaneously. In the pages that follow, we consider each of these options in turn: group-comparison statistics (parametric and nonparametric) and correlational statistics (parametric and nonparametric). We also briefly describe some of the more common model-testing analyses. This will allow you to start adding the names of the appropriate statistics to your analysis plan.

Consider Group Comparison Statistics: Parametric Statistics

ANOVA and the *t* test are widely used parametric statistics for examining differences between groups. If you decide one of them is appropriate for your analysis, you must then select among their numerous variations.

Analysis of Variance and *t* Tests

To work out the specifics of selecting a parametric group comparison statistic, first ask yourself how many independent variables will be involved in answering your particular research question. Next ask yourself how many levels (conditions or groups) will be included with each independent variable. To do this, break each independent variable into the discrete groups it includes (e.g., condition: priming for recall, priming for recognition, no priming [three levels]; time: pre-, post-, follow-up [three levels]). Finally, for each independent variable, ask yourself whether the levels involve *different* groups of people being compared with each other (as with the condition-independent variable) or the *same* group being compared with itself on the same variable under different conditions (e.g., at different points in time, after exposure to different experimental stimuli; as with the time type of independent variable). Once you have answered these questions, you can use the flowchart in Figure 9.1 to identify the most appropriate statistic for your analysis.

Following the steps in Figure 9.1 leads you to the most suitable initial choice. The flowchart then instructs you to examine whether your data meet the assumptions of the statistic. If not, you must ascertain whether the statistic is robust to any violations of its assumptions you might be making *or* whether there is some way of transforming the data or adjusting the statistic to alleviate the problem. Many students approach data transformation warily. However, using a logarithmic, square root, or other sort of transformation to meet the assumptions of a nonrobust statistic is not cheating. In fact, it may help guard against Type I or Type II errors.

If you cannot figure out a way to compensate for assumptions that you violate, the flowchart directs you to seek an alternative statistic with fewer assumptions. Of course, along with fewer assumptions may come lower power. Usually, parametric statistics are more powerful than nonparametric ones, so you will generally want to use a parametric test. Maxwell and Delaney (2004) pointed out, however, that this—like most rules of thumb—is an oversimplification: In some cases, a nonparametric approach can be more powerful than its parametric alternative. Which is the more powerful will depend on the characteristics of your data set. If it's a toss-up and if you are a statistical novice, let pragmatic considerations prevail: Pick the one that you or your statistics consultant knows better.

Let's work through the steps listed so far in this chapter with an example. Suppose, as a preliminary way of examining your data, you wish to see

Figure 9.1

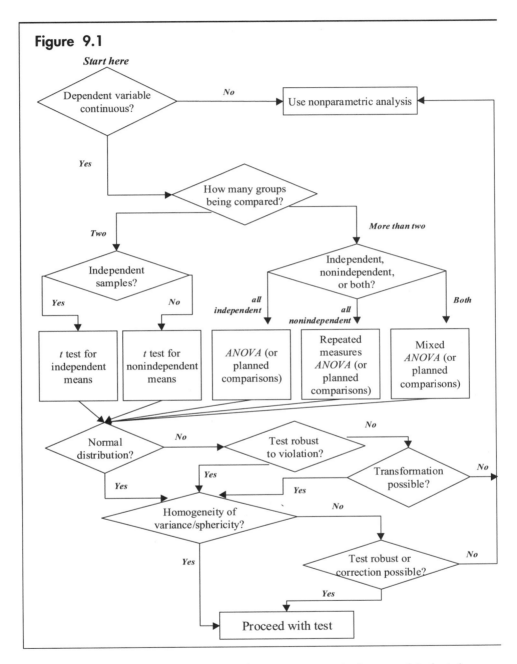

Flowchart for selecting appropriate parametric statistics for group comparison studies (assumes analysis of a single dependent variable). ANOVA = analysis of variance.

whether men and women differ in their responses to a management style questionnaire (on which scores can range from 30–150). For the purposes of this analysis, you have one independent variable (gender) with two levels (male and female). Because you will be comparing groups, your probable analysis will be either a t test or an ANOVA. As you only have two groups to compare, a t test will be most suitable. Moreover, because different participants are in the two groups, a t test for independent samples will likely be appropriate. Incidentally, with only two groups, t tests and ANOVAs are mathematically equivalent.

Now, do your data meet the assumptions of a t test? Those include homogeneity of variance in your groups (i.e., the standard deviations in the two groups are roughly equal), independence of observations, and a normal distribution of your dependent variable (management style scores) in the population to which you wish to generalize. If you have produced a frequency distribution of the scores for each of your groups, you will have a pretty good idea whether the homogeneity and normality assumptions are tenable. You can also do specific statistical tests for homogeneity and normality (e.g., to examine whether your distribution has problems with skew or kurtosis). If your data meet these assumptions, you can then proceed to perform the analysis. Exhibit 9.2 lists the assumptions of some of the most common parametric statistical tests and some of the conditions under which the tests are and are not robust to violations.

Now let's take a more complex example. Suppose your research involves testing whether insight-oriented individual therapy leads to better marital satisfaction than problem-solving individual therapy. Your dependent variable is the score on a marital satisfaction scale. The two independent variables are type of treatment (two levels: insight-oriented versus problem-solving therapy) and time (three levels: pre- vs. posttreatment vs. follow-up). The first independent variable involves comparing different groups of participants; the second involves comparing a group with itself at different points in time. If you follow the flowchart in Figure 9.1, you will find yourself at the "mixed ANOVA" box: one between-subjects factor (treatment) and one within-subjects factor (time). Your likely analysis is a 2 (treatment) × 3 (time) mixed ANOVA.

By looking at Exhibit 9.2, you see that, although the results of the treatment comparison are likely to be robust to violations of the assumptions of homogeneity of variance, the analyses involving the time factor are not. Thus, you will need to examine your variances for homogeneity. You can do this by using one of a number of tests described in most statistics books (e.g., Keppel & Wickens, 2004; Maxwell & Delaney, 2004; see the list at the

Exhibit 9.2

Assumptions of Common Parametric Statistical Tests

Statistical Test	Assumptions
t-test	Homogeneity of variance, underlying normal distribution (generally robust to both of these but NOT with repeated measures and very unequal *ns*), independent scores within cells (not robust)
Analysis of variance	Homogeneity of variance, underlying normal distribution; repeated measures ANOVA also assumes homogeneity of covariance and sphericity (circularity); ANOVA generally robust but NOT with repeated measures and very unequal *ns*; may also not be robust with small samples (Tabachnick & Fidell, 2001); independence of scores within cells (not robust)
Analysis of covariance	Homogeneity of variance, independence of scores within cells, underlying normal distribution (generally robust with relatively equal cell sizes, > 19 df for error, two-tailed test, and no outliers; Tabachnick & Fidell, 2001), linear relationship between covariate and dependent variable, homogeneity of regression (i.e., relationship between dependent variable and covariate is the same in each cell), covariates are reliably measured (violation of this assumption leads to loss of power), independence of covariate and independent variable(s) is highly recommended; repeated measures ANCOVA also assumes homogeneity of covariance
Multivariate analysis of variance	Multivariate normal distribution, homogeneity of variance for each dependent variable and variance-covariance matrix (not robust if cell sizes are unequal), linear relationships among all dependent variables, absence of multi-collinearity (among dependent variables) and singularity (among dependent variables)
Pearson correlation	Continuous dependent variables; independent observations

continued

Exhibit 9.2, continued

Assumptions of Common Parametric Statistical Tests

Statistical Test	Assumptions
Multiple linear regression	Absence of multicollinearity (not robust) and singularity, multivariate normal distribution, homoscedasticity, linear relationships between predictors and criterion (interactions between predictors can be included), predictors measured without error (violation leads to underestimates of regression coefficients [betas]), no errors of specification
Structural equation modeling	Absence of multicollinearity and singularity, multivariate normal distribution (robust Chi Square tests available), linear relationships (some other sorts of relationships can be modeled)

---

end of this chapter for additional suggestions). Standard statistical software programs such as SAS and SPSS will calculate most of these tests. If group variances are not homogeneous, you can adjust your degrees of freedom to accommodate this problem using one of several procedures (see Maxwell & Delaney, 2004). The result is that the statistic often becomes more conservative (i.e., decreases the probability of a Type I error) as a way of protecting against the bias introduced by heterogeneity of variances. This means you will have to have greater differences between your groups to achieve the same level of statistical significance you would have had if the assumptions had not been violated. In addition, the F^* and W tests (Maxwell & Delaney, 2004) are alternatives. These variations of the F test produce unbiased results when variances are unequal, both with equal- and unequal-n cells. These are not suitable if your design involves repeated measures, however.

Planned Comparisons

But wait! The box in the flowchart also says planned comparisons are an option. As an alternative to the standard ANOVA approach, you can select a certain set of comparisons you wish to make among pairs of means. You do this in advance, before you collect the data. In effect, you state that you expect certain means to differ in certain directions and wish to test only these differences. No other comparisons are important to you. This permits the option of doing planned comparisons in place of an omnibus or overall

ANOVA. This has the advantage of giving you more statistical power, because you restrict in advance the number of tests you will do. It has the disadvantage of making it more difficult to snoop through the data later on for something interesting that did not involve an *a priori* hypothesis, however. This is because there is no free lunch! True, you get more powerful tests to use for your planned comparisons. But the trade-off is that later snooping requires you to use more stringent tests. In general, planned comparisons make sense if you have well-defined hypotheses with good support in the literature. They may also make sense if you have a complex design in which only a few means are expected to differ and most are not (e.g., if you are running a lot of control conditions). But if your study is more exploratory, you may prefer not to restrict yourself in exchange for greater power. Most statistics books that discuss ANOVA also discuss how to do planned comparisons. Note that several different ways of doing planned comparisons exist, depending on how you select among groups you wish to compare.

Post Hoc Tests

What if you elect not to do planned comparisons? Don't put away your statistics books yet! You need to select a post hoc test. This will allow you to see which mean differences are contributing to any significant effects you find. For example, suppose with the treatment outcome study described earlier, you find a significant main effect for time and an interaction between time and mode of treatment. You will need post hoc tests to see (a) what contributed to the main effect for time (your main effect for time tells you that differences exist among pretreatment, posttreatment, and follow-up means, but not which pairs differ) and (b) which difference in group means contributed to your interaction effect.

An interaction means that the differences between groups are not the same at all of the levels of the independent variables. In this example, a time × treatment interaction could mean that changes between pretreatment and posttreatment means are not the same for both treatments. Or it could mean that differences between posttreatment and follow-up means are not identical in the two treatments. Somewhere among the six means the interaction examined (pre–insight, pre–problem-solving, post–insight, post–problem-solving, follow-up–insight, follow-up–problem-solving) are some significant differences. You will need to find out where these are, however. A post hoc test helps you do this.

Many post hoc tests exist. You can evaluate them in terms of their power, their robustness to violations of their assumptions, and the situations in which each is most appropriate from a conceptual point of view. Maxwell and Delaney (2004) and Kirk (1995) have provided good overviews of different options and compare and contrast these options. If you are using either within-subjects or unequal-*n* designs, which are not robust to violations of homogeneity of variance and normality assumptions, look for a post-hoc test appropriate for these designs.

ANCOVA and MANOVA

But what about ANCOVA and MANOVA, you ask? Should I be using them? Analysis of covariance (ANCOVA), multivariate analysis of variance (MANOVA), and multivariate analysis of covariance (MANCOVA) all provide alternatives to *t*-test and ANOVA statistics. We consider each.

Essentially, an ANCOVA is an analysis of variance with the statistical influence of one or more variables (called *covariates*) removed from the dependent variable. In theory, an ANCOVA is what you would get if you could do the ANOVA with the level of the covariates controlled by randomization. (In practice, this situation is more complex, as we shall see.) When such control is not possible, ANCOVA may be a suitable alternative to an ANOVA. This is true when there is a strong relationship between your dependent variable and another variable that is related to your independent variable. Remember, you want to say something about the effect of a particular independent variable on your dependent variable. You do not want this relationship to be the result of some other variable that you failed to hold constant. A good example is the relationship between race and academic achievement. There is also a strong relationship between socioeconomic status and academic achievement as well as between socioeconomic status and race. If you do not control for socioeconomic status, you might conclude that race and academic achievement are related when they are not.

Because an ANCOVA decreases your error variance by extracting variance that is due to the relationship between the covariate and the dependent variable (Tabachnick & Fidell, 2001), your independent variable may be more likely to show a significant effect. For example, suppose you investigate the effects of three different reading programs on reading scores. You know, however, that IQ correlates highly with reading scores. It may have such a strong relationship that, unless you control for it in some way, this relationship will prevent you from seeing any differences between your three interventions. In essence, doing an ANCOVA with IQ as a covariate will allow you to extract the relationship between IQ and reading from your analyses, making an effect of your independent variable easier to detect.

Researchers sometimes also advocate use of ANCOVA when some variable emerges after the fact as a potential confound (as in the example of race and socioeconomic status) and you want to remove its influence statistically. As another example, consider the outcome study comparing insight-oriented and problem-solving treatments described earlier. Suppose you found that, despite random assignment, the insight-oriented group had significantly more years of education than the other group. Suppose further that education level correlated with therapy outcome. In such a situation any differences favoring the insight-oriented group could be due to education and not therapy. To protect against this you might want to use years of education as a covariate. Theoretically this removes the potential impact education may have on, say, marital satisfaction, so you can see the effects of your treatment independent of the effects of education. There is some dispute as to the appropriateness of this procedure, however, because ANCOVA can produce hard to interpret or even misleading results in certain cases, as we discuss later.

There are several other things you should know about ANCOVA. First, using ANCOVA to control for potential confounds only makes sense if there is a significant correlation between the covariate and the dependent variable. If there is no correlation, the *suspected* confounding variable really isn't one. It thus offers no viable alternative explanation for any differences between your treatment groups. Furthermore, the results of the ANCOVA will not differ much from the ANOVA results (but you will lose a degree of freedom—i.e., a bit of power—by including the covariate). Second, ANCOVA only controls for a linear relationship between the covariate and the dependent variable—a confound could still exist if there is a curvilinear relationship between the covariate and your dependent variable. Third, using ANCOVA when your covariate may be related to or caused by differences in your independent variable poses major interpretive problems (see Maxwell & Delaney, 2004, for discussion). Fourth, interpretive problems also emerge if you use ANCOVA and your groupings do not involve random assignment (i.e., your study is not a true experiment), an issue Huitema (1980) explored in detail. Perhaps because of these interpretive problems, some recommend that ANCOVA only be used to extract variance between the dependent variable and the covariate and not to control for unanticipated (or anticipated) confounds. Thus, although ANCOVA can be a powerful and useful procedure, interpreting its results can be less than straightforward. If ANCOVA seems like a possible analysis to you, examine what it can and cannot do. Huitema (1980), Maxwell and Delaney (2004), and Shadish et al. (2002, chap. 8) have all covered ANCOVA. Further, Huitema (1980) provided formulas for several post hoc tests that can be used with ANCOVA.

What about MANOVA? A MANOVA resembles an ANOVA, except that multiple dependent variables are examined all at once. A MANOVA for the insight-oriented versus problem-solving study, for example, might examine reported satisfaction with communication, sexual interaction, and instrumental tasks (three dependent variables). A MANOVA basically asks the question, "Do the various factors (independent variables) make a difference for this *group* of dependent variables?" Conceptually, MANOVA procedures create a synthetic variable that combines the information in all the dependent variables that are included in the analysis, then analyzes the synthetic variable, and finally tells you about the significance of main effects and interactions for that synthetic variable. This means you will know whether your independent variable affected the synthetic variable, but not whether it affected any one of the individual variables making up the synthetic one.

Frequently, investigators attempt to control inflated Type I error rates by doing a MANOVA. Type I error can increase when you do many statistical tests on numerous separate dependent variables, thereby increasing the likelihood that at least one will be significant solely as a function of doing so many tests. Because MANOVA treats those dependent variables as a group, the investigators conduct fewer analyses and thus reduce the likelihood of Type I error. If the MANOVA is significant (so the logic goes), the investigator can then proceed to do a series of individual ANOVAs on each of the dependent variables to see what produced the significance, much as one can do a post hoc test comparing specific groups following a significant ANOVA. Alternatively, the investigator can use a step-down procedure, eliminating variables one by one to see which accounted for the effect (Tabachnick & Fidell, 2001).

Huberty and Morris (1989) challenged the logic of this approach. They asserted that MANOVA does not uniformly protect against Type I error and is appropriate primarily when the investigator is interested in the dependent variables as a system or when the dependent variables are conceptually related and assess the same or similar underlying constructs. Multiple

ANOVAs, so their argument goes, are preferable when dependent variables are conceptually independent, when doing exploratory research, when previous studies have used separate univariate analyses (so your data will be comparable with those of previous investigators), and when examining whether groups are equivalent (e.g., on possible confounding variables). So what is our recommendation? If your dependent variables are conceptually related, a MANOVA may make sense if you can meet its assumptions or if the particular type of MANOVA (e.g., repeated measures) is robust with regard to violations of its assumptions. If your dependent variables are not conceptually related, remember that you can correct your alpha level to protect against Type I error if need be (more on this later). If you still choose MANOVA in this circumstance, make sure you have a good reason and can counter Huberty and Morris's (1989) excellent points.

Nonparametric Statistics

Let's suppose your data do not fulfill the assumptions required for an ANOVA. What do you do now? Nonparametric statistics, fortunately, may come to your rescue. If you were planning to use a between-subjects ANOVA but your ordinal data are not suitable for one, the Kruskal–Wallis test is a nonparametric alternative. Appropriate for ordinal data, it is equivalent to the Wilcoxon Rank Sum and the Mann-Whitney U tests when only two groups are being compared (Maxwell & Delaney, 2004). Although the Kruskal–Wallis statistic makes no assumptions about underlying distributions, it *does* implicitly assume homogeneity of variance. For this reason, Maxwell and Delaney (2004) recommend the F^* and W tests when variances are not homogeneous, particularly with unequal cell sizes. Joint ranking or pairwise ranking tests (Maxwell & Delaney, 2004) can be used to compare pairs of cells, in the same way that post hoc mean comparisons are used with ANOVAs.

If your design involves repeated measures and only one (repeated) independent variable, Friedman's test (Maxwell & Delaney, 2004) may be appropriate. Like the Kruskal–Wallis test, it analyzes rank orders of participants' scores and so requires ordinal data. With categorical data, the most appropriate analysis is often a χ^2 test or cross-classification analysis (Rodgers, 1995). When there are several levels of an independent variable or when you have more than one independent variable, you may wish to do the equivalent of a post hoc test if your chi-square is significant. This can be done using z tests for proportions. Alternatively, the more complex nonparametric equivalents of ANOVA strategies (logit or log-linear analysis) may be appropriate.

Consider Correlational Statistics

If your design involves looking at relationships among variables in a single group of individuals rather than comparing discrete groups, the first step in selecting a statistic is to decide what is being related to what. If you have two variables that you wish to relate, a bivariate (i.e., two-variable) correlation will be appropriate. If you have a set of variables (i.e., more than one) that you wish to associate with one or more different variables, a regression strategy or model-testing approach may be the best choice.

Bivariate Correlations (Parametric and Nonparametric)

The simplest measures of association are bivariate correlation coefficients. If your data on both variables can be considered interval or ratio, a Pearson product-moment correlation (r) may be suitable. Keep in mind, however, that the Pearson correlation involves rank ordering, and will not take into account systematic mean differences in the two sets of data. Such differences may be important. For example, suppose you wish to correlate the data of two individuals who independently observed the same individuals' head-banging frequency. You would be interested not only in whether they saw the same individuals as higher or lower in head banging but also in whether both observers reported the same frequencies of head banging for each individual jointly observed. In such a case, you might prefer a correlation that takes into account mean differences (e.g., the intraclass correlation coefficient; von Eye & Mun, 2005).

If measuring *one* of your variables produces ordinal data and measuring the other yields ordinal, interval, or ratio data, a Spearman rank-order procedure would be more suitable than a Pearson correlation. If one of the variables is dichotomous, a point-biserial correlation will be appropriate. If both are dichotomous, the correlation between them is called the *phi* (Φ) coefficient. Note that the formula for r produces the *point-biserial* and *phi* coefficients (as special cases), so telling a computer to give you an r

statistic with dichotomous data will produce a correct *point-biserial* or *phi* coefficient (Cohen, Cohen, West, & Aiken, 2003).

Regression Strategies

Regression analyses basically select one variable called the *criterion variable* (also sometimes termed the *dependent* or *outcome variable*) and one or more *predictor* (*independent*) *variables*. When two or more predictors are used, regression procedures develop an equation that describes the best way of combining the predictors. This indicates how well you could guess a person's score on the criterion variable if you knew the scores on the predictors and used the equation to combine them. Regression might be appropriate, for example, if you wished to analyze whether rates of particular therapist behaviors were associated with treatment outcome; whether age, social competence, Graduate Record Exam (GRE) scores, and undergraduate grade point average (GPA) were associated with graduate school GPA or professional licensing exam scores; whether various demographic and cognitive measures were related to rate of recovery from cancer surgery; and so on. Although it can be used with a single predictor, regression more commonly involves multiple predictors. Thus, this parametric version of regression is called *multiple regression*.

Parametric Multiple Regression

Parametric versions of multiple regression analysis basically produce a list of those variables that enhance your ability to predict the criterion over your best guess if you knew nothing about your participants' scores on the predictors (this best guess, by the way, would be the mean of the criterion variable). The analysis procedures take into account the fact that some of the predictors may correlate with each other and are therefore redundant. Thus, each significant predictor variable contributes unique (nonredundant) information (i.e., information that goes beyond that which the previous predictors added). Dichotomous as well as continuous variables can be used as predictors, but for parametric versions of multiple-regression procedures, the criterion must be a continuous variable. (Nonparametric versions of regression [logit analysis and logistic regression] are mentioned later.) Categorical variables that have more than two levels can also be used as predictors, but these must be treated specially (see Cohen et al., 2003). More complex variations of regression even allow you to assess the effects of interactions between different predictor variables (i.e., whether one variable moderates the relationships between the second variable and the criterion variable). Aiken and West (1996) described how to create, analyze, and interpret interactions in regression analyses.

Many different forms of regression exist. Most have to do with the order in which you enter your predictor variables into the regression equation. They can be entered one by one or in one or more groups. Different forms of regression also vary in the ways the analysis tests each variable to see whether it contributes any new information (above and beyond the information contained by other variables in the equation) in predicting the criterion variable.

In *hierarchical multiple regression,* you specify the order in which the variables go into the equation in advance, on theoretical or methodological grounds. The analysis extracts the amount of variance associated with the first variable, then goes on to do the same with the second, and so on. You can either specify the order in which each and every individual variable will be entered or group variables into subsets and then enter the subsets, letting the analysis sort out the order within each set.

For example, one of our students wished to predict in-law satisfaction based on parental marital satisfaction and the quality of the relationship (cohesion) between the parent and child. "In-law satisfaction" was his criterion variable. He first entered several demographic variables (as a set) in a hierarchical multiple regression analysis. Then he entered a single measure of social desirability. Finally, he entered the marital satisfaction and cohesion measures (as a set). He chose this order of entry because he wished to control for demographic characteristics and the tendency to respond to self-report measures in a socially desirable way. He also wanted to look at the relationship between marital satisfaction, cohesion, and in-law satisfaction, holding demographic and social desirability variables constant. Put another way, his results told him whether knowing the marital satisfaction and cohesion scores gave him any new information, over and above that provided by the demographic and social desirability measures. He had no reason for ordering his variables *within* sets, however.

Hierarchical multiple regression is also sometimes used to test mediation hypotheses—hypotheses that state that the relationship between two or more variables is explained by a third variable, called the "mediator." For example, suppose you propose that low academic achievement is related to high school dropout and that this relationship is explained by (mediated by) students' poor attitudes toward school and by lack of connection to teachers and school activities. Baron and Kenny (1986) and Holmbeck

(1997) described what has come to be the classic analytical approach to testing these kinds of mediation hypotheses using regression analyses. Mac-Kinnon, Lockwood, Hoffman, West, and Sheets (2002) have criticized these approaches for lack of power. The alternatives they proposed, however, also make use of regression strategies.

An alternative to hierarchical multiple regression is *stepwise regression*. In this procedure, purely computational decision rules identify which variable predicts the criterion variable best, then which variable adds significantly after that, and so on. Whereas with hierarchical multiple regression you specify the order in advance, with stepwise regression the computer does the ordering. If the student in the example just cited used a stepwise procedure, he would have entered all of his variables and let the computer tell him the order in which they predicted in-law satisfaction.

There are various ways of doing this ordering, and you will need to instruct the computer which procedure to use. These include *forward entry* procedures, *forward stepwise* procedures, and *backward deletion* procedures. Most, but not all, stepwise approaches use procedures that add and delete variables, testing how well each variable performs as the analysis proceeds. A crucial point is that regression analyses can be performed in many different ways. Examine the options and their pros and cons in light of the purposes of your analyses, and then make an informed decision.

Cohen et al. (2003) pointed out several disadvantages of using stepwise procedures. First, when large numbers of predictors are used, the approach seriously capitalizes on chance. Second, the results using these procedures may not replicate in a second sample. Third, depending on the rules used to enter and remove predictor variables, results may be quite misleading. Fourth, using stepwise procedures means you can avoid having to think through the logical relationships among your predictors and criterion variable. This is a bit like using ANOVAs and post hoc comparisons to snoop through your data rather than making the effort to preplan and specify exactly what you want to examine in advance.

One may justify stepwise procedures more readily under certain conditions: (a) when the sample is large, (b) when replication is possible (either with a second sample or by randomly splitting the sample in two), and (c) when the research goal is not based in theory (as in some applied research, when the goal may simply be to predict a phenomenon and not explain it; Cohen et al., 2003). Tabachnick and Fidell (2001) characterized stepwise procedures as model-building techniques; early studies in an area would use these. They view hierarchical procedures as hypothesis-testing techniques;[1] investigators would use these when a research area matures enough to allow reasonable predictions.

Regression procedures, like all parametric statistical tests, have certain conditions, which, if you fail to meet them, can cause problems. First, multiple regression procedures assume the absence of multicollinearity. Multicollinearity occurs when two or more of the predictor variables are highly intercorrelated—a situation that produces an unstable regression equation (i.e., the weights associated with each of the predictor variables are unlikely to be replicated in a new population).[2] If you have a multicollinearity problem, you could select the most important predictor from among the correlated variables or explore whether you can legitimately combine the correlated variables into a single score.

A second condition you must satisfy in using multiple regression is that predictor variables cannot be combinations of other predictor variables (this is termed *singularity*). In other words, you cannot use scores for hitting, swearing, punching, and total aggression as predictors: The last is a combination of the first three. Third, regression assumes linear relationships between each predictor and the criterion (but multiple regression can be used to test interactions among predictor variables, too). Fourth, multiple regression assumes an underlying multivariate normal distribution. This means that not only is each predictor normally distributed, all possible combinations of the predictors are as well. A fifth assumption involves homoscedasticity: The prediction made by the regression equation is comparable at different points on the regression line. Fortunately, one can check the last three assumptions by examining the residuals. An analysis of residuals essentially looks at the difference between each score as predicted by the regression equation and the score you actually got in your data (each difference is called a *residual*). Different patterns of residuals at different points on the regression line have implications for the assumptions of multiple regression (see Tabachnick & Fidell [2001], for graphic representations of patterns that indicate difficulties).

---

[1] You can combine stepwise and hierarchical procedures. That is, you can enter a series of subsets of variables hierarchically but use stepwise procedures to figure out the order of variables within each subset.

[2] One common guideline is that bivariate correlations above .7 may suggest a multicollinearity problem (e.g., Tabachnik & Fidell, 2001). Note that a bivariate r below .70 does not guarantee the *absence* of multicollinearity, however: Two predictor variables might be only moderately correlated with a third predictor when looked at individually but might be more highly correlated when combined. SPSS and SAS can calculate indexes (e.g., tolerance levels) to test combinations of variables for multicollinearity; Cohen et al. (2003) discuss these issues as well.

Final assumptions of multiple regression can be more difficult to satisfy. First, regression assumes that you have included all relevant predictors and that none of the predictors is irrelevant (Licht, 1995). Failure to meet this is called a specification error. In addition, multiple regression procedures assume that variables are measured without error.

These assumptions seem impossible to meet: If you knew everything that was and was not related to the criterion variable, why do the research? And how many variables can be measured without error? The truth is, researchers proceed to use regressions in spite of the fact that no one can meet these assumptions fully. But rather than ignoring them, practical recommendations for dealing with them include thinking about the degree to which the assumptions are met (Klem, 1995). Licht (1995) recommended using theory and past data to select appropriate predictors, and selecting the most reliable and valid measures available to minimize measurement error.

Nonparametric Versions of Regression

Logistic regression resembles multiple regression in that a number of predictors are related to a single criterion variable. Predictors can be continuous or not, but unlike multiple regression, the criterion variable is categorical, not continuous. In addition, the mathematics underlying logistic regression are more closely aligned with nonparametric than parametric statistics and differ greatly from those underlying parametric versions of multiple regression. Thus, nonparametric regression statistics tell you about how well obtained frequencies in a particular cell fit the expected frequencies, rather than about how much of the variance each predictor variable accounts for in the criterion. A similar procedure, logit analysis (a version of log-linear analysis) is more restrictive than logistic regression in that all variables (predictors and criterion) must be categorical variables.

Discriminant Function Analysis

Discriminant function analysis (DFA) has many of the same uses as logistic regression but involves parametric statistics. DFA is most useful when you wish to predict discrete group membership (considered the dependent variable) from a set of variables (considered the independent variables or predictors). For example, you may wish to assess how well several MMPI scores predict psychiatric diagnosis or whether you can derive a way to combine demographic data with scores assessing attitudes toward work and the company to predict which prospective employees will and will not quit during the first year on the job. These questions resemble group-comparison questions in that you will divide your sample into two or more discrete groups to form your dependent variable (e.g., antisocial personality disorder vs. control; those who leave the company versus those who stay). They resemble regression questions in that you want to examine whether a combination of variables will allow you to separate the groups. A DFA can be useful in these situations, if you meet its assumptions (see Exhibit 9.2); otherwise, logistic regression may be a more viable alternative.

Essentially, DFA examines the predictors (independent variables) and formulates an equation that weights each one to maximize correct classification of participants into groups (the dependent variable). As with regression, variations of DFA exist. Mathematically, DFA is closely related to MANOVA. One important consideration involves whether you want the computer to test certain variables before others (hierarchical DFA) or whether you want the computer to order the variables statistically (step-down DFA or direct ["standard"] DFA; see Tabachnick & Fidell, 2001).

Factor Analysis

We assumed in the previous pages that you have some variables you designated as independent variables and some as dependent variables, and you are interested in how the independent variables and dependent variables relate to one another. Maybe you do not view your data in terms of independent and dependent variables, however. Perhaps you are interested in numerous variables without specifying causal or predictive relationships among them. If so, another set of correlationally based statistics might be more suitable. Factor analysis and its sibling, principal components analysis, summarize patterns of correlations among a set of variables. Investigators often use these to reduce a large set of variables or items to a smaller number or to test hypotheses about the underlying structure among variables. For example, an investigator developing a new questionnaire may wish to reduce the 50 items to a few homogeneous subscales before looking at differences between groups.

Issues involved in using factor analysis are too numerous and complex to cover (see Fabrigar, Wegener, MacCallum, & Strahan, 1999; Floyd & Widamon, 1995; and Preacher & MacCallum, 2003, for excellent overviews of some these issues). One issue does warrant mentioning, however: sample size. Common rules of thumb require a minimum of 5 participants per item (variable) or 100 participants in total, whichever is higher. MacCallum, Widamon, Zhang, and Hong (1999) criticized these rules, showing that the number of participants required depends on the degree to which the factor structure accounts for variance in the items and on the extent to which each factor is measured by a reasonable number of items. If the analysis accounts for a reasonable amount of variance (i.e., communalities around .50) and there are at least six or seven items for each factor, a sample of 100 to 200 may be sufficient according to MacCallum et al. With fewer numbers of items per factor, more participants will be needed. In addition, many investigators recommend replicating a factor analysis to be sure of the findings. Are you willing to recruit enough participants to do the analysis right? If not, do not promise to solve the problem of too many variables by conducting a factor analysis to create a more manageable number of scores. A better solution is to think through whether all those measures are necessary in the first place, especially given the great likelihood that they do not measure different constructs in the first place.

A second important consideration is whether to use exploratory or confirmatory factor analysis (CFA). Exploratory factor analysis allows the computer to determine the best-fitting organization of variables; this may or may not make conceptual sense. Principal components and principal-axis factor analyses are both examples of exploratory factor analysis. In contrast, confirmatory factor analysis is a model-testing technique in which you specify which variables load on which factors, then test your theoretical model against the actual data. The consensus is that exploratory factor analysis is most appropriate in the initial stages of measure development, whereas confirmatory analysis is more appropriate for testing clear theories of how items or scores are organized and with well-developed measures (Floyd & Widaman, 1995).

Model-Testing Approaches

As mentioned earlier, model-testing approaches differ from the other statistical approaches covered in this chapter in that they test whether the actual data fit a theoretical model proposed by the investigator. Possibly the best-known model-testing analysis in psychology is Structural Equation Modeling (SEM). CFA is one application of SEM. With CFA, you might tell the computer which items from a questionnaire are supposed to make up different subscales. The analysis tells you whether they do.

SEM can also be used as an alternative to multiple regression to test mediation hypotheses. To illustrate, consider the mediation example we described earlier, where you propose that attitudes and feeling disconnected mediate the relationship between low academic achievement and dropping out of high school. You are hypothesizing a rather complex set of relationships in this instance—that achievement is related to dropout, that achievement is also related to poor attitudes and lack of connections, and that attitudes and feeling disconnected are also related to dropout. Furthermore, you speculate that you can explain the relationship between achievement and dropout if you also know something about the students' attitudes and connections. SEM permits you to test all of these relationships in one analysis.

SEM can also be used to examine even more complex models than this. For example, SEM is increasingly being used instead of path analysis. Path analysis looks at direct and indirect relationships between predictors and criterion variables. A typical simple path model might speculate that A leads to B, which leads to C, but that A also leads to C directly. This model says there is an indirect relationship between A and C that B explains, and a direct relationship in which B plays no role. Mediation analyses can be thought of as subsets of path analytic strategies. Complex path models are possible, too. For example, A could lead to B, which leads to C, which leads to D. Typically this kind of model used regression methods to calculate direct and indirect path coefficients that showed the relationships among variables (Klem, 1995), but SEM is more often used in contemporary research to test this kind of model if sample sizes are sufficient.

Many investigators also use SEM when they use multiple measures of the same constructs and wish to estimate relationships among the constructs (sometimes called "latent variables") rather than the actual measured variables (also known as the "observed variables" or "indicators"). This is because, conceptually speaking, SEM combines features of factor analysis (creating a synthetic or latent variable based on the observed scores) with features of regression analysis (examining the extent to which one variable or set of variables predicts another). With this sort of model, you tell the computer (a) which variables measure which latent construct and (b) how you expect the constructs to be related. How well the model fits depends on how well you got both (a) and (b) right.

Model-testing approaches all share the requirement that you tell the computer in advance how you expect variables to relate to one another. The analytical strategies then test the extent to which the relationships you predict fit the covariation pattern existing in the data. The test statistic is a chi square, but here, a significant chi square means that your predictions deviated significantly from the actual data. In fact, this is one of those rare times that you will be hoping for a nonsignificant result from your statistics!

The problem with this approach, however, is that whether the chi square is significant depends both on how much difference there is between your model and the actual data *and* on your sample size. The larger the sample, the smaller the difference the chi square test will be able to detect. A cruel twist of fate is that statisticians generally recommend large samples for SEM. This increases the chances of finding your model doesn't fit, even though the lack of fit may be by a rather trivial amount. If you paid attention solely to the chi square result, you might discard your model prematurely.

Fortunately, unhappy investigators and statisticians are aware of this conundrum, and have devised some ways around the large sample/ significant chi square issue. The solution is a boatload of different goodness of fit indicators (see Ullman, 2001, for a description of different classes of fit indicators). And yes, this means you have to choose the fit indicators you will use. Many recommend using more than one. Each has its own recommended cutoff scores as well (see Raykov & Marcoulides, 2000, chap. 1, for rules of thumb for some of the more common indicators).

Structural equation modeling has several advantages. A big one is that it permits you to test many relationships simultaneously in a single analysis rather than running many individual ones. This reduces Type I error. Another is that it forces you to articulate a theory or model you wish to test in advance. Finally, if you use multiple indicators of the same construct (some recommend a minimum of three indicators/construct), SEM tests relationships between the construct score and other variables. In so doing, it removes some of the measurement error from your model, which should result in greater statistical power.

SEM is not for every data set, however. First and foremost, sample size is an issue. Rules of thumb are hard to come by, but in general, samples need to be large. In general, the more complex the model, the smaller the effect sizes you expect, the more missing data you have, and the more skewed the data, the larger the sample required. In our experience, published studies using SEM rarely have fewer than 100 to 150 participants. Ullman (2001) indicated that a sample of 200 "may be adequate" (p. 659) for parsimonious models; Thompson (2000) also suggested at least 10 to 15 participants for each observed variable. Second, novices may fall in love with the idea of testing complex models with SEM. Not only do these demand large samples, but they also are prone to a variety of problems. The result is a computer printout with ominous messages such as "the model cannot be identified" and output that either is missing key statistics or looks odd in some other way. We strongly recommend that you take a course that includes a large dose of SEM, get some experience doing SEM, start collecting and reading articles and books on the approach (e.g., Thompson, 2000), and line up some good consultation on SEM if you are new to it and are likely to use it in your thesis or dissertation.

Set Your Alpha Levels

Now that you have selected an analysis plan, you are ready to begin, right? Not quite! Take a look at the plan to see how many analyses it will take to test your hypotheses. Will you have to run 3 analyses or 30? If you are closer to the latter than the former, remember that running lots of statistical tests increases the chance of making Type I errors, a problem called experiment-wise error.

There are several solutions to this problem. First, you can see whether you really need to conduct all of those statistical tests: Is there another viable analytical approach that will permit you to test the hypotheses with fewer analyses? Perhaps you can use SEM in place of several regression equations or use regression in place of lots of correlations, for example. A second alternative is to reexamine your hypotheses to see if you are trying to do too much in one study. If so, pare down your hypotheses to those that are most important and viable (see Wilkinson & The Task Force on Statistical Inference, 1999, for related discussion).

A third common method is to adjust your p value downward based on the number of tests you wish to run, using the Bonferroni method or some alternative (see Keppel & Wickens, 2004). This adjustment comes at a price, however, and the price is statistical power. So go back and redo those sample size calculations (power analyses) with the new p value. Don't be surprised if the number of participants you need increases dramatically.

Another solution that Keppel and Wickens (2004) suggested is to consider your hypotheses carefully. If each hypothesis truly tests something separate from the others, they suggest you retain an alpha level of .05 for all analyses. If, on the other hand, your hypotheses fall into families (for example, you have five hypotheses, two of which seem logically related, the other three of which fit together as a separate "family"), you should adjust your alpha levels by family.

What counts as an analysis for purposes of examining experiment-wise error? Most students will do three sets of analyses: preliminary analyses, hypothesis-testing analyses, and supplemental analyses (to explore the data further, usually in search of explanations for the results of hypothesis-testing analyses). In considering Type I error, we focus primarily on hypothesis testing. We generally recommend setting alpha at .05 for preliminary analyses, because the purpose of these analyses is usually to look for confounds or problems, and here Type II error is more important than Type I (we don't want to conclude there are no covariates that warrant control when in fact there *are* a few potential confounds). In fact, one could argue that *p* values should be increased, not decreased, in these circumstances. With supplemental analyses, you could adjust your *p* value or not, depending on your philosophy. If you are truly on a fishing expedition and want to be cautious, adjust your alpha downward. If, on the other hand, you are afraid of missing something important, keep your alpha at .05. If you do the latter, however, do not overinterpret isolated findings with small or medium effects—there is a good chance they are spurious. Instead, look for consistencies across related supplemental analyses and large effects, which are less likely to be the result of chance.

As you can see, you have a number of options. Think through the approach you wish to take and incorporate that approach into your analysis plan.

Be Careful With Nonindependent Data

Although appropriate statistics exist for most questions and types of data, be wary about special circumstances that can complicate your statistical life. The first and most important comes from a basic assumption of many parametric *and* nonparametric statistics: independence of observations. Keppel and Wickens (2004) defined this clearly: "This assumption says that what one subject does has no effect on any other subject's performance" (p. 134). This assumption is important because violating it biases the results by leading to underestimates of standard errors of the statistics. This in turn increases the likelihood of Type I error.

You may remember from your introductory statistics courses that one common violation of this assumption occurs when the dependent variable comes from the same participants being tested more than once, in within-subjects designs. A common example of this would involve a treatment and control group who are pretested on the dependent variable of interest, receive either an experimental or a control manipulation, then are post-tested on the same dependent variable. Well-developed methods exist for handling this issue when making group comparisons (e.g., *t*-tests for nonindependent samples, repeated-measures ANOVAs). Regression analyses can handle longitudinal data from two time points, usually by using data from Time 2 as the dependent variable and the data from Time 1 as a predictor or control variable. More complex modeling approaches such as hierarchical linear modeling (Raudenbush & Bryk, 2002; Singer & Willett, 2003) can also handle longitudinal data collected at multiple time points. Handling nonindependence is more complex, however, in three situations. First, repeated measures nonparametric analyses are rare. For example, suppose you want to test which of three products the same set of participants chooses under three different experimental circumstances. Your dependent variable is categorical (which product participants select), but data are not independent because each participant is exposed to all three conditions. Although there probably is some statistic to use in this circumstance, we don't know what it is, and we can safely say that the many textbooks we have perused do not include one.

Here is a second complicating situation. It involves exposing participants to more than one condition (creating a repeated measures design in which one independent variable is a treatment condition and the dependent variable is a repeated-measures variable) and looking at whether participants who vary on a second, continuous variable differ in how they respond to the manipulation. For example, one of our students, Laura Goyer, asked boys to view two sets of videotapes: one set in which stimulus boys engaged in "normative" discussions of everyday topics and another set in which boys talked about more deviant activities. She observed boys' affective expressions as they viewed the different discussions. She was interested in whether disruptive and delinquent boys respond differently to the two types of videos. Ideally, she wanted to examine the interaction between delinquency (a continuous variable) and the type of tape boys viewed (a within-subjects experimental variable). Because she could not locate an appropriate statistic, Laura used her delinquency measure to classify boys as high, medium, or low in delinquency and disruptiveness. Then the analyses were simple: She conducted 3 (delinquency level) × 2 (type of discussion) mixed ANOVAs, with type of discussion treated as a repeated-measures variable.

A third problem situation arises when investigators fail to recognize they have violated the assumption of independence. Recall Keppel and Wicken's (2004) definition of independence: One participant's performance on the dependent variable has no effect on another's performance. In some between-subjects designs, even though each participant contributes only one dependent variable, independence is not a viable assumption.

These circumstances occur when the participants come from the same group, and something about the nature of the group likely causes participants' performance to be affected by that of others. For example, consider studies in which researchers observe interactions between dating couples or small groups of individuals interacting together. Clearly what one person does affects another's performance; the data from people dating each other or interacting together cannot be assumed to be independent. When classrooms or groups of individuals receive interventions as a group, how one person responds to treatment likely influences how others respond. Situations in which several family members participate, people interact in groups, and interventions address groups of individuals who are likely to influence one another are the most frequent situations in which data cannot be assumed to be independent. In these circumstances, the most common solution involves some sort of multilevel or hierarchical analysis (e.g., Raudenbush & Bryk, 2002) that can deal with the nonindependence. These analyses are complex, however, and may require specialized software.

What is our take-home message? Approaches to nonindependent data are not as plentiful, well developed, and readily available as statistics based on the assumption of independent data. Virtually all statisticians seem to agree that the assumption of independence must be taken seriously, however. Therefore, make sure you have worked out how to deal with nonindependence problems from the outset. You may need to redesign your study, as Laura did. Another choice is to turn a within-subjects independent variable into a between-subjects variable. Alternatively, you may be able to discover how to analyze data in ways that get rid of the nonindependence problem. For example, you might average data from both members of a dating couple and use "couple" as your unit of analysis. Finally, you may need to seek out and learn approaches that are unfamiliar to you.

Beware of Causal Terminology

Be careful about allowing the name or nature of the statistic to dictate your reasoning about causality. For example, some students mistakenly believe that significant ANOVAs mean that the independent variable "caused" the changes in the dependent variable. Not so. Yes, differences in levels of the independent variable *relate* to differences in the dependent variable. Whether you can say the independent variable *caused* the differences, however, depends on your design, not the statistics used to test relationships between variables. If you didn't manipulate the independent variable, you cannot legitimately ascribe causal status to it.

In this vein, some refer to structural equation modeling as "causal modeling," an unfortunate moniker that produces droves of inappropriate inferences. Most SEM is based on data collected at a single point in time. Similarly, path analysis based on cross-sectional data is simply a fancy correlational analysis. So is regression in which one or more variables "predict" an outcome and all the variables are measured concurrently. Ditto for mediation analyses. No matter the lingo used to describe the statistic, a correlation is just a correlation. Your design, not your statistic, determines whether you can say that your independent variable caused changes in your dependent variable.

Use Consultation Prudently

At this point, you may have some idea of which statistics are suitable for your study. If so, you may wonder whether you have selected correctly. Go to the library or to good Internet sites and read about some of your potential statistics in more detail. Check out your selections with other students or faculty members to see if they agree with your choices.

What should you do if you still feel clueless and need additional help? Are you allowed to get help or consultation on statistics, and for what purposes? The answers to these questions depend on the degree of consultation involved. "Consultation" can range from asking your chairperson, another graduate student, or a statistics professor on your faculty a few isolated questions about particular aspects of your analyses to hiring someone to select, program, and run the analyses for you. These extremes are different in how much of the work is done by the consultant versus by you, the one who is earning the degree.

Consultation is healthy. Most faculty members consult colleagues with more knowledge about a particular statistical procedure than their own and learn from the experience. Seasoned researchers frequently write statistical consultation into the budgets of their grants. We consulted with several colleagues in writing this chapter. Consultation with faculty and graduate students to point you in the right direction about the ins and outs of particular analyses generally falls within the boundaries of accepted professional practice. In fact, figuring out what you do not know and then finding out the answer by reading and consulting with a colleague is an important part of the professional repertoire. Most students will seek consultation in selecting their statistics or in verifying their choices.

But what about more than mere consultation? This is a complex question. Ideally, students do all of the work themselves, with occasional advice. Unfortunately, at some schools, the statistics classes may not have taught the students well. In addition, the student may have had a great deal of difficulty with the material, the student's chairperson may be as frightened of statistics as the student, or the computer facilities and consultation needed for complex analyses may not be available. In these cases, expecting the student to figure out what to do with the data and then conduct the analyses without assistance may be unrealistic.

Regardless of how you use consultation, remember that ultimately you must be responsible for the statistics in your project. This means that you must know why one particular statistic and not another is suitable, what computer program was used and what choices were made in analyzing your data, how things such as missing data were handled, what the computer output means, whether the analyses were done correctly, and how to interpret the findings. In other words, whether you actually perform the analyses or not, you must know what was done, inside and out, and be responsible for the accuracy of the results as well as their interpretation. Your consultant will not be the one on the hot seat during your proposal meeting and oral defense!

What should you do if you need more than occasional advice? First, we recommend that you do as many of the analyses as you can yourself. If you have appropriate computer resources but no understanding of the particular statistic, you might consult with someone regarding choosing the statistic, programming, and reading the output. You would score, reduce, and enter the data yourself, and run the analyses (perhaps with the assistance of a computer consultant who can help you find errors in your program statements). Second, we recommend consultation specifically aimed at teaching the skills you lack. This might be more appropriately termed *tutoring* than *consultation*. At the end of this tutoring, you should be prepared to pass an examination on what you did, why you did it, the assumptions and characteristics of the statistics you used, and what you found.

In fact, just such an examination may occur in your oral defense. "Well, I really am not sure about exactly what was done; I'll have to ask the person who ran the statistics" is *not* a good way to answer a statistics question in your final orals. You and you alone—not the person who assisted you— must defend your thesis or dissertation before your committee. It is your competence to do research, not your consultant's, that your committee assesses. You, and not a helper, will be earning your degree. Therefore, get the assistance you need to learn and understand what you are doing, but do as much as you can on your own and take full responsibility for ensuring that the statistics have been selected and calculated correctly.

Even if someone will assist you with all of your analyses, prepare your data yourself. Enter the data into the computer after talking with your consultant about how to do it. This will help you understand what the raw data look like. It will also prompt you to think about important issues, such as how to handle missing values. You can also detect outliers—extreme scores that can distort your results and that you might want to handle carefully. We also recommend that you do preliminary analyses yourself, looking at means, standard deviations, frequency distributions, and so on. As mentioned earlier, frequency distributions help you determine whether various statistics are appropriate, and they can alert you early on that you need to alter your statistical plans. We will say more about preliminary analyses in chapter 10.

Seek Additional Assistance If You Are Still Confused

Still confused about what statistics you should use after reading this chapter? You probably are not alone. Statistical material is not equally comprehensible to all readers. Books, professors, and disciplines have different language systems for talking about analyses. Not only is the notation different, sometimes people even use different names for the same analysis. We could not cover every statistic or even every variation on the basic ones we mentioned.

Undoubtedly, many of you will need additional assistance at this point. One additional source in decision making is to use decision trees, such as the one in Figure 9.1, based on information compiled from statistics texts and other decision-making aids, including those described in this discussion. Yates (1982) provided similar information in table form to help students select appropriate statistics. Andrews, Klem, Davidson, O'Malley, and Rodgers (1981) provided an extensive decision tree for selecting appropriate statistics. Their material includes correlational, nonparametric, and parametric tests; provides a reference for each statistic they mention; and refers you to statistical packages that will do the analyses you select. They cover repeated measures (within-subjects) statistics only minimally, however. Tabachnick and Fidell (2001, pp. 27–29) provided a decision tree for multivariate techniques, including correlational strategies.

Another idea is to examine recent articles in well-respected journals that present studies like the one you are proposing and see what kinds of analyses they used. Be sure to look for examples that have variables and types of measures (e.g., suitable for parametric analyses or not) that resemble yours. They should also have a similar design.

We recommend that you use these tools like you use this chapter—as a way to get ideas that you later confirm or reject through appropriate reading and consultation. Your chairperson, statistics professor, graduate student colleagues, and local consultants may provide additional assistance in helping you make sure you've selected the best statistical tools to use in your project.

Supplemental Resources

Comprehensive Statistics Textbooks

Grimm, L. G., & Yarnold, P. R. (Eds.). (1995). *Reading and understanding multivariate statistics.* Washington, DC: American Psychological Association.

Grimm, L. G., & Yarnold, P. R. (Eds.). (2000). *Reading and understanding MORE multivariate statistics.* Washington, DC: American Psychological Association.

Keppel, G., & Wickens, T. D. (2004). *Design and analysis: A researcher's handbook* (4th ed.). Upper Saddle River, NJ: Pearson Prentice-Hall.

Kirk, R. E. (1995). *Experimental design: Procedures for the behavioral sciences* (3rd ed.). Pacific Grove, CA: Brooks/Cole Wadsworth.

Maxwell, S. E., & Delaney, H. D. (2004). *Designing experiments and analyzing data: A model comparison approach* (2nd ed.). Mahwah, NJ: Erlbaum.

Mertler, C. A., & Vannatta, R. A. (2005). *Advanced and multivariate statistical methods* (3rd ed.). Glendale, CA: Pyrczak.

Pedazhur, E. J. (1997). *Multiple regression in behavioral research: Explanation and prediction* (3rd ed.). Orlando, FL: Harcourt Brace.

Siegel, S. (1956). *Nonparametric statistics for the behavioral sciences.* New York: McGraw-Hill.

Tabachnick, B. F., & Fidell, L. S. (2001). *Using multivariate statistics* (4th ed.). Needham Heights, MA: Allyn & Bacon.

Winer, B. J., Brown, D. R., & Michels, K. M. (1991). *Statistical principles in experimental design* (3rd ed.). New York: McGraw-Hill.

More Specialized References

Aiken, L. S., & West, S. G. (1996). *Multiple regression: Testing and interpreting interactions.* Thousand Oaks, CA: Sage.

Andrews, F. M., Klem, L., Davidson, T. N., O'Malley, P. M., & Rodgers, W. L. (1981). *A guide for selecting statistical techniques for analyzing social science data* (2nd ed.). Ann Arbor, MI: Survey Research Center, Institute for Social Research, University of Michigan.

Baron, R. M., & Kenny, D. A. (1986). The moderator–mediator variable distinction in social psychological research: Conceptual, strategic and statistical considerations. *Journal of Personality and Social Psychology, 51,* 1173–1182.

Bruning, J. L., & Kintz, B. L. (1987*). Computational handbook of statistics* (3rd ed.). Glenview, IL: Scott, Foresman.

Cohen, P., Cohen, J., West, S. G., & Aiken, L. S. (2003). *Applied multiple regression/correlation analysis for the behavioral sciences* (3rd ed.). Mahwah, NJ: Erlbaum.

Fabrigar, L. R., Wegener, D. T., MacCallum, R. C., & Strahan, E. J. (1999). Evaluating the use of exploratory factor analysis in psychological research. *Psychological Methods, 4,* 272–299.

Floyd, F., & Widaman, K. F. (1995). Factor analysis in the development and refinement of clinical assessment instruments. *Psychological Assessment, 42,* 286–299.

Gorsuch, R. L. (1983). *Factor analysis.* Hillsdale, NJ: Erlbaum.

Holmbeck, G. N. (1997). Toward terminological, conceptual, and statistical clarity in the study of mediators and moderators: Examples from the child–clinical and pediatric psychology literatures. *Journal of Consulting and Clinical Psychology, 65,* 599–610.

Huitema, B. E. (1980). *The analysis of covariance and alternatives.* New York: Wiley.

Jaccard, J., Becker, M. A., & Wood, G. (1984). Pairwise multiple comparison procedures: A review. *Psychological Bulletin, 96,* 589–596.

MacCallum, R. C., Widamon, K. F., Zhang, S., & Hong, S. (1999). Sample size in factor analysis. *Psychological Methods, 4,* 84–99.

MacKinnon, D. P., Lockwood, C. M., Hoffman, J. M., West, S. G., & Sheets, V. (2002). A comparison of methods to test mediation and other intervening variable effects. *Psychological Methods, 7,* 83–104.

Newton, R. R., & Rudestam, K. E. (1999). *Your statistical consultant: Answers to your data analysis questions.* Thousand Oaks, CA: Sage.

Preacher, K. J., & MacCallum, R. C. (2003). Repairing Tom Swift's electric factor analysis machine. *Understanding Statistics, 2,* 13–43.

Raudenbush, S. W., & Bryk, A. S. (2002). *Hierarchical linear models: Applications and data analysis methods* (2nd ed.). Thousand Oaks, CA: Sage.

Raykov, T., & Marcoulides, G. M. (2000). *A first course in structural equation modeling.* Mahwah, NJ: Erlbaum.

Singer, J. D., & Willett, J. S. (2003). *Applied longitudinal data analysis: Modeling change and event occurrence.* New York: Oxford University Press.

Thompson, B. (2000). Ten commandments of structural equation modeling. In L. G. Grimm & P. R. Yarnold (Eds.), *Reading and understanding MORE multivariate statistics* (pp. 261–283). Washington, DC: American Psychological Association.

Wilkinson, L., & The Task Force on Statistical Inference. (1999). Statistical methods in psychology journals. *American Psychologist, 54,* 594–604.

✔ To Do . . .

Selecting Appropriate Statistics

☐ Beef up your statistical knowledge early

— Find comprehensible statistics books, Web sites, and articles

— Get experience doing statistical analyses

☐ Examine your study

— Identify questions you wish statistics to answer

— Make a list of variables you plan to analyze

— Identify the nature of each variable (categorical, ordinal, interval, ratio)

— Identify independent and dependent variables for each question

☐ Identify whether dependent variables are suitable for parametric or nonparametric analyses

☐ Create an analysis plan

— Match statistics to research questions, hypotheses, and variables

— Select among group-comparison statistics

— Select among correlational statistics

☐ Set your alpha levels

☐ Be careful about assuming causality

☐ Use consultation prudently

☐ Assume responsibility for your statistics

☐ Seek assistance if you are not sure

— Look at decision trees

— Read stats books and check out Web sites

— Look at articles that used designs like yours

— Talk to your mentor, stats professor, or knowledgeable students

10

Collecting, Managing, and Analyzing the Data

Y ou've finished the proposal, your committee has approved it, and now it's time to collect the data—to do what you promised to do in your method section. The promises may have been easier to make than to keep, however. How much difficulty you have keeping them will depend in part on careful planning to minimize potential hassles. Chapter 3 described planning steps you could take early in your project. In this chapter we provide more advice for avoiding and coping with common problems fledgling researchers encounter as they put their plans into practice.

Before you rush out to recruit participants, take time to pilot test and fine-tune your procedures, train any research assistants (RAs) you have working with you, develop a data storage and management plan, and arrange for equipment and facilities. In this chapter, we discuss each of these steps in more detail. In addition, make sure you obtain *written approval* from your institutional review board (IRB) for the protection of human (or animal) participants before you even advertise for or recruit human participants.

Pilot Test Your Procedures

If you have not already pilot tested your procedures, now is the time to do it. Pilot work is important because what you plan to do may look good on paper but not work well when you try it out with real participants. For example, the procedure you thought would take 15 minutes may take an hour for some participants. The equipment may not work the way you thought it would, or participants may not understand your carefully crafted instructions. Even if your procedures run smoothly, pilot work will alert you to issues you need to train your RAs to handle. It is hard to train someone to use procedures that you do not know intimately yourself.

Who should serve as pilot participants? If you will have no problem recruiting a sufficient sample for the research, designate the first few participants you recruit as pilots. Do not include their data in the study, because normally you will treat them differently than later participants. If participants who meet your criteria are scarce, use individuals who have characteristics that match your target population as much as possible but who would not qualify as participants in your actual study. For example, in our work with children, we often recruit children of colleagues or of graduate students to serve as pilot participants. Other graduate students, undergraduate RAs, and friends may be willing to serve as pilot participants for some or all of your procedures.

The specific purposes of pilot testing are (a) to ensure that participants will respond in accord with instructions, (b) to uncover and decide how to handle unanticipated problems, (c) to gauge how long participants will take to finish their tasks, and (d) to learn how to use and to check the adequacy of your equipment. Now is the time to fine-tune your procedures and work out the bugs. To facilitate this, you will want to ask your pilot study participants to give you feedback, something that usually does not occur during the study proper. Ask your participants whether the instructions were clear, what difficulties they had following the instructions, whether anything about the environment or the experimenter's behavior interfered with their performance of the task, and so on. In addition, watch your participants as they complete your procedures. Do they perform as you instructed? Based on their feedback and your observations, make suitable changes and run the next pilot participant. Again, ask for feedback. Keep adjusting your procedures until you are satisfied the study will run smoothly. Keep written notes to use in training any assistants you might involve.

If you use human judges or observers to rate or record participants' responses, collect pilot data to use when you train them. For example, videotape the kinds of interactions observers will be recording on the playground or collect samples of written open-ended responses that raters will later code. Having these samples will allow your assistants to practice during training on real data. This is important because real data often pose difficulties you may not anticipate when you make up training materials. Perhaps this is why interobserver agreement often drops when observers begin to observe "real" participants after training (e.g., Taplin & Reid, 1973). Train assistants to deal with these problems *before* you start collecting the data needed for your thesis or dissertation.

Pilot testing occasionally turns up a problem that requires a major change in design or procedures. Your clever use of an experimental confederate, for example, may be blatantly transparent to the pilot participants. Your experimental manipulation of participants' motivation may not motivate them, and so on. Your chairperson must approve all changes in procedures and design. If you propose a major change, you may need to meet again with your entire committee. At a minimum, you should circulate a memorandum outlining the changes you propose and asking committee members to agree to the changes in writing. In addition, changes in procedures may require you to alter your consent form and to apply to your IRB for approval of the changes.

Recruit and Train Assistants

Thesis and dissertation studies are big undertakings. Ordinarily, they require assistants of one sort or another. For example, you may need others to serve as experimenters, raters, observers, confederates, and the like. These individuals may be undergraduate students working for credit, paid assistants, other graduate students, or friends and relatives who have a perverse interest in your being indebted to them in a major way.

These assistants should first be told—preferably in the form of a written agreement that you and they sign—exactly what you will require of them and what they will receive as a result of their role in the project. This should include the full nature of their duties; the times you will ask them to work; the duration of their involvement; compensation for services (if any); and, if they are students working for credit, how you will evaluate them. We also recommend full disclosure of things that can get them "fired" from the project.

Be honest, direct, and realistic with prospective assistants. Remember that collecting data may take longer than you plan, that participants may not show up, and that training takes time. Leading prospective assistants to believe that their duties will be minimal and later dumping extra work on them can create resentment. If someone does not have enough time to meet your requirements, let him or her opt out in the beginning. This is better than having assistants quit after you spend considerable time training them because the project is more work than you told them it would be.

Timing is important. A common error involves recruiting assistants too early. They then have nothing to do for several weeks or months. When the project is finally ready to go, typically several can no longer participate. A good rule of thumb is to begin recruiting assistants after (a) your committee approves your proposal, (b) you have arranged a source of participants, (c) your training materials are ready, and (d) your initial pilot testing is complete. An approved proposal ensures that your procedures will not change much as a result of a committee member's suggestions, and a source of participants usually means that you can begin collecting data as soon as you train your assistants.

Your proposal may dictate certain types of assistants—for example, a female confederate, a graduate-student therapist, or a child model. In addition to screening for qualities that relate to your design, select assistants who are dependable. You want RAs to be on time and to keep other commitments. With undergraduates, we sometimes assess this by asking about their job experience, on the assumption that individuals who have held part-time or full-time jobs have had to learn and demonstrate reliable performance. Another quality to look for is good judgment: Ideally, your RAs should do what you would do when an unanticipated problem confronts them. For example, if RAs will be observing in the school setting, they will need to dress appropriately, interact professionally with the school office staff and teachers, and refrain from complaining if a teacher asks them to leave the classroom because it is time for a test he or she forgot to mention earlier. Although high-level general intellectual functioning is a wonderful quality in an RA, dependability, social skills, and good judgment may be more important.

After you recruit your RAs, train them well. Research has shown that several procedures contribute to skill acquisition and performance: instruction, modeling, rehearsal, and feedback. Explain tasks to your RAs, show them (though role playing, video, or other means) how to do them, and have them practice as you give feedback. If your assistants must perform complex duties, break tasks down and have them learn and practice small steps that cumulate to mastery of the complete task.

As an example, Sharon Foster and some of her students trained other graduate students to interview children about incidents involving peer provocation (Dumas et al., 1992). Interviewers had to learn a complex coding system for scoring the children's responses as well as the format for conducting a semistructured interview. The first step was for interviewers to review the written coding manual. They then practiced coding pilot responses, beginning with easy responses and progressing to more difficult ones. The research team had previously coded each series of responses. Trainers checked interviewers' responses for accuracy against these criterion coding decisions and provided feedback to the trainees. After interviewers demonstrated 85% or higher agreement with the master coding on all categories on a series of examples, they learned how to interview the children. Trainers described and modeled each of the skills (e.g., asking precise questions and paraphrasing the child's statements) for the interviewer–trainees. Trainees then role-played portions of interviews with trainers (who provided feedback) to learn the skill on which they were being trained. After mastering all of the component skills, interviewers practiced complete interviews with pilot participants and with the investigators. They were ready to interview actual participants when they completed two different mock interviews with two different investigators that required minimal correction.

Because knowledge of experimental hypotheses has been tied to biased data (e.g., Rosenthal, 1969), keep your RAs as unaware as possible about the different conditions of your study. If you cannot make sure they are not aware of your conditions, at least make sure they do not know your hypotheses. At the same time, tell them enough so they can perform their duties adequately. To figure out whether a piece of information is inappropriate to share, ask yourself, "Could this information conceivably influence in a negative fashion the way this assistant interacts with participants or scores the data?" If the answer is "yes," do not give the assistant the information. It is also important to avoid experimenter-condition confounds. This occurs when different experimenters are exclusively responsible for different conditions. When this happens, you cannot be sure your findings are the result of your independent variable or differences in your experimenters.

When students are working for credit, make the experience an educational one. You can do this by teaching the fundamentals of research design and procedures (without revealing your hypotheses, of course!). Thus, students can learn about the importance of standardized procedures, the concept of experimental control, why and how data on interobserver agreement are important, and so on. You may also be able to help undergraduate students learn the ins and outs of graduate school life, application procedures, and the like, or you may be able to mentor other graduate students who are not as far advanced as you are. As much as possible, we like to give students a variety of duties as RAs, so that they can observe and experience many aspects of the research process.

Build in Ethical Safeguards

Presumably, you thought through a number of ethical issues when planning your study and obtaining IRB approval. Now is the time to make sure your RAs understand research ethics and how they apply to your study. Review the material on research ethics in chapter 7. Remember to inform your assistants about the importance of confidentiality. They should not talk about human participants' data or behavior with others outside the project. Be sure to tell them not to chat about participants with fellow assistants in public places: Prospective participants may overhear their comments.

Instructing yourself and others is only part of this process, however. Having procedures in place to ensure ethical conduct is also important. Think about how you will store the data, make sure no names are on data forms, and so on. If you are working with children in school settings, how will you collect consent forms from teachers? How will you make sure you don't accidentally run a participant who does not have parental consent? How will you obtain assent from the children themselves and make sure that they have the opportunity to ask questions and demur if they decide they do not wish to participate?

In addition to developing procedures that ensure confidentiality and informed consent, make sure to monitor the way you and others conduct the research. If you are using assistants, this can take the form of sitting in on or listening to tape recordings of their interviews with participants to check that they really are obtaining informed consent and explaining participants' rights in language the participants can understand. Likewise, sit in on or listen to tapes of debriefing sessions to make sure your assistants tell participants the essential details of the experiment in which they have just participated.

If you are following clinical samples over time, be especially sensitive to the possibility of changes for the worse in participants' clinical picture. Scheduled contact to check on this will permit you to make an appropriate referral if they do get worse (Yates, 1982).

Schedule Settings and Arrange Materials

After you finalize your procedures and establish a timetable for starting the project, work out final logistic details. The checklist at the end of this chapter lists a number of steps to take in preparing to run participants. It prompts you to think about how you are going to keep the project running smoothly from week to week and to plan accordingly. Such planning involves ensuring that you have a physical location to run participants at appropriate times. If you are running animals in a long series of trials over a specific time period, make sure someone will be available to run the animals during weekends and vacations.

If you are purchasing measures or other copyrighted materials, order these in advance (be sure to ask about discounts or freebies for starving students working on dissertations). Similarly, if you need equipment, make sure it will be available when you need it and have a backup plan in case equipment suddenly fails or disappears. If several people will take equipment to different sites, make rules for checking out and returning equipment to a central spot in a timely fashion so that you can locate missing tape recorders, and so on. Have a plan for preventive maintenance, such as cleaning video- or audiotape heads and replenishing batteries.

Copy and organize all forms. Ideally, when a participant arrives, the experimenter should pull out a file with all the forms and information for that participant arranged in the proper order. Normally, this file will contain copies of the consent or assent form, any special instructions to the experimenter (e.g., a note designating the participant's condition), and questionnaires to be completed. Write the participant's code number on all pieces of data, in case these pieces get separated later. If your procedures are complex, include in the file a checklist (e.g., stapled to the inside of the file) listing the tasks and measures to be completed. As the participant completes each task, the experimenter can check the appropriate spot on the checklist. Create a method of checking for missing data as participants or RAs turn in forms. For example, in studies using questionnaires, we scan through the items when the participant turns in the research forms. When we see a blank item, we ask the person whether he or she accidentally or intentionally left the answer blank (in the latter case, we say "that's fine, you don't have to answer anything you don't want to").

Arrange a place to store the data as they come in. To ensure confidentiality, keep data in a locked room (at a minimum), and preferably in a locked filing cabinet. Make sure RAs know the rules and the procedures for filing data (e.g., all data must be filed immediately after running a participant—not carried around in a car; no raw data may leave the building). You should also file consent forms in an organized way and check periodically to make sure you have forms on file for all participants. If there is a key that codes their names with identifying numbers, make sure it is up to date and kept in a separate, locked place. Incidentally, consider the possibility of fire and other disasters and whether it makes sense to keep a separate set of the data somewhere else.

Think, too, about easy ways of keeping track of how many participants have been run as the study progresses (a publicly posted cumulative graph of accomplishments motivates everyone), and of informing others involved in the project about what is happening that week. For example, one of us often conducts research involving individual sessions with children in school settings. Sometimes schedules must change from week to week because of teacher requests, RA availability, student absence, and the school schedule. When you cannot have a master schedule to follow every week, take Thursday or Friday to schedule RAs for the following week. Do this after checking with the school secretary about field trips, teacher conference days, and other times the children will not be available. Late Friday or early Monday, the experimenter or the lead RA takes the schedule to the school and verifies it with the teachers, making last minute changes and leaving copies with the teachers, the principal, and the school's administrative assistant. A finalized copy goes to RAs via e-mail and on the lab wall. Next to the schedule is a list of children with parental permission who have not yet participated. RAs cross off the names of children they saw when they bring in the data each day.

Another detail to think about involves transferring the data to computer-usable form. Unless you are doing a single-organism study with no statistics involved, eventually you will need to do this. Although some researchers like to wait until all data are collected, we prefer to get data ready for and into the computer as they come in. That way, individuals running participants can also be responsible for recording their own data, and the process is not as tedious as it is when all data are recorded at once. We discuss methods for recording data later.

One exception to our "do it as you go" advice arises if observers or raters will code videotapes or written responses. Observer (rater) drift can distort data if a coding scheme is not implemented carefully. This occurs when two or more human judges gradually drift consensually in how they use a coding system over time (Romanczyk et al., 1973). This can happen if they discuss problems using the coding scheme and evolve implicit decision rules that do not appear in the original coding manual. If everyone "drifts" as a group (i.e., consensually), interrater or interobserver agreement figures will be high and will not detect the drift. Most important, data that come in later in the project will be coded differently than early data, creating a potential confound for longitudinal, time-series, and pre–post designs. Thus, assembling all the data first and coding tapes or responses in random order later ensures that drift and time of data collection are not confounded. Another way to combat drift is to continue meeting as a group and scoring stimuli that were criterion scored before the study began, while providing feedback regarding agreement with the criterion (DeMaster, Reid, & Twentyman, 1977). This process is called *recalibration*. Recalibration is important for any project involving human judges, and it is crucial when data must be coded as they come in rather than randomly at some later time.

Plan for the Unexpected

No matter how carefully you plan, things will go wrong. One important step is to identify the most probable areas in which unexpected events might occur. In our experience, there are three: participants, personnel, and equipment. What unexpecteds can you expect in each of these? With respect to participants, there are two basic considerations: recruitment and appointment keeping. Remember the rule of the threes: Allow three times as much time as you think it will take to recruit enough participants.

You might be saying this doesn't apply in your case because you already have the permission of the instructors of three college classes that will provide more than enough participants for your administration of the XYZ Scales. Perhaps so, but what if the class is cancelled one day because the instructor is ill and the next class cannot be used because an exam is scheduled? Or what if a lower percentage of class members volunteer to participate than you expected? Maybe you plan to do your recruiting by calling people on the phone. Do you know the average number of times you need to call someone to reach them? Do you have any pilot information to indicate what kind of response rate you can expect?

Once you schedule your participants, do you have any way of ensuring they show up? Do you have some idea what the typical no-show rate is for studies such as yours? What will you do if someone fails to keep an appointment? Will you schedule a makeup or decide not to run the risk of a repeat offense? Take a clue from physicians and dentists. They give you a little card with the exact day and time of your appointment. Some even call you to remind you of the appointment a day or two before it occurs. Have you made arrangements to do this for your participants?

Despite your best efforts, some participants will not keep their appointments. How will you use this unexpected time? If you are thinking it will be a good time to get caught up on your sleeping or recreational pursuits or to study for a class, consider another possibility. This is time set aside for working on your research. If a participant fails to appear, this is not really "free" time. It only looks that way. You will have to make up this session some time later if you plan to keep the project on schedule. That will take time away from some other research-related activity you had planned. Anticipate the occasional no-show and plan to do some research-related work during that time. Revise the introduction to get it ready for the final version. Write a more detailed method section now that you have had experience running the study. Input your latest data into the computer. Chase down that final elusive reference at the library. If you keep to the task this way, you will minimize the time wasted by no-shows and you will not be derailed from accomplishing your goal.

Another area of potential surprises involves RAs or other project-related personnel. Being human, they get sick, fail to keep *their* appointments, forget to collect or enter an important piece of data, and so on. How will you handle these oversights? Standard personnel management practices are the best advice. Start with the selection of the best people you can get. Who these are may depend on such factors as how you will compensate them. If you can pay them a reasonable amount in money or academic credit, you can select higher caliber people and expect more from them. If you cannot pay, consider nonmonetary rewards. The barter system sometimes works well. You agree to help someone with his or her data analyses if she or he will run participants for you. Or how about a home-cooked meal for every six participants run?

To avoid problems when an assistant calls in sick or takes a vacation, cross-train your RAs. Make sure each knows at least one other person's job so you can arrange substitutions when needed.

In addition, plan time for frequent monitoring. In addition to monitoring for implementation of research ethics procedures, check the data as they come in. Make sure your assistants are following research procedures to the letter. Even conscientious assistants make errors, and spot-checking their performance can allow you to catch these before they get out of control.

Finally, expect surprises from your equipment. You can anticipate all of these. Some (e.g., projector bulbs burning out, having difficulty hooking the projector to the computer) are more likely than others (e.g., someone stealing the polygraph), but it is best to assume that breakdowns will happen and be prepared for them. In case you are thinking that you are doing low- or no-tech research and equipment is not involved, think again. What about the car that gets you back and forth to the research site? What about the computer that you are using for word processing and data analyses? A couple of years ago, one of us had three hard disk crashes on different computers in the same year. Do you have plans for backing up documents and data on different computers maintained in different locations?

The Department of Redundancy Department is a good place for dealing with all three of these sources of potential surprises. Cross-training of RAs is an example of the redundancy principle. Have more participants, personnel, and equipment ready to do the job than you think you will need. Arrange in advance to borrow or rent equipment to use temporarily while yours is being repaired. Have a plan to notify your backup or on-call RAs in case the primary one gets sick. The National Aeronautics and Space Administration (NASA) exemplifies the principle of redundancy in its manned flights into outer space. When one system fails, a backup system immediately assumes its functions. Run your research this way. In fact, run your life this way, and you will suffer fewer unpleasant surprises!

Collect the Data

Finally, the first participant arrives, or you run your first animal. The procedures run smoothly, the participant stays for the entire session, and everyone is where they should be at the right time, doing what they are supposed to do. Time to kick back and have some fun while the RAs take over, right? Well, not quite.

A key to keeping the process running smoothly is to *supervise it closely*. This does not mean micromanaging your RAs. But you do need to make sure they are performing their duties correctly and in a timely fashion. This ordinarily means setting objectives and arranging a schedule for yourself and your assistants, then regularly assessing progress toward those objectives and compliance with the work schedule. Reward RAs with positive comments and other signs of appreciation for successful performance. Similarly, talk with RAs about any performance problems in a courteous but firm fashion early in the process, to prevent problems that can easily occur without adequate supervision. Encourage RAs to bring up any difficulties they encounter early on, too. Problems in procedures, data coding, and other aspects are best handled as soon as you discover them. Regular meetings of project staff provide good forums for discussing progress and logistics.

Also, be sure to check your data as they come in to see that they are being collected correctly. If you do this in the presence of RAs, control your desire to exclaim positively over data that look positive and to weep over those that do not. These behaviors can prompt the assistants to produce biased data that may make you happier but may not reflect participants' actual performance (O'Leary, Kent, & Kanowitz, 1975).

If your data will be processed extensively or handled by different people, consider how you will track who has completed what. For example, suppose you will be collecting, transcribing, and scoring audiotaped data based on interviews. Tapes will have to be logged in as they are collected, then out again for transcribing. Transcripts will need to be stored and then checked out later for scoring. How will you organize and track these procedures? Spreadsheet programs such as Excel or Calc provide one way; lower tech versions such as checklists are another.

If you collect your data in an applied setting, check periodically with contact people in the setting to make sure everything is running smoothly. Doing so will catch potential difficulties early in the process. We cannot emphasize this enough: One RA who fails to attend to protocol may sour those in the setting on research and even get you tossed out! Apprise key personnel in the setting of changes in schedules and thank them formally (we do it in writing as well as in person) when you complete your data collection. If you promised to show them the results, let them know when you should have the data analyzed, and be sure to go back and present your findings. Your performance as a researcher affects whether an applied setting will allow future students and faculty to use their facilities.

Finally, keep a research log of unusual things that happen during data collection, decisions that you make, informal observations, and the like. Jot down ways you wish you had done the study differently. These may come in handy later, when you write your discussion section—particularly if you have unusual results. Looking back at your observations as you were running the data may help you to identify possible reasons for your findings.

Score, Check, and Analyze the Data

As you get ready to start data collection, think through how you will score your data and transfer them to computer-analyzable form. A good rule of thumb is that the fewer the steps between the raw data and the computer, the better. One good idea, therefore, would be to have your participants record their answers directly into a computer. This requires that you have access to computer equipment and programming for your measures, that your measures are suitable for this process, and that your participants are sufficiently computer-savvy (or computer-trainable) to follow the procedures. In addition, if your measures are generally administered in paper-and-pencil form, responses to your measures should be reliable and valid when computer-administered. If direct computer entry is not feasible, consider mark-sense forms that can be machine scored. The scores are stored in computer-compatible formats that permit manipulation and analysis without any hand-scoring or data entry by you. If neither direct entry nor mark-sense technology is available, you and your assistants could enter the data directly from questionnaires or scoring sheets into the computer, without the middle step of writing the scores on large data sheets.

Before beginning to enter data, write out instructions (i.e., a "code-book") to be followed in entering data. These should specify the name of each variable in computerese (i.e., the name you give the variable for statistical analyses), a description of the data to which the name refers, and how to score the variable. For example, your codebook might indicate that you should enter responses to an ethnicity question on the demographic form under the variable called "ethnic," entering the number "1" for African American, "2" for Asian American, and so on.

Consider the computer program you will be using as you plan how to code your data in computer-readable form. Each program has different rules about how to arrange the data. If you administer the same measure repeatedly over time to each participant, be sure to check how your program handles repeated-measures data. Some programs work better with repeated measures data on different data lines, others with all data from the same participant on the same data line. Also check how your program handles missing data. The two most common ways are to delete cases with missing values on either a listwise or pairwise basis. The first approach deletes all data for a particular participant if some are missing. With the second approach, participant data are disregarded for any pair of variables for which one has missing data. For example, if relaxation practice times were missing for 2 of 80 participants, correlations involving relaxation practice and other variables would be based on 78 rather than 80 participants. The participant's data would still be included in analyses involving variables other than relaxation practice, however. We discuss issues related to missing data in a later section of this chapter.

If you are a computer neophyte or are unfamiliar with the program you plan to use, consult with someone more knowledgeable about your particular analyses for suggestions about how to set up your computer data file. How-to guidebooks are also available for some of the major programs (e.g., Pallant, 2001, for SPSS; Delwiche & Slaughter, 2003, for SAS). Most of these provide basic instruction in how to set up data files, manage data (e.g., do variable transformations), and interpret output, and they also review some of the basics of statistics.

Similarly, if you intend to purchase software for yourself, shop carefully. Be aware of your analyses, and ask questions that pertain to them before purchasing anything. Some software companies such as SPSS have demonstration seminars you can attend online for free to see if the analysis will accommodate your data. Checking in advance is particularly important if you are doing unusual or cutting-edge analyses; even large software packages may not offer the options you wish to use. Make sure to ask whether graduate students can purchase the software at reduced rates and whether you will get a full version of the program or a version with some restrictions (e.g., it will only handle a limited number of cases or variables).

Free software is sometimes available online. You may be tempted to download some of this instead of investing in more standard software packages. Some of this has been created by capable, high-minded professionals who wish to make it freely available. For example, Mx (http://www.vcu.edu/mx) is a programming language for doing structural equation modeling. In our experience, most often these freebies are specialized or intended for individuals who are quite familiar with computer programming and creating and solving the formulas involved in statistical analyses. In addition, because creators of this shareware generally contribute their time, rarely do these programs have the documentation and user support that more costly statistical programs provide. If you are an experienced stats or computer junkie and this doesn't scare you off, more power to you. If you are a novice, you might be better off sticking with a more widely used package.

What data should you record in a computer file? We recommend putting in anything that you could conceivably want to analyze, whether you planned an analysis with the variable or not. For example, we always code the identity of the person who ran the participant, although we rarely use this variable in analyses (but we just might, if the data looked strange and we wanted to find out if one particular experimenter was responsible). Code individual items of questionnaires if you want the computer to derive subscales, if you wish to compute internal consistency scores on your scales, or if you think you might want to group items in a different fashion later. If none of these is relevant, you may choose to record only summary scores. A good rule of thumb is to record data at as molecular a level as your resources will allow. You can always aggregate later, but you can't always disaggregate.

You must verify data for accuracy *every step along the way that involves human recording*. We routinely verify all of our data at the data-entry stage by having them checked for accuracy by someone else. One easy and efficient way to do this involves working in pairs where one reads the data and the other enters the data, then the two change places to verify. Some statistical-analysis programs permit duplicate entry of the same data and signal you if the original and duplicate entries do not match. You can also run summary statistics on each variable to look for ns that are not what you expect them to be and for out-of-range values (e.g., a value of 42 on a 1–5 scale!).

Verification does not stop with data entry. If you score your questionnaires by hand to get summary scores, someone should check the scoring. If you write a variable transformation program to compute subscale scores, calculate a few by hand to make sure you did not make an error in creating the transformation. Now is the time to be obsessive–compulsive. We personally have detected major errors in recording and calculations, even among some of our most competent students—errors sufficient to change the results and interpretation of the analyses. Remember, the computer cannot tell you whether you scored the data correctly. It will only analyze what you give it. As the saying goes, garbage in—garbage out.

After you record and verify your data, it is time to perform the analyses. Haul out your analysis plan, discussed in chapter 9. Complete the preliminary analyses before you go on to test your hypotheses. As noted in chapter 9, preliminary analyses generally involve such things as checking (a) the assumptions of the analyses you plan to use to test hypotheses, (b) the reliability and validity of your measures, (c) unintended confounds, (d) whether methodological details such as order or sequencing have posed problems that you need to solve, (e) the distributions of your variables, and (f) the extent of missing data and whether missingness is related to other variables in your study. The results of these analyses help you decide whether to test your hypotheses as planned or whether you need to rethink your hypothesis-testing plan.

Start by spending some time looking at your data. If you are examining groups of participants, get scatterplots of correlations among variables. Look at how each group of participants scored on major variables, whether the distributions of different groups overlapped, and if so, how much. Look at frequency distributions of variables. This kind of early data exploration provides a good feel for the data and will probably help you interpret more complex statistical findings later.

Before diving into your main analyses with group designs, you should check whether your groups are equivalent on demographic characteristics and other potentially confounding variables. In correlation studies, correlate demographic variables with your independent or predictor variables. If the demographic variables (or other potential confounding variables) are related to your independent variables, you can then correlate the potential confound with your dependent variables. If uncorrelated, the potential confound is not linearly related to the dependent variable and is unlikely to influence your analyses. A significant correlation indicates that you might need to control for that variable, however, either through a design change (e.g., using the confounding variable as an additional independent variable) or statistically (e.g., using analysis of covariance; but see our discussion of this in chapter 9).

Also, check whether your data meet the assumptions of the statistics you plan to use. If not, check whether your proposed analysis is robust with regard to violation of the assumption. If not, take appropriate actions (e.g., transform the data or select an alternative analysis). Return to chapter 9 for a discussion of the assumptions of various statistics.

Finally, look for missing data and figure out how you want to handle them. As you entered data into the computer, you undoubtedly noticed that a person omitted a question here and there. You may lack data for entire measures for some individuals. How should you deal with these missing data?

This sounds like an easy question, but actually, the answers are fairly complex. They depend on the reasons data are missing in the first place. Are your missing data (a) related to both the independent and dependent variable (nonignorable missingness, MNAR), (b) related to the independent variables but not the dependent variable ("missing at random," MAR), or (c) related to neither the independent nor the dependent variables ("missing completely at random," MCAR). Schafer and Graham (2002) provided an extensive overview of options for dealing with missing data under these different conditions. We borrow heavily from their analysis and strongly recommend that you soldier through their comprehensive discussion for an in-depth look at this issue.

Once you have figured out in your preliminary analyses whether your data are MCAR, MAR, or MNAR, you have several different choices in how to handle missing data. One of the most common is listwise deletion, mentioned earlier: any data missing at all, and the person's data, are not used. The practical disadvantage of this approach (lowered N) will be particularly obvious if you worked and slaved for every participant in your study. In addition, unless the data are missing completely at random, the results will produce biased estimates of population parameters under most circumstances (Schafer & Graham, 2002). If few data are missing, however, this is an option.

A second common method of dealing with missing data is used when responses to items on multi-item scales are missing. Here a common procedure is to substitute the average of other available indicators of a construct—for example, use the mean of remaining scale items if one or more items is missing, sometimes called unweighted means estimation (Winer, Brown, & Michels, 1991). Schafer and Graham (2002) reported that this can produce biased results, but the biases are relatively small when the remaining items are intercorrelated highly (i.e., have high internal consistency). Another strategy involves using regression equations to estimate replacement values (Farrell, 1999).

Substituting a value for the missing piece of data is one method of imputation—making a good guess as to what the missing data would have been. Another way of dealing with missing values involves multiple imputation methods in which many plausible values are generated for each piece of missing data, and the results are then averaged. Although multiple imputation methods are generally held to be superior to single imputation methods (Schafer & Graham, 2002), these newer methods are only now being incorporated into mainstream software. Finally, maximum likelihood methods can be used; these are statistical techniques that use available data to make their best estimates of what the statistical parameters of the population might be. These methods are only suitable when data are missing at random (or completely at random). They are available through many widely used statistical packages.

Learn to Use Your Software

Doing your analysis allows you to learn not only about statistics but also about the ins and outs of the software you are using. If this is your virgin journey into a program or type of analysis, *be prepared for frustration*. Some of the most powerful computer programs have user-unfriendly help menus loaded with technical jargon but short on the details of how to handle common types of data. Anticipate that you will run into difficulties and be pleasantly surprised if you do not. Remember, you are not alone. And you are not stupid because you cannot get the machine to do what you want. We have had to learn several data analysis programs in our combined seven decades as faculty members, and have discovered that it usually takes about seven tries the first time through a new analysis with a new program to get it right!

If you are not familiar with the statistics you will be using, find someone who knows the software *and* the analyses you plan to use and who will help you or at least give you an example of their programming statements. Preferably, this will be your chairperson or another student in your program. Do your analyses when that person is available to help. Physical availability is best, because your consultant will probably want to see the printouts and any error messages that you have received.

As you tell the computer what to do, take the time to tell it how to label your printouts and your variables. Give them names you will remember 5 years from now. Labeling the levels of your independent variable as *A* and *B* may make sense to you now, but you will not remember what *A* and *B* stand for next month. It takes some time and imagination, but programming the computer to label the top of each page with the name of the project and to give each independent and dependent variable a meaningful name will pay off later in the intelligibility of your printouts. You will already have arrived at this conclusion independently if you have spent time staring blankly at computer file names several years after you created them, trying to remember what they meant.

If your statistics program is the point-and-click variety (e.g., SPSS), learn to use syntax and save syntax files. Computer syntax is the language used by the program to tell the computer what to do. Often this language is hidden from view in the interest of making the program easier to use. Learn how to get the syntax you use, to save it, to recall it, and to reuse it. If you save your instructions to the computer, you can reconstruct your analyses with minimal effort.

Why is this important? Recall the "it takes seven times to get it right" observation. Suppose you create summary scores for all of your variables, and then discover that some of these scores look odd. If you have syntax files saved, you can go back and check your work. If not, you have no way of checking for errors except by completely redoing the analyses. Suppose you discover late in the process that someone failed to enter data for one of the participants, and that you need to rerun all of your analyses—or you want to see if your analyses produce similar results if you filter out possible problem participants or outliers. With syntax files, rerunning analyses takes minutes, not the hours it would take to recreate the analyses if you had to start again from scratch.

In addition, remember to investigate and check the default values your program uses for the analyses you conduct. Default values are the choices the computer makes for you if you do not tell it otherwise. The more complex the analysis, the more the analysis is based on choices about how to calculate the results. For example, factor analysis involves many choices about how to extract factors, whether factors are allowed to be correlated, and so on. Different statistical analyses have different choices, so software for each analysis may have different default values built in. Computer programmers try to program in the most widely accepted or common defaults. Many statisticians have gotten tenure by debating the pros and cons of these alternatives, however, so the default value is not always the best choice for every situation. You, not the creators of SPSS or SAS, will be responsible for the details of your statitstics and whether the default values are appropriate for your data and purposes. Most programs allow you to override the defaults, so it's a good idea to figure out which options to select for the analyses you run.

After you examine your data and the results of your preliminary analyses, determine whether you need to modify your hypothesis-testing plan. Now is a good time to check with your chairperson if you have run into snags and to discuss how to handle the statistical or methodological problems you have encountered. Do this *before* you test your hypotheses to prevent biased decision making. It's not a good idea to pick one statistic or approach over another just because one turns out the way you like and the other does not. Better to make the decision beforehand.

As you run your hypothesis-testing analyses, figure out what sample sizes and degrees of freedom the computer should be using, and check the printout to see if the computer's figures match your own. If not, look for errors in programming or data entry. Ask your chairperson or someone else more knowledgeable than you are to check your printouts for possible errors, too. Keep notes on any unusual features of your data or decisions you make so you will be able to reconstruct your thinking later on (e.g., excluding outliers from analyses; transforming variables).

Finally, don't forget to calculate effect sizes and confidence intervals (Wilkinson & The Task Force on Statistical Inference, 1999). For nonsignificant findings, examine your power as well. Most computer programs will do this for you if you specify that you need this information. Effect sizes will help you interpret the magnitude of your findings further down the road. Many serious statisticians see these as far more important than whether your p values were less than your designated alpha (e.g., .05). Power will permit you to assess one reason for any nonsignificant results. Confidence intervals will help you compare your findings with those of others.

Conduct Supplemental Exploratory Analyses

Do not be surprised if, as you analyze your data, you come up with additional questions and need to perform analyses beyond those you originally proposed. The results of a study rarely turn out exactly as predicted and often lead to questions about why. Additional analyses frequently help you answer such questions. Expect to do supplemental analyses to help you understand your data more fully. The results of these exploratory analyses may or may not wind up in the final version of your thesis or dissertation, depending on what they tell you and how they qualify the interpretation of the analyses you planned. You may wind up running additional analyses later, too, once you start writing the results and discussion—topics of the next two chapters.

Supplemental Resources

Guides to Statistical Software

These are guides for relative newcomers to SPSS and SAS. Good sources for more advanced guides are reviews and book lists contained on major book retailers' Web sites (e.g., Amazon.com, Barnesandnoble.com).

Delwiche, L. D., & Slaughter, S. J. (2003). *The little SAS book* (3rd ed.). Cary, NC: SAS.

Green, S. B., & Salkind, N. J. (2004). *Using SPSS for Windows and Macintosh: Analyzing and understanding data* (4th ed.). Upper Saddle River, NJ: Prentice-Hall.

Pallant, J. (2001). *SPSS survival manual: A step-by-step guide to data analysis using SPSS.* Philadelphia: Open University Press.

UCLA Academic Technology Services. *Statistical computing resources.* Retrieved November 15, 2005, from http://www.ats.ucla.edu/stat. [UCLA Statistics Department Web site; has some great information on SAS, SPSS, and STATA basics.]

Missing Data

Schafer, J. L., & Graham, J. W. (2002). Missing data: Our view of the state of the art. *Psychological Methods, 7,* 147–177.

✔ To Do . . .

Collecting, Managing, and Analyzing the Data

☐ Obtain IRB approval in writing

☐ Finalize procedures and materials

— Develop stimulus material

— Complete preinvestigation manipulation checks

— Pilot test procedures

— Have changes in procedures approved by your chairperson, committee, and/or IRB

☐ Arrange settings and equipment

— Obtain location for study

— Schedule location for study

— Obtain equipment for study

— Write and post rules for equipment use

— Obtain locked data storage facility

— Secure computer and software for data analysis

— Develop system for scheduling assistants, participants, rooms, equipment, and so forth.

— Make arrangements for running participants during vacations, weekends, and so forth.

☐ Arrange for participant recruitment

— Finalize participant recruitment arrangements

— Make up participant recruitment forms

— Initiate participant recruitment/order animals

☐ Arrange forms and tracking procedures

— Duplicate consent/assent forms

— Duplicate other forms

— Develop system for keeping track of participants

— Arrange filing system for raw data and participant information

☐ Recruit and train assistants

☐ Plan for the unexpected

— Participants

— Personnel

— Equipment

☐ Collect the data

— Schedule regular meetings with assistants

— Supervise assistants' performance

— Identify probable problems early

☐ Score the data

— Verify scoring

☐ Enter the data

— Write up system for coding data into computer

— Create codebook

— Develop a data verification plan

— Verify data entry

— Look for unusual values and verify them

— Check accuracy of transformation programs

☐ Analyze the data

— Obtain help if unfamiliar with computer programs

— Investigate the defaults and alternatives your statistical analysis software uses for your particular analyses

— Review your analysis plan

— Conduct preliminary analyses

— Examine missing data and determine how to deal with them

— Conduct hypothesis-testing analyses

— Conduct exploratory analyses

— Calculate effect sizes, power, and confidence intervals

— Label variables and printouts

11

Presenting
the Results

You collected all your data, analyzed them (incorrectly, at first; correctly, at last!), and now you are ready to present them to the world. Well, maybe not the world just yet. For the time being, you will be happy to get them down on paper so that this section of your writing will be out of the way and you can move on to the discussion section.

If all has gone well and you have followed our advice closely up to now, the task of preparing your results section should be easy. That is because you should already have prepared it, at least in skeleton form, for your proposal. Remember how shocked (and probably resistant!) you were to the suggestion that you mock up a results section to include in your proposal? Well, now comes the payoff. The mock results section should have been helpful in clarifying your design and planned analyses. Now it will be useful once again in providing the framework for the real results section. In fact, if you took our advice seriously and prepared complete mock results for your proposal, most of your work has already been done. Producing a results section now should be mainly a job of erasing the imaginary data and filling the space with real data. Let's look at the kinds of information you will want to include in your results section and how you might want to organize it for maximum clarity.

249

Restrict your presentation to data related to the purposes of the study. Avoid the temptation to inject analyses that are interesting but tangential. One area in which many ignore this suggestion has to do with the instrumentation needed to produce the data for the major hypotheses. For example, as part of ensuring the adequacy of your measures, you may collect psychometric information of one type or another. (Chapter 8 discussed several instances in which you might address reliability and validity issues in your study.) Suppose, for example, your major dependent variable involves ratings by others. To show these data are adequately reliable for additional analysis in examining the major hypotheses of the study, you compare the data from independent raters. The results of these comparisons are important in showing how sound your methodology was. They are not directly relevant to your major hypotheses, however, unless your study was about interrater reliability for this particular measure. The best place for these data is in the method section where you are describing your dependent measures. Similarly, place data related to the characteristics of your sample and the demographic equivalence of any groups you compare in the participants subsection of the method section. Be aware, however, that some disagree with us on this point, so be sure to check with your chairperson. Having gotten some of these methodological issues out of the way, you are ready to focus on your primary data.

Do Some Basic Housekeeping

It helps to think of your results section as analogous to having guests for dinner. Think of the guests as your primary data, the numbers you will present to support your initial hypotheses. To get ready for these guests you need to do a bit of housekeeping. The first thing you do is confirm that you have everything you need for the evening. We call this the complications/qualifications/limitations (CQL) portion of the results section. This is where you identify missing data, participant dropout, and any occurrences that might affect the representativeness of your sample. We discuss ways of treating missing data in chapter 10. The CQL portion of your results is the place to mention whether and how many data are missing and how you have dealt with this problem. If participants have dropped out, tell us who and whether they compromise the equivalence of any groups you are comparing. Such a compromise results when there is differential dropout or disproportionately more participants going AWOL from some groups than others. This is also the place to mention other inadvertent factors that might bias your outcomes.

Now that you know you have all the ingredients for a successful dinner party, take a moment to examine the quality of those items. Are you using real butter or margarine? Is the wine of high caliber? Take time to stand back and look at your data critically. Are there obvious problems with them? Do you need to correct these problems before conducting your statistical analyses? We are not talking about snooping through your data to identify and discard those that do not support your hypotheses. As Wilkinson and The Task Force on Statistical Inference (1999) have noted, "Data screening is not data snooping" (p. 597). For example, looking at the distributions can alert you to the need for transformations of scores that will allow you to use your planned statistical analyses appropriately.

Here, too, is the place to describe whether your data meet the assumptions underlying the statistics you planned to use. Describe the steps you took to determine this, the results, and any changes to your analytical plan based on the outcomes. Although it has long been a practice to use statistical approaches to testing whether your data meet underlying assumptions, the American Psychological Association (APA) Task Force on Statistical Inference (Wilkinson et al., 1999) argued the superiority of a graphical analysis instead. This is good advice. It is consistent with the suggestion that you undertake visual screens of the quality of your raw data before jumping into your statistical analyses.

Present Your Primary Analyses

Your dinner guests have arrived, you've served the hors d'oeuvres, and now everyone is eagerly anticipating the main course. This is where you present the major types of data related to the hypotheses you examined in your study. In addition, you will include the statistical treatments you used to make sense of your data. You will want to be complete, but think lean and mean at the same time.

Brevity will be enhanced if you present your results in an orderly, logical way. Avoid presenting individual scores or raw data unless, of course, your study involves a single-subject design. Retain the raw data for later consultation if needed; place it in an appendix if you must. As Yates (1982) observed, keeping your raw data available in easily analyzable form can be important, especially for any subsequent analyses that might be requested by editors of journals to which you eventually submit the research for publication. Confine the results section to data and their statistical treatment. Reserve the implications of the results for the discussion section.

Happily, there is nothing mysterious about results presentations. Once you have decided what to include and what to avoid, the rest is rather mechanical.

Sequence the Results

Organizing your results section really started back at the hypothesis-formulation stage. Recall our strong statements concerning hypotheses. Assuming that you produced some hypotheses before starting your research (as chap. 4 recommended), you most likely listed them in order of importance. If so, you simultaneously produced the general organization of the rest of your write-up, especially the results section, without even knowing it. When presenting your primary analyses, describe the results in the order of the importance of the hypotheses. Present the data used to test each, along with the relevant statistical analyses. If you used numerous dependent measures or analyses for each hypothesis, consider using subheadings. Each subheading could be a shortened reference to the hypothesis being tested. As a general strategy, state your conclusions, and then follow immediately with the data and statistical analyses supporting your conclusions. For example, you might say "boys were found to spend more time in types of play involving large muscle activity. This can be seen in Table 11.1, in which the means for boys for all three games involving such activity are significantly higher than for girls (main effect for gender [1, 59] = 4.62, $p < .05$)." Some authorities may suggest that you organize your results by major dependent measure. This seems to us to be logically less suitable than by hypothesis

Table 11.1

Levels of Self-Disclosure by Gender Following Exposure to Disclosing or Nondisclosing Models: Means and Standard Deviations

Model	Female		Male	
	M	*SD*	*M*	*SD*
Disclosing	7.60	2.34	4.85	2.02
Nondisclosing	4.76	1.89	2.67	1.93

Note. n = 22 per group.

because you are not studying the measures themselves. Rather, you are using them as a vehicle for testing your hypotheses. If, however, you have several measures related to each hypothesis, you might want to organize them by subheading within hypotheses (e.g., self-reported data; parent-reported data). Even if you do not use subheadings within subheadings, decide on an order for presenting the results for each measure and then stick with that order monotonously when you present the results for the rest of the hypotheses.

Sometimes, the clearest way of organizing your results is by analysis. For example, suppose you have three hypotheses that pertain to the percentage of variance three variables will account for in a multiple-regression equation. In this case you may wish to summarize all three hypotheses, then present the results of the one multiple regression. This way you avoid redundancy and still keep your results tied to your hypotheses.

Include Relevant Information

For each analysis you conduct, include the name of the statistic and its particulars. Particulars for ANOVA, for example, include the factors, how many levels of each, whether any factors involved repeated measures, and the name of any post hoc test you used. Include important statistical values (e.g., F, t, and p) for all significant effects. Indicate the p values you selected as cutoffs for determining statistical significance and state the basis for their selection. Some will want you to include this information for nonsignificant effects as well, perhaps in an appendix. Also, include means, standard deviations, and sample sizes for each dependent variable. For correlational studies, include these for the sample as a whole, unless the sample was subdivided for analyses (when you will want means, sample sizes, and standard deviations for each subsample). It is also desirable to present effect sizes for your primary analyses. This is because p values do not tell us about the strength of a relationship or the magnitude of an effect (see Wilkinson et al., 1999; APA, 2010). In addition, provide confidence intervals (e.g., 95% confidence interval [CI] = $1.08 - 2.77$) for your test statistics.

If you compare groups of participants, present means, standard deviations, and sample sizes appropriate to each significant effect. For example, if a gender × grade ANOVA shows a main effect only for gender, make sure you present these types of data for gender (collapsed across grade). You may also wish to present the same data for each grade–gender cell in an appendix. What information should you include in a table or figure and what goes in the text? In general, means and standard deviations most often go in tables, unless there are so few of them they can be accommodated easily in the text. Statistical values (e.g., *F*s) may go in the text or a table, depending on which is easier to follow. Place the names of statistical tests and describe their particulars in the text.

Word Your Results Clearly

Remember, the results section is the place for maximum clarity. This is not the time to be creative or to look for the most prose-worthy way of saying things. A good rule to follow is, "Be monotonously repetitive!" Decide on a particular sentence structure that most clearly presents the results of a particular type, and stick with that structure for all results that are similar. For example, if your study uses a 2×2 factorial design and involves three different dependent variables that you analyze using ANOVA, present the results for each dependent variable in exactly the same way. Thus, if gender was one of your independent variables, you might present any results for it first, followed by those for your second independent variable, followed by the interaction, if any. Stick with this order as you lay out the data for each of your dependent variables. Moreover, if you discuss data for females first for the first dependent variable, discuss them first for all the rest. Consistency and symmetry will aid greatly in understanding your results. The reader will follow your presentation more easily if you minimize variety in sentence structure and write clearly and concisely.

Moreover, consistency in presentation allows the reader to return much more easily to previously read sections to check for understanding or comparison against later results. In addition to being monotonously repetitive, it is a good idea to write English rather than statistical sentences (Yates, 1982). Make it a habit to put the statistics related to a conclusion or finding at the end of the sentence. For example, "Males were less likely to notice differences in facial expression than females ($M_{males} = 5.2$; $M_{females} = 3.5$), $F(1, 29) = 6.49$, $p < .05$." This is much easier to read than "The mean for the males on the Test of Facial Cue Reading was 5.2, which the ANOVA $F(1, 29) = 6.49$, $p < .05$, revealed to be significantly higher than the females' mean of 3.5."

Notice in our first example that we also talked about the dependent variable when comparing males and females, not the specific measure of it. This is acceptable when there is a single measure for a particular variable. If there is more than one, it is a good idea to precede the first example with something such as, "With respect to differences in facial expression, males were less likely to notice differences in facial expression than females on the Test of Facial Cue Reading." This could then be followed with the results on the second measure; for example, "However, there were no differences on the videotape measure of visual affect (M_{males} = 12.4; $M_{females}$ = 13. 1), $F(1, 29)$ = 1.56, p = .14."

Follow Conventions Concerning the Presentation of Statistics

Generally accepted rules or conventions govern how you are supposed to present the results of statistical tests. Remember our rule about being monotonously repetitive to aid reader understanding? Adhering to conventions in presenting statistics is based on exactly the same logic. Readers should not be distracted from understanding your findings by having to figure out your creative way of presenting statistics. Recommendations about such presentations in psychology (and most of the social and behavioral sciences) have been documented in the *Publication Manual of the American Psychological Association* (APA, 2010). We have given you some examples of statistical results presented according to APA style in the preceding section. The general rule when presenting inferential statistical information in the text is to give the symbol of the statistic followed by the degrees of freedom (e.g., $F[1, 29]$), then the value of the statistic (e.g., 6.49), and finally the probability level (e.g., $p < .05$). A zero is not used before the decimal in probability levels. When a chi square is used, the degrees of freedom and sample size are reported in parentheses; for example, $\chi^2(4, N = 86)$ = 9.67, $p < .05$. Space does not allow us to discuss all of the many other conventions concerning the presentation of statistics in the text of papers. The *Publication Manual* gives more details.

Discuss Supplemental Analyses

Analyses related to your principal hypotheses often lead to additional questions you can examine with more analyses. If you have the data to address these and the questions are germane to the primary focus of your study, we recommend including supplemental analyses at the end of your results section. This can be an important addition to your dissertation or thesis. Often, it is fertile ground for stimulating new theorizing that can lead to hypothesized relationships to explore in further research. Do not allow your excitement about these new possibilities to divert you from the task of clearly and thoroughly addressing the questions posed in the present research, however. Remember, serendipitous findings, although potentially important, should not displace your principal hypotheses that have an ancestry in careful review and theorizing about existing research in the area.

Prepare Appropriate Tables

Because tables are more difficult (and therefore more expensive) to typeset, most journal editors will resist including them except for important findings and ones that cannot be presented in the text. In a thesis or dissertation, you have more latitude because they are not going to be typeset.

A well-crafted table can assist readers immeasurably in understanding your results, especially if the results are complex. Do not merely cut and paste a table (or figure) from the printout of your computer software into your dissertation or thesis. These are rarely in the precise format, size, or quality expected in your particular school. It is too bad this easy way is problematic, because skillfully constructing tables and figures takes a good deal of practice. The best advice we can give you about preparing tables is found in the five Ps referred to in chapter 3: Prior planning prevents poor performance. First, think about the effect you want your table to have on the reader. If you are presenting data on a dependent measure to show the impact of one or more independent variables, decide which of the latter you want to emphasize most. For example, suppose you are studying the effects of exposure to disclosing and nondisclosing models on subsequent self-disclosure of therapy candidates. Suppose further that you have included gender as a secondary independent variable. You probably used a 2 (type of exposure) × 2 (gender) ANOVA to examine your data. In a simple four-group comparison such as this, you might present the data in the text and not use a table. If you use a table, however, you might arrange your data the way we have in Table 11.1. Or you might arrange your presentation as we have in Table 11.2. Which of these two tables gives more emphasis to modeling?

If you said Table 11.2, you would agree with most readers. In general, it is easier to make side-by-side than up–down comparisons.

This was a straightforward example. Suppose we complicate it a bit by adding additional dependent measures. For example, we might differentiate types of self-disclosure. We might have content related to (a) sex and intimacy, (b) money, and (c) professional ambition. How would we represent

Table 11.2

Levels of Self-Disclosure by Gender Following Exposure to Disclosing or Nondisclosing Models: Means and Standard Deviations

Gender	Disclosing model		Nondisclosing model	
	M	SD	M	SD
Female	7.60	2.34	4.76	1.89
Male	4.85	2.02	2.67	1.93

Note. n = 22 per group.

data for all three types of content under the different modeling conditions for males and females? Table 11.3 shows one possibility.

How easy is it to see the impact of the major independent variable, namely, modeling, in this presentation? True, the two model conditions are still presented side by side. But how about comparing the disclosing and nondisclosing conditions? One would need to do this measure by measure. This would require finding a mean on the left and looking across to its counterpart on the right, ignoring the means in between. It might help to place your forefingers on the respective columns, but a different arrangement of the table might make the evaluation of the major independent variable easier.

Table 11.3

Levels of Self-Disclosure for Three Types of Content Following Exposure to Disclosing or Nondisclosing Models for Females and Males: Means and Standard Deviations

Gender	Disclosing model						Nondisclosing model					
	Sex/ intimacy		Money		Prof'l amb.		Sex/ intimacy		Money		Prof'l amb.	
	M	SD	M	SD	M	SD	M	SD	M	SD	M	SD
Female	5.20	2.01	4.80	1.98	4.75	1.87	3.26	1.67	3.91	1.56	3.84	1.73
Male	3.35	1.77	5.92	1.96	5.87	2.15	2.67	1.78	5.13	2.21	5.46	2.04

Note. n = 25 per group. Prof'l amb. = professional ambition.

Table 11.4

Self-Disclosure for Three Types of Content Following Exposure to Disclosing or Nondisclosing Models: Means and Standard Deviations

Gender	Disclosing model		Nondisclosing model	
	M	*SD*	*M*	*SD*
Female				
Sex/Intimacy	5.20	(2.01)	3.26	(1.67)
Money	4.80	(1.98)	3.91	(1.56)
Professional ambition	4.75	(1.87)	3.84	(1.73)
Male				
Sex/Intimacy	3.35	(1.77)	2.67	(1.78)
Money	5.92	(1.96)	5.13	(2.21)
Professional ambition	5.87	(2.15)	5.46	(2.04)

Note. n = 25 per group.

Now, consider the layout represented in Table 11.4. It is much easier to compare the effects of model disclosure in this arrangement because one can make side-by-side comparisons for females and males on each dependent measure by reading down the columns. Moreover, an overall comparison of disclosing versus nondisclosing model conditions could easily be made by taking the mean of the entries in each column.

In theses and dissertations, it is generally better to use more rather than fewer tables. Include ones that are central to interpreting your results in the results section; place less central ones in the appendixes. The APA *Publication Manual* requires tables to be included at the end of a manuscript after the footnote page. When the paper is typeset, tables are presented close to where they are discussed in text. Some schools often allow more latitude in table placement. We prefer tables to appear in the text as near to where they are being described as possible, just as they would in a published paper. This facilitates reading, because there is no need to switch back and forth between text and the end of a long thesis or dissertation to find the relevant table.

When constructing tables, keep an eye out for readability. Allow sufficient space between entries, line up columns of numbers on decimal points, and avoid splitting tables across pages if possible. Tables presented vertically in portrait format are less cumbersome than ones presented in landscape fashion, requiring the reader to turn the page sideways, but a single-page landscape table is usually preferable to a vertical table that must be continued on the next page. Sometimes, the difference in vertical versus landscape presentation can turn on the need for precision in your data entries. In behavioral science it is rarely necessary to present data beyond the second decimal place. Omitting extra digits saves space and avoids the appearance of pseudoscientific writing. If you do use the landscape format, be sure the title of the table appears along the binding side of the page (i.e., the left-hand side).

Speaking of titles, write one that is brief and explanatory at the same time. Avoid including information in the title that also appears in headings of the table itself. As an illustration, compare the titles of Tables 11.3 and 11.4. These tables present the same information, just arranged in different ways. The title for Table 11.3 errs on the side of excess detail. In part, this is the result of duplicating information that occurs in the headings of the table itself. Note that brevity was purchased in the title of Table 11.4 by omitting reference to the secondary independent variable, gender. This was not a great information loss because the table headings convey this anyway. Also, words such as *levels* and *scores* can generally be omitted because they are easily inferred from a glance at the table. Note that we prefer to state the dependent variable first, followed by the major statistics presented in the table. Thus, "Self-Disclosure by Gender Following Exposure to Disclosing and Nondisclosing Models: Means and Standard Deviations" is clearer than intermixing statistics and dependent variables in the same segments of the title. This is our "substance first, statistics second" guideline.

As we said, the preparation of effective tables takes practice. The *Publication Manual* provides many more details concerning tabular presentations. It even includes a checklist specific to tables (see APA, p. 150). Consult this valuable resource before beginning your initial drafts. Bailer and Mosteller (1988) and Nicol and Pexman (2010) provided other good sources of sample tables for a variety of analyses. It is also helpful to look at professional journals to see how others have presented tables like yours for analyses. Use the clearest as models. Also, you will benefit from trying out different arrangements and then having other people look at them and tell you how easy they are to interpret.

Once you have decided on a particular layout, present all similar data in tables set up exactly the same way. Remember our advice to be monotonously repetitious in presenting your results? The same applies to tables. Do not tax the reader or yourself with different formats when the first, painstakingly prepared one can serve nicely as the template for many others. Also, remember to present only the most important data in tabular form. Save the data from individual participants and other detailed peripheral information for your appendixes.

Prepare Suitable Figures

The other major type of illustration you will want to consider is a figure. Anything that is not text or a table will fall into this category, including graphs, charts, photographs, and drawings. Because figures typically are more difficult to prepare (more time, more money) than text or tables, you will want to use them sparingly. Certain types of information are difficult to convey any other way, however, and you will have to rely on figures for these. For example, one of us had a student who, for his master's thesis, evaluated approaches to teaching mealtime skills to individuals with mental retardation. The professionally prepared drawings that appeared in the thesis because figures greatly facilitated communicating the topography of the utensil grip the participants learned (Nelson, Cone, & Hanson, 1975). Also, figures portray interactions among independent variables and trends over time or over dosage levels most effectively.

Ask yourself the following questions before you decide to use figures:

1. What do you want the figure to communicate?
2. Can you communicate it more effectively by text or tabular presentation?
3. Will the figure duplicate information already provided in other ways?
4. How will the figure complement information presented in other forms?
5. What type of figure (e.g., graph, drawing, or photograph) will be best?
6. If using a graph, what type of graph (e.g., histogram, bar, or line) will be the best?
7. How will you have the figure produced (e.g., drawn by hand yourself, prepared with software, created by a professional draftsperson)?

You are ready to begin preparing your figures once you have answered these questions. As with tables, there are a number of conventions applied with varying consistency to figures. Let's spend a few moments reviewing these. We will not discuss the various types of charts and graphs you might select. Good descriptions are presented in the *Publication Manual* (2010) and by Parsonson and Baer (1978), Tufte (2001), and Cleveland (1995). We cover only a few high points of graphic presentation, mixing generally accepted convention with some preferences of our own.

Start your graph with Cartesian coordinates (i.e., lines at right angles to one another). The dependent variable will be represented on the vertical or *y* axis (ordinate); the independent variable or time, on the horizontal or *x* axis (abscissa). A rule of thumb is that the length of the *y* axis should be approximately two thirds the length of the *x* axis. The *y* axis should include the entire range possible on the dependent variable. For example, if you are presenting percentages, the intercept of the axes should be at 0 and the last number on the ordinate should be 100, unless, of course, your percentages could exceed 100. If your scores actually occupy only a portion of the entire range, consider showing a discontinuity or interruption in the ordinate. Figure 11.1 illustrates these points.

The data in the top portion of the figure (a) give a somewhat different impression than those in the bottom half (b). This is because they do not emphasize just how far from being 100% appropriate the verbal behavior actually is. In (a), the pre- to posttest changes shown by the first two data points seem quite large. When the "distance to go" is made clear by including the entire range, as in (b), the impression of the impact of the intervention is likely to be different.

The units on the axes should be equally distant from each other. On the *x* axis, this would be true for units showing equal amounts of time passage. Notice in Figure 11.1 that the distances between Pre- and Posttest 1 and Pre- and Posttest 2 are identical. The distances from posttest to follow-up differ from the pre- to posttest distances, however, and reflect the different amounts of time involved.

Units on the axes are indicated by grid or tick marks starting at the axis and extending toward the inside of the figure slightly. Some authorities (e.g., APA, 2010; Parsonson & Baer, 1978) prefer the tick marks to extend toward the outside of the figure. Others prefer to extend them toward the inside. In any event, the vertical axis should not extend beyond the last tick mark. Both axes are labeled clearly, giving the name of the variable being measured and the units of measurement. In Figure 11.1, appropriate verbal behavior is the variable, and it is measured in terms of percentage. Place axis labels parallel to the axes, and place tick mark numbers or labels horizontally.

Figure 11.2 illustrates additional conventions. Again, notice the discontinuity in the ordinate. This time we also show a discontinuity on the abscissa.

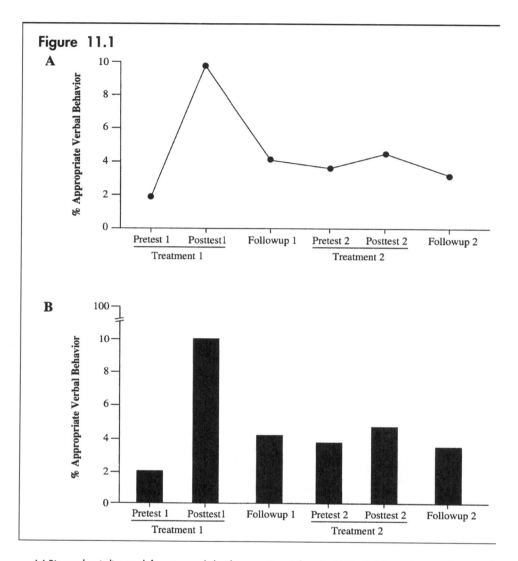

(a) Discrete data in line graph format, no scale break on an attenuated *y* axis. (b) Identical data in bar graph format, with scale break. Reprinted from "The Analysis and Presentation of Graphic Data," by B. S. Parsonson and D. M. Baer, 1978, *Single Subject Research* (p. 117), San Diego, CA: Academic Press, Copyright 1978, with permission from Elsevier.

Notice that the general layout of the data in Figure 11.2 communicates the type of design (*A-B-A-B*) used in the study. Notice also that each of the phases is labeled and separated by a dashed vertical line. It is useful to name the phases descriptively (e.g., *feedback*) as this communicates more information than generic labels (e.g., *treatment*). Figure 11.2 presents data

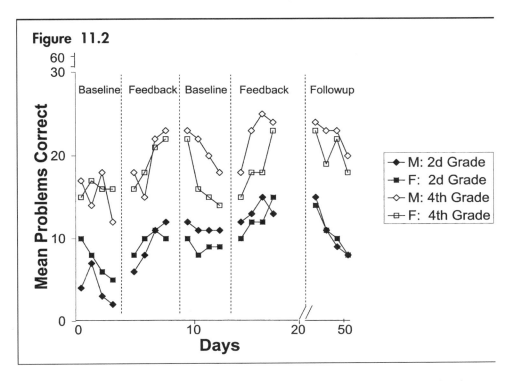

Mean subtraction problems correct for second- and fourth-grade boys and girls across four phases of the study and at follow-up.

from four groups. Generally, four lines in a line graph would be the maximum for readability. If the data are close, however, even four may be too many. Note also that we have included a legend for the groups. It is a good idea to put a box around a legend and include it within the area defined by the axes. If space does not allow this, the next best location is usually to the right of the figure.

Once you decide on symbols for your lines on the graph, be consistent. In Figure 11.2, we used squares for girls and diamonds for boys. We also kept these same symbols for both grade levels, using open and filled versions to indicate fourth and second grades, respectively. If you use more than one figure, keep the symbols consistent. That is, always represent boys with diamonds, girls with squares, fourth graders with open symbols, and so on.

Figure 11.2 also illustrates some other useful conventions. Data points are not connected *between* phases, allowing easier evaluation of differences between phases. Missing data would be indicated by a blank space. Points on either side of the missing data would not be connected across the missing day. The lines within the axes should be narrower than the axes themselves. Sometimes you may wish to present the results for more than one dependent variable in the same figure. This can be tricky when the scale of measurement differs for the variables. Figure 11.3 illustrates a solution for this problem. In this figure, we use two ordinates, with one line of the figure being referred to the left ordinate, and the other to the right. This shows graphically the different directions of change associated with the treatment for each of the dependent variables. This presentation makes it easy to compare the variables, and the entire presentation is more economical than drafting two different figures.

Finally, you want to select the type of graph that is most appropriate to your data. Generally, line graphs are inappropriate for data that are discontinuous. The top half of Figure 11.1 illustrates this. As Parsonson and Baer (1978) pointed out, the "actual data path between temporally distant plotted points is unknown" (p. 117). In such cases, the bar graph shown in the bottom half of the figure is more appropriate.

The last step for most of us in creating a figure is deciding how to caption it. With manuscripts submitted for publication, APA style requires

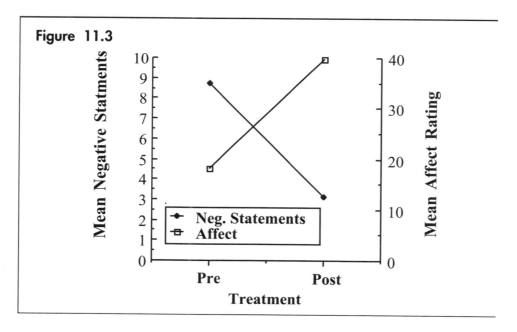

Figure 11.3

Mean negative statements (left ordinate) and affect ratings (right ordinate) for the depressed clients at pre- and posttreatment assessments.

that figure captions be included on a separate page that is placed at the end of the manuscript. The figures themselves are also placed at the end, so this is consistent. In theses and in dissertations, you may have more latitude in placement. As with tables, we prefer figures to appear in the text near where they are being discussed. The caption for the figure would then appear just below it.

Figure captions serve two purposes. They provide a title for the figure and explain the figure itself. Figures and their captions are designed to stand by themselves. That is, the reader should not have to search the text to understand the data the figure presents. In composing a caption, describe the contents of the figure. This can usually be accomplished in a brief sentence or phrase. As the *Publication Manual* suggests, explanatory information may also be included in parentheses appearing at the end of the caption or strategically placed within it. An example of a "too brief" caption for Figure 11.3 is "*Figure 11.3.* Verbal behavior and affect levels preand post-treatment." Compare this caption with the one actually provided with the figure.

Just as was true for tables, crafting figures well takes repeated practice. The *Publication Manual* covers many additional details pertaining to figures. It also includes a useful checklist specifically for figures (see APA, 2010, p. 167).

As with tables, it is a good idea to try out different versions of figures before committing to final production. Ask friends or your committee chairperson for their reactions. Revise the figure and then draw it, create a final version with software, or have it drawn professionally. A time-effective way to develop alternate forms of figures is with computer programs. Most major statistical software packages (e.g., SPSS, SAS) and many spreadsheet programs (e.g., Excel, Calc) include graphing capabilities. Cutting and pasting from statistical programs often does not produce suitable figures, however: The figures must first be edited so the font, line thickness, and so forth, are suitable.

The advent of personal computers and associated graphics software has made the production of publishable-quality figures much easier We recommend that you take the time, preferably early in your graduate career, to learn to produce graphs and simple figures using computers. This will be well worth your effort both in terms of time savings and in the cost of having a professional draftsperson do the work for you. Besides, it is always good to have a few graphs lying around the house showing the success of your exercise or weight-loss program! We mention figure-drawing capabilities of major spreadsheet programs here because these are increasingly adequate for all but the most complex figures you will produce. We mention several other figure-composing computer programs at the chapter's end as well. We do not present an exhaustive listing of such software, however, because our experience is that these programs come and go fairly quickly, and a list would soon be out of date, as we found with software listed in the first edition of this book. A good source of information about currently useful software is other students doing graphs/figures for their own theses or dissertations, or staff of the computer center of your school.

If you decide to take the old-fashioned hand-drawn route to figure production, a number of materials available commercially will make your job easier. Among these, the most useful are blue-lined graph paper and rub-on, press-on, or dry-transfer lettering systems. The graph paper can be of immeasurable help in lining up and spacing the elements of your figure, and its blue lines will not show when photocopies are made of the finished product. Most university bookstores carry such paper in various sizes and have lettering kits, as well. The latter will often include press-on lines to be used as axes and symbols to be used as points in line graphs. Yates (1982, pp. 165–171) provided some useful suggestions for the do-it-yourself figure drafter.

Supplemental Resources

Books and Papers

Carr, J. E., & Burkholder, E. O. (1998). Creating single-subject design graphs with Microsoft Excel. *Journal of Applied Behavior Analysis, 31,* 245–251.

Henry, G. T. (1994). *Graphing data.* Thousand Oaks, CA: Sage.

Heppner, P. P., & Heppner, M. J. (2004). *Writing and publishing your thesis, dissertation, and research.* Belmont, CA: Thompson-Brooks/Cole.

Tufte, E. (2001). *The visual display of quantitative information* (2nd ed.). Cheshire, CT: Graphics Press.

Wallgren, A., Wallgren, B., Persson, R., Jorner, U., & Haaland, J. (1996). *Graphing statistics & data.* Thousand Oaks, CA: Sage.

Wilkinson, L., & The Task Force on Statistical Inference. (1999). Statistical methods in psychology journals. *American Psychologist, 54,* 594–604.

Software

Excel: http://www.ms.com (Note: Excel is the spreadsheet application in Microsoft's Office suite of programs. It contains the charting functions for the suite. Chart in OpenOffice contains the charting functions for all of the applications in the OpenOffice suite, including Calc, the OpenOffice spreadsheet application. If you are unfamiliar with charting in either of these suites, we recommend you explore OpenOffice first. It is free, and completely compatible with files created in Microsoft's Office.)

OpenOffice: http://www.openoffice.org/

SINGWIN: program for analyzing sgl-S design data, including stats and graph construction; see Bloom, M., Fischer, J., & Orme, J. E. (2005). *Evaluating practice: Guidelines for the accountable professional* (5th ed.). Boston: Allyn & Bacon.

✔ To Do . . .

Presenting the Results

☐ Present data related to purposes of the study

☐ Present results in an orderly, logical way

—Order and sequence the results

- Present preliminary analyses

- Present primary analyses

- Present supplemental analyses

—Include relevant information

- Name of statistic

- Relevant details about the statistic

- Statistical values for significant effects

- Means

- Standard deviations

- Sample size

- Effect sizes

- Confidence intervals

—Word your results clearly

—Follow conventions in psychology regarding presentation of statistics to create well-designed, clear tables

☐ Prepare well-crafted, clear figures

12

Discussing
the Results

As you near the end of your analyses, start thinking again about writing. A good way to ease back into writing is to revise your literature review and method sections first and then to work on the results and discussion sections.

Revise Your Literature Review and Method Section

If you did a thorough, high-quality literature review during the proposal stage and gathered your data in a timely fashion, it should need few changes. Nonetheless, you will need to peruse the major journals in your area to add literature that has been published since your proposal meeting and to see which in-press citations have been published so that you can update the references. In addition, there may be changes to make that your committee requested during the meeting. If you produced an abbreviated literature review for the proposal, you now must pay your dues and do that comprehensive literature review you put off.

Just as a well-done literature review at the proposal stage means fewer revisions later, a detailed, clearly written method section in the proposal can be easily revised at this point by doing four things. First, if you wrote your method section in the future tense, change to the past tense now. Second, alter your descriptions of participants, procedures, and so on, if there are differences between what you actually did and what you had planned to do. Third, add details about your actual population (e.g., a description or table of participant characteristics for each group you included). Fourth, describe any analyses you conducted to show the adequacy of your measures (e.g., interrater agreement data for your study). Even if you have relatively few revisions to make at this point, be sure to review your literature review. This will refresh your memory about how your study fits with existing literature, a topic you will revisit when you discuss your findings in the discussion section.

Write Your Discussion

The last big chunk of writing you do will probably be your discussion section. Students sometimes tell us they don't know what to say in the discussion—they said everything already. It is easy to understand why they believe this, but it really is not so. The discussion section is where you interpret your findings, place them in the context of your hypotheses and the literature you reviewed, and examine critically their implications and limitations. To assist you in this process, we pose numerous questions that may apply to your study. As you read them, think about the answers. Keep notes on your thoughts and consider integrating these points into your discussion section.

Summarize Your Findings

Most discussion sections begin with an integrative summary of the results. This should not reiterate your statistics; you should not state F and p values, nor should you reiterate technical details of the analyses. Instead, describe your results clearly, using as little statistical jargon as possible. It might be tempting to say, "There was a significant main effect for condition on the vigilance and recall variables." But first apply the layperson test: How would you describe your results to educated people outside the field so that they will understand them? "Students told to expect a later memory test were more vigilant and showed better recall than those who were not" would pass the layperson test.

One good way to organize your summary of the results is around whether they did or did not support each of the hypotheses or research questions. This summary can lead logically to a discussion of the various reasons you found what you did (or did not). Discuss hypotheses in the order that you originally listed them in your literature review in the subsection on research questions and hypotheses. Briefly, restate each hypothesis so the reader will not have to turn back to the earlier section. This should mirror the order in which your results section unfolded as well. This organizational structure is most appropriate when each hypothesis or set of hypotheses is conceptually distinct. Beware, however, that unless you are careful, hypothesis-by-hypothesis discussion can lead to repetitive, unintegrated discussion.

An alternate way of summarizing the results is to present major findings together. This is a more challenging route to pursue but often produces a richer discussion because it forces you to think thematically. Here, ask yourself how the findings cut across variables and measures. Once you've identified cross-cutting themes, write about them. For example, Laura Goyer (2005) asked boys of varying delinquency levels to view videotapes of other boys talking together. She compared boys' reactions to tapes characterized by high rates of rule-breaking with those involving more normal discussion. She proposed a series of hypotheses based on how she thought delinquent and nondelinquent boys would differ in their observed and self-reported affective reactions to the different types of discussions. She collected supplemental observational and paper-and-pencil data, as well as looking at boys' attention and interpersonal judgments of the boys in the videotapes.

Laura's results did not support her initial hypotheses: Delinquent and nondelinquent boys did not differ in any of their responses to the videos on either the dependent variables involved in her hypotheses or on her supplemental variables. Instead, virtually all of the variables differed depending on whether the tape showed rule-breaking or normative talk. Thus, it made much more sense for Laura to organize all of her findings around the two main themes of her findings: the difference between the two types of discourse and the failure to find the predicted differences related to delinquency level. She integrated contrasted results for affective and supplemental dependent variables within each section.

Do not forget adventitious findings—results of analyses you did not plan originally or did not expect to be significant. Sometimes the unexpected provides the most interesting outcome. If you compared groups of individuals, did you find any unexpected differences between the groups? Did these differences relate to your dependent variables? For example, one of our students (Sikora, 1989) examined the relationships among divorce, recent life changes, and preschool children's behavior with peers. Unfortunately, the children of divorced parents and of adults who indicated a great deal of life change came from significantly poorer families than the control children. Surprisingly, divorce and reported life change related little to behavior, but socioeconomic status correlated strongly with it. This relationship, therefore, became a major focus of the discussion that followed, despite the fact that Sikora's hypotheses had not even mentioned socioeconomic status.

Interpret Your Findings

Summarizing the results is only one part of their interpretation. What do they mean? What do your results tell you about the relationship between the independent variables and the dependent variables? Were there relationships? Did they apply to several or only selected dependent variables? Were there confounds or mediators that accounted for the findings? Some of you will be lucky. Your study will turn out exactly as you predicted. Interpretations will come easily because you thought about them when you designed the study. If you are among these lucky few, you can progress to discussing alternative explanations for your findings and exploring what they mean for theory, practice, and the world at large.

The majority of you, however, will be less fortunate. Some things will turn out as you hoped; others will not. All this means is that some things did not happen as predicted. Be grateful: This gives you lots to talk about! In this case, you should consider *which* variables showed predicted relationships and which did not. Then consider *why* this was the case. Do significant variables share any commonalities? Point them out. Why did nonsignificant variables turn out that way? In other words, compare and contrast the significant with the nonsignificant findings. Examine why the differences exist and what these differences might tell you about the phenomena you are studying.

Consider these explanations for why your measures do not all agree: (a) instrumentation problems (Did you measure the dependent variables well? Were measures reliable enough to detect true effects?); (b) inadequate documentation or manipulation of the independent variable (You *think* you assessed or manipulated it well, but did you *really* do so? Was the "dose" of the independent variable strong enough to make a difference?);

(c) inadequate sample size (Was your sample large enough to detect an effect?); (d) specific procedural aspects of the study may have suppressed the effects of the independent variable; and (e) true relationships between the independent and dependent variables differ from the ones you predicted (Do you need to rethink how the independent variable works? Do additional mechanisms or mediators need to be proposed?). Consider each of these in turn, discussing reasons why it is or is not a plausible explanation for your failure to find what you expected. If you kept a log while you were collecting and analyzing your data, haul it out and see if your observations give you some ideas. As you consider these explanations, think about how you might be able to use some of your results to provide evidence for or against them. Consider conducting supplemental analyses for this purpose. For example, if you used a relatively new measure for your study, one with minimal reliability and validity information, you may be able to correlate that measure with other measures used in the study that have known reliability and validity data. These correlations might support the validity of the new measure or they might challenge it.

Occasionally, a student will find no significant results at all, even after months of toil. If this is you, look for reasons this may have occurred. Consider the factors just described. Conduct whatever supplemental analyses of your data are possible to check out hunches for the lack of findings. For example, suppose your data are highly variable and you suspect that only a subset of your participants responded to your independent variable as predicted. Analyze data for that subset only. If you suspect certain demographic variables were responsible for your lack of findings, correlate the problem demographics with your dependent variables. Be sure to present these analyses in the results section and discuss them as supplemental (and, if your sample sizes are quite small, preliminary).

Do not despair if you find little to crow about. Science advances through an accumulation of information. Some of that involves failed predictions. Failed predictions can be as important as supported predictions in a well-designed study with adequate sample size and reliable and valid measures. In these cases, failed predictions may suggest that the framework that led to the hypotheses needs revision. Remember, however, that the absence of significant findings does not confirm the null hypothesis. Consider a full range of plausible explanations.

In the absence of significant findings in other areas, you can always correlate your demographic variables with your dependent variables and your dependent variables with each other. This will provide additional information to discuss in the absence of more substantive findings.

Place Your Findings in Context

Your study is not the only research dealing with the issue you investigated. In fact, you probably spent many a page describing related studies when you wrote your literature review. Do not, therefore, write your discussion as though your study was the only one in the field! As you summarize and describe your results, consider how they do and do not fit with your earlier literature review. To do this, think about how your study compares with earlier research in terms of population characteristics, measurement tools, independent variables (and how they were verified), research design, and procedures. Then, think about whether your results converge with, clarify, or contradict past findings.

If your study converges with others, differences between your methods and those of others may indicate ways your study *extends* earlier findings. For example, imagine that researchers have repeatedly found that couples' attributions measured in the laboratory correlate with marital satisfaction. Fortunately, you found something similar using daily logs of attributions. Now you can discuss how well the relationship holds using measures taken daily in the natural environment.

Your results might also clarify contradictions in the literature. If so, point this out. Often researchers can explain contradictory findings as they examine new and finer grained distinctions in population parameters, measurement domains, and independent variables. If you make these kinds of distinctions, your findings can help others understand existing literature better. Suppose, for example, previous studies used men and women as participants, without looking for gender differences. You examine these gender differences, and they are significant. This has two important implications: (a) future research should consider gender as an important variable and (b) past research may have *failed* to find effects when genders were combined, because of the variance attributable to gender. Past samples made up mainly of men would likely show patterns for the male gender, whereas those made up mainly of women would show patterns for the female gender.

If you don't find what others found, consider why. What are the differences between your study and others'? Consider methodological explanations: Could different measures, procedures, or samples account for the discrepancy? Discuss what your failure to replicate others' results says about limitations to the generalizability of their findings. Do your findings suggest new distinctions might need to be made in the literature in the future? If your failure to replicate previous findings is not an artifact of problems with your procedures or measures, you may have discovered something important about the phenomenon you examined.

Consider, as well, what your research contributes to the existing literature. Remember, a dissertation is supposed to contribute new knowledge. A thesis may provide less novel information but should certainly add to what is already known. Regardless of how familiar the study now seems to you, it adds to the literature in some way. Point this out. What did you do that no one else did? How did this improve on past investigations? And what did this improvement yield in terms of findings?

Consider the Implications of Your Findings

What do your findings imply? How do they improve our understanding of the phenomenon you investigated? How should they alter the way we think about the issues you researched? When you think about the implications of your findings, consider how they might speak to theory, research, and practice.

With respect to theory, think first about the prevailing theoretical models in your research area. What do these models postulate? What are their implicit assumptions? What would these theories predict about your findings? Are your results consistent with one or more of these theories? Why or why not? Your findings do not prove or disprove a theory: They just support or fail to support it. Although it would be nice if your findings were consistent with only a single theory, they may be explained equally well by more than one. That's fine—discuss this fact and describe how future researchers might design studies to pit the two explanations against one another.

With respect to research methodology, remember, understanding of a phenomenon advances as important distinctions are made. Did your study imply any new distinctions or any factors that are important to control in additional investigations? For example, consider Sikora's (1989) dissertation on preschool children described earlier. Her finding that socioeconomic status correlated consistently with social behavior implies two things: (a) future researchers in peer relations should control for socioeconomic status and (b) they should describe that characteristic of their participants.

Research also advances with improvements in design and measurement. Do your results have implications in these areas? If you used observational measures when others used only self-reports, do your results indicate that future studies should follow your lead? Research often progresses from general to specific, and from weak designs to strong. To illustrate, suppose you used a longitudinal design and failed to find what cross-sectional studies have found. You may use your results to lobby for the continued use of stronger designs that yield results that are more conclusive.

What do your findings have to say for practice in your field? If you are a psychology student, for example, what do they say for the clinical, educational, or industrial/organizational practice of psychology? Who might be interested in your findings, and why? How should these potential readers change their thinking or practice based on your findings? Even disappointing results can indicate that applied psychologists should consider your issue more carefully than they have. For example, suppose your findings challenge customary assumptions about problems experienced by adult offspring of individuals with alcoholism. Or suppose they question the accuracy or even the existence of repressed memories. What would this mean for mental health professionals using interventions based on these assumptions? What would it mean for the lay public reading undocumented pop psychology books full of these "facts?"

Some studies have more implications for practice than others, to be sure. Studies that involve clinical or business populations, for example, are likely to have a great many practical applications; basic science investigations in physiological psychology may have none. If your findings have potential implications for applied work, be sure to consider their limitations as well. You may want to speculate about the generalizability of your findings. If you do, be sure to acknowledge your speculations and to describe the kind of research that would be necessary to bridge the gap between your findings and the applications you discuss.

This brings us to the important issue of the role of speculation in discussion sections. Many students err in their discussion by sticking too closely to their data. As a result, there is little or no discussion in their discussion section! When you talk about your findings, balance scientific skepticism with speculation. In practice, this means it is all right to speculate, but don't stray too far from the data. Also, be aware of the assumptions you are making when you speculate, and point them out. It is desirable to justify your logic with your own findings or those of others, whenever possible. The keys are to be explicit about your speculations and to discuss evidence for and against them, when such evidence exists.

Include a Limitations Subsection

A discussion section is certainly a place to brag (subtly, of course) about the quality of your project and the importance of your findings. Temper this boasting with the recognition that your study is not perfect, however. Writing a "humility" subsection, as one of our colleagues refers to it, allows you to point out the limitations of your study. This has two wonderful benefits: (a) it demonstrates that you understand research methodology and the inevitable trade-offs that accompany research decisions and (b) it might preempt your committee from tearing your study to pieces.

Limitations of your study generally come from two sources: (a) decisions made about how to conduct the study in the first place and (b) problems that came up when running it. Decisions about criteria for subject inclusion, procedures, measures, and design all may carry limitations as well as strengths. In this section of the discussion, consider those trade-offs. Of course, you may have anticipated some of the potential problems and taken steps to circumvent them. If so, you can now point out (humbly, to be sure) how you dealt with the potential limitation.

Unavoidable problems that limit your findings may also have come up as you collected your data. Your sample may have been smaller than planned, limiting your statistical power. Consent rates may have been low. Participants may have dropped out. Different groups of individuals may have differed on demographic variables. Perhaps you overlooked some other confound that you should have assessed. Observations conducted in the natural environment may not have been reliable. True, these were headaches during the study. Now, however, they provide material for your humility section. Remember, the key word is *discuss*. This is not a complaint section. Whining about the problems you encountered will not interest your reader. Discussing how they may or may not have affected your outcomes will.

Think about possible limitations in four major areas. The first lies in the design of the investigation and involves issues of internal validity: limitations in whether you can attribute causal status to the independent variables, potential confounding variables, and so on. The second lies in external validity: generalizing your findings to other populations, tasks or situations, levels of your independent variable, nonexperimental settings, and so on. The third involves the reliability, validity, and scope of your measures, along with response sets or other problems in measurement that may have contributed to your findings. The fourth involves the statistical analyses you selected. You may not have limitations in all of these areas, but you should consider each as you appraise the strengths and weaknesses of your study.

Note Internal Validity Concerns

Design issues always involve compromises. Any design that is relational/ quasi-experimental and does not involve random assignment of the independent variable does not permit you to say that the independent variable "caused" differences in the dependent variable. *Unless you manipulated it, you cannot say, unequivocally, that the independent variable affected any of your dependent variables.* If your research is nonexperimental, you must consider alternative explanations for relationships between your independent and dependent variables. These include reverse causation (the variable called the dependent variable caused the independent variable), third-variable causation (a confound caused both the independent and dependent variable), and reciprocal or circular causation (increases in the independent variable caused changes in the dependent variable; increases in the dependent variable also caused changes in the independent variable). To be sure, if you controlled potential confounds, you may be able to rule out some of these explanations. This will give you stronger support for a causal hypothesis than if you failed to control these variables. However, you still cannot make unequivocal causal statements in such designs.

Problems in attributing causality also occur when a mixed design is used. These designs involve at least one independent variable that is experimental (i.e., manipulated by you) and another that is not. For example, consider a study in which older and younger participants complete one of two experimental memory tasks. Differences in performance between the two tasks can be attributed to differences you created in the conditions. But differences related to age cannot necessarily be ascribed to age per se, because age was not manipulated. You can review specific considerations regarding internal validity that attach to particular designs by looking at Kazdin's (2003) and Shadish, Cook, and Campbell's (2002) books on experimental and quasi-experimental designs.

You might also discover, in retrospect, that you failed to collect certain kinds of information that would help make sense of your findings. Or there may be a potential confound that you did not control. Here is a good place to mention this, if you did not discuss it earlier.

Note External Validity Limitations

Even the best, most carefully controlled experimental designs are not without limitations. The control necessitated by true experiments usually entails some compromises in external validity. Generalizability across situations, stimuli, and procedures to important real-life situations is often a good issue to discuss.

Other elements of investigations, regardless of design, can also limit their generalizability. These include the characteristics of the population and the specific operationalization of the independent variable (would your findings generalize to other operationalizations or variations?). Analog and laboratory studies have limits on the generalizability of their findings by the very nature of the controls incorporated in them.

Note Measurement Issues

Your measures, too, may have limitations, such as insufficient reliability and validity information for your population. Using self-report as a surrogate for observable behavior of another type in the absence of data showing correspondence is another common problem. Possible reactivity to measurement procedures, insufficiently reliable ratings or observations, missing data, and possible biases that could influence your results (e.g., response sets, such as social desirability) may also be considered if they are potential problems. Finally, consider whether your measures do a good job operationalizing your variables: Did you select an instrument that was less than perfect for your purposes (perhaps because it has been widely used in the literature)? If so, consider how its imperfections might affect your results.

Note Statistical Problems

Perhaps there are problems with your analyses. Did your data meet the assumptions of the statistics? Were your statistics overly conservative or overly liberal? Did your sample size limit the power of your statistics to detect anything but the strongest effects? Did you control for Type I error by limiting the number of statistical tests you performed, setting your alpha level to control for the number of tests you used, or using appropriate multivariate procedures? Did you use a new statistical procedure that lacks full elaboration of its assumptions and its problems? Ideally, you encountered none of these statistical problems. If you did, however, revisit your results section and take care of the problem before you give your completed write-up to your committee. If, after doing these things, minor statistical concerns remain, discuss these in your limitations subsection.

A danger in writing limitations sections is that you may come to believe that the many limitations of the study make its findings worthless. This is rather unlikely. As you write, remember that no research is perfect. The results of each study must be considered in light of its limitations. Final conclusions are reached based on a body of evidence, not a single investigation. Remember, the choices you made seemed the best at the time. Furthermore, every weakness may have a corresponding asset as its flip side. For example, controlled laboratory experiments gain tight experimental control at the expense of external validity, whereas natural-environment and quasi-experimental studies gain generalizability at the expense of internal validity. Keep a balance. Consider both the pros and cons of your choices as you acknowledge the limitations of your study.

Include Comments About Future Directions

Ordinarily, your discussion section will end by pointing out directions for future research. Here you tell others the questions and issues to examine in light of the results you have just presented.

Researchers often say that each study raises more questions than it answers. In your writing to this point, you should have thought of many questions that warrant future research. Organize and elaborate them in this section of your discussion.

Most discussion writers think easily of extending the study to other populations. You can go beyond this with several additional questions. Ideally, the first place for these will be the theory underlying your study. What additional independent variables need more research? What additional levels of existing independent variables should investigators explore? What important dependent variables should they examine, and what is the best way to assess them? What design improvements are needed? What methodological changes should researchers make in future studies?

In addition, what new distinctions might be made in population characteristics, independent variables, and dependent variables? These distinctions can suggest future research comparisons. For example, perhaps your results indicate that a certain form of cognitive–behavioral therapy affects different types of thoughts in different ways. The logical next steps would be to develop reliable and valid ways of measuring different classes of thoughts, implement the form of cognitive–behavioral therapy, and see how it influences these different measures.

A good way to think about future directions is to ask yourself what follow-up studies you would do, given your results. What questions do your findings provoke? What more do you need to know to understand fully the issue you set out to address in your study? What would you do with unlimited resources? Here is the place to dream. Ground your dreams in reality, though, and be sure you can justify why the information gleaned from your menu of future studies would be important for theory, research, or practice.

Tips to Organize and Write Your Discussion

After you have thought through the points you wish to make in your discussion, organize your thoughts into cogent prose. You may find, as many of our students do, that this stage is much easier than writing the literature review. If so, enjoy it! You have probably learned a lot about scientific writing in the process of doing your dissertation.

Do not become complacent, however. Avoid some of the common problems found in discussion sections. Taking time to work out a logical organization will help with your writing as well.

Critique Your Ideas

As you consider your conclusions, play the devil's advocate. What would a critic say in response to your points? Anticipate the criticisms and weave your rebuttals into your discussion. This both fills up pages and demonstrates your intellectual agility—assuming, of course, your logic is sound!

Remember to show the steps in your logic. Do not assume that simply presenting your findings will make your conclusions obvious. If you make assumptions in drawing your conclusions, point them out. Your conclusions may seem simple once you arrive at them, but remember how much thinking it took to figure out what the results mean. Assume you need to guide your reader through the same process.

Avoid Common Problems

A series of common problems often characterizes the discussion sections of dissertations, theses, and published articles. Avoid the following errors:

1. *Do not discuss nearly significant or nonsignificant findings as though they were significant.* They were not, even if they might have been in the right direction. Thus, a statement such as, "The finding that boys were more active than girls approached significance. Boys' greater activity could be the result of . . ." treats a nonsignificant finding as though it were significant. You may, however, consider whether power problems limited your ability to detect effects. Saying something like, "Boys' activity level failed to differ significantly from that of girls. This may have been due to the relatively small sample size, however, and the difference approached significance. Future studies should explore this question with a larger sample . . ." would be more acceptable.

2. *Do not use causal language when discussing relational findings.* Many writers describing relational studies pay homage to the problems of assuming causation in their obligatory limitations section, but they use terms such as *affect, influence,* and *produced* throughout the discussion! If your study was not a true experiment, replace verbs that imply causation with words and phrases such as "correlated with," "was associated with," and "related to."

3. *Do not equate statistical significance with effect size.* A p value of .05, .01, or .00001 is in part a function of the magnitude of effect relative to chance, but it is also influenced by sample size. With a sample of 100, for example, correlations of .19 will be significant at the .05 level. Yet the two variables share less than 4% of their variance! When discussing correlations, be especially careful to focus your discussion on the magnitude of significant correlations. The same applies to differences between means—the magnitude of the p value tells you nothing about the magnitude or practical significance of differences between groups. So avoid saying that a difference was "highly significant," and discuss your effect size instead.

4. *Avoid language that assumes the self-report or informant reports of events means the actual events occurred.* Stating "clinic mothers reported that their children were more deviant than did non-clinic mothers" is preferable to saying that "clinic children were more deviant than non-clinic children." The more precise language also suggests two alternative explanations for your findings: Clinic children actually behaved more deviantly, or one or both sets of mothers see or report behavior in biased ways.

5. *Do not present new analyses for the first time in the discussion section or discuss results that were not reported in the results section.* If you wish to

discuss a supplemental analysis, first describe the test and its outcomes in the results section.

6. *Do not simply regurgitate the results section.* As we have emphasized repeatedly, go beyond mere summary to interpret, synthesize, analyze, and critique your findings. Show your reader your logic as you go along, and acknowledge speculation when you engage in it.

Select an Appropriate Organization

There are many ways of organizing the discussion section, but two common structures work well, in our experience. The first more or less follows the headings listed in the previous sections of this chapter. Thus, you progress from summary to interpretation and implications, to integration with existing literature, to limitations, and finally, to future directions. The second structure involves organizing the discussion around major findings, and integrating implications, others' findings, and specific limitations into your discussion of each finding. Exhibit 12.1 presents two hypothetical outlines for a discussion section that follow these different formats. Be sure to end your discussion section with a wrap-up paragraph. This should pull the discussion together and highlight some of your main points, without being a summary. End the discussion as you began it—with general statements. Be upbeat. One of our favorite endings involves emphasizing the importance of a full understanding of the area under investigation, to remind the reader of how comprehension of the processes or individuals under investigation will improve theory, research, or practice. Then, having written your last sentence, congratulate yourself and celebrate! You deserve it!

Produce the Final Product

Usually after writing your discussion you will breathe a sigh of relief as you turn in your draft to your chairperson. Now is a good time to deal with the final details to get your manuscript in defense-ready shape. Check your references. Make sure everything in the text is in the reference list and vice versa. Write your abstract (check your local requirements and *Dissertations Abstracts International* for length and format requirements), revise your table of contents (don't forget to add lists of figures and tables), and prepare your title page and signature sheets. Usually you will be required to submit a complete copy of the thesis or dissertation, minus acknowledgments and dedication pages, to your committee before your defense.

Exhibit 12.1

Two Hypothetical Outlines for a Discussion Section

Outline 1: Findings organized by hypotheses

I. Summary and integration of results
   A. Hypothesis 1
   B. Hypothesis 2
   .
   .
   .
   Z. Additional findings

II. Explanations for findings
   A. Hypothesis 1
   B. Hypothesis 2
   .
   .
   .
   Z. Additional findings

III. Integration of findings with past literature
   A. Convergent findings
      1. Description of how findings converge with relevant findings of others
      2. Explanations of convergence
      3. Implications of convergence
   B. Divergent findings
      1. Description of how findings diverge from relevant findings of others
      2. Explanations of divergence
      3. Implications of divergence
   C. Contributions of findings to literature
      1. How findings resolve current issues
      2. What findings suggest about new distinctions and controls

IV. Implications of findings
   A. Theoretical implications
   B. Research implications
   C. Applied implications

V. Limitations
   A. Design and internal validity
   B. External validity and generalizability
   C. Analyses and statistical power
   D. Measurement

VI. Future directions

continued

Exhibit 12.1, continued

Outline 2: Findings organized thematically

I. Summary and discussion of findings
  A. Finding 1
    1. Summary and fit with hypotheses
    2. Explanation of finding
    3. Convergence or divergence with past literature
      a. Explanations for convergence or divergence
      b. Implications of convergence or divergence
    4. Limitations related to finding
    5. Specific research needed to clarify or extend finding

    .
    .
    .

  Z. Finding *n* (topics covered as above)
II. General implications of findings
  A. Theoretical implications
  B. Research implications
  C. Applied implications
III. General limitations of study (covers issues not discussed under specific findings)
  A. Design and internal validity
  B. External validity and generalizability
  C. Analyses and statistical power
  D. Measurement
IV. Future directions

Check your local requirements for other details that need to be taken care of to graduate. You are almost to the finish line. This is no time to let ignorance of some form or requirement keep you from crossing it.

Supplemental Resources

Heppner, P. P., & Heppner, M. J. (2004). *Writing and publishing your thesis, dissertation, and research.* Belmont, CA: Thompson-Brooks/Cole. [Provides samples of write-ups of different sections of a discussion section.]

✔ To Do . . .

Discussing the Results

☐ Revise your literature review

☐ Revise your method section

— Change future to past tense

— Alter descriptions to match what you actually did

— Add demographic and other information

☐ Summarize your findings

— Avoid technical detail

— Use clear language

☐ Interpret your findings

☐ Place your findings in context

— Consider how your findings converge with, clarify, or contradict past findings

☐ Consider the implications of your findings

— Theoretical implications

— Methodological implications

— Applied implications

☐ Include a humility subsection

— Consider internal validity issues

— Consider external validity issues

— Consider measurement issues

— Consider statistical issues

☐ Include comments about future directions

☐ Use these tips:

— Be a critical thinker

— Avoid common problems

- —Select an appropriate organization
- ☐ Polish the final document
  - —Revise table of contents
  - —Write abstract
  - —Add any additional sections
  - —Check your references

13

Managing Committee Meetings: Proposal and Oral Defense

The thesis or dissertation candidate commonly has two formal meetings with the committee: once to present and discuss the proposal, and again to defend the final outcome. The proposal meeting occurs *before* you begin to collect data. The oral defense occurs *after* you have analyzed your data and written up your project. Although proposal meetings are not always required, oral defenses of the dissertation are. Defenses of master's thesis research may be more variable.

During the proposal meeting, committee members and the student meet to discuss the proposed research. Usually this occurs after the student has prepared a complete proposal (i.e., literature review, methodology, proposed data analyses, references, and appendixes) and the chairperson is satisfied with this product. The student then submits the document to the committee and schedules a 1- to 2-hour meeting after some agreed-on interval, often a minimum of 2 weeks.

Proposal meetings generally follow one of two formats: (a) an implicit problem-solving format or (b) a minidefense model. In the problem-solving model, the meeting largely revolves around committee members asking questions to clarify the proposal, raising potential problems they see with the project, and suggesting alternative procedures, measures, and so on. The underlying theme is cooperative; committee members work with the student and chairperson to produce a better product. In the minidefense model, committee members expect the student to defend the content of the proposal; the focus is on students' skills at articulating the rationale for various aspects of the proposal and defending the choices they have made. In many ways this resembles the oral defense. With both models, committee members expect that the proposal may be altered based on their discussion. Of course, meetings can contain a mixture of problem-solving and mini-defense components.

The oral defense is generally more formal than the proposal meeting. This formality results in part because its major purpose involves evaluating whether you have the research competence to be granted the master's or doctoral degree. This evaluation is based on both the written document and on your performance in the oral defense. Thus, committee members will ask you in your defense to explain what you did, what you found, what it means, and to discuss your research intelligently in the context of others' findings in the area. They will be looking for evidence that you (a) understand what you did and why, (b) can think about your project from a scientific (as opposed to a commonsense or intuitive) perspective, and (c) can describe what you did to others. In general, faculty members expect more expertise and polish from dissertation than from master's-thesis students. Although some students believe that these meetings are pro forma exercises, we know students who have failed their oral defense. Others have been sent back to the drawing board after a disastrous proposal meeting. We therefore recommend taking both the proposal meeting and the defense seriously and preparing appropriately.

Prepare for the Proposal Meeting

Departments vary widely in how they structure proposal meetings and oral defenses. Therefore, investigating local rules and norms is essential to prepare adequately for these meetings. Exhibit 13.1 presents a series of questions to ask other students and faculty about the proposal meeting and the oral defense. The answers to these questions will give you a good idea of the logistics, variability, tone, and scope of these meetings.

Know the Format

The format and length of proposal meetings differ from department to department. In some you will be asked at the outset to provide a brief formal

---

Exhibit 13.1

Information to Seek About the Proposal Meeting and Oral Defense

- When does the meeting usually occur in the dissertation process?
- Who schedules it, reserves the room, and arranges any equipment?
- How far in advance should committee members get the written document?
- What forms need to be filed before having the meeting? How far in advance?
- Is there any sort of formal review of the document or the defense by nonmembers of the committee (e.g., sending out the dissertation for formal external review, appointing an extra member to the committee for the defense)? If so, what form does this take and how is it arranged?
- What is the general format of meetings? Does each committee member ask all of his or her questions one after the other, or do members take turns?
- Who chairs the meeting?
- How long is the meeting?
- Are students expected to bring refreshments?
- Does the student make a formal presentation? How long? What is included? Are overheads/slides expected?
- Do questions focus only on the dissertation, or do they pertain to other areas as well?
- Who records suggestions regarding changes in the proposal/dissertation?
- What is the general tone of meetings? Do members respond to your answers?
- What are the rules about quorums? Do all committee members have to be present?
- Can a member be included via telephone or videoconference? If so, who arranges these?
- Who else may attend besides the committee and the student?
- How does the meeting end?
- What forms must be signed at the meeting? Who provides these and where can you obtain copies?
- What happens after the meeting? How do you alter the document to reflect changes?
- Must committee members approve changes in the documents themselves after you make alterations, or can the chair do this?

---

overview of your proposal. Such an overview should summarize your rationale for the study and focus primarily on the methodology you plan to use. Following the overview, committee members will ask questions. These will take three basic forms: (a) What do you plan to do? (asking for greater clarity or expanded information); (b) Why are/aren't you doing _____? (inquiring about rationales and decision-making);

and (c) What will you do about _____? (stating a problem that the member believes is likely to arise). Ordinarily these questions will focus on the study itself, but committee members may also raise questions about why your research question is important; findings in the general area in which you are working; methodological issues related to your measures, design, and procedures; and statistical matters. Committee members will also make suggestions they believe will improve the project.

You, not your chairperson, should answer these questions and respond to suggestions. The best preparation for questions, of course, is to know exactly what you are doing and why you have selected the methods you have and not others. Be sure to think about methodological and theoretical reasons for your choices as well as practical ones. Present these reasons first when articulating your responses to committee members' questions. Committee members do not respond well to answers such as, "I'm including 20 participants per group because I need to finish soon and don't have time to run more than that," or similar answers that imply that you put convenience above scientific integrity. An answer such as, "I did a power analysis based on pilot data. My pilot data suggest that my effect will be quite strong and the power analysis showed this n should be sufficient to detect it" will come across much better.

Committee members' suggestions about improving the study may vary considerably in quality and in the work required to accomplish them. In responding to these suggestions, ask yourself first whether and how each suggestion would add to the quality of your research. If it would add substantially, you may want to follow it, even if it involves significant extra work. If it involves altering an aspect of the methodology you have already thought about, it is fine to discuss the pros and cons of the suggestion with committee members. Never dismiss a suggestion simply because you are horrified by the amount of work it will entail.

Does this mean you have to add independent and dependent variables to your study at the whim of committee members? No. You might respond to an unreasonable request by saying, "That would be an interesting aspect of this issue to address, but I believe it is beyond the scope of this study. I will certainly comment on it in the discussion section," and then pray that your chairperson backs you up. In addition, you can raise practical issues, although you should discuss these from a scientific perspective as much as possible. The following example illustrates how this might be done tactfully.

I agree that restricting my sample to middle-class, married, employed females who have just given birth to their first children and have a reliably diagnosed Major Depressive Disorder (and no concomitant medical or psychological problems) would be the best way to do the study, but such a homogeneous sample is not available to me here in Podunk in sufficient numbers to do the study. I tried to expand the participant parameters in ways that wouldn't jeopardize the findings. Do you see special problems with this, or can you suggest ways that will allow me to recruit a larger sample?

Responding competently to committee members' suggestions requires that you be a quick thinker and reasonably articulate. If you have difficulties in either of these areas, take the time you need to think through a suggestion. One way to buy time is to restate the suggestion or question: "So, you are suggesting that. . . ." You can then comment on the pros and cons of the idea. By the end of this process, you may have an opinion. A second way to buy time is to say, "Give me a minute to think about that." Then sit quietly and think about what you want to say. Either your committee will sit quietly, or—more likely—another committee member or your chair will jump in with a comment or opinion.

Make Sure Someone Takes Notes

You and your committee will undoubtedly agree to changes in your proposal during the proposal meeting. Someone should write down these changes. Before the meeting, clarify with your chairperson who will do this. In addition, have the changes read aloud before ending the meeting, because this helps make sure everyone concurs with them.

At the end of the meeting, one of several things may happen. You may be asked to leave the room so your committee can discuss the proposal meeting. Your committee may formally approve your proposal (ordinarily with the suggested revisions, which must be either typed and circulated or incorporated into a revised version of the proposal). In some cases, the committee members return the proposal to the student for more work before they will approve it. In rare cases, the proposal will be disapproved. Outright disapproval can occur if the study is fatally flawed, the committee believes that the proposal demonstrates incompetence in research design or scientific writing, or the study poses major ethical problems. The student usually then has the option of preparing another proposal, perhaps with a new committee.

Prepare for the Oral Defense

As with the proposal, departments vary widely in their rules and unwritten traditions regarding the thesis or dissertation defense. As with the proposal meeting, investigation will help you know what to expect and how to prepare. Here we provide a general overview to get you started in this process.

Know the Format

The oral defense usually begins with a formal presentation. We discuss these later. Because dissertation orals are usually open to the academic community, some people present may not have read the document. For this reason, plan your presentation as though it were a talk you were about to give to a room full of professionals at a regional or national conference. Just as you would have a strict time limit at a conference, find out your time limit for the presentation and rehearse your talk so you will stay within those limits. You might decide to use audiovisual aids, such as slides, overhead transparencies, or presentation software (e.g., PowerPoint™ or AutoPilot) as part of your presentation.

After you describe what you did and what you found, questions will begin. As in the proposal meeting, you will be asked about your procedures, why you did certain things, what you found, and how you arrived at your conclusions. You may also be asked to comment on alternative explanations offered by committee members. Finally, you will be asked "thought questions," most of which revolve around the larger issues involved in your research. Exhibit 13.2 lists typical generic questions you might be asked at an oral defense. Be prepared for questions that focus on the details of your specific topic, methodology, and statistical approach as well.

At the end of the meeting, the committee will excuse you and any visitors from the room. They will then discuss the written document and your oral performance. Discussions can be brief or lengthy. Lengthy discussions do not mean you are in trouble: Faculty members may be arguing about a minor point of your findings or methodology and not about your performance! Usually committee members will require changes in the written product after the defense (otherwise some believe they haven't done their job properly). Expect this and do not be dismayed. As with the proposal meeting, someone should write down these suggestions for revision and review them aloud to ensure all agree. After committee members conclude their discussion, they will call you back into the room and tell you the results of their deliberation. You may pass both of the written and the oral

---

Exhibit 13.2

Common Oral Defense Questions

- What do you see as the problems in your study? What limitations do these impose on what you can say? How would you correct these in future studies?
- If you want to improve this measure, procedure, and so on, how would you do it?
- You note that your results approached significance, but did not reach it. What could you have done differently to increase the likelihood of significant findings?
- Are you sure about the degrees of freedom for the *F*-test in Table _____? It seems to me these should be _____.
- Which current theory or model best explains your findings?
- How would someone using a _____ theoretical framework interpret your results?
- How do you explain the discrepancy between your findings and those of Dr. X?
- What implications do your results have for future research methodology in this area?
- What do you see your study contributing to the literature?
- What have you learned about this area from doing this research?
- What would be the next logical study to do as a follow-up to this one (or to clarify a hard-to-interpret finding)?
- What implications, if any, do your findings have for applied psychological practice?
- If you had your study to do over again, with unlimited resources, how would you do it?
- What do you plan to do next with your data?

---

requirements, pass one but not the other, or fail both. In some departments and schools, you remediate a failure with a second try. If you are in the "passed both" category, pop the champagne corks and start the celebration!

How can you increase the chances you'll be celebrating at the end of your orals? First and foremost, prepare a good written document. If the manuscript you hand to your committee is thorough, thoughtful, well written, and carefully prepared (e.g., clear, dark print, table of contents includes page numbers, no missing references, American Psychological Association [APA] style, no spelling errors, tables match the text), you will begin your orals with a favorable impression based on your excellent document. Do not let your personal eagerness to finish or your personal timetables mislead you into pressuring your chairperson or committee to meet when your written document needs more work, because this is likely to backfire (Yates, 1982). Just because you decided to take time off to make some extra money and are now anxious to finish, do not assume your committee shares your sense of urgency. A chairperson who does not think your document is ready is unlikely to back you up if you find yourself in hot water for lack of preparation. Second, prepare for the defense by informing yourself thoroughly about what is likely to happen, planning your talk, and rehearsing how you will deal with probable questions. Third, develop an action plan for managing excess arousal that can interfere with optimal performance. The pages that follow explore these topics in detail.

Prepare Your Talk

The talk you give at the start of your oral defense will set the tone for the rest of the meeting. It is worth your time to write or outline this talk and then practice until you can give a professional-sounding, coherent overview of your study in the time available. Time limits of 10 to 20 minutes for this talk are common, but in some departments a half hour or more is the norm.

The major parts of your talk will usually parallel the sections of an APA-style publication, and will include introduction, method, results, and discussion sections. For a 20-minute talk, allow about 3 minutes for introducing your study, 6 to describe your methods, 6 for your results, and 5 for your discussion; for a 45-minute presentation, you might want approximately 10, 20, 10, and 5 minutes, respectively, to cover each of the four sections. Do not feel wedded to a four-section, one-by-one presentation of introduction, methods, and so forth. Remember, a talk is not the same as a written document. If your talk is fairly brief, you may want to integrate some of these sections—for example, present results and discuss them briefly as you go. In general, you will spend more time on the method and results sections than the other two.

Some polished speakers like to start presentations by telling a joke. This breaks the ice and indicates your humanity and that you have a sense of humor. If you are not a joke teller, however, this is probably not the time to launch a career as a comedian. Another ice-breaking strategy is to thank the committee for coming and openly acknowledge (with a smile) your sheer terror at standing before them. Make eye contact with members of the audience early and often.

Start at the beginning. Tell the audience how you got interested in this particular research. Keep it professional and brief. Your colleagues are not interested in the fact that you have always had a problem with weight yourself, or that it runs in the family, and so on. Something more along the lines of "Dr. Bulimarex and his research group, of which I am a member, have studied whale blubber for the past three years. We became interested in why some people eat more of it than. . . ."

Then launch into a brief review of the relevant research in the area, setting the context for your particular study. Recall the discussion in chapter 5 about organizing your literature review in the form of a funnel, starting broadly and leading the reader skillfully to the conclusion that the absolutely next most logical study to do in the area was the one you are about to describe. In the short time allowed in your oral presentation you will not be able to start close to the mouth of the funnel. Instead, assume some familiarity with the general area and concentrate your introduction on the literature most relevant to your own research. Briefly summarize the progression of studies that led up to yours, pointing to major findings. Give a general integrative overview rather than a boring litany of names and dates. Then review the shortcomings of previous research and lay the groundwork for your own study and how it was designed to overcome some of these. Be humble. Every study, including yours, will have problems. Do not go overboard in criticizing others or you might be setting yourself up for a similar fate during the question period that follows. If you have included a table summarizing research studies in the literature review section of your dissertation, you might present it now, assuming time permits. Your audiovisual equipment can help.

When you have skillfully led the audience to the conclusion that your study is the logical next step for research in this area, state your research question and specific hypotheses. An overhead or slide may assist with this. Then move into your methodology. Follow the customary APA format, starting with a description of your participants and research setting. Describe recruitment procedures and inclusion/exclusion criteria. Mention informed consent. Next, describe your independent variable(s) and dependent measures. Again, slides of any unusual apparatus and transparencies of your tests, checklists, or observation codes are useful if time allows. Mention the reliability and validity of your measures, and indicate how you trained raters or observers, if used, and how you assured their continued high reliability during the data collection phase. Weave in a description of your procedures for handling each participant and for debriefing them after they have participated.

At this point, your design likely will be clear. In case it isn't, describe it now. Verbal description will suffice for straightforward designs. More complex ones may require a diagram on a slide or transparency.

You will obviously not be able to present every detail of your methodology in the brief time available. Leave out details that listeners will not be able to follow or that are less important to your study. In an observational study, for example, knowing the word-for-word definitions of each observation category will be unnecessary. If you are not sure what to include, pick the 10 most important facts to mention, and add to this list until you fill your allotted time for the methods section.

Next present your results. Do this in the order in which you introduced your research hypotheses. If you used multiple dependent measures to test each hypothesis, decide an order for their presentation and stick with this order as you come to each hypothesis. As with the methods section, you will have more data than time will permit you to present. Cull through it carefully and select only those data that pertained most directly to testing your hypotheses or that yielded the most important findings. When many variables show the same patterns of results, summarize these rather than going through each variable one by one.

Here more than anywhere, simple is best. Do not state your F and p values in your talk. Just present the name of the analysis and its findings—in plain English. One way to keep your presentation simple is to present only those data that relate to your hypotheses and major findings. You need not present every analysis you did. Nor do nonsignificant findings ordinarily warrant more than brief mention. Again, ask yourself what's most important, see how much time it takes to go over those findings, and add only if time permits. Better to be selective and clear than to throw every number in your study at the audience and risk confusing them.

Either during or after presenting your results, discuss their implications. Do this in the order in which you stated your hypotheses originally, which should be the order you just used to present the results. Begin your discussion with a restatement of the purpose of the research, and then launch into the first hypothesis. If you had many hypotheses, see if you can integrate findings relevant to several of them at once. Refer frequently to how your research fits with studies of others, and note how your results might alter prevalent thinking in the area.

In addition to an enthusiastic discussion of the implications of your findings, include a brief humility section. Acknowledge some of the inevitable shortcomings of your research and lay the groundwork for future improved studies. Be careful not to be overly self-critical. Acknowledge obvious shortcomings and point out limits to the generalizability of your findings. The latter is always a safe place to be humble because all studies have some limitations in this regard. A good way to end your presentation is by giving two or three specific suggestions for future research, unless you have integrated these into your discussion earlier.

Prepare Audiovisual Materials

It is hard to imagine a research presentation that lasts longer than 5 minutes without some form of audiovisual assistance. Audiovisual aids can help get your message across and keep your audience awake and interested. The number and type of audiovisual aids you use depends on your setting and the length of your talk. Even a 10-minute presentation can benefit from a few overheads, slides, or handouts, however.

We have developed several guidelines for using audiovisual aids over the years. First, select a medium of presentation that is readily available and reliable. For presenting textual material, including tables of numbers, figures, and assessment instruments, overhead transparencies are one choice to consider. Overhead projectors are generally available, transparencies are relatively inexpensive to prepare, and most copiers and laser printers will make them. Their ease of preparation and low cost mean you can revise readily as new data or better ways of presenting the material occur to you, although not as readily as you can with computer-based slide presentations. In addition, the room can often stay fully illuminated when viewing over-heads but may need to be dimmed for slides.

Slides are also an effective medium. With the advent of computerized slide presentations, they are even less expensive than overheads as long as the necessary equipment is available. Slides can convey the research context more adequately than overheads and make the presentation more real to the audience. For example, showing pictures of a child sitting in front of the experimental apparatus or of the intersection in which data on seat belt usage were taken can do a lot to bring your presentation to life. You can also alter slides easily if you want to change your presentation after you rehearse it. In addition, we recommend that students make backup slides of material that they will not present in their talk but they may need in the defense. Examples of these include copies of measures, frequency distributions of variables, and tables of data that will not be used in the presentation but might be useful if your committee asks certain questions. Computerized slide presentations are increasingly becoming the norm at professional presentations, so it is advantageous to master this medium.

Videotape provides another good way to bring life to your presentation. This especially flexible medium does, however, require the appropriate equipment. Some computer presentation programs allow you to integrate video into a data presentation, for example. If you mix a slide presentation with playing DVDs or VCR tapes, indexing systems on some of these allow you to advance or return to specific locations to reshow a particular table or segment of experimenter–participant interaction. If you decide to use DVDs or videotapes, make sure viewers can see and hear clearly throughout the room, just as with transparencies and slides.

If you are using computerized presentations for the first time, our advice is to follow the old military KISS maxim: "Keep it simple, stupid." The Murphy's law of research presentations is that anything that can go wrong will, especially where equipment is concerned. If you are using a system such as PowerPoint™ or AutoPilot, rehearse all details more than once before the orals. Make sure you know how to transfer your presentation to the computer you will use to show the slides, hook up the computer, and get the projector running. We also recommend that you have a set of overheads as backup just in case of last-minute equipment failure, and arrange for an overhead projector to be in your defense room. Whatever equipment you use, check it out again, immediately before your presentation. Know where a backup can be found in case something breaks or a bulb burns out (it happens, believe us!). Sit in different parts of the room to check sound and picture quality. Coordinate with anyone who will be assisting to dim lights, change transparencies, or distribute handouts.

We have seen both excellent *and* mind-numbing slide presentations at oral defenses and at conferences. In the mind-numbing category are presentations that contain too many slides (each containing too many words), try to present too much data on a slide, or use fonts that are too small to read easily from the back of the room. Too much text or data are particular problems because they force the audience either to listen to the speaker and ignore the slide (which cannot be read and digested simultaneously) or to read the slide. Presentations in which the presenter merely reads the slide can also be deadly. Remember, these are aids to your oral presentation, not substitutes for it.

So be selective. Instead of putting the entire rationale for your study on a slide, use key phrases that highlight your ideas. Avoid the temptation to make slides of tables from your thesis or dissertation just because they are readily available or you love the way they look in your text. Most often, this information will not be easy to digest when it appears briefly on a screen. Pare down the tables, putting the data in several new slides if you absolutely need them to make a point. Keep your tables uncluttered. It is better to use more tables with fewer numbers in them than the reverse. Leave out nonessential statistical details (e.g., F values, beta weights). Make sure that any numbers on slides or overheads will be readable from the back of the room.

Develop Strategies to Handle Questioning

Many students are terrified when they think about being questioned during their oral defense. This terror can be managed by knowing something about what committee members will probably ask (see Exhibit 13.2) and by writing out and rehearsing your answers ahead of time. Developing general strategies for responding to questions can also help. We described some of these strategies in the proposal meeting section of this chapter; we list others next.

Respond to questions professionally in your role as a scientist. Even if you know your committee members well, now is not the time to joke around informally. As Yates (1982) cogently pointed out, now is not the time to get angry or defensive either, even if the question seems pointless or unnecessarily antagonistic. Again, pretend your committee is a professional audience at a national convention, and comport yourself accordingly.

Another good thing to remember is to take your time. As in the proposal meeting, rephrase hard-to-follow questions to make sure you understand them. Give complete answers that show your thought processes. And remember, your committee members may have missed something you said in the document or may ask what seem to you at this point to be easy questions.

Answer questions succinctly. Answer the question you were asked, not the question you wish you had been asked. Do not give long lectures. In particular, do not throw in fancy jargon or mention concepts you do not understand fully. Using a term incorrectly invites probing questions to see if you understand what you are talking about.

Most students are faced with one or more convoluted, hard-to-follow questions in their oral defense. If you don't understand the question, other committee members may not, either! Take the time to paraphrase confusing questions to make sure you heard them correctly and to allow the questioner to correct any misperceptions you might have.

Expect a few questions with no right or wrong answers. These thought questions may require speculation. It is fine to speculate as long as you acknowledge this. Presenting speculations as though they were facts is a sure way to elicit intellectual attacks from committee members.

Do not be surprised if you are unsure of answers to some of the questions. If you really do not know the answer to something, say "I don't know," or "I'm not sure" rather than guessing. An occasional "don't know" won't flunk you (unless, of course, this is in response to questions such as, "who were your participants?" and "what measures did you use?"). A stupid guess, on the other hand, communicates two things: (a) you did not know the answer and (b) you failed to recognize your ignorance.

Expect a certain amount of grandstanding. One of our colleagues, Albert Farrell, tells his students to remember that committee members ask questions during the orals for three reasons. The first, and rarest, is because they genuinely want to know the answer to the question. The second, more common reason is that they want to know if *you* know the answer to the question. The third reason is that they want to show other committee members that *they* know the answer to the question. Grandstanding, as reflected in the last reason, often takes the form of lengthy questions or responses to your answers, and does not imply that you have handled yourself incompetently. Do not try to compete with the grandstander. Just let faculty grandstanders do their thing, make an appropriate comment like "that's a really important/interesting/intriguing point," and move on.

Correctly reading whether committee members like your answers is hard to do. We recommend you spend your time trying to provide good answers rather than evaluating what committee members think of your performance. A committee member may smile congenially and nod but be dissatisfied with your response, and another may sit stony-faced and love what you are saying. Sitting in on others' defenses will help you see whether the general tone of these meetings at your school is somber or lively. One dependable indicator that things are going well is the occurrence of frequent, lively exchanges among committee members and between you and them. Most likely this means everyone is having a good time and that you are doing fine. The absence of lively exchange, however, does *not* mean that you should start searching the help-wanted ads for a new profession!

Finally, find out what materials you can take with you to your defense. Definitely take a copy of the complete document you gave to your committee to defend; questions such as "what do you mean by such and such on page ____?" are common. If allowed, we recommend you also take your printouts, copies of measures, and the articles you used in the literature review, and even copies of notes you made in preparation for your oral defense. Stash these unobtrusively under your table or in a corner. We have heard questions during orals about whether the numbers in Table 462 really were correct, whether Smith and Jones really produced a 3- and not a 4-factor structure with the *XYZ* measure, and what items were included on a particular dependent measure. If you suspect you might need to refer to one of these items during your defense, see if you can take it with you.

Rehearse Your Oral Defense

The oral defense is important enough, particularly for the doctorate, to spend some time rehearsing. If possible, schedule a mock oral defense, so you can practice both your oral presentation and responses to audience questions. Fellow graduate students (especially those who have been through or observed an oral defense) and your chairperson are ideal audience members, if you can persuade them to spare the time. A little wine always helps!

Before giving your mock presentation, ask your chairperson to review an outline of your talk. After suitable changes, conduct your rehearsals. We recommend the two-rehearsal format in which you give the talk once to yourself, audiotaping or videotaping it for later review, and once for an audience. Review the tape of the first rehearsal with timer in hand before doing the second one. Time the lengths of the various sections and the total talk, and plan where you will expand or economize the next time around.

For both rehearsals, prepare completely ahead of time. Have your notes and audiovisual equipment ready to use, and use them as you plan to during the actual presentation. Select a place to rehearse that is as much like the orals setting as possible. Conduct the rehearsal at the same time of day. You may even want to have a "dress rehearsal" and wear the clothes you plan to wear during your defense. The more cues from your eventual presentation context that you can build into your rehearsal, the more useful the rehearsal will be.

After your talk, get your audience to ask you questions like those you anticipate your committee members will ask. Prime your audience to ask questions you fear (e.g., about theoretical or statistical issues) because this is a low-risk time to practice and get feedback.

Allow enough time for your mock orals to get reactions from the rehearsal audience at the end. Prepare a few items to ask about the talk and about how you handled questions. Review these when you view or listen to your own tape as well. Exhibit 13.3 presents a simple checklist of some important behaviors to note during the presentation and questioning. You might even ask your rehearsal audience to fill out a checklist similar to this as a way of directing their attention to specific aspects of your presentation. In addition, ask them for their general reactions and suggestions for changes. You may want to ask a friend to take notes for you based on this discussion.

If a specific portion of the talk worries you (e.g., how clearly you described the design of the study or presented the results of the factor

Exhibit 13.3

Checklist of Important Behaviors for Oral Presentations and Responses to Questioning at Proposal Meetings and Defenses

Yes No   **For oral presentations:**

☐ ☐   1. Did you make an appropriate opening comment?

☐ ☐   2. Did you vary your voice level and intonation throughout?

☐ ☐   3. Did you smile appropriately?

☐ ☐   4. Did you make eye contact with the audience?

☐ ☐   5. Did you look energetic, peppy, and forceful, avoiding sitting down or leaning your chin on your palm on a table?

☐ ☐   6. Did you speak from carefully prepared notes and avoid reading your talk?

☐ ☐   7. Did you make major points clearly?

☐ ☐   8. Did you use good transitions between sections of the talk?

☐ ☐   9. Did you allocate your time appropriately?

☐ ☐   10. Were your audiovisual assists clear and easy to read from all parts of the room?

☐ ☐   11. Were any additional audiovisual materials needed?

☐ ☐   12. Did you minimize "uhs," "ahs," throat clears, and other speech interrupters?

☐ ☐   13. Did you use advance organizers, in other words, tell your audience where you were going at the beginning?

☐ ☐   14. Could your audience follow your results easily?

☐ ☐   15. Did you keep your talk simple and to the point?

☐ ☐   16. Did you avoid unnecessary detail?

☐ ☐   17. Did you avoid distracting mannerisms (excessive movement, fiddling with clothing, mustache, or hair?)

☐ ☐   18. Did you use scientific vocabulary appropriately?

☐ ☐   19. Did you explain complex procedures clearly?

Yes No   **For oral questioning:**

☐ ☐   20. Did your answers address the questions?

☐ ☐   21. Were your answers concise?

☐ ☐   22. Did you appear confident during questioning?

☐ ☐   23. Did you qualify your remarks appropriately (e.g., acknowledging speculation as such)?

☐ ☐   24. Did you respond nondefensively to antagonistic questions?

☐ ☐   25. Did you rephrase hard-to-understand questions before attempting to respond?

analysis), solicit the audience's reaction. Ask how it might have been done differently. Be open and reflective and avoid defensiveness. Remember, these are your friends. They are doing you a favor. Hear their suggestions and take their comments seriously.

Manage Your Arousal Constructively

The oral defense (and for some, the proposal meeting) seems to produce at least twinges of anxiety even in the most eloquent speakers. Some students experience overwhelming anxiety as they think about the oral examination. Some arousal is normal: The oral defense is the last step toward an important degree, it is an evaluative situation, and the rules for what to expect and how to handle the defense are ambiguous. One expert on anxiety, David Barlow, theorized that "a sense of unpredictability and uncontrollability is at the heart of anxiety" (Barlow, 2000, p. 1254). Although the defense is neither completely unpredictable nor uncontrollable, it *is* true that you will not be the only one in charge of the process.

Because of this, we do not say you must go through the proposal meeting or orals without heightened arousal. Indeed, we believe the old inverted U-shaped arousal function is relevant to the oral defense—a medium level of arousal facilitates performance by helping to focus one's attention to the task. Too much arousal, however, can impede your ability to think on your feet and to express yourself clearly. One key to a successful proposal meeting and oral defense lies in managing your arousal constructively.

Researchers for many years have described three sometimes related but more often nonconvergent elements of anxiety (e.g., Barlow, 2000; Lang, 1971). The first, the cognitive component, involves the subjective experience of anxiety: the things you say to yourself about the situation and how you label your feelings. The second, the physiological component, pertains to the physical substrate of arousal (e.g., increased heart rate and nervous system activity, perhaps noticed by you as sweaty palms or shortness of breath). The final component, the motor, relates to your observable performance (e.g., pacing, clearing your throat, making eye contact with the audience). Managing these three components can help you deal more effectively with the proposal meeting and oral defense.

Manage Your Thoughts

Two general cognitive factors can contribute to "orals anxiety": (a) fear of the unknown (what will they ask? will I be able to answer?) and (b) irrational thinking (I'm sure I'll fail and be unemployed for the rest of my life). To see if either of these haunts your thoughts, think about the orals. Listen to what you say to yourself. Does this self-talk revolve around fear of the unknown or the potential catastrophic consequences of failure? If your self-talk pertains to either of these, read on.

If the ambiguity and uncertainty of oral presentations worry you, make the process less ambiguous. Reading this chapter should help. In addition, talk with people who have gone through the process about what happened during their orals. Gather a list of common questions from other students and from your chairperson, and add these to the ones in Exhibit 13.2. Dissertation defenses are open to the public, so go to some in your department to see what they are like (choose someone who is likely to pass so that you can see a successful coping model). All of these preparations together should decrease the ambiguity of the situation for you substantially, and you will feel better prepared.

What about irrational thinking? More than four decades ago, Ellis (e.g., Ellis & Harper, 1961) proposed the notion that irrational beliefs are associated with feelings of depression, anxiety, anger, and the like. One key irrational belief related to anxiety involves catastrophic thinking: "If things do not turn out as I wish, it will be just awful." A second relates to perfectionism: "I must handle myself flawlessly in all circumstances." Either of these beliefs can be associated with performance anxiety, and together they can be quite debilitating.

The key to dealing with irrational self-talk is to challenge it and talk back more rationally. First, let's look at perfectionism. Do you really have to handle your orals perfectly? No, you just have to handle them competently. Correcting a misstatement, taking time to think through your answers, and encountering occasional problems understanding or answering a question will not lead you to fail your orals. Recognize and plan for the fact that you may not be as articulate on your feet as you are on paper. That is perfectly natural and no one expects you to be.

What about catastrophes? Some students fear they will not be able to answer questions correctly. They then say to themselves, "I will fail the orals. Then all my work will be down the drain and I will be homeless and unemployable and no one will love me." Let's examine the assumptions behind these thoughts more rationally. First, what is the evidence you will not be able to answer the questions? You know what you did, right? You know *why* you did it, right? At this point, you should know more about your specific topic area than anyone in the room, with the possible exception of your chairperson. A reasonable prediction is that you will be able to answer most questions easily and that a few will be more difficult for you. Believe it or not, it is even possible to have fun during your orals: It can be intellectually stimulating and enjoyable to have a group of bright individuals discuss your project with you for a couple of hours.

Will occasional difficulty with a question lead you to fail the orals? Probably not. Overall, you are likely to handle the easy questions well and the difficult questions satisfactorily. After all, the best predictor of future behavior is past behavior, and if you have done well in graduate school, you will likely do fine in the orals, too. Even if you flub a question or two, you are unlikely to fail your orals. Remember, the faculty have an investment in you. They really want you to succeed.

And what if you do fail? What is the worst that can happen? Many schools allow students to retake the orals if they fail them and pass the written portion of the dissertation or thesis. The worst that would happen then would be that you would be embarrassed by having to retake your exam. Embarrassment is rarely fatal and, no doubt, you would survive. Unless you have forged ahead in your program despite repeated feedback that you should hang on to your day job, completely flunking at this point is unlikely.

Manage Your Physiology

Another key to managing anxiety is to reduce your arousal level. Working on irrational thoughts may help reduce your arousal. In addition, many techniques work directly to modulate physiological arousal, including progressive relaxation, meditation, autogenic training, self-hypnosis, exercise, breathing training, biofeedback, and pleasant imagery. See the supplemental resources at the end of the chapter for some good workbooks to consult about some of these.

To manage the physiological components of your anxiety, experiment and find a strategy that works for you. Some like to visualize the threatening scene ahead of time, while seeing themselves performing deliberately and competently. Many athletes are trained in this form of imagery or visualization. Others can lower their anxiety by sitting in a quiet place, closing their eyes, and imagining a relaxing setting like a favorite beach or place in the mountains. Or perhaps it will work for you to move from the tips of your toes to the top of your head (or the reverse), deliberately tensing and relaxing each body part as you come to it. Many medical centers and universities offer instruction in relaxation or biofeedback that may prove helpful if these skills do not come easily to you. Smith (2005) and Davis, Robbins-Eshelman, and McKay (2000) have provided instructions in book form.

A final way to manage your physiology is to breathe in ways that reduce rather than exacerbate anxiety. Under stressful conditions, many people breathe faster and more shallowly than usual, and this can lead to physical sensations associated with anxiety (e.g., dizziness, numbness in hands; Gevirtz, 2002). The solution to this is to breathe slowly and deliberately from the diaphragm, a large muscle under the ribcage. Many forms of yoga teach this type of breathing. You can learn to breathe with your diaphragm by placing your hand on your stomach, then inhaling so your stomach goes out, and exhaling so it goes in. Imagine that you are inflating then deflating a balloon. Several minutes of sitting quietly and focusing on regular diaphragmatic breathing (try for 5–7 complete breaths/minute) helps many people reduce the fear butterflies.

In addition to selecting and learning a skill to manage your physiological arousal, schedule time to use it right before your oral defense. One student we know scheduled her doctoral defense so she would have time for a vigorous workout and shower before it started!

Another way of managing one's physiology involves drugs. Taking a pill is easier than learning arousal reduction skills, but some drugs carry the risk of also slowing your cognitive processes. We do not recommend pharmacological coping aids unless you are certain that they will not create untoward side effects in the situation.

Manage Your Motor Behavior

The final component of anxiety, the motor component, has to do with how you appear to others. Remember, the motor, physiological, and cognitive components of anxiety need not covary. Thus, although inside you may be shaking, this does not have to show in your behavior. Many of the best performers confess to feeling anxious inside—anxiety that their audiences cannot detect.

As with most of our advice, the key to looking like a professional in your orals lies in planning and practice. Remember the five "P's": prior planning prevents poor performance. Think of which of your professors or fellow students come across professionally and emulate the behaviors that give that impression. Remember, you do not have to feel like you are competent—you just need to *pretend* that you feel that way. Rehearsal, too, can help considerably. Exhibit 13.4 presents Paul's (1966) Timed Behavioral Checklist for Performance Anxiety. You can use this to identify performance cues that make you look anxious that you might try to minimize. Use it to

Exhibit 13.4

Timed Behavioral Checklist for Performance Anxiety

Rater: _____

Name: _____

Date: _____ Speech No. _____ I.D. _____

Behavior Observed Time Period	1	2	3	4	5	6	7	8	9	10
1. Paces										
2. Sways										
3. Shuffles feet										
4. Knees tremble										
5. Extraneous arm and hand movements (swings, scratches, toys, etc.)										
6. Arms rigid										
7. Hands restrained (in pockets, behind back, clasped)										
8. Hand tremors										
9. No eye contact										
10. Face muscles tense (drawn, tics, grimaces)										
11. Face "deadpan"										
12. Face pale										
13. Face flushed (blushes)										
14. Moistens lips										
15. Swallows										
16. Clears throat										
17. Breathes heavily										
18. Perspires (face, hands, armpits)										
19. Voice quivers										
20. Speech blocks or stammers										

Comments:

rate a videotaped version of your talk; you may be surprised at how calm you can appear. Many of us look much more competent than we feel.

Serious Anxiety Problems

As we've said, some anxiety during an oral defense is normal, even desirable. If you generally experience serious anxiety in public speaking or other social situations, however, you may want to obtain treatment for your anxiety before you get to the oral defense. For minor cases of speech anxiety, participating in Toastmasters can be useful (http://www.toastmasters.org). This is an international organization with chapters in many towns and cities. Contact the chapter nearest you. For more serious cases, seek assistance from a qualified, competent professional who specializes in empirically supported strategies for anxiety management. Many professional organizations (e.g., Association for Behavioral and Cognitive Therapy, Anxiety Disorders Association of America) have Web sites with referral information about mental health professionals who specialize in treating anxiety disorders. The Anxiety Disorders Association of America also lists a number of recommended self-help books.

Reread Your Document

Finally, we recommend that you reread your document in the last week or two before your defense. You may have written some sections of the document months or even a year or two before the defense. Do you remember exactly how you scored the data? Handled missing values? Screened participants? Do you know exactly where to look in your document to find details related to measures and analyses? Do you remember important details of the key studies that guided your work and that are most similar to your own? Can you discuss them knowledgeably?

If the answers to any of these questions is "no," you need to refresh your memory about what you wrote and your procedures for collecting and analyzing the data so that you won't fall on your face in your defense. One student we know, for example, almost failed her defense when she could not answer a question about whether she had reverse-scored some of the items in a key questionnaire she had used. This scoring error would have explained some unusual results—along with invalidating them. She *had* scored her data correctly, but in the heat of the moment, she could not remember her scoring procedures. Because she defended the project well otherwise, the committee passed her provisionally, pending review of her scoring procedures. Had she scored the data incorrectly, she would have been required to redo the defense with a new document. The key point, however, is that she could have avoided all this had she reviewed her document and procedures during the week before the defense. We've seen other students handle similar questions with ease because they knew their document inside and out. Prior planning prevents poor performance!

Remember, proposal meetings and oral defenses can be terrifying or they can be enjoyable and productive. As with virtually every step of the research process, some advance investigation and preparation can increase the chances that this aspect of your project will go smoothly and successfully.

Supplemental Resources

Defense Process and Tips

Pyrczak, F. (2000). *Completing your thesis or dissertation*. Los Angeles: Author.

Managing Anxiety

Anxiety Disorders Association of America. (2005). Retrieved November 17, 2005, from http://www.adaa.org/

Bourne, E. J. (2001). *Anxiety and phobia workbook* (3rd ed.). Oakland, CA: New Harbinger.

Davis, M., Robbins-Eshelman, E., & McKay, M. (2000). *The relaxation and stress reduction workbook* (5th ed.). Oakland, CA: New Harbinger.

Greenberger, D., & Padesky, C. (1995). *Mind over mood: Change how you feel by changing the way you think*. New York: Guilford Press.

Smith, J. C. (2005). *Relaxation, meditation, and mindfulness: Self-training manual*. Morrisville, NC: Lulu Press.

Toastmaster's International. (2005). Retrieved November 17, 2005, from http://www.toastmasters.org/

✔ **To Do . . .**

Managing Committee Meetings

☐ Prepare for the proposal meeting

— Know the format (use Exhibit 13.1)

— Make sure notes get taken

☐ Prepare for the formal defense

— Know the format (use Exhibit 13.1)

— Prepare your talk

— Prepare your audiovisual materials

— Develop strategies to handle questions (use Exhibit 13.2)

— Rehearse your oral defense (use Exhibits 13.3 and 13.4)

— Manage anxiety constructively

— Reread your final document

14

Presenting Your Project to the World

I t's over. You've defended your research, made the necessary revisions, and presented the required copies to the librarian. Whew! Now, on with your life, right? Wrong! Well, at least not without ever looking back at your project. You began a research process months and possibly years ago when you started looking for an idea that could be molded into the project you've just completed. That process, as Yogi Berra once said, isn't over until it's over. And research, in a sense, is never really over. As Figure 14.1 shows, research is a cyclical process that begins with a question and begins again, when the answers to that question have been presented to the research community. In truth, your study probably raised additional questions that you or others will pursue in the future. So research is probably best thought of as an evolutionary process rather than as something with definite boundaries and end points.

Nonetheless, there are times when major portions of research (e.g., specific studies in a program; specific thesis or dissertation projects) are complete and can be shared with others. When should you present yours? Usually, as soon as possible after your oral defense. We encourage speed, because you will have a natural tendency to let down after your defense, and you risk never touching your document again. This is a mistake. For one thing, the research process is aborted if results are not disseminated,

Figure 14.1

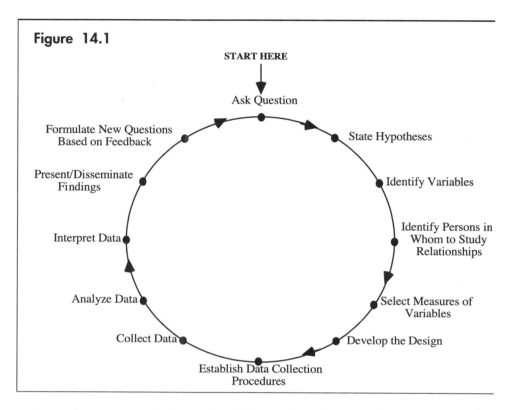

The research cycle. From *Evaluating Outcomes: Empirical Tools for Effective Practice* (p. 41), by J. D. Cone, 2001. Washington, DC: American Psychological Association. Copyright 2001 by the American Psychological Association.

as Figure 14.1 makes clear. If this happens, you never really complete the research cycle. As a result, others have no opportunity to learn from your work. If your study evaluated an existing program, there are ethical concerns related to timely disclosure of your results. You may have a responsibility to both a sponsor and to program participants to present your findings within a reasonable period after completing the evaluation.

As we said in chapter 4, research is a cumulative process. Each study builds on those that have gone before. If yours is not there for others to see, they cannot build on it. Nor can they come to you with questions that might improve the quality of their own research. In addition, sharing your results with others communicates something important about how you value the time and effort you have expended and the sacrifices you have asked others to make on your behalf. Was it really so bad that you never want to talk about it again? Were all those sacrifices only for the sake of a diploma to hang on a wall?

Finally, on a less lofty, more practical note, presenting and publishing your work may help you in the job search now or in the future. Any potential employer will be impressed that you took the time and were organized enough to present your findings. If you plan an academic career, want to apply for postdoctoral research fellowships, or are interested in research-oriented clinical internships, having some presentations, publications, and submissions on your vita may be essential to the success of your application. If you just finished a master's thesis and want to apply to doctoral programs, note that most faculty look favorably on students who took the initiative to present and publish their theses.

Although some master's research will lack the necessary scope for publication, many thesis and dissertation projects will be suitable for presenting at a conference and publishing in a journal. Assuming we have convinced you to share the good news of your findings, let's talk strategy for a minute. How should you go about disseminating your research to the scientific and other communities?

Present It First, Publish It Later

The ideal progression with respect to research dissemination is to present your findings to groups of professionals and get their feedback, incorporate this feedback into your own thinking about the research, and then prepare a formal submission for publication. This permits the research to benefit from the gradual shaping provided by the peer-review process. In addition, presenting (particularly at conferences) inevitably leads to conversations with others interested in your work, expanding your professional network and providing support and encouragement for your efforts. Think about the Big Names you wrote about. Wouldn't it be a thrill if one of them came up and complimented you on your study?

A continuum of outlets exists for presenting research results. At one end are informal discussions of your findings with other students over coffee. At the other is the formal presentation of your research to the Committee for Nobel Laureates at the Nobel Institute in Stockholm. In between, there are departmental colloquia, research presentations during job interviews, informal media presentations (e.g., as a guest on a radio or television show) and formal presentations at state, regional, national, and international professional conferences. Most of us spend our research careers at the lower end of the continuum, leaving the American Psychological Association (APA) Distinguished Scientist, President's Medal, Nobel Prize, and other high-level presentations for the truly gifted, rare few in psychology capable of reaching such lofty heights.

Many departments routinely schedule colloquia during which students, faculty, or invited visitors present their research to anyone interested in attending. If yours does, we recommend presenting your findings in this forum as soon as possible after completing your defense. In effect, this will be your second presentation, because you already gave one and entered the peer review process when you met with your committee for your defense.

You may be thinking, "Okay, okay, I'll present a paper, but I think I'll skip the opportunity for local presentation because the audience is probably not important enough for me to bother." In reality, presentations at home are sometimes the most challenging, because members of the local audience are more likely than others to know some of the real issues and to feel comfortable discussing them with you. Thus, they are less likely to pull punches in questioning you about your research procedures and findings. You might be thinking, "I have to see these people every day. What if my research presentation is absolutely horrid? Do I want to have to slink along the hallways or come to school only at night to avoid the scorn or pity of my colleagues?" These concerns are quite normal, and they are the kind of thinking that leads some to say that if you can present at home, you can present anywhere.

Beyond the department, there are state-level professional meetings, as well as regional, national, and international meetings. Where you choose to submit your research will depend on a number of factors, including whether the meeting invites research presentations, the schedule (i.e., time of year the meeting is held), the cost of attending, and professional advantages. Assuming the meeting welcomes research presentations, the most important of these considerations may be the professional advantages that can accrue. If you are likely to be looking for a job immediately after completing your study, you should consider submitting your research to a meeting that may help you find a position. If your interest is in an applied position and you have definite geographic requirements, consider a state or regional meeting. These often have placement facilities and procedures for arranging interviews with representatives of agencies currently hiring in the geographical area represented at the meeting. Even if no formal placement facilities exist, presenting at a state or regional meeting will expose you to individuals in the desired geographical area and increase your chances of hearing about suitable positions.

If your career aspirations tend toward the academic, consider submitting an abstract to a national convention. The annual meetings of the American Psychological Society or the APA include job-placement functions, as do meetings of disciplines and of specialized groups such as the Association for Behavior Analysis, Society for Research in Child Development, and the Association for Behavioral and Cognitive Therapies. You can find out about the timing of these conventions by looking through recent issues of publications from these organizations or by going to their Web sites. Be warned that abstracts often must be submitted long before the conference. For example, the Association for Behavioral and Cognitive Therapies, which meets in November each year, usually requires that submissions be received by March. The APA requires submissions to be received by mid-November for its meeting, which is ordinarily held the following August. Presenting your study in a forum such as these obviously takes some advance planning. This is such an important part of the dissertation–job-finding sequence, however, that we strongly recommend that you build such a presentation into the time schedule you developed in chapter 3.

When you begin exploring presentation possibilities, you will find that most professional organizations entertain a number of different presentation formats. These include poster presentations, individual papers presented orally, papers presented as part of organized symposia, workshops, panel discussions, and invited addresses. The first three will be the most relevant for research presentations. Submissions of individual projects such as a thesis or dissertation are often most appropriate for poster sessions or paper presentations. If your study is part of a research program, you may be able to talk your chairperson into organizing a research symposium that includes several presentations around a particular theme. If you are an advanced student with some experience presenting, consider organizing a symposium yourself. Your study might be included as one of the submissions.

In general, symposia are reserved for more seasoned researchers, each of whom has a program of research and summarizes one or more studies from that program in the presentation. We will therefore focus our suggestions in the following section on paper presentation and poster session formats.

Pare to Prepare for Presentation

In the subheading for this section, we emphasize "paring" because much of getting a thesis or dissertation ready for dissemination involves just that: paring it down to a manageable size. The dictionary defines the process quite appropriately: "to trim off an outside, excess, or irregular part of . . . ; to diminish or reduce" (Merriam-Webster OnLine, n.d.).

If you wish to present your research at a conference, you will have to submit an abstract of your study. Producing a good abstract requires that you pare your 100 or more pages to just one or two. The abstract accompanying your thesis or dissertation is a good place to begin. The abstract should contain the rationale for your research, methodology, results, and brief reference to its significance and implications. Approximately 60% of the allocated words should describe method and results. These sections should communicate the most important details of the study, because this is what the program committee will use to decide whether to accept or reject your paper. For this reason, make clear to the reviewer what you did and the methodological soundness of your procedures. Exhibit 14.1 presents an abstract that was submitted and accepted for presentation at a meeting of the APA. It was based on a student's dissertation (Ben-Horin & Foster, 2001). It is typical of such submissions and might be a useful model in planning your own.

Assume that a program committee or group recognizes the worth of your research and schedules your presentation at a conference. Or someone invites you for a job interview. The next round of paring involves producing your talk or poster. Preparation for these two events differs somewhat. However, both have much in common with the preparations necessary for the proposal and defense meetings discussed in chapter 13.

Oral Presentations

First, consider how much of your study you should present. That depends on a number of factors. How much time will you have? Who is likely to be in the audience? Will audiovisual or computer equipment be available? Ask these questions before preparing any presentation. Regional or national meetings will allow you 10 to 20 minutes for your talk and usually provide overhead or slide projectors. Some are beginning to make PowerPoint™ or AutoPilot presentation equipment available as well, although you might have to bring your own laptop to attach to it. During job interviews or at

Exhibit 14.1

Sample Abstract for a Poster Presentation

*Psychopathy and Relational Aggression Among
Incarcerated Women*

Improvements in understanding and detecting psychopathy in female inmates require corresponding improvements in conceptualizations of how women act out aggressively. Contemporary research suggests that relational aggression (which involves harm to individuals' relationships with others) is equally or more likely to be found among females than males. Furthermore, relational aggression has many of the same correlates as physical aggression. Because of these findings, and because of the manipulative nature of relationally aggressive behavior, we speculated that relational aggression might be an important but overlooked factor in female psychopathy. Furthermore, assessment of relational aggression might improve the usefulness of the measures of psychopathy among female inmate populations in predicting negative outcomes—in this study, institutional misconduct.

The present study used a correlational design to examine the relationships among psychopathy, relational aggression, and institutional misconduct in female inmates. Female inmates ($N = 64$; 20 African American, 27 Caucasian, 17 other) who had been incarcerated at least 2 months in minimum, medium, and maximum security units within a county jail participated. Psychopathy was measured by the Psychopathy Checklist—Revised (intraclass correlations between independent raters = .93, .70, .90 for total PCL–R scores, Factor 1 scores, and Factor 2 scores, respectively). Peer nominations assessed relational aggression, physical aggression, and prosocial behavior within each unit. Rule violations in the jail (divided by amount of time in jail) were counted from inmates' files to measure institutional misconduct (interrater agreement = 1.00). Psychometric analyses of the peer nomination instrument (adapted from a measure for college students) showed excellent reliability (coefficient alphas = .95, .95, .92 for relational aggression, physical aggression, and prosocial items, respectively) and good evidence of construct validity: relational aggression correlated significantly with physical aggression and prosocial behavior, $r = .83, -.33, p < .05$, but not with the trait version of the State-Trait Anxiety Inventory $r = .14$, n.s.

Results indicated that relational aggression correlated significantly with institutional misconduct, $r = .38, p < .05$. Although relational aggression was significantly related to psychopathy total and factor scores, these relationships disappeared when ethnicity was controlled. Inspection of correlations within ethnic groups suggested that relational aggression and psychopathy were unrelated for Caucasians but moderately related for African American inmates, although the relatively small samples within these groups prohibits firm conclusions. Hierarchical regression

continued

Exhibit 14.1, continued

Sample Abstract for a Poster Presentation

analyses indicated that Factor 2 of the psychopathy measure predicted institutional misconduct, but only for African American women. Contrary to prediction, relational aggression failed to capture significant incremental variance in predicting institutional misconduct over and above ethnicity and psychopathy measures.

The findings of this study suggest that relational aggression could be an important but overlooked component of psychopathy in females—particularly African American females. Currently, antisocial personality disorder criteria and the PCL–R criteria for psychopathy do not contain items or content specific to females. Assessment of relational aggression could expand on the current conceptualization of psychopathy in women by capturing in its description nonviolent women who act out aggressively through relationally aggressive behaviors. In addition, the present findings highlight the importance of examining ethnicity as a possible moderator of the relationships among aggression, psychopathy, and outcome variables such as institutional misconduct or recidivism.

Note. Abstract submitted by H. Ben-Horin and S. L. Foster and accepted for presentation at the annual meeting of the American Psychological Association, 2001. Used with permission of the authors.

local departmental research colloquia, expect an hour to be allocated. In these cases, plan to hold your remarks to 45 minutes to allow time for questions, late starts, arguments with your equipment, and so on. Again, chapter 13 presents numerous suggestions for preparing an oral presentation, and we won't repeat them all.

When we discussed the oral defense, we emphasized the benefits of practicing your talk. The same logic applies in this case. Because all you need is a group to listen to you, the audience can consist of practically anyone. The most useful include your chairperson or other faculty members, graduate student colleagues, and significant others. Other good possibilities for dress-rehearsal audiences would be undergraduate classes you or your colleagues are teaching, or research seminars or journal clubs at an agency where you are doing a practicum or internship.

Poster Presentations

Most regional or national professional organizations are more likely to accept individual studies for presentation during poster sessions than during a series of oral talks. The advantage of this format is that you can discuss your work with interested individuals who circulate among the posters in your session. You display the essence of your information on a piece of heavy poster board (approximately 3' high × 5' long) that most often looks like a free-standing bulletin board. For a poster session, you will need to prepare a visual layout of your study that parallels the organization and content that you would present orally or in a formal journal submission. Researchers type the various sections of their papers—namely, abstract, introduction, method, results, and so on—and attach them to the poster. Poster presentations are usually grouped around a particular theme (e.g., human learning; assessment and diagnosis). Numerous presenters display their posters for a designated time period (e.g., 1.5 hours) in the rooms of the conference center dedicated to poster presentations. As the author, you are expected to stand beside your poster and discuss it with members of the audience as they wander by.

The rules governing poster presentations vary somewhat from conference to conference. In general, most poster guidelines specify that (a) the type size must be readable at a distance of 2 to 3 feet; (b) handouts of the complete presentation must be available at the poster site; and (c) at least one author of the paper must be present throughout to discuss the poster. Incidentally, presenters commonly run out of handouts. Plan for this by having a tablet or other means by which interested individuals can leave their address so that you can mail or e-mail information to them later. If you plan to use snail mail, one time-saving way of doing this is to provide a page of self-sticking labels and have people write their addresses right on the labels. Student members of the Association for Behavior Analysis made a study of the quality of poster presentations and produced a checklist that can be quite helpful in preparing posters. Exhibit 14.2 contains a modified version of this checklist.

To decide what goes into your poster, first set some page or word limits. You will note that Item 11 in the checklist recommends 250 words, maximum. We suggest no more than one page for the introduction to and rationale for the study; two pages for the method; one or two pages for the results, supplemented by no more than three tables or figures; and one page for discussion. The checklist recommends no more than a single table. We suggest keeping the combination of tables and figures to three or fewer. Sometimes, results and discussion can be combined. Because your pages will have large type, concise, clear prose is essential. Remember, your readers will want to walk by, read the paper quickly, and get the gist of the study. They can look over your handout (which should at a minimum reproduce

---

Exhibit 14.2

Poster Preparation Checklist

Category Item

General
___ 1. All elements are legible from 6 feet
___ 2. A Sans Serif font is used
___ 3. All elements are in landscape
___ 4. Poster is ordered in titled sections (methods, results, discussion)
___ 5. 250 total words, maximum

Title
___ 6. Title capitalization is used
___ 7. All caps are used for titles of more than one line

Authorship
___ 8. Author(s)' names are complete
___ 9. Author(s)' affiliations are listed
___ 10. Author(s) are grouped by affiliation

Text Body
___ 11. 45 letters per line, maximum
___ 12. 6 lines in a paragraph, maximum

Captions
___ 13. All figures have captions
___ 14. Captions are descriptive

Figures
___ 15. 4 bar graph categories or 4 lines of data, maximum
___ 16. Data points on line graphs are clearly visible from 6 feet
___ 17. No lines in the background of graphs
___ 18. Multiple data lines have different data points or colors
___ 19. Multiple categories on a bar graph have different fill or colors
___ 20. If single-subject data are presented, line graphs are shown
___ 21. Horizontal and vertical axis labels are present on line graphs
___ 22. Text and scales are self-explanatory
___ 23. If more than one color is used, the contrast is sufficient
___ 24. Grouped data include measure of variability (e.g., error bars)

Tables
___ 25. No more than 1 table total

Note. Adapted from http://www.abainternational.org/sub/membersvcs/Student-news/Studentpres. asp.

the poster text but preferably provide a more detailed description of the study) some other time. We find it useful to use the abstract as a basis for the poster and build up, adding additional details in order of importance until we have met our page or word limits.

If you have attended poster sessions already, you have probably been dazzled by the variety of presentation styles. Remember, when you give such a presentation, you represent not only yourself but your coauthors and school as well. The visual appearance of your poster makes an important statement that complements its written content. Most of us have seen hand-written or poorly typed poster presentations and been thankful that they did not have our school's name attached to them. At the other extreme, some brightly colored Las Vegas-style posters clearly represent style over substance. Taste, clarity, and ease of reading are the most important criteria applicable to posters, given that the program committee has considered their content important enough to be accepted in the first place.

Our suggestions for successful posters conform to these criteria. First, follow the guidelines provided by the program committee. This is not the place to get creative. Remember, they have their rules for a reason. Second, keep it simple. You will have to carry your poster with you to the conference, often on an airplane. You will have to set it up and take it down in approximately 15 minutes. The only materials you can count on being provided will be the poster board to which you attach your materials. Be sure to take along a supply of pushpins or tacks. Unless your school has a department that will produce a beautiful poster for you, low-tech may work best. The lowest tech approach involves preparing poster elements as typed pages with enlarged print, then attaching them to stiff colored backing with a half- or three-quarter-inch border around the entire page. Use the same colored backing throughout. As a rule, keep each section (abstract, intro-duction, etc.) on a separate page. If two pages are needed, consider using a backing large enough to include both typed pages. Grouping in this way helps browsers read the presentation. Tack or pin your material to the poster board in the usual left to right sequence. If diagrams, figures, or other elements differ in size and a smooth left-to-right flow is difficult, consider using large arrows between sections to guide the reader's eye.

If all of this sounds too much like the last (only?) art class you ever took, consider taking a disk of your presentation to a copy shop and asking them to prepare a single, large photo or printed sheet containing the entire thing. You can roll this up in a mailing tube and carry it on the plane with you. Putting up the poster is then a simple process of unrolling and pinning. The major drawbacks of this approach are cost and the minor inconvenience of lugging the mailing tube to and from the conference.

Publish Your Study After Presenting It

After you have presented your findings to various professional audiences and received feedback from them, plan to submit your study for publication. Speed and brevity are again two important considerations at this point. As discussed earlier, avoid the temptation to shove your document in a drawer and forget about it. Capitalize on the completion momentum and write it up for publication as soon as possible. A good rule of thumb is to present the paper and submit it for publication within 12 months of your defense.

Select a Journal

Prepare your research for publication by first selecting an appropriate journal. Your committee chairperson may suggest an appropriate outlet. Possibly, your study is part of a research program that normally directs its submissions to one or two journals. You undoubtedly are already familiar with one or more outlets for research of the type you have completed because you noticed them when doing your literature review. Which journals publish most of the research in this area?

Be aware that journal "pecking orders" exist, with some journals being harder to publish in than others. Many journals of the APA, for example, receive hundreds of submissions each year and have 80% or higher rejection rates. Editors of these journals often are looking for reasons to reject manuscripts, simply to get through the stacks of material that are submitted. If your study did not turn out as well as you wanted or had some obvious problems, you might want to try a less selective or more specialized journal and avoid the pain of an almost certain rejection. If your findings and methodology are solid, and if you have a thick skin and don't mind the fact that you may have to revise and submit the article to your second-choice outlet, you may want to try for a more prestigious or widely circulated journal. Chairpersons and committee members with experience publishing in your area can advise you about how likely different journals are to accept your submission.

When you have selected the appropriate journal, get a copy of its instructions to authors. These can usually be found toward the front or back of each issue or online at the journal's Web site. They describe the type of work the journal publishes, along with format and submission requirements. These are reasonably consistent across journals in the behavioral sciences, and many format requirements conform closely to those of the *Publication Manual of the American Psychological Association* (APA, 2010). Pay attention to the types of work considered appropriate by the journal, however. You will save yourself considerable time by sending your manuscript to the most appropriate outlets. It usually takes 60 to 90 days for your paper to be reviewed. Rejection for inappropriateness and delays of this length can be avoided by careful journal selection in the first place.

Prepare the Manuscript

As with preparing a presentation, paring is essential to get your study ready to submit to a journal. Many research-based journal articles contain a maximum of 25 double-spaced manuscript pages of text. Journals that publish primarily reviews of the literature (e.g., *Psychological Bulletin, Developmental Review, Psychological Review,* and *Clinical Psychology Review*) often accept longer papers. Some data-type journals (e.g., medical publications) require considerably shorter articles. In any event, your submission will require shortening your thesis or dissertation. Examine your target journal to estimate average article length. If a paper is too long, shorten it by stating points clearly and directly, confining the discussion to the specific problem under investigation, deleting or combining data displays, eliminating repetition across sections, and writing in the active voice (APA, 2010).

An important warning: Do not simply cut and paste from your thesis or dissertation. This leads to disjointed papers. As we mentioned earlier, one idea is to build up from your poster presentation or abstract rather than pare down from your thesis or dissertation. To create a compact poster, you had to include only the most important details. Add the next most important points, then the next, and so on, until your paper approximates the target length.

As you write, consider the specific requirements and typical content of articles appearing in the journal you have selected. How much emphasis do authors give to theoretical issues, to methodological ones, to discussion? Tailor your paper to the specific requirements of the journal, both explicit and implicit, whenever possible.

Be sure to attend to details. If a phrase or sentence is not clear to you, it will not be clear to the reviewer who has never heard of your work. Have a colleague read your paper, checking in particular for inadequate or unnecessary detail and for clarity. In addition, proofread and follow APA publication requirements meticulously. A sloppy paper leads many to wonder how carefully the research was conducted.

Discuss with your chairperson and other coauthors how to orchestrate the write-up. Often, the student writes a first draft, and coauthors edit it and make comments. Making a publicly agreed-to schedule for completion of drafts helps get the manuscript ready in a timely fashion.

Decide Authorship

Standard 8.12 of the "Ethical Principles of Psychologists and Code of Conduct" (APA, 2002; see Appendix, this volume) governs authorship issues. Usually, dissertations and theses are submitted for publication under the joint authorship of the student and the chair of the student's committee, with the student as first author. As noted in the APA's *Publication Manual* (APA, 2010), authorship is accorded those who make "substantial scientific contributions" to the research and is not reserved for those who do the actual writing. In general, the term "substantial professional contributions" includes activities such as suggesting the problem or hypotheses, writing major portions of the paper, conducting the statistical analyses, suggesting the research design, providing one's own archival data, or arranging access to participants. Minor intellectual contributions and clerical and other forms of nonintellectual contributions (e.g., building an apparatus, collecting data, and making suggestions for statistical analyses) can be acknowledged in footnotes. The significance of the contribution each person makes generally determines the order of authorship, with the person making the greatest contribution listed first. With rare exceptions, "a student is listed as principal author on any multiple-authored article that is substantially based on the student's doctoral dissertation" (APA, 2002, p. 1070).

At the same time, the Ethics Committee of the APA has indicated that second authorship for committee chairs may be considered obligatory if they designate the primary variables, make major interpretative contributions, or provide the database. It also noted that authorship is a courtesy if the chair suggests the general research area, is substantially involved in the development of the design and dependent measures, or contributes substantially to writing the published report. It goes on to say that authorship is not acceptable if the chairperson's only contributions consist of editorial suggestions, encouragement, or the provision of physical facilities, financial support, or critiques (APA Ethics Committee, 1983). For this input, acknowledgment in a footnote or introductory statement is appropriate. Fine and Kurdek (1993) discussed authorship determination for nonthesis/dissertation papers in more detail. Shawchuck, Fatis, and Breitenstein (1986) suggested a process to follow in working out authorship arrangements.

Refer to authors in the text of the paper by ordinal position of authorship, not by reference to professional seniority (for example, "All children were observed by the first author"). This is obvious when one remembers the requirement to order authors by significance of contribution, because it is quite often the case that junior authors make greater contributions, especially to their own doctoral dissertations.

It is sometimes difficult to ascertain the relative significance of contributions among authors at the completion of a particular research endeavor. As a result, disputes about authorship or order of authors are common, and they are not pleasant. A good way to avoid them is to decide at the *beginning* of a collaborative research effort just who is going to do what and what the relative contributions mean in terms of eventual authorship.

In fact, dissemination is such an important part of the research process that it is unwise to leave issues regarding presentation and publication unspoken. Especially with dissertations, a good deal of both the student's and faculty's time will be devoted to the research, and its completion demands some form of presentation at least, and publication at best. After deciding on your research question, think about making a formal agreement with your chairperson (perhaps in writing) covering jointly determined plans for dissemination. The agreement should state what forms dissemination will take; the approximate time after completion these forms will be pursued (recall the 12-month rule); individual responsibilities of the student, the chair, and any others who will be involved; and the order of authorship you anticipate. The agreement should also provide contingencies should one or more of the parties alter the level or timing of their participation. A clear, written agreement produced in advance can do much to prevent strained relationships later. And it will do a lot to ensure the project advances all the way to publication.

Submit the Manuscript

When you are ready to send your slimmed-down opus to the previously selected journal, consult the journal's guidelines for authors once again to determine the exact submission procedures to be followed. If manuscripts are to be sent to the journal editor, make sure to find out the name and address of the current editor; some journals change editors every 3 to 5 years. Submit the required number of copies to the address provided in a recent issue of the journal. Be sure that your copies are legible and complete and that pages are in the proper order. Do not staple or otherwise bind pages together. A paper clip will suffice. Accompany your submission with a cover letter indicating that the paper is not simultaneously being considered by any other journal. If the journal has a provision for anonymous (or blind) reviews and you are requesting one, state this in the letter. Mention that all participants (human or animal) have been treated in accord with the ethical standards of the APA concerning research. If any copyrighted material appears in your submission, be sure to enclose copies of any permission you have to reprint or adapt it. Finally, indicate a phone number and address where you can be reached. If your address changes while the article is under review, notify the editor handling the submission promptly.

Editors of most journals assign papers to an associate editor with expertise in the general area the research addresses, reserving a few papers to handle themselves. The associate editor then seeks comments from between two to five peer reviewers. One or more of these will usually be an expert on your specific topic. These individuals provide written comments about the strengths and weaknesses of the paper and recommend whether the journal should publish it. Most editors will acknowledge receipt of your manuscript in writing. Some will tell you who is handling the manuscript (i.e., the editor or one of the associate editors, sometimes referred to as the "action editor") and a date by which you can expect to receive the reviews and the publication decision. About 90 days turnaround time is common, but journals with many submissions may have longer delays.

If you have not heard from the journal within a week or two of the target date, call or write to the person handling your manuscript and inquire politely about its status. The associate editor may have had trouble finding reviewers, a reviewer may be late, or the associate editor may be behind. Polite, repeated inquiries at 2-week intervals can prompt a slow editor to complete the review process on your manuscript in a more timely fashion.

When you receive an editorial decision, your work is not over. Journal editors ordinarily use four categories of response. The least frequent is an outright acceptance with no requirement for revision. The most common is a rejection, accompanied by one or more reviews, usually anonymous, detailing the reviewers' reactions to the paper. A third type of decision involves conditionally accepting the paper based on your agreeing to make certain changes. The fourth type of decision is really no decision at all. It involves telling the authors that the reviewers and editor could not decide. The paper had a number of strengths, but it also had enough weaknesses that an acceptance, even with the promise of changes, could not be rendered at this time. The editor encourages the authors to revise the paper as suggested by the reviewers and resubmit it for additional consideration. In such cases, the editor often treats the paper as a new submission, sending it through the entire review process again.

The revise–resubmit verdict often devastates first-time submitters, who conclude that their paper is ultimately doomed. In reality, such a decision from a good journal that has a high rejection rate can be excellent news. It means your paper was good enough to get a second chance! If you and your coauthors think it is possible to make the suggested changes within a reasonable amount of time, your best bet is to resubmit to that journal. If you have significant disagreement with the changes recommended or they will take too much time, you may prefer to revise and submit the paper to another journal. Be aware that your chances of acceptance should increase with each submission if you improve the manuscript as suggested by the various reviewers and editors.

Pick Yourself Up, Dust Yourself Off, and Start All Over Again

Because approximately 80% of the papers submitted to the best journals are rejected, it is reasonable to assume that your study may meet a similar fate the first time you submit it. Even if the study is not rejected, it will likely receive criticisms. First-timers often react to such criticism with excessive anger or depression. Stay centered at this point. Be constructive. Act out the advice of the old Dorothy Fields and Jerome Kern song in the subheading of this section. See the rejection as an opportunity to get back in the game, and at a higher level of participation. In interpreting reviewers' comments, it is helpful to remember several points. First, editors ask reviewers to indicate how the paper can be improved. This can seem like criticism, but it is usually constructive commentary on how to make things better. Second, whereas strengths can often be stated briefly, it takes more space to explain a weakness. Third, the review tradition emphasizes critical rather than laudatory commentary. For these reasons, it is likely that most comments you receive will focus on weaknesses of the manuscript. Even papers that are published in excellent journals usually go through at least two revisions to handle reviewers' criticisms. Don't take the comments personally.

The high likelihood of initial rejection is another good reason for getting your project ready for submission as soon after your defense as possible. The bad news is that you may have to try again, revising your paper and sending it out one more time. The good news about a rejection is that it is usually accompanied by excellent suggestions from experts in your area about how the paper and your research can be improved. If you attend to these carefully and make the changes that are appropriate, you will increase your chances for acceptance of your next submission considerably. Even more important, attending to the comments of these experts can improve your own critical thinking and any future research you might do in this or other areas.

Incidentally, it is considered professionally unacceptable to submit your manuscript to a second journal without revision. Different journals sometimes use the same reviewers, and these hard-working colleagues do not take kindly to seeing a paper a second time when its authors have not bothered to respond to suggestions for improving the first version. The peer-review process is an important mechanism for the advancement of science, and it behooves all of us to respect it.

When (as is likely) you do receive a rejection the first time you submit the paper, you may be inclined to put the paper away and forget about it. This is a natural reaction. After all, although some of the comments of the reviewers simply reflect their misunderstanding of what was done or found, some are rather telling criticisms of the study as well. You might be tempted to conclude that the research is so flawed it is not worth disseminating further. Avoid this temptation. Remember, a committee of scholars at your school approved what you have done and contributed substantially to it. It must have *some* merit. Most carefully conceived and conducted research efforts have something worth sharing with the professional community. When you get your reviews, we suggest you read them and show them to your chair. Set a time to discuss them after a week or so. During this cooling off period, put the reviews away and forget about them until just before meeting with your chair. At this point, you will have a fresh, somewhat less defensive perspective. You will be ready to offer suggestions about how the reviewers' concerns can be addressed in a revision. When you do meet with your chair, you can decide jointly how each of the concerns will be handled and who will be responsible for each. If you do not have a resubmit option from the initial journal, decide where to send the revised version and consult that journal's instructions to authors.

Consider Dividing Major Projects for Multiple Submissions

Approach the submission of your research for publication systematically. This is especially critical with a dissertation that can produce multiple scholarly products. In fact, you might have a publication program worked out from the very beginning. You might decide at the outset that your literature review will be of such comprehensiveness and quality that it will warrant submission to a discussion or review-type journal, such as *Psychological Bulletin*. In addition, you might develop a piece of apparatus or computer software for conducting your study that could be described in a separate paper submitted to an appropriately specialized journal. You might produce treatment manuals describing your intervention programs in sufficient detail to warrant publication as a short book. Or you might develop and produce sufficient information about a new assessment instrument that you could write a stand-alone article describing it. All of these spin-offs from the major thrust of your research could be parts of your publication program.

If you consider submitting more than one paper from your dissertation, you will want to consult the APA's warnings about duplicate publication (APA, 1983, 2002). Duplicate publication involves work that has been "published in whole or in substantial part in another journal or in any readily available work" (APA, 1983, p. 167). If, for example, you submit the literature review section of your thesis or dissertation separately, it must be substantially different from the introduction or other sections of the research paper submission. Prudence dictates informing the editor receiving either submission of the second paper so that the editor will have the opportunity to decide whether duplicate publication is an issue.

Note that we are talking about submitting papers describing relatively independent parts of the larger project. We do not advocate "piecemeal publication of several reports of the results from a single data base . . ." (APA, 1983, p. 168). This practice often constitutes duplicate publication (because of substantial overlap). There are legitimate instances (e.g., results of individual assessment occasions in a longitudinal study) in which multiple publications from the same database would be warranted, however, and we encourage you to consult the APA's *Publication Manual* (2010) for more discussion of these.

Weigh the Benefits of Dissemination in the Popular Press

Up to now, we have restricted our discussion to disseminating your findings to professional audiences. The general public may be an appropriate audience as well. Not only does the profession generally benefit from informing the public of significant research in the academic community, but you may benefit personally. For example, imagine you have an interest in the relatively new area of behavioral finance. This discipline studies how emotional and cognitive behavior can influence the investment decisions people make (e.g., Shiller, 1999). Suppose also that you complete a dissertation that shows substantial individual differences in the extent to which people spread hypothetical large sums of inherited money across different investments or concentrate it in one or two. Moreover, you show that willingness to diversify is positively correlated with scores on a measure of risk aversion. Media interviews could inform the public of this finding and include carefully worded implications it might have for personal investing. Articles citing your work might appear in the business section of major city newspapers. Being mentioned as a potential expert in this area could help your beginning career in the psychology of personal finance!

If you are pursuing an academic career, you can also benefit from having information about your work appear in the popular press. If your research requires cooperation of local agencies, schools, and so on, a good way to be introduced can sometimes be a newspaper story about the "fascinating research of Dr. Blank, newly appointed assistant professor at O.U.K.D." Timing the appearance of such a story to precede your contacting the agencies might go a long way toward opening some doors.

We speak in this instance of stories in local newspapers and appearances on radio or local television talk shows. These do not usually involve publication of major portions of your findings. There are other popular outlets (e.g., magazines or trade books), however, in which a substantial part of an applied research project might be published. These may or may not be appropriate to your professional objectives.

Warnings are in order. These are not peer-reviewed journals and, thus, will not carry much weight in the academic community. In addition, it is easy to lose control of the content of stories appearing in popular media. Your carefully phrased, appropriately qualified interpretations can be sensationalized rather quickly into more newsworthy proclamations that go way beyond the scope of your study. Ask to have final approval of any article or story based on your research, especially if it includes direct quotes from you. Finally, it is well to consider that previous publication in popular outlets such as these might foreclose publication in professional journals because of the duplicate publication prohibition. Weigh your dissemination options carefully. Develop a plan or program that involves multiple publications, if appropriate, and multiple dissemination outlets, both professional and popular, if appropriate. If you decide to reach the public through the media, be sure to follow the APA guidelines for appropriate public presentation. Include sequencing and time lines in your plan and consider using the project planning software discussed in chapter 3.

Dissemination is the important last step in the research cycle. Do not avoid it in your natural inclination to get the dissertation process behind you and move on with your life. Your research benefited from the fact that others presented and published their work. You learned from their advances and from their mistakes. Now allow others to learn from you. Besides, publishing your results provides another reason to celebrate. And, face it, it's fun to see your name in print!

Supplemental Resources

General Publishing Guidelines/Suggestions

American Psychological Association. (2010). *Publication manual of the American Psychological Association* (6th ed.). Washington, DC: Author.

McInerney, D. M. (2001). *Publishing your psychology research: A guide to writing for journals in psychology and related fields.* Thousand Oaks, CA: Sage.

Research Ethics

American Psychological Association. (2002). Ethical principles of psychologists and code of conduct. *American Psychologist, 57,* 1060–1073.

Suggestions for Preparing Poster Presentations

Association for Behavior Analysis. (2005). *Student committee: Poster presentations.* Retrieved November 18, 2005, from http://www.abainternational.org/sub/membersvcs/Student-news/Studentpres.asp

University of Washington School of Public Health. (2005). *Creating a poster using MS PowerPoint.* Retrieved November 18, 2005, from http://depts.washington.edu/mphpract/ppposter.html

✔ To Do . . .

Presenting Your Project Publicly

☐ Submit your research for presentation

—Meet with chairperson and decide authorship

—Identify outlet and due dates for submissions

—Submit an abstract

☐ Prepare your presentation

—Identify format and length of oral talks

—Identify page limits for posters

—Create a clear, readable poster

—Prepare handouts to accompany poster

—Obtain tablet, push pins, etc., to use during poster session

—Provide means for obtaining addresses to send paper later

☐ Publish your study

—Select a journal

—Examine instructions to authors

—Write the manuscript

—Submit the manuscript

—Be ready for criticism and don't let it get you down

☐ Divide major projects for multiple submissions

☐ Consider dissemination in the popular press

Appendix: Selected Ethical Standards Relevant to the Conduct of Research in Psychology

2.05 Delegation of Work to Others

Psychologists who delegate work to employees, supervisees, or research or teaching assistants or who use the services of others, such as interpreters, take reasonable steps to (1) avoid delegating such work to persons who have a multiple relationship with those being served that would likely lead to exploitation or loss of objectivity; (2) authorize only those responsibilities that such persons can be expected to perform competently on the basis of their education, training, or experience, either independently or with the level of supervision being provided; and (3) see that such persons perform these services competently. (See also Standards 2.02, Providing Services in Emergencies; 3.05, Multiple Relationships; 4.01, Maintaining Confidentiality; 9.01, Bases for Assessments; 9.02, Use of Assessments; 9.03, Informed Consent in Assessments; and 9.07, Assessment by Unqualified Persons.)

3.04 Avoiding Harm

Psychologists take reasonable steps to avoid harming their clients/patients, students, supervisees, research participants, organizational clients, and others with whom they work, and to minimize harm where it is foreseeable and unavoidable.

Adapted from "Ethical Principles of Psychologists and Code of Conduct," by the American Psychological Association, 2002, *American Psychologist, 57,* pp. 1060–1073. Copyright 2002 by the American Psychological Association.

3.08 Exploitative Relationships

Psychologists do not exploit persons over whom they have supervisory, evaluative, or other authority such as clients/patients, students, supervisees, research participants, and employees. (See also Standards 3.05, Multiple Relationships; 6.04, Fees and Financial Arrangements; 6.05, Barter With Clients/Patients; 7.07, Sexual Relationships With Students and Supervisees; 10.05, Sexual Intimacies With Current Therapy Clients/Patients; 10.06, Sexual Intimacies With Relatives or Significant Others of Current Therapy Clients/Patients; 10.07, Therapy With Former Sexual Partners; and 10.08, Sexual Intimacies With Former Therapy Clients/Patients.)

4.01 Maintaining Confidentiality

Psychologists have a primary obligation and take reasonable precautions to protect confidential information obtained through or stored in any medium, recognizing that the extent and limits of confidentiality may be regulated by law or established by institutional rules or professional or scientific relationship. (See also Standard 2.05, Delegation of Work to Others.)

4.02 Discussing the Limits of Confidentiality

(a) Psychologists discuss with persons (including, to the extent feasible, persons who are legally incapable of giving informed consent and their legal representatives) and organizations with whom they establish a scientific or professional relationship (1) the relevant limits of confidentiality and (2) the foreseeable uses of the information generated through their psychological activities. (See also Standard 3.10, Informed Consent.)

(b) Unless it is not feasible or is contraindicated, the discussion of confidentiality occurs at the outset of the relationship and thereafter as new circumstances may warrant.

(c) Psychologists who offer services, products, or information via electronic transmission inform clients/patients of the risks to privacy and limits of confidentiality.

4.04 Minimizing Intrusions on Privacy

(a) Psychologists include in written and oral reports and consultations, only information germane to the purpose for which the communication is made.

(b) Psychologists discuss confidential information obtained in their work only for appropriate scientific or professional purposes and only with persons clearly concerned with such matters.

4.07 Use of Confidential Information for Didactic or Other Purposes

Psychologists do not disclose in their writings, lectures, or other public media, confidential, personally identifiable information concerning their clients/patients, students, research participants, organizational clients, or other recipients of their services that they obtained during the course of their work, unless (1) they take reasonable steps to disguise the person or organization, (2) the person or organization has consented in writing, or (3) there is legal authorization for doing so.

5.01 Avoidance of False or Deceptive Statements

(a) Public statements include but are not limited to paid or unpaid advertising, product endorsements, grant applications, licensing applications, other credentialing applications, brochures, printed matter, directory listings, personal resumes or curricula vitae, or comments for use in media such as print or electronic transmission, statements in legal proceedings, lectures and public oral presentations, and published materials. Psychologists do not knowingly make public statements that are false, deceptive, or fraudulent concerning their research, practice, or other work activities or those of persons or organizations with which they are affiliated.

(b) Psychologists do not make false, deceptive, or fraudulent statements concerning (1) their training, experience, or competence; (2) their academic degrees; (3) their credentials; (4) their institutional or association affiliations; (5) their services; (6) the scientific or clinical basis for, or results or degree of success of, their services; (7) their fees; or (8) their publications or research findings.

(c) Psychologists claim degrees as credentials for their health services only if those degrees (1) were earned from a regionally accredited educational institution or (2) were the basis for psychology licensure by the state in which they practice.

6.01 Documentation of Professional and Scientific Work and Maintenance of Records

Psychologists create, and to the extent the records are under their control, maintain, disseminate, store, retain, and dispose of records and data relating to their professional and scientific work in order to (1) facilitate provision of services later by them or by other professionals, (2) allow for replication of research design and analyses, (3) meet institutional requirements, (4) ensure accuracy of billing and payments, and (5) ensure compliance with law. (See also Standard 4.01, Maintaining Confidentiality.)

6.02 Maintenance, Dissemination, and Disposal of Confidential Records of Professional and Scientific Work

(a) Psychologists maintain confidentiality in creating, storing, accessing, transferring, and disposing of records under their control, whether these are written, automated, or in any other medium. (See also Standards 4.01, Maintaining Confidentiality, and 6.01, Documentation of Professional and Scientific Work and Maintenance of Records.)

(b) If confidential information concerning recipients of psychological services is entered into databases or systems of records available to persons whose access has not been consented to by the recipient, psychologists use coding or other techniques to avoid the inclusion of personal identifiers.

(c) Psychologists make plans in advance to facilitate the appropriate transfer and to protect the confidentiality of records and data in the event of psychologists' withdrawal from positions or practice. (See also Standards 3.12, Interruption of Psychological Services, and 10.09, Interruption of Therapy.)

8. Research and Publication

8.01 Institutional Approval

When institutional approval is required, psychologists provide accurate information about their research proposals and obtain approval prior to conducting the research. They conduct the research in accordance with the approved research protocol.

8.02 Informed Consent to Research

(a) When obtaining informed consent as required in Standard 3.10, Informed Consent, psychologists inform participants about (1) the purpose of the research, expected duration, and procedures; (2) their right to decline to participate and to withdraw from the research once participation has begun; (3) the foreseeable consequences of declining or withdrawing; (4) reasonably foreseeable factors that may be expected to influence their willingness to participate such as potential risks, discomfort, or adverse effects; (5) any prospective research benefits; (6) limits of confidentiality; (7) incentives for participation; and (8) whom to contact for questions about the research and research participants' rights. They provide opportunity for the prospective participants to ask questions and receive answers. (See also Standards 8.03, Informed Consent for Recording Voices and Images in Research; 8.05, Dispensing With Informed Consent for Research; and 8.07, Deception in Research.)

(b) Psychologists conducting intervention research involving the use of experimental treatments clarify to participants at the outset of the research (1) the experimental nature of the treatment; (2) the services that will or will not be available to the control group(s) if appropriate; (3) the means by which assignment to treatment and control groups will be made; (4) available treatment alternatives if an individual does not wish to participate in the research or wishes to withdraw once a study has begun; and (5) compensation for or monetary costs of participating including, if appropriate, whether reimbursement from the participant or a third-party payor will be sought. (See also Standard 8.02a, Informed Consent to Research.)

8.03 Informed Consent for Recording Voices and Images in Research

Psychologists obtain informed consent from research participants prior to recording their voices or images for data collection unless (1) the research consists solely of naturalistic observations in public places, and it is not anticipated that the recording will be used in a manner that could cause personal identification or harm, or (2) the research design includes deception, and consent for the use of the recording is obtained during debriefing. (See also Standard 8.07, Deception in Research.)

8.04 Client/Patient, Student, and Subordinate Research Participants

(a) When psychologists conduct research with clients/patients, students, or subordinates as participants, psychologists take steps to protect the prospective participants from adverse consequences of declining or withdrawing from participation.

(b) When research participation is a course requirement or an opportunity for extra credit, the prospective participant is given the choice of equitable alternative activities.

8.05 Dispensing With Informed Consent for Research

Psychologists may dispense with informed consent only (1) where research would not reasonably be assumed to create distress or harm and involves (a) the study of normal educational practices, curricula, or classroom management methods conducted in educational settings; (b) only anonymous questionnaires, naturalistic observations, or archival research for which disclosure of responses would not place participants at risk of criminal or civil liability or damage their financial standing, employability, or reputation, and confidentiality is protected; or (c) the study of factors related to job or organization effectiveness conducted in organizational settings for which there is no risk to participants' employability, and confidentiality is protected or (2) where otherwise permitted by law or federal or institutional regulations.

8.06 Offering Inducements for Research Participation

(a) Psychologists make reasonable efforts to avoid offering excessive or inappropriate financial or other inducements for research participation when such inducements are likely to coerce participation.

(b) When offering professional services as an inducement for research participation, psychologists clarify the nature of the services, as well as the risks, obligations, and limitations. (See also Standard 6.05, Barter With Clients/Patients.)

8.07 Deception in Research

(a) Psychologists do not conduct a study involving deception unless they have determined that the use of deceptive techniques is justified by the study's significant prospective scientific, educational, or applied value and that effective nondeceptive alternative procedures are not feasible.

(b) Psychologists do not deceive prospective participants about research that is reasonably expected to cause physical pain or severe emotional distress.

(c) Psychologists explain any deception that is an integral feature of the design and conduct of an experiment to participants as early as is feasible, preferably at the conclusion of their participation, but no later than at the conclusion of the data collection, and permit participants to withdraw their data. (See also Standard 8.08, Debriefing.)

8.08 Debriefing

(a) Psychologists provide a prompt opportunity for participants to obtain appropriate information about the nature, results, and conclusions of the research, and they take reasonable steps to correct any misconceptions that participants may have of which the psychologists are aware.

(b) If scientific or humane values justify delaying or withholding this information, psychologists take reasonable measures to reduce the risk of harm.

(c) When psychologists become aware that research procedures have harmed a participant, they take reasonable steps to minimize the harm.

8.09 Humane Care and Use of Animals in Research

(a) Psychologists acquire, care for, use, and dispose of animals in compliance with current federal, state, and local laws and regulations, and with professional standards.

(b) Psychologists trained in research methods and experienced in the care of laboratory animals supervise all procedures involving animals and are responsible for ensuring appropriate consideration of their comfort, health, and humane treatment.

(c) Psychologists ensure that all individuals under their supervision who are using animals have received instruction in research methods and in the care, maintenance, and handling of the species being used, to the extent appropriate to their role. (See also Standard 2.05, Delegation of Work to Others.)

(d) Psychologists make reasonable efforts to minimize the discomfort, infection, illness, and pain of animal subjects.

(e) Psychologists use a procedure subjecting animals to pain, stress, or privation only when an alternative procedure is unavailable and the goal is justified by its prospective scientific, educational, or applied value.

(f) Psychologists perform surgical procedures under appropriate anesthesia and follow techniques to avoid infection and minimize pain during and after surgery.

(g) When it is appropriate that an animal's life be terminated, psychologists proceed rapidly, with an effort to minimize pain and in accordance with accepted procedures.

8.10 Reporting Research Results

(a) Psychologists do not fabricate data. (See also Standard 5.01a, Avoidance of False or Deceptive Statements.)

(b) If psychologists discover significant errors in their published data, they take reasonable steps to correct such errors in a correction, retraction, erratum, or other appropriate publication means.

8.11 Plagiarism

Psychologists do not present portions of another's work or data as their own, even if the other work or data source is cited occasionally.

8.12 Publication Credit

(a) Psychologists take responsibility and credit, including authorship credit, only for work they have actually performed or to which they have substantially contributed.

(b) Principal authorship and other publication credits accurately reflect the relative scientific or professional contributions of the individuals involved, regardless of their relative status. Mere possession of an institutional position, such as department chair, does not justify authorship credit. Minor contributions to the research or to the writing for publications are acknowledged appropriately, such as in footnotes or in an introductory statement.

(c) Except under exceptional circumstances, a student is listed as principal author on any multiple-authored article that is substantially based on the student's doctoral dissertation. Faculty advisors discuss publication credit with students as early as feasible and throughout the research and publication process as appropriate. (See also Standard 8.12b, Publication Credit.)

8.13 Duplicate Publication of Data

Psychologists do not publish, as original data, data that have been previously published. This does not preclude republishing data when they are accompanied by proper acknowledgment.

8.14 Sharing Research Data for Verification

(a) After research results are published, psychologists do not withhold the data on which their conclusions are based from other competent professionals who seek to verify the substantive claims through reanalysis and who intend to use such data only for that purpose, provided that the confidentiality of the participants can be protected and unless legal rights concerning proprietary data preclude their release. This does not preclude psychologists from requiring that such individuals or groups be responsible for costs associated with the provision of such information.

(b) Psychologists who request data from other psychologists to verify the substantive claims through reanalysis may use shared data only for the declared purpose. Requesting psychologists obtain prior written agreement for all other uses of the data.

8.15 Reviewers

Psychologists who review material submitted for presentation, publication, grant, or research proposal review respect the confidentiality of and the proprietary rights in such information of those who submitted it.

References

Aiken, L. S., & West, S. G. (1996). *Multiple regression: Testing and interpreting interactions.* Thousand Oaks, CA: Sage.

Ambady, N., & Rosenthal, R. (1992). Thin slices of expressive behavior as predictors of interpersonal consequences: A meta-analysis. *Psychological Bulletin, 111,* 256–274.

American Psychiatric Association. (1994). *Diagnostic and statistical manual of mental disorders* (4th ed.). Washington, DC: Author.

American Psychological Association Ethics Committee. (1983). *Authorship guidelines for dissertation supervision.* Washington, DC: Author.

American Psychological Association. (2002). Ethical principles of psychologists and code of conduct. *American Psychologist, 57,* 1060–1073.

American Psychological Association. (2010). *Mastering APA Style: Student's workbook and training guide* (6th ed.). Washington, DC: Author.

American Psychological Association. (2010). *Publication manual of the American Psychological Association* (6th ed.). Washington, DC: Author.

Anastasi, A., & Urbina, S. (1997). *Psychological testing* (7th ed.). Upper Saddle River, NJ: Prentice-Hall.

Andrews, F. M., Klem, L., Davidson, T. N., O'Malley, P. M., & Rodgers, W. L. (1981). *A guide for selecting statistical techniques for analyzing social science data* (2nd ed.). Ann Arbor, MI: Survey Research Center, Institute for Social Research, University of Michigan.

Antony, M. M., Orsillo, S. M., & Roemer, L. (2001). *Practitioner's guide to empirically based measures of anxiety.* New York: Kluwer.

Anxiety Disorders Association of America. (2005). Retrieved November 17, 2005, from http://www.adaa.org/

AskOxford.Com. (n.d.). Retrieved March 7, 2005, from http://www.askoxford.com/concise_oed/dissertation?view=get

Association for Behavior Analysis. (2005). *Student committee: Poster presentations.* Retrieved November 18, 2005, from http://www.abainternational.org/sub/membersvcs/Studentnews/Studentpres.asp

Association for Support of Graduate Students (1995). Tips for writing a literature review. *Thesis News, 4,* 8–9.

Bailer, J. C., & Mosteller, F. (1988). Guidelines for statistical reporting in articles for medical journals: Amplifications and explanations. *Annals of Internal Medicine, 108,* 266–273.

Bakeman, R., & Gottman, J. M. (1986). *Observing interaction: An introduction to sequential analysis.* Cambridge, England: Cambridge University Press.

Barlow, D. H. (2000). Unraveling the mysteries of anxiety and its disorders from the perspective of emotion theory. *American Psychologist, 55,* 1245–1263.

Barlow, D. (2002) *Anxiety and its disorders: The nature and treatment of anxiety and panic* (2nd ed.). New York: Guilford Press.

Barlow, D. H., Allen, L. B., & Choate, M. L. (2004). Towards a unified treatment for emotional disorders. *Behavior Therapy, 35,* 205–230.

Barlow, D. H., & Hersen, M. (1984). *Single-case experimental designs: Strategies for studying behavior change* (2nd ed.). Elmsford, NY: Pergamon Press.

Baron, R. M., & Kenny, D. A. (1986). The moderator–mediator variable distinction in social psychological research: Conceptual, strategic and statistical considerations. *Journal of Personality and Social Psychology, 51,* 1173–1182.

Beck, A. T., Rush, A. J., Shaw, B. F., & Emery, G. (1979). *Cognitive therapy of depression.* New York: Guilford Press.

Bellack, A. S., & Hersen, M. (1977). Self-report inventories in behavioral assessment. In J. D. Cone & R. P. Hawkins (Eds.), *Behavioral assessment: New directions in clinical psychology* (pp. 52–76). New York: Brunner/Mazel.

Bell-Dolan, D. J., Foster, S. L., & Sikora, D. M. (1989). Effects of sociometric testing on children's behavior and loneliness in school. *Developmental Psychology, 25,* 306–311.

Bem, D. J. (1995). Writing a review article for *Psychological Bulletin. Psychological Bulletin, 118,* 172–177.

Ben-Horin, H., & Foster, S. L. (August, 2001). *Psychopathy and relational aggression among incarcerated women.* Paper presented at the annual meeting of the American Psychological Association, San Francisco.

Billingsley, F., White, O. R., & Munson, R. (1980). Procedural reliability: A rationale and an example. *Behavioral Assessment, 2,* 229–241.

Bloom, M., Fischer, J., & Orme, J. E. (2005). *Evaluating practice: Guidelines for the accountable professional* (5th ed.). Boston: Allyn & Bacon.

Bolker, J. (1998). *Writing your dissertation in 15 minutes a day.* New York: Henry Holt.

Bollen, K., & Lennox, R. (1991). Conventional wisdom on measurement: A structural equation perspective. *Psychological Bulletin, 110,* 305–314.

Bourne, E. J. (2001). *Anxiety and phobia workbook* (3rd ed.). Oakland, CA: New Harbinger.

Bruning, J. L., & Kintz, B. L. (1987). *Computational handbook of statistics* (3rd ed.). Glenview, IL: Scott, Foresman.

Burka, J., & Yuen, L. (1983). *Procrastination: Why you do it, what to do about it.* Cambridge, MA: Da Capo Press.

Butcher, J. N., Graham, J. R., Haynes, S. N., & Nelson, L. D. (Eds.). (1995). Special issue: Methodological issues in psychological assessment research. *Psychological Assessment, 7,* 227–413.

Cairns, R. B., & Green, J. A. (1979). How to assess personality and social patterns: Observations or ratings. In R. B. Cairns (Ed.), *The analysis of social interactions* (pp. 209–226). Hillsdale, NJ: Erlbaum.

Campbell, D. T. (1960). Recommendations for APA test standards regarding construct, trait, and discriminant validity. *American Psychologist, 15,* 546–553.

Campbell, D. T., & Fiske, D. (1959). Convergent and discriminant validation by the multitrait–multimethod matrix. *Psychological Bulletin, 56,* 81–105.

Carr, J. E., & Burkholder, E. O. (1998). Creating single-subject design graphs with Microsoft Excel. *Journal of Applied Behavior Analysis, 31,* 245–251.

Christensen, T. C., Barrett, L. F., Bliss-Moreau, E., Lebo, K., & Kaschub, C. (2003). A practical guide to experience-sampling procedures. *Journal of Happiness Studies, 4,* 53–78.

Clarke, G. N., Lewinsohn, P. M., Hops, H., & Seeley, J. R. (1992). A self- and parent-report measure of adolescent depression: The Child Behavior Checklist Depression Scale (CBCL–D). *Behavioral Assessment, 14,* 443–463.

Cleveland, W. S. (1995). *Visualizing data.* Summit, NJ: Hobart Press.

Cohen, J. (1983). The cost of dichotomization. *Applied Psychological Measurement, 7,* 249–253.

Cohen, J. (1988). *Statistical power analysis for the behavioral sciences* (2nd ed.). Hillsdale, NJ: Erlbaum.

Cohen, J. (1992). A power primer. *Psychological Bulletin, 112,* 155–159.

Cohen, P., Cohen, J., West, S. G., & Aiken, L. S. (2003). *Applied multiple regression/correlation analysis for the behavioral sciences* (3rd ed.). Mahwah, NJ: Erlbaum.

Cone, J. D. (1977). The relevance of reliability and validity for behavioral assessment. *Behavior Therapy, 8,* 411–426.

Cone, J. D. (1978). The Behavioral Assessment Grid (BAG): A conceptual framework and a taxonomy. *Behavior Therapy, 9,* 882–888.

Cone, J. D. (1992). Accuracy and curriculum-based measurement. *School Psychology Quarterly, 7,* 22–26.

Cone, J. D. (1999a). Observational assessment: Measure development and research issues. In P. C. Kendall, J. N. Butcher, & G. N. Holmbeck (Eds.), *Handbook of research methods in clinical psychology* (2nd ed., pp. 183–223). New York: Wiley.

Cone, J. D. (Ed.). (1999b). Special section: Clinical assessment applications of self-monitoring. *Psychological Assessment, 11,* 411–498.

Cone, J. D. (2001). *Evaluating outcomes: Empirical tools for effective practice.* Washington, DC: American Psychological Association.

Cone, J. D., & Dalenberg, C. (2004). Ethics concepts in outcomes assessment. In M. E. Maruish (Ed.), *The use of psychological testing for treatment planning and outcomes assessment* (3rd ed.). Mahwah, NJ: Erlbaum.

Cooper, H. (1998). *Synthesizing research: A guide for literature reviews* (3rd ed.). Thousand Oaks, CA: Sage.

Cronbach, L. J. (1990). *Essentials of psychological testing* (5th ed.). New York: HarperCollins.

Cronbach, L. J., Gleser, G. C., Nanda, H., & Rajaratnam, N. (1972). *The dependability of behavioral measurements.* New York: Wiley.

Crowne, D. P., & Marlowe, D. (1960). A new scale of social desirability independent of psychopathology. *Journal of Consulting Psychology, 24,* 349–354.

Darley, J. M., Zanna, M.P., & Roediger, H. L. (Eds.). (2003). *The compleat academic: A career guide* (2nd ed.). Washington, DC: American Psychological Association.

Davis, G. B., & Parker, C. A. (1979). *Writing the doctoral dissertation: A systematic approach.* Woodbury, NY: Barron's.

Davis, M., Robbins-Eshelman, E., & McKay, M. (2000). *The relaxation and stress reduction workbook* (5th ed.). Oakland, CA: New Harbinger.

Delwiche, L. D., & Slaughter, S. J. (2003). *The little SAS book* (3rd ed.). Cary, NC: SAS.

DeMaster, B., Reid, J., & Twentyman, C. (1977). The effects of different amounts of feedback on observer's reliability. *Behavior Therapy, 8,* 317–329.

Dent, C., Galaif, J., & Susman, S. (1993). Demographic, psychosocial, and behavioral differences in samples of actively and passively consented adolescents. *Addictive Behaviors, 18,* 51–56.

DeVellis, R. F. (2003). *Scale development: Theories and applications* (2nd ed.). Thousand Oaks, CA: Sage.

Dionne, R. R. (1992). *Effective strategies for handling teasing among fifth and sixth grade children.* Unpublished doctoral dissertation, California School of Professional Psychology, San Diego, CA.

Dumas, M. D., Dionne, R. R., Foster, S. L., Chang, M. K., Achar, M. S., & Martinez, C. M., Jr. (1992, November*). A critical incidents analysis of strategies for handling peer provocation* *among second-, fifth-, and eighth-grade children.* Paper presented at the annual meeting of the Association for Advancement of Behavior Therapy, Boston.

Edwards, A. L. (1957). *The social desirability variable in personality assessment and research.* Hinsdale, IL: Dryden Press.

Edwards, A. L. (1970). *The measurement of traits by scales and inventories.* New York: Holt, Rinehart & Winston.

Edwards, A. L. (1990). Construct validity and social desirability. *American Psychologist, 45,* 287–289.

Einstein, A. (1974). *The universe and Dr. Einstein.* New York: Lincoln Barnett.

Ellis, A., & Harper, R. A. (1961). *A guide to rational living.* North Hollywood, CA: Wilshire.

Fabrigar, L. R., Wegener, D. T., MacCallum, R. C., & Strahan, E. J. (1999). Evaluating the use of exploratory factor analysis in psychological research. *Psychological Methods, 4,* 272–299.

Farrell, A. D. (1999). Statistical methods in clinical research. In P. C. Kendall, J. N. Butcher, & G. N. Holmbeck (Eds.), *Handbook of research methods in clinical psychology* (2nd ed., pp. 72–106). New York: Wiley.

Ferma, E. K. (2005). *Peer influences on body image related concerns: The role of social comparison.* Unpublished doctoral dissertation, Alliant International University, San Diego, CA.

Finch, C. L. (2001). *The relationship among relationally aggressive behavior, emotion and social cognitions in preadolescent females.* Unpublished doctoral dissertation, Alliant International University, San Diego, CA.

Fine, M. A., & Kurdek, L. A. (1993). Reflections on determining authorship credit and authorship order on faculty–student collaborations. *American Psychologist, 48,* 1141–1147.

Fink, A. (2002). *The survey handbook* (2nd ed.). Thousand Oaks, CA: Sage.

Fischer, J., & Corcoran, K. J. (2000a). *Measures for clinical practice: Adults.* New York: Free Press.

Fischer, J., & Corcoran, K. J. (2000b). *Measures for clinical practice: Couples, families, and children.* New York: Free Press.

Fisher, C. B., Hoagwood, K. Boyce, C., Duster, T., Frank, D. A., Grisso, T., et al. (2002). Research ethics for mental health science involving ethnic minority children and youth. *American Psychologist, 57,* 1024–1040.

Floyd, F., & Widaman, K. F. (1995). Factor analysis in the development and refinement of clinical assessment instruments. *Psychological Assessment, 42,* 286–299.

Foster, S. L., Bell-Dolan, D. J., & Burge, D. A. (1988). Behavioral observation. In A. S. Bellack & M. Hersen (Eds.), *Behavioral assessment: A practical handbook* (3rd ed., pp. 119–160). Elmsford, NY: Pergamon Press.

Foster, S. L., & Cone, J. D. (1995). Validity issues in clinical assessment. *Psychological Assessment, 7,* 248–260.

Foster, S. L., Laverty Finch, C., Gizzo, D., & Osantowski, J. (1999). Practical issues in self-observation. *Psychological Assessment, 11,* 426–438.

Foster, S. L., & Martinez, C. R., Jr. (1995). Ethnicity: Conceptual and methodological issues in child clinical research. *Journal of Clinical Child Psychology, 24,* 214–226.

Frick, R. W. (1996). The appropriate use of null hypothesis testing. *Psychological Methods, 1,* 379–390.

Gantt charts. (2005). Retrieved November 17, 2005, from http://www.ganttcharts.com/index.html

Galvan, J. L. (1999). *Writing literature reviews.* Los Angeles: Pyrczak.

Galvan, J. L. (2004). *Writing literature reviews: A guide for students of the social and behavioral sciences* (2nd ed.). Los Angeles: Pyrczak.

Gevirtz, R. (2002). Physiological perspectives. In B. Horwitz (Ed.), *Communication apprehension: Origins and management* (pp. 114–136). Florence, KY: ThompsonDelmar Learning.

Goldman, B. A., & Mitchell, D. F. (Eds.). (2003). *Directory of unpublished experimental mental measures* (Vol. 8). Washington, DC: American Psychological Association.

Gorsuch, R. L. (1983). *Factor analysis* (2nd ed.). Hillsdale, NJ: Erlbaum.

Goyer, L. E. (2005). *Responsiveness to deviancy training among highly deviant, moderately deviant, and non-deviant early adolescent males.* Unpublished doctoral dissertation, Alliant International University, San Diego, CA.

Green, S. B., & Salkind, N. J. (2004). *Using SPSS for Windows and Macintosh: Analyzing and understanding data* (4th ed.). Upper Saddle River, NJ: Prentice-Hall.

Greenberger, D., & Padesky, C. (1995). *Mind over mood: Change how you feel by changing the way you think.* New York: Guilford Press.

Grimm, L. G., & Yarnold, P. R. (Eds.). (1995). *Reading and understanding multivariate statistics.* Washington, DC: American Psychological Association.

Grimm, L. G., & Yarnold, P. R. (Eds.). (2000). *Reading and understanding MORE multivariate statistics.* Washington, DC: American Psychological Association.

Grusec, J. (1991). The socialization of altruism. In M. S. Clark (Ed.), *Prosocial behavior* (pp. 9–33). Newbury Park, CA: Sage.

Guilford, J. P. (1956). *Fundamental statistics in psychology and education.* New York: McGraw-Hill.

Hartmann, D. P. (1982). Assessing the dependability of direct observational data. In D. P. Hartmann (Ed.), *New directions for methodology of social and behavioral science: Using observers to study behavior* (pp. 51–65). San Francisco: Jossey-Bass.

Hayes, S. C., Barlow, D. H., & Nelson-Gray, R. O. (1999). *The scientist practitioner: Research and accountability in the age of managed care* (2nd ed.). Boston: Allyn & Bacon.

Haynes, S. N., Richard, D. C. S., & Kubany, E. (1995). Content validity in psychological assessment: A functional approach to concepts and methods. *Psychological Assessment, 42,* 238–247.

Helmes, E., & Holden, R. (2003). The construct of social desirability: One or two dimensions. *Personality and Individual Differences, 34,* 1015–1023.

Henry, G. T. (1994). *Graphing data.* Thousand Oaks, CA: Sage.

Heppner, P. P., & Heppner, M. J. (2004). *Writing and publishing your thesis, dissertation, and research.* Belmont, CA: Thompson-Brooks/Cole.

Hersen, M., & Bellack, A. S. (Eds.). (1988). *Dictionary of behavioral assessment techniques.* Elmsford, NY: Pergamon Press.

Hochhauser, M. (1999). Informed consent and patients' rights documents: A right, a rite, or a rewrite? *Ethics and Behavior, 9,* 1–20.

Hoier, T. S. (1984). *Target selection of social skills for children: An experimental investigation of the template matching procedure.* Unpublished doctoral dissertation, West Virginia University, Morgantown.

Hoier, T. S., & Cone, J. D. (1987). Target selection of social skills for children: The template matching procedure. *Behavior Modification, 11,* 137–163.

Holmbeck, G. N. (1997). Toward terminological, conceptual, and statistical clarity in the study of mediators and moderators: Examples from the child–clinical and pediatric psychology literatures. *Journal of Consulting and Clinical Psychology, 65,* 599–610.

Horowitz, M. J., Wilner, N., & Alvarez, W. (1979). Impact of Event Scale: A measure of psychosomatic stress. *Psychosomatic Medicine, 41,* 209–218.

House, A. E., House, B. J., & Campbell, M. D. (1981). Measures of interobserver agreement: Calculation formulas and distribution effects. *Journal of Behavioral Assessment, 3,* 37–57.

Huberty, C. J., & Morris, J. D. (1989). Multivariate analysis versus multiple univariate analyses. *Psychological Bulletin, 105,* 302–308.

Huitema, B. E. (1980). *The analysis of covariance and alternatives.* New York: Wiley.

Hunter, J. E., & Schmidt, F. L. (2004). *Methods of meta-analysis* (2nd ed.). Newbury Park, CA: Sage.

Inderbitzen-Pisaruk, H., & Foster, S. L. (1990). Adolescent friendships and peer acceptance: Implications for social skills training. *Clinical Psychology Review, 10,* 425–439.

Jaccard, J., Becker, M. A., & Wood, G. (1984). Pairwise multiple comparison procedures: A review. *Psychological Bulletin, 96,* 589–596.

Johnston, J. M., & Pennypacker, H. S. (1993). *Strategies and tactics of human behavioral research* (2nd ed). Hillsdale, NJ: Erlbaum.

Kaplan, R. M., & Saccuzzo, D. P. (2005). *Psychological testing: Principles, applications, and issues* (6th ed.). Belmont, CA: Wadsworth.

Kazdin, A. E. (2003). *Research design in clinical psychology* (4th ed.). Boston: Allyn & Bacon.

Kelley, M. L., Reitman, D., & Noell, G. H. (2002). *Practitioner's guide to empirically based measures of school behavior.* New York: Kluwer.

Kelley, T. L. (1927). *Interpretation of educational measurements.* Yonkers-on-Hudson, NY: World Book.

Kent, R. N., O'Leary, K. D., Diament, C., & Dietz, A. (1974). Expectation biases in observational evaluation of therapeutic change. *Journal of Consulting and Clinical Psychology, 42,* 774–780.

Keppel, G., & Wickens, T. D. (2004). *Design and analysis: A researcher's handbook.* (4th ed.). Upper Saddle River, NJ: Pearson Prentice-Hall.

Kerlinger, F. N. (2000). *Foundations of behavioral research.* (4th ed.). New York: Harcourt Brace.

Kirk, R. E. (1995). *Experimental design: Procedures for the behavioral sciences* (3rd ed.). Pacific Grove, CA: Brooks/ColeWadsworth.

Klem, L. (1995). Path analysis. In L. G. Grimm & P. R. Yarnold (Eds.), *Reading and understanding multivariate statistics* (pp. 65–97). Washington, DC: American Psychological Association.

Koyre, A. (1965). *Newtonian studies.* Cambridge, MA: Harvard University Press.

Krathwohl, D. R. (1988). *How to prepare a research proposal: Suggestions for those seeking funds for behavioral science research* (3rd ed.). Syracuse, NY: School of Education, Syracuse University.

Kuhn, T. (1970). *The structure of scientific revolutions* (2nd ed.). Chicago: University of Chicago Press.

Lakin, A. (1974). *How to get control of your time and your life.* New York: Signet Books.

Lang, P. J. (1971). The application of psychophysiological methods to the study of psychotherapy and behavior modification. In A. E. Bergin & S. L. Garfield (Eds.), *Handbook of psychotherapy and behavior change* (pp. 75–125). New York: Wiley.

Licht, M. H. (1995). Multiple regression and correlation. In L. G. Grimm & P. R. Yarnold (Eds.), *Reading and understanding multivariate statistics* (pp. 19–64). Washington, DC: American Psychological Association.

Lipsey, M. W., & Wilson, D. B. (2000). *Practical meta analysis.* Thousand Oaks, CA: Sage.

Lord, C. (2005). *Indirect aggression and social support among elderly retirement community residents.* Unpublished doctoral dissertation, Alliant International University, San Diego, CA.

MacCallum, R. C., Widamon, K. F., Zhang, S., & Hong, S. (1999). Sample size in factor analysis. *Psychological Methods, 4,* 84–99.

MacKinnon, D. P., Lockwood, C. M., Hoffman, J. M., West, S. G., & Sheets, V. (2002). A comparison of methods to test mediation and other intervening variable effects. *Psychological Methods, 7,* 83–104.

Maher, B. A. (1978). A reader's, writer's, and reviewer's guide to assessing research reports in clinical psychology. *Journal of Consulting and Clinical Psychology, 46,* 835–838.

Mahoney, M. J., & Mahoney, B. K. (1976). *Permanent weight control.* New York: Norton.

Maxwell, S. E., & Delaney, H. D. (2004). *Designing experiments and analyzing data: A model comparison approach* (2nd ed.). Mahwah, NJ: Erlbaum.

McBurney, D. H. (1990). *Experimental psychology* (2nd ed.). Belmont, CA: Wadsworth.

McBurney, D. H. (2004). *Research methods* (6th ed.). Belmont, CA: Brooks/Cole.

McInerney, D. M. (2001). *Publishing your psychology research: A guide to writing for journals in psychology and related fields.* Thousand Oaks, CA: Sage.

Meltzoff, J. (1998). *Critical thinking about research: Psychology and related fields.* Washington, DC: American Psychological Association.

Mertler, C. A., & Vannatta, R. A. (2005). *Advanced and multivariate statistical methods* (3rd ed.). Glendale, CA: Pyrczak.

Merriam-Webster OnLine. (n.d.). Retrieved March 7, 2005, from http://www.m-w.com/cgi-bin/dictionary?book=Dictionary&va=dissertation&x=19&y=16m

Miller, D. C. (2002). *Handbook of research design and social measurement* (6th ed.). Newbury Park, CA: Sage.

Murphy, K. R., & Myors, B. (2004). *Statistical power analysis* (2nd ed.). Mahwah, NJ: Erlbaum.

Murphy, L. L., Plake, B. S., Impara, J. C., & Spies, R. A. (Eds.). (2002). *Tests in print VI.* Lincoln: University of Nebraska.

Myers, J. L., DiCecco, J. V., White, J. B., & Borden, V. M. (1982). Repeated measurements on dichotomous variables: *Q* and *F* tests. *Psychological Bulletin, 92,* 517–525.

Nagy, T. F. (2005). *Ethics in plain English: An illustrative casebook for psychologists* (2nd ed.). Washington, DC: American Psychological Association.

National Institutes of Health. (2005a). *Guidelines for the conduct of research involving human subjects at the National Institutes of Health.* Retrieved November 7, 2005, from http://ohsr.od.nih.gov/guidelines/graybook.html

National Institutes of Health. (2005b). *Regulations and ethical guidelines.* Retrieved November 7, 2005, from http://ohsr.od.nih.gov/guidelines/45cfr46.html

Nelson, G. L., Cone, J. D., & Hanson, C. R. (1975). Training correct utensil use in retarded children: Modeling vs. physical guidance. *American Journal of Mental Deficiency, 80,* 114–122.

Neuman, W. L. (1997). *Social research methods: Qualitative and quantitative approaches* (3rd ed.). Boston: Allyn & Bacon.

Newton, R. R., & Rudestam, K. E. (1999). *Your statistical consultant: Answers to your data analysis questions.* Thousand Oaks, CA: Sage.

Nezu, A., Ronan, G. F., Meadows, E. A., & McClure, K. S. (2000). *Practitioner's guide to empirically based measures of depression.* New York: Kluwer.

Nicol, A. A. M., & Pexman, P. M. (2010). *Presenting your findings: A practical guide for creating tables.* Washington, DC: American Psychological Association.

Nunnally, N. C., & Bernstein, I. H. (1994). *Psychometric theory* (3rd ed.). New York: McGraw-Hill.

Oetting, E. R. (1986). Ten fatal mistakes in grant writing. *Professional Psychology: Research and Practice, 17,* 570–573.

O'Leary, K. D., Kent, R. N., & Kanowitz, J. (1975). Shaping data congruent with experimental hypotheses. *Journal of Applied Behavior Analysis, 8,* 463–469.

O'Shea, H. (2003). *Assessment of aggression in children: An exploration of self and peer report methods.* Unpublished dissertation proposal, Alliant International University, San Diego, CA.

Pallant, J. (2001). *SPSS survival manual: A step by step guide to data analysis using SPSS.* Philadelphia: Open University Press.

Parsonson, B. S., & Baer, D. M. (1978). The analysis and presentation of graphic data. In T. R. Kratochwill (Ed.), *Single subject research* (pp. 101–165). San Diego, CA: Academic Press.

Paul, G. L. (1966). *Insight vs. desensitization in psychotherapy.* Stanford, CA: Stanford University Press.

Paul, G. L. (1969). Behavior modification research: Design and tactics. In C. M. Franks (Ed.), *Behavior therapy: Appraisal and status* (pp. 29–62). New York: McGraw-Hill.

Paulhus, D. L. (1991). Measurement and control of response bias. In J. P. Robinson, P. Shaver, & L. S. Wrightsman (Eds.), *Measures of personality and social psychological attitudes* (pp. 17–59). San Diego, CA: Academic Press.

Paulhus, D. L. (2002). Socially desirable responding: The evolution of a construct. In H. I. Braun, D. N., Jackson, & D. E. Wiley (Eds.), *The role of constructs in psychological and educational measurement* (pp. 49–69). Mahwah, NJ: Erlbaum.

Pedhazur, E. J. (1997). *Multiple regression in behavioral research: Explanation and prediction* (3rd ed.). Orlando, FL: Harcourt Brace.

Pedhazur, E. J., & Schmelkin, L. P. (1991). *Measurement, design, and analysis: An integrated approach.* Hillsdale, NJ: Erlbaum.

Plagiarism: What it is and how to avoid it. (n.d.). Retrieved February 4, 2005, from http://www.indiana.edu/~wts/pamphlets.shtml

Plake, B. S., Impara, J. C., & Spies, R. A. (Eds.). (2003). *The fifteenth mental measurements yearbook.* Lincoln: University of Nebraska.

Preacher, K. J., & MacCallum, R. C. (2003). Repairing Tom Swift's electric factor analysis machine. *Understanding Statistics, 2,* 13–43.

Pyrczak, F. (2000). *Completing your thesis or dissertation.* Los Angeles: Author.

Raudenbush, S. W., & Bryk, A. S. (2002). *Hierarchical linear models: Applications and data analysis methods* (2nd ed.). Thousand Oaks, CA: Sage.

Ray, W. J. (2006). *Methods: Toward a science of behavior and experience* (8th ed.). Pacific Grove, CA: Brooks/Cole.

Raykov, T., & Marcoulides, G. M. (2000). *A first course in structural equation modeling.* Mahwah, NJ: Erlbaum.

Research and Education Association. (1981). *Handbook of psychiatric rating scales.* New York: Author.

Roberts, R. E., Lewinsohn, P. M., & Seeley, J. R. (1991). Screening for adolescent depression: A comparison of depression scales. *Journal of the American Academy of Child and Adolescent Psychiatry, 30,* 58–66.

Robinson, J. P., Shaver, P. R., & Wrightsman, L. S. (Eds.). (1991). *Measures of personality and social psychological attributes.* San Diego, CA: Academic Press.

Rodgers, W. (1995). Analysis of cross-classified data. In L. G. Grimm & P. R. Yarnold (Eds.), *Reading and understanding multivariate statistics* (pp. 169–216). Washington, DC: American Psychological Association.

Romanczyk, R. G., Kent, R. N., Diament, C., & O'Leary, K. D. (1973). Measuring the reliability of observational data: A reactive process. *Journal of Applied Behavior Analysis, 6,* 175–184.

Rosenthal, R. (1969). Interpersonal expectations: Effects of the experimenter's hypothesis. In R. Rosenthal & R. L. Rosnow (Eds.), *Artifact in behavioral research* (pp. 181–277). San Diego, CA: Academic Press.

Rosenthal, R. (1991). *Meta-analytic procedures for social research.* Newbury Park, CA: Sage.

Rosenthal, R. (1995). Writing meta-analytic reviews. *Psychological Bulletin, 118,* 183–192.

Rossi, J. S. (1990). Statistical power of psychological research: What have we gained in 20 years? *Journal of Consulting and Clinical Psychology, 58,* 646–656.

Rudestam, K. E., & Newton, R. R. (2001). *Surviving your dissertation* (2nd ed.). Thousand Oaks, CA: Sage.

Sales, B. D., & Folkman, S. (Eds.). (2000). *Ethics in research with human participants.* Washington, DC: American Psychological Association.

Sanchez-Hucles, J., & Cash, T. F. (1992). The dissertation in professional psychology programs: 1. A survey of clinical directors on requirements and practices. *Professional Psychology: Research and Practice, 23,* 59–61.

Sandler, R. B. (2000). *Plagiarism in colleges in the USA.* Retrieved February 2, 2005, from http://www.apa.org/

Saving your thesis when support goes down the drain. (1995). *Dissertation News, 3,* 1–7.

Schafer, J. L, & Graham, J. W. (2002). Missing data: Our view of the state of the art. *Psychological Methods, 7,* 147–177.

Schwarz, N., & Oyserman, D. (2001). Asking questions about behavior: Cognition, communication, and questionnaire construction. *American Journal of Evaluation, 22,* 127–160.

Severino, J. (2002). *Gay and straight men's attributions to simulated antigay and nonbias victimization.* Unpublished dissertation proposal, Alliant International University, San Diego, CA.

Shadish, W. R., Cook, T. D., & Campbell, D. T. (2002). *Experimental and quasi-experimental designs for generalized causal inference.* Boston: Houghton Mifflin.

Shaw, R. (2002). Grammar checkers: Helpful or harmful? *USA Today.* Retrieved November 17, 2005, from http://www.usatoday.com/tech/news/2002/07/15/tech-grammar-full.htm

Shawchuck, C. R., Fatis, M., & Breitenstein, J. L. (1986). A practical guide to the assignment of authorship credit. *Behavior Therapist, 9,* 216–217.

Shiffman, S. (2000). Real-time self-report of momentary states in the natural environment: Computerized ecological momentary assessment. In A. A. Stone, J. S. Turkan, C. A. Bachrach, J. B. Jobe, H. S. Kurtzman, & V. S. Cain (Eds.), *The science of self-report: Implications for research and practice* (pp. 277–296). Mahwah, NJ: Erlbaum.

Shiller, R. J. (1999). Human behavior and the efficiency of financial markets. In J. B Taylor & M. Woodford (Eds.), *Handbook of Macroeconomics* (Vol. 1, pp. 1305–1340). Amsterdam: Elsevier.

Shuller, D. Y., & McNamara, J. R. (1976). Expectancy factors in behavioral observation. *Behavior Therapy, 7,* 519–527.

Siegel, S. (1956). *Nonparametric statistics for the behavioral sciences.* New York: McGraw-Hill.

Sikora, D. M. (1989). *Divorce, environmental change, parental conflict, and the peer relations of preschool children.* Unpublished doctoral dissertation, West Virginia University, Morgantown.

Singer, J. D., & Willett, J. S. (2003). *Applied longitudinal data analysis: Modeling change and event occurrence.* New York: Oxford University Press.

Smith, J. C. (2005). *Relaxation, meditation, and mindfulness: Self-training manual.* Morrisville, NC: Lulu Press.

Smyth, J. M., & Stone, A. A. (2003). Ecological momentary assessment research in behavioral medicine. *Journal of Happiness Studies, 4,* 35–52.

Sobell, M. B., Bogardis, J., Schuller, R., Leo, G. I., & Sobell, L. C. (1989). Is self-monitoring of alcohol consumption reactive? *Behavioral Assessment, 11,* 447–458.

Solso, R. L., & MacLin, M. (2002). *Experimental psychology: A case approach* (7th ed.). Boston: Allyn & Bacon.

Sternberg, D. (1981). *How to complete and survive a doctoral dissertation.* New York: St. Martin's Press.

Stone, A. A., Kessler, R. C., & Haythornthwaite, J. A. (1991). Measuring daily events and experiences: Decisions for the researcher. *Journal of Personality, 59,* 575–607.

Stone, A. A., Turkan, J. S., Bachrach, C. A., Jobe, J. B., Kurtzman, H. S., & Cain, V. S (Eds.). (2000). *The science of self-report: Implications for research and practice.* Mahwah, NJ: Erlbaum.

Stuart, R. B. (Ed.). (1977). *Behavioral self-management: Strategies, techniques and outcome.* New York: Brunner/Mazel.

Suen, H. K., & Ary, D. (1989). *Analyzing quantitative behavioral observation data.* Hillsdale, NJ: Erlbaum.

Sweetland, R. C., & Keyser, D. J. (Eds.). (1983). *Tests: A comprehensive reference for assessments in psychology, education and business.* Kansas City, MO: Test Corporation of America.

Sweetland, R. C., & Keyser, D. J. (Eds.). (1997). *Tests* (4th ed.). Austin, TX: PRO-ED.

Tabachnick, B. F., & Fidell, L. S. (2001). *Using multivariate statistics* (4th ed.). Needham Heights, MA: Allyn & Bacon.

Taplin, P. S., & Reid, J. B. (1973). Effects of instructional set and experimental influence on observer reliability. *Child Development, 44,* 547–554.

Thomas, L., & Krebs, C. J. (1997). A review of statistical power analysis software. *Bulletin of the Ecological Society of America, 78,* 126–139.

Thompson, B. (2000). Ten commandments of structural equation modeling. In L. G. Grimm & P. R. Yarnold (Eds.), *Reading and understanding MORE multivariate statistics* (pp. 261–283). Washington, DC: American Psychological Association.

Thompson, B. (Ed.). (2003). *Score reliability: Contemporary thinking on reliability issues.* Newbury Park, CA: Sage.

Toastmaster's International. (2005). Retrieved November 17, 2005, from http://www.toastmasters.org/

Tracy, B. (2004). *Time power: A proven system for getting more done in less time than you ever thought possible.* New York: AMACOM.

Tryon, W. W. (1998). Behavioral observation. In A. S. Bellack & M. Hersen (Eds.), *Behavioral assessment: A practical handbook* (4th ed., pp. 79–103). Needham Heights, MA: Allyn & Bacon.

Tufte, E. (2001). *The visual display of quantitative information* (2nd ed.). Cheshire, CT: Graphics Press.

UCLA Academic Technology Services. (n.d.) *Statistical computing resources.* Retrieved November 15, 2005, from http://www.ats.ucla.edu/stat

Ullman, J. B. (2001). Structural equation modeling. In B. F. Tabachnick & L. S. Fidell (Eds.), *Using multivariate statistics* (4th ed., pp. 653–771). Needham Heights, MA: Allyn & Bacon.

University of Washington School of Public Health. (2005). *Creating a poster using MS PowerPoint.* Retrieved November 18, 2005, from http://depts.washington.edu/mphpract/pp poster.html

Vernoff, J. (2001). Writing. In K. E. Rudestam & R. R. Newton (Eds.), *Surviving your dissertation* (2nd ed.). Thousand Oaks, CA: Sage.

von Eye, A., & Mun, E. Y. (2005). *Analyzing rater agreement: Manifest variable methods.* Mahwah, NJ: Erlbaum.

Wallgren, A., Wallgren, B., Persson, R., Jorner, U., & Haaland, J. (1996). *Graphing statistics & data.* Thousand Oaks, CA: Sage.

Webb, E. J. (1961). The choice of problem. *American Psychologist, 16,* 223–227.

Webb, E. J., Campbell, D. T., Schwartz, R. D., & Sechrest, L. (1966). *Unobtrusive measures: Nonreactive research in the social sciences.* Chicago: Rand McNally.

Weisberg, H. F., Krosnick, J. A., & Bowen, B. D. (1996). *An introduction to survey research, polling, and data analysis* (3rd ed.). Newbury Park, CA: Sage.

Whalen, C. K., Jamner, L. D., Henker, B., & Delfino, R. J. (2001). Smoking and moods in adolescents with depressive and aggressive dispositions: Evidence from surveys and electronic diaries. *Heath Psychology, 20,* 99–111.

Wiggins, J. S. (1959). Interrelationships among MMPI measures of dissimulation under standard and social desirability instructions. *Journal of Consulting Psychology, 23,* 419–427.

Wilkinson, L., & The Task Force on Statistical Inference. (1999). Statistical methods in psychology journals. *American Psychologist, 54,* 594–604.

Winer, B. J., Brown, D. R., & Michels, K. M. (1991). *Statistical principles in experimental design* (3rd ed.). New York: McGraw-Hill.

Wolfe, V. V. (1986). *Paternal and marital factors related to child conduct problems.* Unpublished doctoral dissertation, West Virginia University, Morgantown.

Wolfe, V. V., Gentile, C., Michienzi, T., Sas, L., & Wolfe, D. A. (1991). The Children's Impact of Traumatic Events Scale: A measure of post-sexual-abuse PTSD symptoms. *Behavioral Assessment, 13,* 359–383.

Yates, B. T. (1982). *Doing the dissertation: The nuts and bolts of psychological research.* Springfield, IL: Charles C. Thomas.

Index

A

A-B-A-B design, 129, 262
Abstracts, 99, 100, 283, 318, 319–320
Abstract services, 101
Accuracy of observation, 165
Ad homonym criticism, 120
Advance organizer, 117
Age, as variable, 195
Alpha levels, 216–217
  and statistical power, 134
Alternate-form reliability, 167, 179
Altruism, as research participant, 169
American Psychological Association
    (APA)
  annual meetings, 317
  ethical guidelines, 157
  Ethics Committee, 326
  Membership Register, 181
  style guidelines, 18, 88, 102
  Task Force on Statistical Interference,
    251
American Psychological Society, 181, 317
Analyses of covariance (ANCOVA)
  and ANOVA, 202–203
  assumptions of, 199
  definition of, 202
  possible difficulties with, 203–204
  reporting results of, 86
  role of, 202–204
Analyses of variance (ANOVA)
  and ANCOVA, 202–203
  assumptions of, 199
  final review of results, 279–280
  vs. MANOVA, 204–205
  methodology, 199
  nonparametric alternatives to, 205–206
  one-way, 129, 132, 135

and planned comparisons, 200–201
  power analysis in, 134
  reporting results of, 86
  2×2 design, 129
  with two groups, 198
  with Type I errors, 196, 204
Analysis plan, 189–195, 241–242. *See also*
    Statistics, Statistical tests
  hypothesis-testing, preliminary, 190
  hypothesis-testing, supplement, 246
ANCOVA. *See* Analyses of covariance
Animal subjects, 91, 131
  ethical guidelines for, 143, 341
  reporting methodology in, 131
  surgery, 138
Annual Review of Psychology, 66
ANOVA. *See* Analyses of variance
Anxiety, in oral defense, 305–310. *See also*
    Defense
  cognitive component of, 305–307
  motor component of, 308–310
  physical component of, 307–308
  serious cases of, 310
Apparatus, research. *See also* Computer-
    ized tools
  planning for, 233
  reporting use of, 136
Appendixes
  debriefing script in, 141
  measurement instruments described in,
    138
  in proposal, 88, 89, 91
  raw data in, 253
Applied research, 209–210
  assistants in, 237–238
Archival sources, 174
Assent forms, 146–149, 152, 153

Assessments. *See* Measures

Association for Behavioral and Cognitive Therapy, 317

Association for Behavior Analysis, 317

Association for Support of Graduate Students (ASGS), 25

Attention-deficit hyperactivity disorder (ADHD), 191

Audiotape recording, 174

Audiovisual materials, in defense, 297, 299–300, 303

Authors, 99

Authorship issues, 326–327, 342

AutoPilot, 300, 318

B

Backward chaining, 33

Baer, D. M., 264

Bar graphs, 262, 264

Barlow, D. H., 305

Behavior, as subject matter, 163–164

Behavioral Measurement Database Service (BMDS), 172

Behavior research, 163, 172
  and construct validity, 169
  instrument validity in, 167
  manipulation checks in, 136–137
  measurement in, 163–164, 171
  publishing, 324
  self-reports in, 164–165, 180–181
  video- or audiotape recording, 174

Bem, D. J., 118

Ben-Horin, H., 320

Between-participants designs, 128, 129, 218–219

Bias
  avoiding, in methodology, 137–138
  educational and racial, 155
  generosity, 165
  from heterogeneity of variance, 200
  of research assistants, 65, 231, 238
  in self-presentation, 177
  in self-reports, 164

Bibliographic references, 97–98

Bibliographies
  compiling, 98
  reference sources for, 98, 100, 102

Biofeedback, 307–308

Bivariate correlations, 206–207

Blind experimenters, 137–138, 141, 231

Blogs, 99

Bolker, J., 116

Bonferroni method, 216

Brevity, 109–110
  in conference presentations, 250, 259

Buros. See Mental Measurements Yearbook

Buros Center for Testing, 172

C

Captions, 265

Causation, 219–220, 282
  language of, misused, 282
  reverse, 278
  types of, 278

Chairperson, 8. *See also* Committee; Defense; Proposal meeting
  approaching, 58–60
  availability of, 54–55
  changes in methodology reported to, 229
  checklist for selecting, 78–79
  as collaborator, 51–52, 76
  committee selection, 76
  communicating with, 50–60
  criteria for selecting, 8, 49–63
  and dissemination of research, 51, 325–326
  and drafts, review of, 50, 54, 74–75, 89–91
  expectations of, 54–55
  expertise of, 50, 52–54
  failure to find, 62–63
  interviewing potential, 58–60
  investigating, 56–58
  in oral defense, 303
  personal problems with, 60–63, 75
  in proposal meeting, 292
  in proposal process, 89–91
  and publishing research results, 324
  relations with committee, 57, 74
  and research authorship, 326–327
  role of, 47–49, 50, 51, 54–55, 74–75
  rules concerning, 50–51
  skill appraisal of, 54–56
  strong, 74–75

Charts, 260

Children, as participants, 172, 230–231
  consent issues, 146, 149, 150–153, 232
  as pilot participants, 228
  scheduling, 234

Chi square, 135, 206, 214–215
Citations, 102–103, 112
Clinical Psychology Review, 66, 325
Clinical research, 276
  measures for, 171–172
Code book, 239
Coefficients
  bivariate correlation, 206–207
  intraclass correlation, 206
  phi, 207
Cognitive ecology, 26–27
Collateral data sources, 178
Committee. *See also* Chairperson; Defense;
      Proposal meeting
  approaching, 76
  as audience, 109
  changes in methodology reported to,
      229
  checklist for selecting, 78
  expertise of, 74
  grandstanding, 302
  interpreting reactions of, 302
  investigating candidates for, 75–76
  involvement models for, 74–75
  potential problems with, 75
  proposal meeting with, 291–293, 294,
      301–302
  in proposal process, 91
  recruiting, 73–76
  relationship with others, 75–76
  relations with chairperson, 57, 74
  role of, 74, 75
  rules concerning, 74
  strong model, 75
Committee meetings, managing, 289–311
Complications/qualifications/limitations
      (CQL), 250
Computerized databases, 98–100
Computerized tools. *See also* Data
      collection
  access to, 23, 238
  for bivariate correlations, 206–207
  for creating figures, 265–266
  data analysis, 87, 239–240, 243–245
  data collection, 238–241
  data entry, 238–239
  data storage, 233–234
  format of summaries from, 241–243
  grammar-checking programs, 14–15
  literacy, 22–23
  for literature searches, 98–100, 107

for power analysis, 135
raw data from, 238–239
in regression analysis, 209
in selecting assessment instruments,
      172
in selecting statistics, 222
spell-checking software, 18
for statistical work, 21, 135, 200, 242
syntax files, 244
time management software, 34, 36
Concurrent validity, 169
Cone, J. D., 141, 169
Conferences, 95, 101, 315
  access to current research in, 101
  oral presentation at, 318–320
  poster presentation at, 320–323
  presenting research at, 315–316
Confidence intervals, 245, 253
Confidentiality, 233, 336–337, 338, 343
Confirmatory factor analysis (CFA), 213
Confounding variables, 20, 133, 138, 205,
      241, 277, 278
  and ANCOVA, 203
Consent forms, 147–149, 150–151, 152,
      153, 233
  and children, 146, 149, 150–153, 232
  passive procedures for, 154–155
Consistency, 254
Constructs, research on
  and dependent variables, 176
  differentiated from behavior, 169
  evaluating reliability of scores, 167–168
  and internal consistency, 175
  measurement in, 163–164, 166
  self-report measures for, 176–177
  validity in, 168–170, 176–179
Construct validity, 168
Consultants, 220–222
Content validity, 168
Continuous data, 194–195
Contract, 82
Control procedures, 138
Control sheet, 103, 107, 108
Convergent validity, 139, 158, 176–179
Cooper, H., 112
Copyright issues, 233
  in proposal, 88
  in publications, 328
Correlational design. *See also* Research
      design
  bivariate, 206–207

Correlational design (*Cont.*)
    causal language in discussion of, 282
    discriminate function analysis, 206,
        211–212
    vs. group comparison, 194
    internal validity issues in, 278, 280
    nonparametric regression in, 211
    nonsignificant results in, 177, 214
    parametric regression in, 207–211
    power analysis in, 134, 135
    presentation of results in, 254
    role of, 128, 191–193, 194
    statistical techniques for, 206–212
Correlational statistics, 206–216
Covariate analysis. *See* Analyses of
    covariance
Covariates, 202
Counseling, 42, 63
Counterbalancing, 129
Cover letter, 327
Criterion-related validity, 168–169
Critical reading
    in literature review, 119–121
    techniques, 103–107
    of your work, anticipating, 281, 298
Cross-training, 236, 237
Current Contents, 97, 98, 100

D

Data analysis, 87, 238–243. *See also* Compu-
    terized tools; Data collection
    computer programs for, 239–240,
        243–245
    missing data, 239, 242–243, 250,
        263–264
    plan for, 86, 241–242
    supplemental, 246
Databases, 97–100
Data collection, 141–142. *See also* Compu-
    terized tools; Data analysis
    codebook, 239
    data entry, 234, 238–239
    ethical safeguards in, 232
    monitoring and supervision in, 236,
        237–238
    settings and materials in, 232–235
    training in, 229–231
    unexpected events in, 235–237

    verification or data verification in,
        240–241
Deadlines, 40–42
Debriefing, 341
Deception, in research, 337, 340–341
Defense, 20. *See also* Anxiety, in oral
    defense
    anxiety management, 305–310
    audiovisual materials, 297, 299–300,
        303
    checklist, 304
    committee role in, 303
    failing, 307
    format of, 289, 294–296
    humility section, 298
    humor in, 296
    information, 291
    of literature review, 297
    materials to bring, 303
    of methodology, 297
    minidefense model, 289–290
    opening talk, 296–298
    preparation, 294–300, 310–311
    presentation in, 318–320
    problem-solving model, 289–290
    purpose of, 289
    questioning in, 295, 301–302
    rehearsing, 303–305
    of research design, 297
    response strategies, 301–302
    speculation in, 276
    suggestions from committee members,
        292
    verbal style in, 298
Dependent variables, 67–68, 133, 134,
    138–140
    adequacy of, 161
    conceptually related, 205
    literature review organized by, 114
    and MANOVA, 133, 204–205
    in methods section, 138–141
    operationalizing, 161–162
    and parametric statistics, 198
    in regression strategies, 207
    reliability of, 138–140
    in research question, 68
    in results section, 254
    results section organized by, 252–253
    and statistical needs, 195
    step-down procedures for, 204

Design. *See also* Research design
  statement, 129
Developmental PsycSCAN, 97–98
Developmental Review, 325
*Dictionary of Behavioral Assessment Tech-
  niques*, 171
Digital Dissertations, 7
Directness, as quality of measure, 162
Direct observation, 164, 165–166
  coding system, 174
  monitoring, 140–141
  and videotaping, 166
Discriminant function analysis (DFA),
  211–212
Discriminant validity, 139, 168, 176–179
Discriminative validity, 168
Discussion section, 269–285
  anticipating critical reading of, 281
  avoiding nonsignificant results in, 282
  causal language in discussion of, 282
  checklist for, 286
  clinical implications in, 276
  comparative analysis in, 274–275
  future directions noted in, 280–281
  generalizability problems noted in, 279,
    298
  implications of results noted in, 275
  interpreting finding in, 272–273
  lack of significant findings in, 272–273
  limitations section of, 283–285
  as manuscript, 277–278
  measurement problems noted in, 272,
    279
  oral presentation of, 296, 298
  organization of, 281–283, 284–285
  research design of, 276
  role of, 269
  speculation in, 276
  statistical research noted in, 279–280
  summary of finding in, 270–272
  supplemental analyses in, 273
  unexpected results noted in, 271,
    272–273
  validity issues noted in, 273, 278–279
  writing style, 270–272, 281–283
Dissertation. *See also* Defense; Thesis
  defense of, 289–290
  definition of, 5–8
  empirical research in, 6
  etiquette of, 58–60, 76–77
  format and length of, 7–8
  as idea source, 67
  length of, 7
  literature review, 122
  literature review in, 84–85
  origins of, 8–9
  preparing for, 11–28
  as reference, 67
  role of, 5–9
  table of contents in proposal for, 88–89
  vs. thesis, 5–6
Dissertation Abstracts International, 51, 97,
  283
Dissertation coaches, 42
Dissertation proposal. *See* Proposal
Dissertations, research ideas in existing,
  67
Doctoral programs, 6–7
Doctor of Psychology (PsyD) programs,
  6, 7
Drafts
  chairperson review of, 50, 54, 74–75,
    89–91
  editing software, 14–15
  role of, 115–116
Drift, in scoring, 234–235

E
Editing
  hiring help for, 15
  for publication, 325–326, 328
  software for, 14–15
Educational Resources Information
  Center (ERIC), 97
Educational Testing Service (ETS),
  database, 172
Effects, size of
  identifying significant, 245, 253, 282
  and power analysis, 134–135
Einstein, Albert, 31
Empirical research, 68
  alternatives to, 7
  guidelines for evaluating, 103–107
Employment opportunities
  interview for, 318
  and presentation of research results,
    316–317
  and publication in popular press, 332
EndNote database, 102

Environmental support, 21–22
ERIC. *See* Educational Resources Information Center
Ethical standards, 142–143, 335–343
Ethics. *See also* Informed consent
    in animal research, 143, 341
    authorship issues, 326–327
    in clinical research, 142–158
    confidentiality issues, 143, 232, 233
    ethnic populations and, 153–154
    guidelines, 142–143, 335–343
    implementation of, 144–158, 232
    managing research participant data, 157–158
    and research assistants, 232, 335–336
    in research design, 144–145
Ethics Code, 142, 145
Ethics in Plain English: An Illustrative Casebook for Psychologists, 144
Ethics in Research With Human Participants, 144
Ethnicity. *See* Race/ethnicity
Evaluation guidelines, 104–106
Experimental design, 128, 130
Experiment-wise error, 216–217
Exploratory factor analysis, 213
External validity, 20, 27, 279. *See also* Validity
    direct assessment, 149

F

Face validity, 168
Factor analysis, 180, 212–213
    role of, 179–180
Faculty. *See also* Committee
    role in topic selection, 47, 49, 50–51
Failed predictions, 272–273
Feedback, 54, 228
Fellowships, 25
Figures
    captions for, 264–265
    checklist for, 265
    content of, 253–254
    convention for presentation of, 260–266
    data between phases in, 263–264
    deciding whether to use, 260
    labeling of, 261–262
    numbers of, 256
    percentages in, 261

    research design depicted in, 129
    software in, 265–266
    tick marks in, 261
    time as measure in, 261
Financial issues
    compensating assistants, 229
    consultation, 220
    hiring blind experimenters, 137–138
    in use of figures, 260
Format
    of appendixes in proposal, 88
    of audiovisual presentation in defense, 299–300, 303
    for computer summaries, 243–245
    for conference presentation, 315–316
    of defense presentation, 294–298
    of discussion section, 283
    of figures, 260–266
    guidelines for, 7–8
    institution-specific, 7–8
    for introducing research questions, 121–122
    for introduction to proposal, 84–85
    for journal submissions, 324–325, 327–329
    of literature review, 84–85, 110
    of method section in proposal, 85–86
    one-chapter, in literature review, 84
    of oral defense meeting, 294–296
    for poster presentation, 320–323
    of proposal meeting, 290–292
    of references section in proposal, 88
    of results section, 252–254
    of results section in proposal, 86–87
    of table of contents, 88–89
    of tables, 256–259
    two-chapter, in literature review, 84
Forms
    for chairperson collaboration, 51
    documenting proposal acceptance, 82
    informed consent, 147–149, 150–151, 152, 153, 233
    organizing, 232, 233
Forward chaining, 33, 209
Foster, S. L., 118, 320
Friedman's test, 205
F tests, 200, 205
Funnel approach, 85, 110, 114

G

Gantt charts, 34–35
Gender, 130
  and parametric work, 194
  as variable, 195, 198
Generalizability, 167, 179, 298. *See also*
      Reliability; Validity
  alternate forms, 139–140
  across settings, 169, 179
  theory of reliability, 168
Generosity bias, 165
Goal lists, 33–34
Goal setting, 32, 33, 116–117
  product vs. process goals in, 116
  time considerations in, 31–34
  visual representations in, 34–36
  in writing process, 109–110
Google, 97, 181
Google Scholar, 100
Graduating, 145
Grammar-checking programs, 14
Grandstanding, 302
Grants, 25, 53
Graphics. *See* Audiovisual materials, in
      defense; Figures; Tables
Group comparison statistics, 195–205
  ANCOVA tests in, 199, 202–204
  ANOVA tests in, 199, 200, 202, 204
  vs. correlational design, 194
  evaluating computer analysis in,
      243–245
  MANOVA tests in, 199, 202, 204–205
  nonparametric statistics in, 205–206
  parametric, 195–205
  planned comparisons to, 200–201
  post hoc tests in, 201–202
  preliminary analyses, 241–242
  presentation of results from, 254
  role of, 194–195
  t tests in, 198, 199
  with two groups, 198, 205
  selecting, 196–201
  selection flow chart of, 197

H

Halo effects, 165
Handbook for Psychiatric Rating Scales, 171
HaPI. *See* Health and Psychological
      Instruments
Harm, avoiding, 335

Hawthorne effect, 141
Health and Psychological Instruments
      (HaPI) database, 172
Hierarchical linear modeling, 218
Homogeneity of variance, 132, 176,
      198–200
  and post hoc tests, 201–202
  testing, 200
Homoscedasticity, 210
Humor, in defense, 296
Hypotheses
  checklist for, 73
  defense of, 298
  definition of, 69
  development of, 69–73
  experimenters blind to, 137–138, 141,
      231
  failed predictions, 272–273
  in discussion section, 284
  identifying statistical needs of, 189
  introducing, 121–122
  null, 70–71, 273
  number of, 72
  and planned comparisons, 200–201
  and presentation of results, 254
  in primary analyses, 252–253
  in proposal, 69–72
  research, 67–69
  types of, 70–71
  variables in, 64, 67–68
  wording of, 71
Hypothesis-testing analyses, 190, 209–210,
      217. *See also* Hypotheses
Hypothetical construct, differences with
      behavior, 163

I

Ice-breakers, 296
Idea log, 37
Illustrations, 260
Impact of Events Scale, 66
Impression management, 177
Imputation, 243
Independence of observations. *See* nonin-
      dependent data
Independent variables
  adequacy of, 161
  and ANCOVA effects, 202
  in correlational design, 194, 195
  in group comparison designs, 194

Independent variables (*Cont.*)
  integrity of, 136–137, 142
  literature review organized by, 113–114
  manipulation checks, 136–137
  and methodological validity, 278, 280
  in methods section, 136–138
  operationalizing, 161–162
  and parametric statistics, 196–198
  research population size, 132–133
  in research question, 68
  and statistical needs, 195, 196–200
Inderbitzen-Pisaruk, H., 118
Indexers, 99
Individual difference research, 176
Indicators, 214
Informal rules, 24–25
Informant ratings, 165, 176
Information management
  confidentiality issues, 143, 232, 233, 336
  consent forms, 145
  ethical guidelines for, 337–338
Informed consent, 145–155, 338–340
Informed consent form, 141, 145–155
  adolescent, 152
  adult, 147–149
  child, 146, 149, 150–153, 232
  elements of, 145–146
  reading level of, 154
Ingenta, 100
Insight-oriented individual therapy, 198, 203
Institutional review board (IRB)
  approval of, 91–92, 155, 227
  full review by, 156
  operations of, 156–157
  requirements of, 142, 145
Instruments. *See* Measures
Integrity, of independent variables, 136–137, 142
Internal consistency, 167, 175–176
Internal validity, 278, 280. *See also* Validity
Internet, 42, 95, 96–97, 172
Interobserver agreement, 140
  correlating differences in, 206
  monitoring, 140–141
  reactivity of, 140
  slippage of, 174
Interpersonal relations, 23–24
  with chairperson, 50–55
  chairperson–committee, 57, 74
  within committee, 75–76

and dissemination of research, 51, 325–326
  ethical guidelines for, 336
  with faculty, choosing chairperson and, 76
  multiple regression analysis of, 208
  skills in, 23–24
Interrater agreement, 140–141
Interview-and-invite strategy, 76
Introduction, to proposal, 84–85
  one-chapter model of, 84, 85
  two-chapter model of, 84
  writing of, 117
Irrational thinking, 26–27, 306

J

Jargon, 270
Jingle fallacy, 180
Job interviews, 316
Joint ranking, 205
Joke telling, 296
Journals
  to improve writing skills, 15–16
  peer-reviewed, 96
  as primary source, 96, 97
  rejection by, 324, 329–330
  in research, 95, 101–102, 223
  submissions to, 324–325, 330–331
Judges, 140, 174
  assessing agreement between, 140
  in pilot testing, 227–228

K

Kappa coefficient, 173
Keyboarding skills, 22–23
Keywords, 98–99
Koyre, A., 23
Kruskal–Wallis test, 205
Kuder–Richardson procedures, 21, 175

L

Laboratory. *See* Research setting
Language-based assessment, 178
Latent variables, 214
Legal issues
  parental consent, 146, 147–149
Letter of recommendation, 53
Levels, 191, 196, 216–217

Limitations subsection, 277–280
Line graphs, 262, 264
Literature review
    computerized searches, 98–100, 107
    critical reading, 103–107
    guidelines for evaluating, 104–106
    identifying major sources for, 95–96
    locating authors, 101
    obtaining reprints, 100–101
    and primary sources, 96
    in related disciplines, 101
    for research ideas, 65–67
    scanning key journal contents, 101–102
    shortage of material for, 113
Literature review section
    checklist for, 124–125
    defense of, 297
    degree of criticism in, 120
    in discussion of results, 269–270
    format, one chapter vs. two, 84
    goals of, 119
    introduction to, 116, 117
    length and format, 109–110
    limiting contents of, 112–113
    meta-analysis in, 119
    organization strategies, 113–115
    outline for, 110–111
    preparing to write, 109–115
    process, 95–123
    in proposal, 84–85
    publication of, 330–331
    research question source, 66–67, 70
    revising, 123, 269–270
    secondary sources in, 95–103
    statement of problem in, 121–122
    subgroupings, 117–119
    writing, 115–123
Logistic regression, 206, 211
Logit analysis, 206, 211
Log-linear analysis, 206
Longitudinal design, 128

M

Manipulation checks, 136–137
Mann–Whitney tests, 205, 206
MANOVA *See* Multivariate analyses of
    variance
Manuscript preparation, 325–326
Manuscript submissions, 327–329,
    330–331

Matching, 129
Math anxiety, 187–188
Measurement, 161–182
    avoiding errors in, 180–181
    characteristics of, 161–162
    limitations of, 279
    reliability of, 139, 167–168
    requirements of, 161–162
    validity of, 139, 168–170
Measurement theory, 19–20, 166
Measures
    adaptation of, 179–180
    availability of, 181–182
    describing, 138–139
    directness of, 162
    score reliability of, 166, 167–168
    sources of, 170–172
    unavailability of, 173–179
    well-known, 139
Media presentations, 316, 331–332
Mediation analysis, 214, 220
MEDLINE, 100
Membership directories, 101
Mental Measurements Yearbook, 170
Meta-analysis, 119
Methodology. *See also* Ethics; Method
    section
    abstracting, 318, 319–320
    chairperson expertise in, 50, 52–54
    comparative analysis of, 274–275
    control procedures, 138
    data analysis, 87, 239–240, 243–245
    data checking, 139–141
    data collection, 238–241
    data management checklist, 247
    defense of, 297
    defining variables, 162–163
    in discussion section, 276
    ethical issues in, 142–157
    implication or results, 275–276
    in literature, critical analysis of,
        119–121
    literature review materials grouped by,
        113–114, 117–119
    major changes in, 229
    perfection in, 27, 40
    pilot testing, 156, 227–229
    reviewed for flaws, 269–270
    review of, in proposal meeting,
        290–291
    and risk to participants, 155–156

Methodology (*Cont.*)
  and setting, 136
  supplemental review of, 217, 246,
      255–256
  skills for, 19–21
  verifying data, 241
Method section. *See also* Methodology;
      Research design
  addressing instrument reliability in,
      167–168
  apparatus, 136
  checklist for, 159
  contents for, 128–142
  independent variables described in,
      136–138
  informed consent procedures in,
      145–155
  judging procedures documented in,
      141–142
  measures (dependent variables) de-
      scribed in, 138–141
  overview, 85–86
  participants described in, 129–136
  in presentation of defense, 296–297
  research design described in, 128–136
  revising, 269–270
  setting described in, 136
  subsections, 128
Method variance, 181
Milestone chart, 31
Minnesota Multiphasic Personality
      Inventory—2 (MMPI-2), 179, 190
Missing at random (MAR), 242
Missing completely at random (MCAR),
      242
Missing data, 239, 242–243, 250, 263–264
Mock oral defense, 303–305
Mock results section, 86–88, 249
Model testing, 193, 213–216
Monitoring
  data collection, 236, 237–238
  scoring, 241
Motor behavior management, 308–310
MS Project, 34
Multicollinearity, 210
Multiple regression, 194, 200, 207–211
  hierarchical, 208–209
  stepwise, 209
Multitrait–multimethod matrixes, 178
Multivariate analyses of covariance
      (MANCOVA), 202

Multivariate analyses of variance
      (MANOVA), 202, 204–205
  vs. ANCOVA, 204
  assumptions of, 199
  and discriminant function analysis, 212
  number of participants needed in,
      133–134
  role of, 204
  and Type I errors, 204
Myth, of methodological perfection, 27,
      40

N
National Library of Medicine, 100
Natural science perspective, 167, 169
Newspapers, 332
Newton, R. R., 40
Nobel laureate error, 26, 46
Nonignorable missingness (MNAR), 242
Nonindependent data, 217–219
Nonparametric regression, 211
Nonparametric statistics, 205–206
Note taking
  idea log, 37
  in oral defense, 294
  in proposal meeting, 293
  in reviewing literature, 103–107
Null hypotheses, 70–71

O
Observation, 164, 165–166
Observed variables, 214
Observer drift, 234–235
Observers, 163, 164, 174
  direct assessment by, 163–164
  in pilot testing, 227–228
  slippage of, 174
  training of, 140
Occam's razor, 72
One-chapter model, 84, 85, 121
Operational definitions, 161
Oral defense. *See* Defense
Oral presentations, 318–320
Organizational skills, 14
Organizational strategies
  by assessment methods, 114
  by design type, 114
  by related variables, 113–114
  for results discussion, 281–283

Originality
   in choosing a topic, 47
   emphasis on, 82
   in writing proposal, 6
Outliers, 222
Outlining, 110–111
Outlines
   for discussion section, 284
   for literature review section, 110–111
   for oral defense, 296
Overhead projectors, 299
Overreading, 107
Oxford English Dictionary, 5

P

Page allocations, 110, 111
Pairwise ranking tests, 205
Parallel organization, 118
Parametric multiple regression, 207–211
Parametric statistics, 194–195. *See also*
      Analyses of covariance (ANCOVA);
      Multivariate analyses of variance
      (MANOVA)
   assumptions of, 199–200
   bivariate, 206–207
   flowchart for choosing, 196–197
   nonparametric alternatives, 205–206
   planned comparisons, 200–201
   post hoc tests, 201–202
   power analysis in, 134
   regression strategies, 207–211
   t tests, 196–199
Parental consent form, 146, 147–149
Parsonson, B. S., 264
Participant drop-out, 250–251
Participants. *See* Research populations
Participants subsection, 85–86, 129–136
Passive procedures, 154–155
Path analysis, 214, 220
Pearson product-moment correlations,
      194, 199, 206–207
Pedhazur, E. J., 71
Peer-reviewed journals, 96
Peer-review process, 315, 330
Perfectionism, 26–27, 306
Performance anxiety, 305–310
Performance anxiety behavioral checklist,
      308–310
Periodicals, 97–98
Personal data assistants (PDAs), 165

Phi coefficient, 206
Photocopying, 103, 106–107
Physiological anxiety management,
      307–308
Pilot data, 174, 176
Pilot studies, 140–141, 145
Pilot testing, 156, 227–229
Plagiarism, 107, 122–123, 342
Planned comparisons, 197, 200–201
Planning
   authorship credits, 326–327
   backward chaining in, 33
   checklist for, 43
   for committee meetings, 290–293
   computerized data collection, 238–241
   for defense, 303
   dissemination of research, 325–326
   ethics considerations in, 338–342
   forward chaining in, 33
   literature review, 95–98
   methodological practice, checklist for,
      247
   outline for literature review, 110–111
   for proposal meeting, 290–293
   for research assistants, 228–229,
      230–231
   for research participants, 233–234
   visual representations in, 35
Podcasts, 99
Point biserial correlation, 206–207
Popular press, 96–97, 331–333
Poster preparation checklist, 322
Poster presentations, 317, 320–323
Post hoc tests, 201–202, 204
Power, statistical
   analysis of, 134–136
   in parametric, vs. nonparametric,
      statistics, 196
   and planned comparisons, 200–201
PowerPoint, 300, 318
Predictive validity, 169
Preliminary analyses, 190, 216–217
Preliminary outline, 110–111
Premack principle, 41, 116
Preparation assessment
   cognitive ecology, 26–27
   computer access, 22–23
   costs and services, 25–26
   environment, 21–22
   interpersonal skills, 23–24
   keyboarding skills, 22–23

Preparation assessment (*Cont.*)
  methodology skills, 19–21
  rules and formalities, 24–25
  time management, 23
  writing skills, 14–19
Preprints, 100–101
Presentation
  figures in, 260–266
  preparing for, 250–251
  primary analysis in, 255–256
  tables in, 256–260
Primary analyses, 251–255
  clarity in, 254–255
  relevant information in, 253–254
  sequencing results in, 252–253
  statistical results in, 255
Primary sources, 96
Principal components analysis, 212
Privacy, 336–337
Procrastination, 38–39, 107, 110
Professional conduct, 142. *See also* Ethics
Professional conferences, 316
Professional development
  and presentation of research, 315–318
  and publication of research, 324–329
  and thesis/dissertation, 8–9
Professional directories, 181
Professional meetings, 316
Program Evaluation and Review Technique (PERT), 34
Project-scheduling software, 34, 36
Proofreading, 18
Proposal. *See also* Chairperson; Committee; Defense
  appendixes in, 88, 89, 91
  checklist of, 304
  committee meeting, 289–290
  as contract, 82
  copyright issues, 88
  de novo instruments in, 140
  elements of, 83–89
  format of meeting, 290–291
  functions of, 81–83
  grounds for rejection, 329–330
  introduction section in, 84–85
  method section in, 85–86
  number of hypotheses, 72
  preparing for, 290–293
  process of, 89–92
  references in, 88
  results section in, 86–88

  role of, 81–83
  table of contents in proposal for, 88–89
PsycARTICLES, 100
Psychological Abstracts, 97, 101
Psychological Bulletin, 66, 325
Psychological Review, 325
PsycINFO database, 97, 100, 172
PsycSCANs, 100
Publication credit, 326–327, 342
Publication of research, 324–333
  authorship credit for, 326–327, 342
  benefits of, 313–315
  checklist for, 334
  duplicate, 342
  ethical standards in, 338–343
  literature review section, 330–331
  manuscript preparation, 325–326
  in popular press, 96–97, 331–333
  preparing for, 325–326
  rejection, 329–330
  selecting journal for, 324–325
  submission of manuscript, 327–329, 330–331
  timing, 324
Publication Manual of the American Psychological Association, 8, 18, 88, 102, 255, 262, 324. *See also* American Psychological Association
PubMed, 100

Q

Quasi-experimental design, 128
Quotations, using, 107

R

Race/ethnicity, 254
  and ethics, 153–154
  as variable, 195
Radio talk shows, 332
Random assignment, 129
  and ANCOVA, 203
Rating scales, 171
Readiness, for research
  checklist, 12–13
  computer skills, 22–23
  interpersonal skills, 23–24
  methodological skills, 19–21
  realism in assessing, 26–28
  statistical knowledge, 189

writing skills, 14–18
Reading level, 154
Recalibration, in scoring, 235
Record maintenance, 337–338
Recruiting
    of participants of, 131
    of research assistants, 228–229
Reference lists, 102, 283
References, 88, 91, 97–98, 283
Regression strategies, 207–211, 218
    backward deletion procedures in, 209
    conditions for, 210
    forward entry procedures in, 209
    forward stepwise procedures in, 209
    hierarchical, 208–209
    logistic, 211
    and multicollinearity, 210
    nonparametric, 211
    parametric multiple, 207–211
    stepwise procedures in, 209–210
Reliability
    addressing in paper, 167–168
    assessing, 167–168
    of dependent variables, 139–140
    evaluating, 166, 167–168
    forms of, 139, 167–168
    generalizability theory of, 167
    internal consistency, 175–176
    reviews of, 171–172
    scorer, 173–174
    temporal stability, 169, 175
    and validity, 168–170
Representativeness rule, 132
Reprints, 100–101
Research assistants (RAs)
    bias in, 65, 231, 238
    ethical guidelines, 232, 335–336
    paid, 56
    training of, 228–229, 230–231
    supervision of, 237–238
    unexpected problems with, 236
Research cycle, 314
Research design, 128–136, 194. *See also*
    Correlational design; Group com-
    parison design; Methodology
    between-participants, 128, 129, 195–196
    classes in, 19–20
    costs of, 25–26
    deciding area of, 46–49
    dependent variables in, 138–141
    description of, 128–129

dissemination of, 313–333
ethical practices in, 335–343
external validity in, 279
and figure formats, 260–266
future directions of, 280–281
identifying limitations of, 277–280
implications of results for, 275–276
of literature, 95–123
methodology and ethics, 127–158
mixed, 278
nonexperimental, 277–278
nonhomogeneous variances in,
    201–202
and number of research participants,
    132–136
oral presentation of, 297
and post hoc tests, 201–202
quasi-experimental, 278, 279
replications of, 67
review of, in proposal meeting,
    290–293
and screening procedures, 131
statement, 129
and step-wise procedures, 209–210
terminology of, 20
within-participants, 128, 129
Research design, 20
Research hypotheses, 70–71
Research log, 238
Research populations, 129–136. *See also*
    Informed consent
accessibility of, 69
animal, 91, 131, 136, 141, 143, 341
assessing availability, 69
assessing characteristics of, 133
bias effects, 137–138
children as, 146–149
classification of, 129–131
consent of, 145–155
data management, 234–235
deceiving, 144
demographic data from, 130, 132
describing, in methods section,
    129–136
ethical research issues, 144–146,
    155–156
factor analysis requirements, 212–213
feedback from, 228
follow-up procedures, 141–142
homogeneous, 132
identified in hypothesis, 69–72

Research populations (*Cont.*)
  instructions to, 141–142
  numbering of, 133–136
  offering inducements to, 340
  in pilot study, 227–229
  potential problems with, 235–237
  recording representativeness of, 131
  recruiting, 131
  risk to, 155–156
  scheduling, 234–235
  screening procedures for, 131
  selection of, 129–133
  sending results to, 141–142
  subpopulations of, 132
Research question, 63–69. *See also* Topic
    selection
  abstract of, 318, 319–320
  animal surgery in, 138
  criteria for framing, 67–69
  description of, in defense, 297
  developing hypotheses for, 69–73
  experimental confederates in, 137
  form of, 63–64
  identifying statistical needs of, 189–191
  and instrument stability needs, 167–168
  intervention in, 138
  in literature review section, 121–122
  no basis for prediction in, 122
  relevance of, 64
Research Readiness Checklist, 12–13, 21
Research setting
  for direct observation, 164
  generalizability, 179
  planning, 232–233
Residual, 210
Results. *See also* Discussion section;
    Publication of research
  abstract of, 318–320
  alternative explanations for, 271
  and type of causality, 278
  discussion of, 284–285
  ethical guidelines for reporting, 342
  forums for presentation of, 315–317
  future direction of, 280–281
  identifying significance in, 281, 282
  implications of, 275–276
  interpreting, 272–273
  lack of significant, 273
  limitations of, 277–280
  literature review, 274–275
  oral defense presentation of, 298

poster presentations, 317, 320–323
  related to theory, 275
  summarizing, 271–272
  supplemental analyses of, 255–256, 273
  unexpected, 272
  writing, 270, 281–283
Results section, 86–88, 249–267
  checklist for preparation of, 267
  contents of, 86–88, 251–252
  mock-up of, 86–88
  oral presentation of, 296
  order of, 252–253
  presentation of figures in, 260–265
  in proposal, 86–88
  repetition in, 254
  statistics in, 252–253, 255
  tables in, 256–259
  writing style of, 254–255
Retesting, 139
Reviewers, 343
Revisions, 123, 269–270
Rights, research participants, 142–145. *See
    also* Research participants
Risk assessment, 155–156
Rudestam, K. E., 40
Rules
  for chairperson selection, 50–51
  committee, 74
  informal, 24–25
  school, 24–25

S

Sample size, 212–213, 215, 272. *See also*
    Power analysis
Sampling strategy, 131
SAS, 21, 200, 239, 246
Scheduling, 232–235
Schmelkin, L. P., 71
Scientific method
  choice of measures in, 162–163
  deductive approach, 69
  hypotheses in, 69–71
  inductive approach, 70
  role of failed predictions in, 273
  in wording research questions, 67–69
Scorer reliability, 173–174.
Scoring
  accuracy of, 230–231
  computer for, 238–243
  drift in, 234–235

frequency distribution in, 198
monitoring of, 236, 240–241
recalibration of, 235
residual difference in, 210
of self-reports, 165
validity in, 168–170
Screening, of research participants, 131
Search engines, 97, 98–100
Search terms, 98
Secondary source, 96
Self-deception, 177
Self-doubts, 40
Self-fulfilling prophecy, 65
Self-monitoring, 163, 165
Self-observations, 165
Self-presentation, 177
Self-report measures, 163, 164, 165, 173,
    176–177
    collateral data sources with, 178
    and construct validity, 176–177
    correlations between, 180–181
    internal consistency of, 176
    potential problems in use of, 278–279
    reporting results from, 202
    scoring in, 167
Self-talk, 40, 306
Sequential analysis, 188
Settings, 232–235
Severino, Joseph, 146
Signature sheets, 283
Single-item measures, 181
Single-participant design, 128
Slides, 299–300
Social desirability measures, 176–177
Social Sciences Citation Index (SSCI), 98
Social SciSearch, 98
Social support, 41–42
Society for Research in Child Develop-
    ment, 317
Socioeconomic status, 133, 162
Solomon four-group, 129, 175
Spearman rank-order, 206–207
Speculation, 276
Speech anxiety, 310
Spelling checker programs, 14, 17–18
Spreadsheets, 238
SPSS, 21, 200, 239, 240, 246
Statistical tests
    limitations of, 279–280
    omitted from hypotheses, 72
    in proposal results section, 86

Statistical techniques. *See also* Analysis
    plan; *names of specific statistics*
academic preparation for, 19–20,
    187–188
alpha levels in, 216–217
analyses of covariance (ANCOVA), 86,
    199, 202–204
analyses of variance (ANOVA), 86, 129,
    132, 135, 198, 199, 200–201, 202–
    203, 204–206, 279–280
applying, 189–195
assumptions of, 241, 279
causal terminology in, 219–220
checklist for selecting, 225
computers for, 239–240
consultation in, 220–222
conventions for presentations, 255
in correlational research design,
    206–216
covariate analysis, 133
data transformation in, 196
defense of, 292, 293, 300
in discussion section, 279–280
fear of, 187
fishing expedition, 217
fluency in, 19
and homogeneity of variances, 198
identifying needs, 189–195
mock results of, 86–88, 249
multivariate analyses of variance
    (MANOVA), 133–134, 199, 202,
    204–205
nonindependent data, 217–219
nonparametric, 205–206
and number of participants, 131–132
parametric, 195–205
in participant analyses, 133–136
planned comparisons, 200–201
post hoc tests, 201–202
power of, 133
in presentation of results, 252–253
in proposal, 86–88
robustness of, 201–202
seeking help with, 222–223
software for handling, 21, 135, 200
supplemental review of, 255–256
teaching of, 187
writing about results of, 254–255
Stepwise procedures, 209–210
Stimulus control, 22
Strong-chairperson model, 74–75

Strong-committee model, 75
Structural Equation Modeling (SEM), 200, 213–216, 220
Students, 57–58, 231
StyleEase, 18
Style guidelines, 7–8
StyleWriter, 14, 15, 16–17, 18
Subheadings, 114
Subjects. *See* Research populations
Subsections, 85–86, 117–119, 122
Supplemental analyses, 217, 246, 255–256
Support groups, dissertation, 41–42
Symbols, 263
Symmetry, 254
Symposia, 317
Syntax files, 244
Systat, 21

T

Table of contents, 283
    in proposal, 88–89, 90
    scanning, in literature review, 101–102
Tables, 256–260
    for audiovisual display, 299–300
    checklist, 259
    content of, 253–254
    conventions for presentation of, 256–259
    number of, 258, 260
    readability of, 258–259
    titles for, 259
Talk, in relation to behavior, 33
Tape recording. *See* Recording evidence
Television talk shows, 332
Temporal reliability, 167, 175
Temporal stability, 139, 175
Terminology, 20, 219–220
Test construction, 166
Test references, 171
Test–retest reliability, 167
Tests in Print VI, 170–171
Thematic organization, 285
Therapy, 42, 53
Theory
    literature review materials grouped by, 113
    relating to results, 275
Thesis. *See also* Defense; Dissertation
    defined, 5–6
    described, 6–8

vs. dissertation, 5–6
    empirical research in, 6
    etiquette of, 58–60, 76–77
    as idea source, 67
    length of, 7
    origins of, 8–9
    reasons for, 8–9
    as reference, 67
    role of, 5–9
    unpublished, 95
Thesis proposal. *See* Proposal
Timeline charts, 34–35, 36
Time management, 23–24, 31–42
    chairperson availability and, 54–55
    checklist, 43
    to complete dissertation, 21
    computer-scheduling software, 36
    Einstein's definition of time, 31
    estimates of, 32–34
    and Gantt charts, 34–35
    increments of work in, 33
    and institutional review board sched- ule, 156–157
    of oral defense, 294, 295, 296, 299
    pilot testing for, 227–228
    and Program Evaluation and Review Technique (PERT), 34
    in publication of research, 324, 327
    in recruiting assistants, 229–230
    scheduling, 34–36
    school rules and, 24–25
    setting goals in, 32, 33–34
    and unexpected disruptions, 31, 235–237
    visual representations, 34–36
    of work requirements, 32–34
Time-series procedures, 33
Title page, 283
Titles, 259, 265
Toastmasters, 310
Tone, 120
Topic selection, 46–49, 62
    access to research population and, 69
    advantages of early start in, 47–48
    chairperson in, 49–54
    checklist for, 78
    criteria for, 48
    ethical considerations in, 144
    existing dissertations/theses for ideas on, 67
    existing literature for ideas on, 65–66

first step, 47–49
idea log for, 37
identifying area of interest, 47
personal considerations, 8–9, 64–65
role of faculty in, 49
sources of ideas for, 64–67
undergraduate experience in, 46, 47
Training
affecting faculty collaborators, 60–61
animal researchers, 143
assistants, 228–229, 230–231, 236–237
coding procedures, 237–238
confidentiality procedures, 232, 233
describing procedures for, 138
ethical research, 232, 335
of observers, 140, 174
pilot testing for, 227–228
Transitions, 118, 120
Transparencies, 299
Treatment validity, 139
t tests
assumptions of, 198–199
role of, 194, 195, 196–199
Tutoring, 221
Two-chapter model, 85, 121
Type I and Type II errors, 196, 204–205,
    215, 216, 217, 279

U

Undergraduate experience, 46. *See also*
    Readiness for research
Undergraduate research paper error, 46
Unexpected outcomes, 238
Ullman, J. B., 215
Unobtrusive measures, 178–179
Unweighted means estimation, 243

V

Vail-model programs, 7
Validity
concurrent, 169
construct, 168, 169
content, 168, 169
convergent, 168
criterion-related, 168
defining, 168–169
of dependent variables, 139–140
discriminant, 168
evaluating, 139, 166, 168–170

external, 20, 27, 270, 279
face, 168
internal, 278, 280
methodological, 20, 278–279
predictive, 169
and reliability, 168
reviews of, 170–172
supplemental analysis of, 255–256
treatment, 139
types of, 168–169
Variables. *See also* Dependent variables;
    Independent variables; Measures
computer analysis of, 244–245
in correlational design, 191. 194
criterion, 207, 209
defining, 67–69, 162–163
dichotomous, 207–208
direst assessment of, 166
in factor analysis, 212–213
in figures, 260–262
in hypotheses, 67, 71, 72
and methodological validity, 278–279
operationalization of, 161–162
outcome, 207
in regression analysis, 207–210
and research design, 132
social desirability, 208
and statistical needs, 189–195
supplemental analysis of, 272–273
in tables, 256–258
and temporal stability, 175
specified in research question, 68
Verb use
in avoiding causal language, 282
tense, 69
Videotape
as manipulation checks, 137
as permanent record, 166, 174
in pilot testing, 228
in oral defense presentation, 299–300
Visualization, 307
Volunteering, 56

W

Web sites, 25, 135, 317
Wikipedia, 99
Wilcoxon Rank Sum, 205
Within-participants designs, 128, 129, 175,
    219

Work habits, 34–36. *See also* Time
    management
  avoiding procrastination, 38, 39, 107,
    110
  of chairperson, 54–55
  in literature review, 103–107
  rewarding good, 41–42
  role of planning in, 36–39
Writer's block, 115
Writing preparation, 109–115
Writing process, 115–123
  introduction, 117
  literature review, 117–121
  outline for literature review, 110–112
  preparation for, 109–110
  procrastination in, 38, 39, 107, 110
  revisions, 123
  role of drafts in, 115–116
Writing styles, 15
  for abstracts, 318
  causal language misused in, 282
  and computers, 17–18
  conventions for statistics, 255
  in discussion section, 270–272, 281–283
  for figure captions, 264–265
  goals of, 109–110
  good qualities of, 295
  journal requirements, 325–326,
    327–329
  in literature review, 84–85, 117–119,
    269–270
  for poster presentation, 320–323
  proposal, 81–82, 83
  references to authors in, 326–327
  in results section, 254–255
  sample, 15
  for self-report results, 282
  skills assessment, 14–19
  for table titles, 259
  wording of hypotheses, 69–71
W tests, 200, 205

Z

z tests, 206

About the Authors

John D. Cone, PhD, earned his BA in psychology from Stanford University and his MS and PhD from the University of Washington. He has taught at the University of Puget Sound, West Virginia University, the University of Hawaii, United States International University, San Diego State University, and Alliant International University. He is a fellow of both the American Psychological Association and the American Psychological Society, a member of the Association for Behavior Analysis, and a board-certified behavior analyst. His research interests include the development of idiographic assessment methodology; autism intervention; and the development, implementation, and evaluation of large-scale service delivery systems, especially those for individuals with developmental disabilities. An executive coach and frequent organizational consultant, he is the author of several books, including *Evaluating Outcomes: Empirical Tools for Effective Practice* (2001). When not being professionally active, John spends his time jogging, working on his 42′ trawler (*Carefree II*), and cruising the waters of the blue Pacific.

Sharon L. Foster, PhD, is a distinguished professor at Alliant International University in San Diego, California. She received her PhD in psychology in 1978 from the State University of New York at Stony Brook after completing a clinical internship at the University of Washington Medical School. She also taught at West Virginia University. She has served as an associate editor for *Behavioral Assessment* and the *Journal of Consulting and Clinical Psychology,* and was a fellow at the Center for Advanced Study in the Behavioral Sciences in 2000–2001. She is the author of four books in addition to numerous articles and book chapters on children's peer relations, assessment and treatment of parent–adolescent conflict, and research methodology.